GETTING BACK TOGETHER

Getting Back Together

by Robert Houriet

Coward, McCann & Geoghegan, Inc.

NEW YORK

Acknowledgment is gratefully extended to the following for permission to reprint from their works:

Trousdale Music Publishers, Inc.: "The Monster," Copyright © 1969 by Trousdale Music Publishers, Inc., 8255 Beverly Blvd., Los Angeles, California 90048. All Rights Reserved. Used by Permission.

Holt, Rinehart and Winston, Inc.: From "Two Tramps in Mud Time" from *The Poetry of Robert Frost*, edited by Edward Connery Lathem. Copyright 1936 by Robert Frost. Copyright © 1964 by Lesley Frost Ballantine. Copyright © 1969 by Holt, Rinehart and Winston, Inc. Reprinted by permission of Holt, Rinehart and Winston, Inc.

A portion of the Preface to this book appeared in somewhat different form in "Life and Death of a Commune Called Oz," in *The New York Times Magazine*, February 16, 1969, Copyright © 1969 by Robert Houriet.

To Mary who stayed home

Acknowledgments

This book happened neither by accident nor as an individual effort; rather it unfolded under the influence, trust and guidance of the hundreds of people I met over the course of a year. The people of the communes opened their homes and lives fully to me at the risk of again allowing their fragile way of life to be distorted and glamorized by the mass media. I earnestly hope that their trust and help will have been equaled by whatever contribution this book makes to the communal movement.

The communes and communities given major coverage read drafts of the manuscript before publication. All but one responded with comments, criticism and factual corrections. It is their book if anybody's.

Within my own Vermont family, the book was also a communal project. While I wrote and mumbled to myself, Lucy re-typed and made acute suggestions and questions. Michael kept the stoves stoked; Mary stayed calm.

Thanks are also due Patricia Brehaut Soliman, my editor, who gave blood, sweat and tears to see the book through to completion, and to the others who read portions of the text: Irv Sternberg of Aurora, Colorado, Ken Brief, night editor of *Newsday*, Herschel O. Engebretson of Glassboro State College, New Jersey, and to Susan Ezell somewhere in the hills of West Virginia.

Finally, deepest thanks to Robert and Betsy Eldridge of Oldwick, New Jersey whose generous hospitality made possible the writing of the final draft.

Contents

Illustrations Follow p. 252 and 284.

Contents

Preface to a Movement

Chicago and the Fall of Oz

America, where are you now?
Don't you care about your sons and daughters?

Don't you know we need you now
We can't fight alone against the monster
         —"The Monster," STEPPENWOLF

From a distance, against the unbroken horizon, the huddled buildings of the prairie town seem set on an island in a flat sea of corn, alfalfa and wheat. Day and night, the eternal soughing of the wind envelops the settlement. Occasionally it rises to shake the loose window frames and doors of the gray paint-peeled clapboard houses and to whip from the unpaved streets swirls of dust.

Built during the lush heyday of the 1920's, Georgeville, Minnesota, was virtually deserted after its lone industry, a cheese cooperative, collapsed in the economic holocaust of 1929. Until two years ago, the two-story red-brick tenement that once housed a bank, dry-goods store and grange hall was left abandoned. Then a new wave of settlers took over the town—hippies, some of them third-generation descendants of Minnesota's original Swedish homesteaders. They rented the main building, purchased two houses for back taxes, and cultivated fields that had long lain fallow. The bank was converted into a crafts store, where they sold their own pottery. Most of them slept on mattresses in one room—the old dry-goods store. During the long winters they sheltered their goats in the bank's snug old vault and held dances in the grange hall.

On the cement facing of the main building, the commune founders splashed in orange day-glow letters a quotation from Proverbs: "Where there is no vision the people perish."

Members of the Georgeville Trading Post have their own words for what they are seeking—as well as escaping. "We don't think of ourselves as dropouts but rather as 'drop-ins,'" said Alan, the only black, a musician with a moppish head of hair. "We believe we are pioneers in a movement that will soon have to include most of civilization. The orthodox culture that we confront is fatally and contagiously diseased."

Two years ago, when the twenty-five fled Minneapolis, none thought of themselves as a movement which would blaze an alternative course to what they saw as America's suicidal drift. They had no time to assess the historical parallels or to make careful plans for the future. Their flight was desperate. They needed no help from Orwell and Huxley to know that America was marching lockstep toward *1984, Brave New World* and ecocatastrophe. How could they resist the all-pervasive, life-consuming monster which they believed urban America had become? Resistance had proved futile. Neither peaceful demonstration nor sporadic gestures of violence could change the mentality of police who threatened to close down their city commune; could vitalize the towering glass apartment buildings and asphalted shopping centers; could breathe life into decayed churches or humanize inflexible corporations. The only option was to split.

Instinctively, they took the escape route so characteristically American—the same path their grandparents had taken in fleeing the grim cities of the Northeast; that the grandparents before them had taken in fleeing Europe's "dark satanic mills," foreclosures, persecutions and wars.

They went back to the land; but this time, they went together. It was a spontaneous, simultaneous movement. Starting from the cities, from Cambridge to Berkeley, they headed for the wide-open country that held the blank promise of a fresh start. They went to the redwood region of the Pacific Northwest, the mesas of the vast Southwest, the rocky abandoned farms of New England.

Between 1965 and 1970, more than two thousand communal groups were established.* Only afterward was it called a movement. At the outset, it was the gut reaction of a generation. Hippie groups living a few country miles apart were unaware of each other's existence and equally unaware of the other utopian experiments in American history. They thought theirs were unique and unprecedented and scarcely knew what name to go by. Some were called tribes; others nests, affinity groups, collectives, intentional communities or simply families.

Eventually most answered to commune, a term to which this generation would give new and broader meaning.

At their inception, communes represented a countermovement. The first phase was an intense reaction against a fragmented, commercialized society whose institutions—from the family on up to the community—had, they were convinced, lost vital, unifying vision.

At their onset, communes looked as though they were simply repeating the past, returning to the secure, natural comfort of a bygone era, escaping upstream to the clean, clear headwaters of the American pioneer experience. But that was only the first lap in a long journey. Somewhere in the line of history, civilization had made a wrong turn, a detour that had led into a cul-de-sac. The only way, they felt, was to drop out and go all the way back to the beginning, to the primal source of consciousness, the true basis of culture: the land. There, they would again move forward, very slowly, careful not to take the wrong turn and keeping to the main road and to the central spirit and consciousness that modern man had lost along the way.

Reexamining, testing, and adapting, they would evolve a

* Estimates vary. A survey by the New York *Times* (December 17, 1970) turned up 2,000 communes in thirty-four states. Dr. Benjamin D. Zablocki, an assistant professor of sociology at the University of California, at Berkeley, put the figure at 3,000 in an interview in the San Francisco *Chronicle* of February 17, 1970.

micro culture—a synthesis of forms, ideas, art and technology. They built smaller, more self-sufficient communities in harmony with the earth. They tested broader, more flexible forms of the family and ways of raising children. They started freer, more creative schools and developed home industries that retained the integrity of individual craftsmanship. They established churches, ashrams and lay orders, revived old religions, and created entirely new ones. Above all, they infused their rediscovered awareness of immanent divinity into every action of daily life, seeking rituals and traditions with which to pass on to their children the timeless vision.

Whether one looks at individuals, single communes or the communal movement as a whole over a five-year span, the impression is that of an evolutionary process marked by fairly distinct phases.

In trying various forms and approaches for this book, the one that finally seemed to fit was that of the odyssey, the journey, the trip—my own. Over two years I covered ten thousand miles and some fifty communal experiments. As it turned out, by accident, my itinerary and personal changes paralleled the communes' evolutionary growth. My trip began as the movement did, tenuously, with two communes that didn't survive a year and were in many respects failures: the family of Oz, covered later in this section, and Bryn Athyn, the major commune of Book One.

In Book Two I found a "together" commune that had successfully integrated tribal consciousness within a workable, flexible structure. Next I went to New Buffalo, a relatively older commune that had arrived at a crossroads of conflict between two waves of communal pioneers. Thereafter, the trip and book diverged from communes whose emphasis was on changing consciousness to communities (Harrad West, a group marriage, and Twin Oaks, a *Walden Two* experiment) which took the opposite tack—reforming the social structures that mold consciousness.

Even before visiting the three spiritual communities in Book Eight, I had become aware that the essence of the communal movement transcended the lens of the objective reporter; that it couldn't be confined by the old frames of socioeconomic analysis. In Oregon, almost a year after starting my "research," I first realized that the contemporary commune was the outward form of a movement in consciousness.

The question that plagued me as a writer was how to go about reporting a movement in consciousness. The question, of course, implied its own contradiction. There was but one consciousness that could honestly be reported, my own. Given the elusive nature of communal life, my only approach was to respond totally to my subject; my only viewpoint in writing to reveal as honestly and completely both my surface reactions and deepest changes.

Traditionally, utopias, both real and fictional, have been depicted through the eyes of shadowy observers—from Ralph Hythlodaye of Sir Thomas More's *Utopia* to Professor Burris of B. F. Skinner's *Walden Two*. Unlike the utopian experiments of the past, the very nature of the American commune demanded more of me. I couldn't don the utopian visitor's cloak of anonymity or his conventional detachment.

The search for a new community—for America—became my own.

My last job was as night editor of the Camden *Courier-Post*, a daily with a 115,000 circulation throughout the south Jersey suburbs of Philadelphia. In 1968 my staff was a dozen or so young college dropouts and graduates. Some of the most talented reporters had begun to grow their hair long and smoke pot. During the night, while the green-eyeshade men of the day city desk slept, we produced what we believed to be a creative flow of copy: series, features, investigative reports and a running account of the black nationalist movement shaking Camden.

One of the most diligent and enterprising reporters was Rocky. A graduate of the University of Pennsylvania, he had taken to wearing wide ties, khaki pants, tweed jackets and tennis shoes, and his hair had begun to curl over the edge of his collar. In the spring of 1968, the first of a series of memos arrived on my desk. They were on thin paper whose color—panicky pink—sent shivers of apprehension through me. They emanated from the executive editor and publisher and urged me to persuade Rocky to cut his hair and standardize his dress.

For two months, Rocky and I played a delaying, compromising game. After each memo, Rocky would trim his hair back above the collar. Finally the ultimatum arrived: a haircut by Monday at 5 P.M. *or else.* As publishers of newspapers go, ours was selectively open-minded and politically liberal, but apparently some of his advertisers and the corporate associates he played golf with had twitted him for employing hippie reporters and questioned if hippies (all of whom were, of course, radicals) could be trusted to report Camden's racial unrest fairly and objectively. The staff and I circulated a petition protesting Rocky's threatened dismissal. It was signed by forty reporters and editors—an impressive show of solidarity that bridged the age and life-style gap—and presented to the executive editor. He was a liberal who'd quit a pervious editorship because he had the incautious courage of his convictions. Now he had a mortgage on a big house and kids in school. Like many good people of his generation, he was torn but noncommital.

When the publisher learned of the petition, he was outraged, for it smelled of the highest perfidy in the newspaper business —a Guild drive. (Actually, none of us had any interest in guilds, unions being one more block to creativity and individuality.) The publisher called me on the carpet and held me responsible for stirring up staff rebellion. I was given the choice of resigning or recanting: confessing to the night staff that I'd made a mistake in judgment and that, for the good of the paper, Rocky should conform to the company's dress code.

Rocky saved me from having to make the decision.

Regretting that he'd caused such a tempest, he cut his hair to the scalp and reappeared in the city room looking like a Buddhist monk. As usual, the editor was conciliatory: all would be forgotten, etc. But as we left his office, Rocky told me that minutes earlier he'd gone into the office of the publisher—who

was out on the golf course—and dumped a bag of shorn hair
on his king-size desk. In a few minutes, his secretary discovered
the hair and began to notify the chain of command. Little button lights on the city desk phones lit up. In record time, the
executive editor ripped a book of carboned memos from his
typewriter and charged into the city room, tearing off dupli-
cates. One was for Rocky, another for me, a third for the managing editor; then he headed toward the business office, strip-
ping off more. They read:

> To: Robert "Rocky" Wilson
> Re: Appearance and behavior
> As of today your employment on the *Courier-Post*
> newspaper has been severed. . . .

A few days later, I quit; and during the next few months,
four other nightside reporters left. In less than a year, almost
all the night staff had departed. I don't often think about returning to the *Courier*, but if I did, I suspect staff morale
would be about the same. The desks, still arranged in rows four
deep, would be interchangeably occupied by reporters, none
of whom I would recognize.

Unemployed, free of assignments, I decided to go to the
Chicago convention, drawn by the instincts of an off-duty fire-
man to a fire. I had the vague intention of doing a free-lance
piece on the McCarthyites, who seemed destined for disillu-
sionment. And I had a craving to be a free-floating observer of
what I guessed might be a symbolic turning point for America.
Lacking press credentials and even interest in the convention itself, I headed for the demonstration taking place in Grant
Park and on Michigan Avenue across from the Conrad Hilton.
The National Guard, bayonets bared, drew the line on the west
side of the avenue, defending the perfect symbol of the establishment—the floodlit magisterial hotel, home of the delegates,
the upper-middle-class gentry who came and went through its
gleaming revolving doors. The center of the street was occupied
by the Chicago Police and the National Guard, their jeeps

mounted with submachine guns. Among them, with their po-
lice-approved credentials dangling from their necks, were the
press.

I decided to defect to the east side of the street, on the sharp
side of the bayonets. For once, I took no notes. I joined the
tortuously slow marches and ran with the thousands of dem-
onstrators as canisters of tear gas popped overhead, clutching
to my nose a strip of cloth torn from a black flag of anarchy. I
talked to people, no longer seeking out the "leaders" and
"spokesmen," but speaking to equals in the blurred experience
that was Chicago: the long dinner lines in church basements
on the North Side; the campfires made of political placards;
the sunrise gathering in Grant Park, singing, "This Land is
Your Land"; and the pervasive hunger for community. "I have
no family other than you," said a nineteen-year-old, who announced his resignation from the Army at a resistance meeting.
His grandfather had been killed in World War II and his father
in the Korean War.

I never wrote the story I had set out to do; if I had, my
conclusions would have been slightly different from the establishment press's analysis. After Chicago, the split in the
youth movement became wider. It was between the political
revolutionaries, the students of Herbert Marcuse, who attacked
the structures of capitalist society that supposedly restrained
man from liberating his consciousness. For them, Chicago
meant release from their liberal beliefs—from the last check
to unbridled terrorism. On the other side of the gap were the
nonviolent hippies who had read Norman O. Brown and were
absorbed in a cultural revolution. For them Chicago underscored the ultimate futility of protest: What good had it all
done if the final choice was Nixon or Humphrey?

Besides, mere protest would not jar the silent majority's
complacent acceptance of political authority. The people who
cheered Mayor Daley had undergone a lifetime of cultural conditioning. Changes in consciousness had to precede the political revolution. Heads had to be changed—first.

The last night in Chicago, I wandered around Grant Park

campfires and asked people where they were going. Many, especially the McCarthy people, were in shock and didn't know where to go next or what to do. Certainly not back to the university. As a last, desperate alternative, a lot of them talked about dropping out of it *all*, going back to the country to live with their friends in psychological exile from Amerika which they'd begun to spell with a *k*.

To a country seemingly entrenched in self-interest, deaf to change and blind to its own danger, they said "Fuck it" and split. If the cities were uninhabitable and the suburbs plastic, they would still have to live somewhere. If the spirit of humane community and culture were dead in urban Amerika, they would have to create their own.

Before coming to Chicago, I'd kept a file on communes—one of several examples of the "decentralist trends" in American society. Most of the clippings dealt with ones that had come under attack. In their infancy, communes provided a very visible target for the foes of hip radicalism. In August, 1968, near Voluntown, Connecticut, a communal farm of draft resisters was attacked at 2:30 A.M. by a squad of armed Minutemen. Wounded in the gun battle that followed were four Minutemen, a state policeman and one member of the farm, which was operated by the New England Committee for Nonviolent Action.

Some of the most notorious instances of repression directed against communes occurred in California, where the movement began. The flower children had begun to flee San Francisco and its Haight-Ashbury district, where, in a run-down area of flophouses and parking lots, they had planted the first seeds of a community. For a while, it flourished, and elsewhere, small hippie ghettos were rising in other slum-torn centers: in Washington's DuPont Circle, in New York's East Village, Minneapolis' West Bank, and Chicago's Old Town.

But in the Haight, as elsewhere, the influx of hippies was followed by pushers, junkies, speed freaks, prostitutes and the Mafia. When the police came on the scene, the flower children were pushed off streets, which had become unsafe for anyone, hip or straight.

In 1967, Lou Gottlieb opened his thirty-acre ranch in Sonoma County, California, to the swarms of Haight-Ashbury refugees. Its purpose, he said, was "to live experimentally in an alternative society for the technologically unemployable." Morningstar Ranch became the first commune to be celebrated in the slick pages of *Time* magazine, and Gottlieb, a forty-seven-year-old dropped-out jazz musician, became the prophet of the Open Land Movement.

Believing that the creation of private property was man's original sin, Gottlieb renounced ownership of the land. He went so far as to transfer the deed "to God." (At first, the county recorder balked but then accepted Gottlieb's amended deed and one-dollar fee. Later he commented: "If Gottlieb wants to waste his money, let him.") On weekends, hundreds descended on Morningstar and camped out in tepees, wrecked cars and plastic-covered huts—in open view of the plush summer houses of ex-urbanites that adjoined the ranch. The neighbors complained to the police of loud music, knife fights, and hippies "copulating and defecating" in the open. A public hearing was held. The county applied its cudgel of health and building laws and declared that Morningstar failed to meet the code's minimum amount of floor space per person. Gottlieb was fined and restrained by court order from allowing more than fifteen visitors on his ranch at any one time.

Each time the police searched the ranch and uncovered more than fifteen people in residence, the court fined Gottlieb for contempt. From September of 1967 to July of 1968, the county levied fines of $14,000. Eventually, Gottlieb paid most of it. Hippies who realized he was running out of cash simply stopped coming to the ranch. One day the county bulldozers appeared and, in the name of public health, leveled all but one of the commune's buildings.

By that time most of Morningstar's population had moved on. A large group emigrated to a "liberated" mesa north of Taos, New Mexico, to form Morningstar East. Others relocated on a

130-acre commune called Wheeler Ranch, just ten miles away near Bodega Bay, which was also land "liberated" by its owner. Eventually, Sonoma County was to turn its bureaucratic sights on Wheeler and uncover even more code violations there than it had at Morningstar.

As California became more urbanized and densely populated by hips and straights alike, its sunny climate grew tense. The hippies were quick to sense the change and began to scout around for other havens. One such group was the Oz family, who traveled east to start a commune near Meadville, Pennsylvania. Some of them had passed through Morningstar, but the core had come together at Holiday, a hip resort of bungalows outside Santa Cruz. Holiday was the typical first-year commune, heavily dosed with drugs, sex, and populated by transients, a number of them pregnant runaway girls. All had grown tired of California's smog, freeways, and, especially, the harassment. But it was mainly the $500 monthly rent that drove the Oz family to seek its own land. So when a friend and sometime merchant marine, William Close, offered them the farm he'd inherited in Pennsylvania, they headed east for the promised land.

After the Chicago convention, I headed home to Philadelphia, stopping along the way in Meadville, Pennsylvania, to check out Oz. I'd clipped the newspaper stories that chronicled the campaign of harassment the townsfolk were waging against the commune. In 1968, it was the familiar story of "straight" society repressing the hip culture; a miniature sequel to Chicago and a dark omen that even hippies' *peaceful* forms of radicalism would not be tolerated. Like Morningstar, Oz's mere existence seemed to elicit violence.

The beginning of every social movement is littered with its false starts and martyrs. Oz was both. In less than six months, the commune was forced to disband and leave Pennsylvania. That wasn't the whole story, I found. The crucial struggles that divided Oz were internal ones.

The commune was located ten miles outside Meadville. I drove slowly along the dirt road until I came to a line of no-parking signs. Set far back was the weather-beaten, Charles Addamsesque farmhouse, with a yin-and-yang symbol painted beside the door. I parked and locked the car. Wearing a gray flannel suit, striped tie and cordovans, I assailed my first commune. My initial encounter was with the tall, gaunt, prophet-like figure who was standing sentry near a trash can. Josh looked up from his Bible when I introduced myself. For half an hour, under his questioning, I explained who I was and what I believed. As we talked, carloads of gawkers rolled by. Josh dispatched them with icy stares and shouted Biblical quotations. He was initially suspicious of me but eventually revealed himself as a fellow writer and showed me his unpublished book *Josh's Sayings,* a compendium of adages and some "improvisations on Marx." Finally, I passed Josh's admission tests and was allowed to enter the farm grounds.

Most of the windows of the house had been broken and not replaced. Inside, plaster had fallen away from sections of the walls. A wood stove stood unconnected. Thousands of flies filled the air with their contented drone. Clothes piled in a corner constituted the free store—yours for the washing. An upstairs room was full of bare mattresses and sleeping bags. (A few couples had their own rooms, closets or tents.)

The backyard was an open-air kitchen: over a campfire bubbled a perpetual stew. Unfinished portions went back into the common pot. The wind sometimes carried a sweet waft from the outhouse, a few steps away in a clump of bushes. There were eleven dogs and an unenumerated population of cats, who leaped on tables to lick bowls and plates. Planted too late, the garden hadn't yielded a great variety of crops. In a clearing at a distance from the main house stood the unfinished shell of a geodesic dome. The commune started to construct the dome, needing a coffeehouse where they could meet and rap with the hundreds of straight and hip tourists from Pennsylvania, New York, Ohio and West Virginia who flocked to Meadville on weekends. Oz, the region's first "hippie commune," and thus a novelty, was sensationalized in the Cleveland, Pittsburgh and Erie newspapers. But as the summer progressed and tourists

continued coming, Oz's popularity also attracted troublemak-
ers and, finally, public harassment. Work on the dome was
suspended.

Most of my time at the commune was spent on its front porch.
It was a perfect vantage point, since most of the members hung
out there—actors on a stage fronting the dirt road where the
outside world assembled to be entertained. Once, a low-slung,
rumbling Chevrolet inched menacingly past. I caught glimpses
of biceps, T-shirts and beer cans. Suddenly, Michael W., who
was sitting beside me, leaped up, waving his arms in the air.
"Why don't you fuck yourselves," he screamed venomously,
repeating his curse until the car backed out of sight and the
others told him to cool it. His anger made my heart race.

Oz was made up of singles, couples and some ten teen-agers
whose status, ages and numbers fluctuated wildly. They ranged
in age from Amy, three, Rebecca's daughter and the commune's
only child, to Cora Lee, forty-two, who had once been married
and had lived the suburban life in Mill Valley, California. After
her divorce, she'd taken up macrobiotics, yoga and practiced
celibacy. Patty-Pooh was blonde and good-looking, the daughter
of a New York stock broker. She had attended a midwestern
college for a year, then had gone West to the coast and worked
for the Berkeley *Tribe*, an underground newspaper. To earn
money for the commune, she made occasional trips to New York
and posed for pornies.

Many of the men of Oz were like Nevada, the prototypical
California hippie: bare-chested and barefoot, he always wore
the same pair of jeans and washed his long auburn hair every
day in the creek. Nevada went quietly about his work, answered
"whatever" to major questions, and taught the others how to
"make love" to the garden. He was also the chief goatherd and
sometimes slept with Ed, the billy.

During his adolescence in Sacramento, Nevada had waged a
campaign of vandalism against automobiles. He would spend
nights toppling the chain-link fences along the freeways. From
the overpasses, he would dump buckets of urine on the cars

whizzing by below. During his senior year of high school, he was arrested for appearing nude one night in the center of a freeway.

The family of Oz seemed strongly linked by a common background and an enraged memory of having been "fucked over" by indifferent parents, joyless schools and a neon environment. Josh's parents had sent him off to prep school, he said, to "get rid of him." At fourteen, Deja had been raped. Kathy had experienced recurring episodes of schizophrenia. Morgan, known as Count Morgan, had escaped the mental institution to which his parents had committed him. Taking too much speed had impaired his neural pathways, causing him to stumble as he walked mooselike through the woods. Wanda was a violent Virgo who took morphine, talked of assassinating George Wallace, and read books on witchcraft. Ross had grown up in a tough section of the Bronx, a war zone for rival street gangs. He liked to take potshots with his rifle at telephone poles and rabbits.

Few would talk of their parents or past, and when they did, it was bitterly. For instance, Michael W.'s description of his mother's suburban house: "You come in the door and walk on this plastic mat that runs from the doorway all the way through the living room. That's so the rug won't get dirty. All the furniture's covered with plastic slipcovers."

Children of transient corporation men, they had grown up in comfortable sterile homes of pseudo-Colonial design in interchangeable suburbs with almost mocking names like Heritage Hills Estates. They were reared in families that were not families at all, communities that were not communities in the literal sense of the Latin *communico,* meaning "to share." "The only time we actually *felt* like a family," said Muffin, "was when we took two-week vacations in the Poconos. The rest of the time, life at home didn't seem—real." Muffin was pregnant. Her old man, David, said they were going to bring the child up in the country. "What a kid sees around him the first time becomes his reality. If it's cellophane and concrete, he accepts that as real. But the Bible makes a clear point that man shouldn't live in cities. . . ."

The family's unofficial spokesman and spiritual leader was

ascetically thin and heavily bearded George Hurd. Though George was the one who talked to the press, consulted lawyers, and drummed up local supporters, he commanded no authority. A few other members sometimes scoffed at him. But everyone respected George—not as a leader but as just another freak in the family. He was understood and accepted as George, a guy who liked to do the spiritual-verbal trip. So why not let him?

The son of a machinist, George was born under Virgo and grew up in a sedate town in Connecticut. Reared a Roman Catholic, he attended Catholic University in Washington, D.C., and alternated his studies between mathematics and courses leading to the priesthood. He dropped out of school and worked as a computer trainee for a life insurance company while taking philosophy and psychology courses at the University of Hartford. Then he left the programmer's job, going to California, where he was an NAACP staff worker. Intellectually, he told me, his interest shifted from Sartre's "negative" existentialism back to a study of religion, especially the Eastern "mind-expanding" faiths. He took LSD to help his spiritual search and was led into a turned-on, all-embracing faith that is essentially Christian: "The words of Christ contain the essential teaching of all religions. The message of love equates Christ-consciousness with Buddha and Krishna-consciousness, and involves the concept of the immanent divinity as opposed to the transcendent one."

While on the Coast, Hurd visited Holiday and made the journey east with its émigrés. When they arrived in Meadville, he urged them to adopt an open, almost proselytizing attitude toward their neighbors. On one of their first days in town, he went to the office of the Meadville *Tribune* and granted an interview on the commune's aims, explaining that they intended to become a model for the counterculture of the future, when capitalism would be replaced by a brotherhood of love and men would strive to attain cosmic consciousness.

These were distinctly disquieting ideas for the residents of Meadville, the county seat of Crawford County, a citadel of Republicanism and fundamentalism. With a population of

20,000, Meadville is the classic Middletown. Its clean streets are lined with green-and-white litter cans. At noon on Sunday, the air fills with chimed hymns from the belfry of the First Baptist Church. Its population is a mix of laborers and white-collar workers employed by Talon, American Brakeshoe and Viscose, the town's major industries. Meadville's conservative stance is offset somewhat by its liberal elements: the professors and students of Allegheny College, located in town, and its progressive local paper.

The town's initial reaction to Oz was tolerant curiosity. In the first months the commune drew many open-minded visitors: college students, car dealers, professors, ministers, doctors, even a friendly deputy sheriff. Some middle-aged couples stayed overnight at the farm. Construction workers brought a case of beer and questions: Why do you wear long hair, take drugs, and hand-spade the garden instead of using a tractor? Many sought answers to deeply troubling and personal problems. A professor of biochemistry, just divorced, spent many weekends at Oz and later credited the family with having prevented him from committing suicide.

Most of Oz's converts were teen-agers who had left homes within a one-hundred-mile radius of Meadville. Many of them signified their membership and adoption of a new family—one of shared experience rather than blood—by dropping their patronyms and assuming new names like Odessa, Dancing Bear, and Vesta, a sixteen-year-old who lived at the commune with her parents' tacit approval.

As the summer progressed and rumors of drugs and social disease at the commune began to circulate, parents forbade their teen-agers to visit Oz. Naturally, the prohibition was an extra enticement, and more came. Soon runaways were arriving at the commune, placing it squarely in the middle of intrafamily and generational wrangles. Hurd ministered to indignant parents and confused adolescents alike. One night two teeny-boppers, unknown to most members of the commune, set up what amounted to a tent of ill repute on the grounds. However, Ross, a member, acted as their pimp. Their clients were local men and boys who spread the word that the hippies supported themselves by prostitution. Soon carloads of red-necks began appearing late at night to offer six-packs in return for "one of your women."

The family began to divide over the issue of the increasing number of visitors. Oz had not established any policy to guide its relations with the outside world. In publicizing the commune as a pilot project for the counterculture, Hurd acted almost alone. From the start, Oz was a "working anarchy" that had no leaders, took no votes, and could only make common decisions when everybody agreed—which was rare. While no one questioned this policy of consensus, nevertheless, scores of issues hung unresolved. The major one was George's concept of an "open commune," which was strongly opposed by at least four other members. They wanted Oz to be self-sufficient and not dependent for income on panhandling visitors. The matter was never settled. A few members, like Josh, acted unilaterally to close the commune—by kicking out visitors he disliked and throwing stones at cars full of the curious. Each member related spontaneously to the outside world. Parmel spent the early summer in a roadside armchair, gladly accepting gifts from whoever came by. The advocates of a closed commune stayed on the porch and shouted abuse at the parade of passing cars churning up a continual dust cloud. Once Patty-Pooh tried to "vibe away" the curiosity seekers by performing a nude dance on the farmhouse roof. Of course it had the opposite effect.

In general there was tacit agreement on the kind of society Oz did *not* want to duplicate. And a wide assortment of escapist fantasies. But when the chips were down, the commune was paralyzed, unable to convert fantasy into workable realities. Although there was much talk of economic self-sufficiency, most of the commune's money came from the capitalist system its members had rejected: allowances, inheritances, tourist handouts. Rebecca sold a few "god's eyes" that she wound from brightly colored yarn on cross-shaped stick frames, but otherwise, little communal craft was evident. When individuals worked, they did so alone. The first floor of the house was nearing collapse. Friendly farmers lent the family jacks and other tools to shore it up, but the repair work, like the geodesic dome, was never finished. Probably more time was spent throwing the I Ching or reading the tarot cards than doing actual farm work.

There was a great deal of fantasy play in the land of Oz, play that verged on living theater. In the backyard, Bodiless George, Ludwig and Dancing Bear pretended to be a gang of revving, rampaging bikers, grunting, "Hey, mama, I wanta beer." Adolph and Deja, who took her name from a Ouija board, existed in a world of astrology and numerology. Adolph spent hours composing songs to accompany each card in the tarot deck. Shortly before noon, when most woke up, there were sessions of dream analysis. Through the day, there were readings from Dr. Seuss, *Winnie the Pooh,* and *The Wizard of Oz.* Another favorite fantasy was to stalk the "monkey demon" in the woods. "After a while, you could see his green eyes glowing in the dark," said Dancing Bear.

But when the demons became real, the family was helpless to cope with them. One night they were invaded by a gang of armed bikers who demanded they turn over one of their women for a gang bang. For a while the family reacted pacifically. George spoke of love and nonviolence. So did the girl, who was finally raped five times. Then the bikers forced Bodiless George to walk barefoot through a fire. The torture might have continued if someone hadn't used a neighbor's phone to call the state police. When police arrived, the bikers had escaped and could not be apprehended.

Oz was not a "together" commune. Most members were pacifists, but a few, like Ross, shot ducks. The summer's one fistfight occurred over visitors and, specifically, over a violation of a short-lived ban on accepting handouts. Most disputes, however trivial, undermined the family's sense of cosmic oneness. Arguments started over things like whether or not to play the battery-operated phonograph (which was later stolen) and whether to allow animals inside the house. Drugs, in the past a bond, were individually used but seemed to give no group support. There were a few orgies, which made some members uncomfortable, but sex seemed to be largely confined to couples and was not a unifying group ritual.

At best, the family bonds were evanescent. George introduced them to natural group rituals. On moonlit nights they stood, hands clasped, in a circle and chanted the Hare Krishna mantra. They danced in the rain, played music on the roof, and held love-ins down by the creek. But most of the family's spirituality was an individual pursuit. Cora Lee spent long hours in her tent doing yoga. Marko practiced a unique form of pantheism. George aimed to incorporate the commune as "the anthropodeic church," a name he coined by combining the Greek root for "man" and the Latin root for "God." However, many of his own communal family regarded the church as a hoax and a ruse to gain them tax exemption and constitutional protection.

Lacking shared beliefs and common work, divided by their ambivalence toward the outside world, Oz drifted into late summer. Meanwhile, the visitors kept coming. The live-and-let-live days were over. Vigilante groups formed. One midnight the house was blasted by shotgun fire. There was an arson attempt.

When one of the family came down with infectious hepatitis, the regional health officer went on the radio to warn people to stay away from Oz. Because thousands had already visited the farm, the broadcast precipitated a hepatitis scare of bubonic plague proportions. As it turned out, there were only 9 cases of hepatitis in Crawford County in 1968, 6 fewer than the 15 reported the year before. Nevertheless, local residents organized a protest meeting at the Summit Township Fire Hall. A sign posted outside read ALL CITIZENS WELCOME, but when twenty hippies from the farm appeared, they were denied entrance. Only Hurd and one other were allowed into the hall and then given a brief time to ask and answer questions. During the meeting, a woman resident bluntly expressed her views on the free inoculations of gamma globulin being given the family: "I would let them live there and die." Later, State Senator James E. Willard pledged he would do all in his power to move the hippies out of the county, hinting that he might even introduce a special bill in the state legislature.

As the harassment intensified, others rallied to Oz's defense. Letters to the *Tribune* ran three to two in favor of tolerating the commune. The most constant supporters were the commune's immediate neighbors, farmers who respected their nonconformist desire to live simply and in organic harmony with the land. Some of the family were live-in workers on several farms in the area. They painted barns and harvested crops and customarily refused cash payment, preferring instead to be paid in kind—so many bushels of wheat in return for harvesting it. Farmers dumped bags of surplus commodities on Oz's porch— soybeans, potatoes, wheat—and gave them tips on how to grow their own. An elderly sage advised the commune on matters herbal and spiritual. One day he waded into the creek with some of the family and treated their burns and skin diseases with his faith-healing techniques—techniques he'd been afraid to practice for fear the villagers would scoff at him.

Those most deeply offended by the hippies' sanitary and moral standards were the residents of the city and the village—those who had flush toilets, mortgages, TV's and preconceived hippie stereotypes. To them Oz represented an unknown, and therefore threatening, subculture. Down the road from the farm I talked to the elderly owner of a modern ranch house who mentioned pointedly that thefts had increased in the area since the hippies moved in and added, "I see them hitching down the road every day; I'd pick them up, but you never know what they'll do next."

In the village of Harmonsburg, two miles away, a mother spoke of her fear that the commune might introduce her teenagers to drugs, "which might change them forever. I don't know . . . they say drugs do that to you."

The long-anticipated raid occurred on the morning of August 16. The Commonwealth of Pennsylvania arrived at 9:30 A.M., when most of the family was still asleep. The police searched frantically around the house and land but evidently found no drugs. "And they were furious," said George. "They smashed furniture, ripped open mattresses, cracked walls." Meanwhile, the family was herded into a school bus and driven into Meadville, singing, "Yellow Submarine." There they were greeted by a hostile, jeering crowd of about two hundred assembled outside the alderman's office. By prearrangement, they were brought there to be arraigned. When word was sent that no drugs had been found, they were charged with maintaining a disorderly house, in violation of an 1860 statute that read: "Whoever keeps and maintains a common, ill-governed and disorderly house or place to the encouragement of idleness, gaming, drinking or misbehavior and to the common nuisance and disturbance of the neighborhood and orderly citizens is guilty of a misbehavior...." A second charge accused the family of corrupting the morals of Vesta, the sixteen-year-old who'd been living at the farm with her parents' consent. Rebecca was charged with neglect and corrupting the morals of her three-year-old daughter, Amy, who was taken away from her and temporarily placed in a foster home. Later, at the custody hearing, the county charged that Rebecca had allowed Amy to be exposed to male nudity, physical filth, foul language, and had permitted her to wander around the farm and woods without adult supervision. Evidence was apparently based on testimony provided by a paid informer who visited the commune in the guise of a simpleton who looked after animals. Additional evidence came from photographs, sold to the district attorney's office by two free-lancers, that showed Amy and family members posing in the style of a Victorian tintype—but nude. The court awarded custody of Amy to her maternal grandmother.

After spending the night in jail, the family was released on bail furnished by one of their liberal middle-class defenders, a doctor. On returning to the farm, they found an injunction posted on the front door of their home forbidding its use for "fornication, assignation and lewdness."

Between the time of their arrest and a hearing on the charges, the family contemplated its future. Was it worth the hassle to fight Crawford County and become a national test case of hip values versus those of straight society? George Hurd and two others thought so and urged that they resist, but the others wanted to get out of town. Their concern was for the members of the family who were being sought by federal agents on charges of draft evasion.

At the hearing in early September, the family was offered a deal by the district attorney, Peter Shafer, the nephew of Governor Raymond Shafer. If they agreed to "remove themselves from the farm and county and not to regroup within the county for a year," the charges against them would be dropped. The family took a poll and accepted the deal. In the next two weeks they scattered across the country.

For me, Oz was an uncomfortable experience. Most of the time I sat on the porch, absorbing the cultural shock, a Boswell among the Hebrideans. It was remarkable that I was able to write any story at all. The family's fate left me doubting whether any commune could survive the violent defensiveness that Oz had elicited from Meadville. Neither community nor commune was exclusively to blame. Oz was as paranoid as Meadville. The *we/they* division they made between themselves and the "outside world" eventually boomeranged. The trauma of breaking away from the establishment—the establishment they believed had in one way or another thwarted their growth and drained their energy—froze them in fantasy land, splintered their faith, blocked their capacity for work.

As a community, Oz was too undefined and otherworldly to survive in a land of red-necks and court injunctions. On the other hand, Meadville was too narrow-minded, too constricted by a rigid code of morality, and suffered from a different kind of paranoia, which perhaps time and familiarity could have relaxed. If not, if the straight community couldn't relax, there was no hope for communes. In 1968 the two subcultures seemed incapable of peaceful coexistence. I left Meadville half believing the cynical conclusion of the townspeople: that even *without* the raid, the commune would have destroyed itself or quietly withered away. Such was the universal fate of utopias that set themselves above the reality of man's nature.

Most of the Utopian communities that started out in this country in the nineteenth century—the Rappites, Zoarites,

Icarians—had failed to endure past the first generation. And compared to contemporary communes, they had much more going for them: shared traditions, skills and religious convictions. Why should the newest wave be spared the fate of the past? In the late sixties there were already scores that hadn't made it, places like Rancho Olompali, Sunrise Hill, Free Folk, Cold Mountain, Pepperland. If fully compiled, the number of the deceased might well outrun the living.

Often, I would chase down a commune, only to find it had already disbanded. For instance, I had heard of one near West Shoakan, New York, started in the euphoric wake of the Woodstock Festival. For two hours I drove up, down and around the Catskills, hunting for the old resort hotel that the commune had taken over. Halfway up a rocky mountain road that scraped at the muffler, I found it—a four-story building with ghostly Victorian trimmings. From the roof of a half-collapsed veranda was draped an American flag and a girdle-clad dressmaker's form wrapped in black plastic. At first I couldn't find anyone, only rusted cars with sprung hoods and, inside the hotel, rats that beat a scrambling retreat before my footsteps.

Most of the commune had split, leaving only Chris and her old man, who also were about to depart. The main room had been stripped bare. During the last frosty nights the members had burned the furniture. Left behind were spotlights and expensive video tape equipment which, Chris explained, the commune had used to record encounters and acid trips. She played an old tape for me. It had been shot in the same room and filmed hours of everyone's pounding the floor in a deafening rhythm. Over the din, I could barely make out the words individuals on whom the camera focused were screaming. Barry talked prophetically: "The house is strife and discontentment— the same as the divided world. When one man has more pleasure, we get jealous. But we all have pleasure. We are God. . . ." (In the background) "No shit!"

I left the video tape blaring and walked down the long hallway, ducking my head into each room. In the last on the left, I found a mattress beside a crate topped with the congealed stub of a scented candle and an ashtray containing two or three roaches. They had burned all their furniture and smoked the last of their grass. On the wall, writ in Magic Marker, was the self-epitaph of a community that never was: FOREVER CHANGE.

I left and drove down the mountain, unable to shake the dank futility of the place. Perhaps along with this generation of crazy romantics, I was pursuing the chimera of a community no more tangible than a puff of pot. Maybe it was better—and easier—to go along witñ the system, to seek momentary pleasure and snatches of love and meaning here and there. Inside a needling voice: "The system you so vehemently protest, surely it isn't the only source of violence and destruction? Go as far as you want—to the ends of the continent, to the tops of mountain roads —and the enemy will follow you. And it will not be the system— not Mayor Daley, Strom Thurmond, or *Time* magazine—but you, man, and your lusts and power trips."

These gnawing doubts were to be borne out by what I saw of communes in their first years: everywhere, a screaming need for privacy, to be alone in a place called your own, one that was sacred and uncommunal. Everywhere, hassles and marathon encounter meetings that couldn't resolve questions like whether to leave the dogs in or out. Everywhere, cars that wouldn't run and pumps that wouldn't pump because everybody knew all about the occult history of tarot and nobody knew anything about mechanics. Everywhere, people who strove for self-sufficiency and freedom from the capitalist system but accepted food stamps and handouts from Daddy, a corporate sales VP. Sinks filled with dishes, cows wandering through gates left open, and no one to blame. Everywhere, instability, transiency. Somebody was always splitting, rolling up his bag, packing his guitar and kissing good-bye—off again in search of the truly free, unhungup community.

After Oz disbanded in 1968, George and a few others stayed in Meadville through New Year's Day. George was on the college-church speaking circuit as a kind of local guru. Then he, Josh, and two others headed west again to California, picking up

Michael and Kathy in Iowa City. Patty-Pooh returned to her parents' penthouse apartment. Muffin and David had their baby in New York and returned to Pennsylvania to buy land for themselves. Adolph came into an inheritance and bought a big black hearse in which he and Deja set out to tour the country. Rebecca went home with her mother to Florida but later split, with Amy in tow, and rejoined George, Cora Lee and others in Santa Fe. Nevada went to a community in western New York that was dedicated to ecology and eugenics and run by semistraight couples, some of whom worked as computer programmers. He was put in charge of the animals. Other members went to Reality, a commune of dropped-out radicals in New Mexico, and to the Georgeville Trading Post. Throughout all these changes of address, the family stayed in touch, held transcendentally together.

The last to split was Marko, who struck out for Alaska. After he left, there was little to indicate the family had ever been there. Months later persons unknown burned the farmhouse to the ground. The only trace left of Oz was a pile of charred timbers. The family was in diaspora, as George called it. But only for a time.

I
New England

After Several False Starts, a Departure

After the Democratic convention and the fall of the house of Oz, I returned to Philadelphia. I still had no job, nor any desire for one, and felt no need to play the attendant roles: pay rent, live in a city, keep my hair cut. So we packed what we could fit into a U-Haul and paid our last respects and bridge token to the "City of Brotherly Love." I was heading my family—Mary, then pregnant, Susan, four, two cats and five kittens—to a summer cabin on our thirty-five acres in northern Vermont. At the time, we thought life at the cabin would be an extended vacation, until we ran through the $5,000 I'd inherited from my aunt and I had to get another job in another city.

At New Haven, we picked up Interstate 91, which parallels the Connecticut River, once the inland waterway, natural power source and shad run of a bygone America. We passed the dumps that are steadily filling in the river's lowland marshes, where native ducks used to nest. At night, the dump fires make an inferno of the sky.

The river slickens past the rows of cylindrical oil tanks at Hartford and flows between wooded bluffs to Springfield. There, the Interstate detours the through traffic back to old U.S. 5 for a sample of classical American highway art: an endless perspective of signs for Mister Donut, Burger Chef, Gas Town, The Steak Inferno, Pizza Hut, Discount City, Pancake House. South of

Hadley, conveyor belts feed coal into a huge electric generating plant that disgorges its SO_2 and soot over the valley, whose tall conifers have given way to ticky-tacky developments interspersed with signs celebrating the world's largest basket factory. We follow the river north, past the site for an atomic power plant at Vernon, Vermont, guided toward the Connecticut's clean, receding headwaters.

At St. Johnsbury we veered away from the river through country populated by more deer than people, past ponds, abandoned apple orchards, and cemeteries claimed by wild roses. The cabin was on a hill that overlooked a pond in one direction and in the other looked north into Canada.

In the fall I wrote a magazine piece on Oz and puttered around the cabin, insulating and preparing for winter. I felt numb. The clash with the newspaper hierarchy replayed in my memory like an overplugged commercial. Much of that fall and following spring, I fished—therapeutically, like Hemingway's Nick Adams—fixing my attention on the immediate. It took a year to recover from the disorientation of having broken from a career in which I'd invested years of education, apprenticeship and much more ego than I had realized. I was stranded on an icecap, out of radio contact with the voices of my inner self. For the time, I heard only silence.

The winter was sometimes lonely. Every night Mary and I played gin rummy. Finally Mary refused to play because I became so emotionally involved with winning. We started attending a Unitarian church in Derby Line. We were the youngest of about twenty regular parishioners, who every Sunday sat in uncomfortable pews and sang the same small selection of hymns. On the wall was a marble plaque commemorating the founder of the local WCTU. Another foray into the community saw me joining the Lion's Club. During the winter I attended a few meetings in a room of a motel-restaurant that had been decorated with fishing nets, colored glass buoys and a little fountain that served as centerpiece for a buffet table.

In many ways we remained city people. We didn't fit into what remnant was left of community in the country. Every Wednesday (double Green Stamp day) we drove our station wagon into town to shop at the Grand Union and pick up the New York *Times* at Piper's General Store. For a time, we were people without a community or culture, who had escaped to an alien country. Self-outcasts of the silent, buttoned-down fifties, Mary and I debated whether or not to attend our tenth college reunions. With misgivings, we went to a Wellesley party hosted by suburban friends and came away feeling even more alienated. In every way, economically, socially and geographically, we had dropped out; but as yet we had not discovered any kind of sub-society to drop into.

After the Oz piece was published in the *New York Times Magazine,* I got a number of feelers from publishers eager to do a commune book. I had nothing else to do and needed a consuming project. But even if there *had* been a commune nearby, we wouldn't have joined. We were hardly freaks. And communes, as I saw them then, were only a "socially significant," salable subject. As a way of life for myself and my family, no thanks.

That was the attitude I took with me on my first expedition into the communes of New England, seeking "material" to write an introductory chapter from which I hoped to reap an advance. I was like a detached observer who touched down on remote planets and was told by their inhabitants that my earth home was counting down to apocalypse.

High in the Massachusetts Berkshires, living in a lean-to cabin, was the Leyden Society, a group of twenty-year-olds who had just given up drugs. They subsisted on brown rice, took plunges in iced-over brooks, and awaited world's end. "Better stay out of Boston and New York," Tom warned me. "And if you go, better wear an aqualung."

At Johnson's Pastures, an open-land commune in southern Vermont, Michael Carpenter was forecasting that the transition from the Piscean to the Aquarian Age would be accompanied by earthquakes and tidal waves that would send people in the cities fleeing to the country. There the communes would train the survivors to live off the land again and to adapt to the new age's higher vibrational energies. In the fall of 1969, Johnson's Pastures looked much like a refugee camp. Scattered over two hundred acres were tar-paper shacks, tree houses and plastic-covered lean-tos. As a whole, in 1969 the entire commune movement in New England looked much the same: very shaky and temporary and undefined.

The Huggs Family, who were the first in Vermont, were living rent-free in a house on land south of Bennington, by the grace of an apple baron. But they weren't a community. After the first frost, most rolled up their sleeping bags and tepees and split to the Virgin Islands or New York City to live on unemployment.

Besides the summer trippers, New England attracted communes made up of people who had belonged to SNCC and SDS. But they had come to conclude that changing the power structure was futile. Now they called for the abolition of central government entirely and began to refer to themselves as anarchists. A very loose term, "anarchism" covered many positions: intellectual and political nihilism, sexual freedom, violence, concern for ecology. Many accepted Paul Goodman's redefinition of modern anarchism as the replacement of a centralized social and political system with a loose network of decentralized, individualistic communities made viable by an enlightened technology that would provide small energy sources and "miniaturized" industries. This could be accomplished, Goodman wrote, not with the violent revolution of the old anarchism, but through "the increased practice of anarchist living." *

Many people who had been in the political movement left New York, Boston and Philadelphia and came to Vermont, where they set up communities in the neo-anarchist fashion. One of the most recent was the Wooden Shoe, founded in 1969 by a group who had vainly tried to radicalize the college com-

* *New York Times Magazine*, July 14, 1969.

munity of Dartmouth in Hanover, New Hampshire. They took their name from the symbol of anarchism, the *sabot*,* rented a pine-paneled, applianced house on the Vermont side of the Connecticut near Hanover, and hired themselves out as work crews to paint and build houses.

Like Vermont's other fledgling communes, the Wooden Shoe was in a formative stage. When I first visited, they were in the middle of a transition from city to country life, from a brand of political anarchism to an ecological one. Jake Guest, their unofficial spokesman, had just read the papers of Murray Bookchin published in *Anarchos*, a New York journal of anarchist philosophy. If SDS couldn't touch off a revolutionary holocaust, steady pollution of the environment might have the same effect, Jake said. "We're slowly and irreversibly destroying the biosphere and life support systems. As long as we have big cities, megapolitan corridors, we're going to have pollution on a massive scale." His solution was Bookchin's: decentralize society. "We've got to get back to small subsistence villages and tribes. Instead of huge sewage plants, we need thousands more outhouses and compost piles."

The people at the Wooden Shoe were preparing to take the plunge. But first they needed to buy their own land; so for now, to earn the money, they had to work within the system. Like most communes that had just taken hold in New England, the Wooden Shoe was biding its time; it was too unformed, too inexperienced to stand as a model of Goodman's decentralized anarchistic community. In a year, I would return to see them after they had made the crucial conversion to the land.

When I started my forays into New England communes, I found few that had managed to weather more than one of the region's harsh winters. An early and well-known experiment that didn't survive was Sunrise Hill, near Conway, Massachusetts. Sunrise was one of several communities that grew out of

* Legend has it that aggrieved French workers clogged the machinery of employers with their own wooden shoes, or *sabots*: hence, sabotage.

an enthusiastic conference on intentional communities * held in June, 1966, at the School of Living in Freeland, Maryland. Sponsored jointly by the school and the New York Federation of Anarchists, it was the first such conference to produce more than idle discussion.

The meeting was remembered as "a miraculous merging of a long-dispersed family," by Gordon Yaswen, who has written a postmortem history of Sunrise Hill.† "Many of us had led a nomadic existence making little commitment in any area," he wrote. At Heathcote, their splintered, unrealized causes—peace, New Leftism, natural diet, rural living, sexual freedom, mysticism, nudism, psychedelics, psychotherapy, art, craftsmanship, Summerhillianism—were merged in a "bacchanalian orgy of full surrender—it was an overwhelming sensation."

After the conference, a group of twenty held long, intense discussions of the ideal form a community should take. "Why don't we do it?" challenged Bryce Ford, who owned a country house near Conway. He offered his own property for their use. Later that summer, members of the discussion group converged at the Conway farm, and the community was born.

The primary influences at Sunrise Hill were anarchism and the mystical vision of community drawn from *Stranger in a Strange Land*, by science-fiction writer Robert Heinlein. The book tells of a Martian who comes to earth and establishes a communal church called a "nest," whose members learn to communicate telepathically, or to *grok: "Grok* means to understand so thoroughly that the observer becomes part of the observed—to blend, intermarry, lose identity in group experi-

---

* During the Depression, intellectuals and Marxists who believed the land was the real source of wealth and common endeavor created several "intentional communities," some of which have survived to today: Celo Community in Burnsville, North Carolina, and Vale in the Antioch, Ohio. In contrast to a hip commune, such intentional communities are made up of older people who maintain separate houses and eschew drugs and occultism. However the term is still used to apply generically to communal experiments of many forms.

† *Sunrise Hill Community: Post-Mortem,* Star Route, Montague, Massachusetts 01351, $1.

ence." They become "water brothers," sharing each other's thoughts, possessions and bodies.*

Sunrise's first ecstatic months soon gave way to conflict. The major one was between Bryce and some other members. Besides donating the farm and his savings, Bryce took an outside job to support the community. However, he was resented by some as an authority figure. At the outset they tried communal child care, but found they had so many conflicting theories of child rearing that "the responsibility for each child's care was returned to his or her parents." Again, at the inspiration of *Stranger in a Strange Land,* all money was kept in an open box, from which members "took what they required, and recorded how much they had spent, and what for." That, too, was abandoned and replaced by conventional accounting procedures.

The philosophy of work was "do your own thing." But in Yaswen's opinion, this policy, or nonpolicy, "worked very badly." The dishes, he notes, were but one example:

There was at first no schedule for the washing of dishes. They were left for the unspecified person who at some time felt "called upon" to undertake them. They *might* be done directly after supper, but they might also be left for the following morning, when everyone had to scramble through them to scrounge up something with which to cook or eat their breakfasts. . . . Under this system, dishes were likely to accumulate until none were left, many being crusted and so left to "soak" for undefined periods.

This led to the phenomenon of the "unlabeled jars."

Since no one knew what was in them and for what end they were destined, no one wished to disturb them, and so with each use or cleaning of counter tops and refrigerator shelves, they were shuttled about. . . . When some courageous soul wished to solve their mystery, it might take asking everyone in the entire community about them before such could be done—carrying them about the house in the process. Often . . . the contents were thrown out only

---

* *Stranger in a Strange Land* (New York, Ballantine Books), p. 206.

after having received the okay of every adult member of the community.

As the summer came to an end, many members realized they couldn't spend all the winter months under the same roof. It was decided that half would live in a new house the group would build. But the leaderless situation and constant disagreements snarled the work. Impatient, some members went off to construct separate houses on the property. When the community broke up in midwinter, three houses had been begun, none had been completed.

From Sunrise's brief history, Yaswen drew some conclusions that might serve as cautionary advice to would-be communitarians. "A neurotic society must produce neurotic individuals and this is no less true for its rebels than it is for its reformers. . . . It is said that happy people don't volunteer to go to war. Neither, I say, do they join communities."

After its demise, in January, 1967, some of Sunrise's members regrouped at Cold Mountain Farm near Hobart, New York. When that settlement was dissolved by a hepatitis epidemic, a few went to live at Bryn Athyn, near South Strafford, Vermont.

Bryn Athyn existed from August of 1967 to December of 1969, becoming for a time New England's oldest commune. It repeated some of Sunrise's mistakes.

Like many communes, Bryn Athyn owed its existence to the inherited wealth of a young patron. Woody Ransom, the original owner of the farm, was one of several heirs to corporate wealth who were responsible for endowing and subsidizing communes and various hip causes throughout the country.*

---

* In addition to Ransom, other hip patrons included: Bill Wheeler, a graduate of Yale, who liberated Wheeler Ranch; Michael Lang, whose Pepsodent inheritance helped underwrite Woodstock; Chick Lonsdale, who subsidized two communes in New Mexico and a foundation that operates Taos' general store, information center and free clinic; Michael Duncan, who bought an entire New Mexico mesa and turned it over to Morningstar East and Reality communes; and Donald C. McCoy, an heir to a West Coast department store fortune, who in eight months plowed $300,000 into Rancho Olompali, a 450-acre commune

After graduating from Harvard, Woody shunned a ready-made niche in the family business, a large Midwestern paper company, to study architecture and write poetry. He bought the farm as an artist's retreat for himself and his wife. After the marriage broke up, he invited friends to join him, took an interest in anarchism, and began to attend anarchist meetings in Hanover.

During the community's first year, waves of people came and went. Most were city people, anarchists, members of sexual freedom leagues, and artsy-craftsy couples on the brink of divorce. A certain "Captain Garbage" named the farm after Bryn Athyn, outside Philadelphia, which had once been a Swedenborgian community. In Welsh, Bryn Athyn means "hill of unity."

The atmosphere was revolutionary. During the summer months, the farm became the retreat and training grounds for the "Motherfuckers," the self-appointed bodyguards of the hip subculture, who were then based in the East Village. At Bryn Athyn, the Motherfuckers held target practice, karate drills, and tested a few bombs.

One day, FBI agents came looking around for a draft violator. Fearful of being jailed for harboring the young man, the group threw the I Ching and decided that Vermont was not the place to launch a revolution. So they departed for New Mexico, then the mecca of communes, leaving behind yet another uncompleted dome.

Meanwhile, others, including some who had passed through Sunrise Hill and Cold Mountain, arrived at Bryn Athyn. All this time, Woody stayed in the background, not asserting his owner's prerogatives. Anarchically, he declared that the land and house belonged to the community. He spent much of his annual income on workhorses, machinery, taxes and general upkeep.

---

near Novato, California. He was later sued by his own family for recovery of what remained of his inheritance. McCoy was quoted in a newspaper story: "I had become a slave to business. I finally realized that if you are unhappy, you are a failure, no matter how much money you have."

In the fall of 1968, Woody left Bryn Athyn—many thought for good. That winter and the following spring the commune managed to pull itself together. Many of its members had read Wilhelm Reich, the controversial psychoanalyst and philosopher who had combined an anarchist philosophy with sexual liberation: monogamy, Reich asserted, was the seedbed of private property, possessiveness, jealousy, competition and war. For a while, Bryn Athyn attained a sexual coziness. "It was very spontaneous almost childish—like siblings who are finally allowed to play with each other's sexual parts without fear or guilt," said one member. "Some of us had the idea that each woman would have many children one by each of the men."

Woody did return, though, and his very presence—his "vibes" —undermined the group's unity. He lost patience with anarchism and the farm's leisurely economic development. To Woody, self-sufficiency was the basis of freedom from corporate capitalism. He began to call meetings in the mornings and to outline specific production goals and timetables. He initiated plans for a huge potato patch, and a maple-sugaring operation, but he didn't help out. "Most of the time, he walked around the woods tying orange strips around trees . . . no one could figure out what for," a member told me. When Woody did work, it seemed to others that he was forcing himself. Often, he'd challenge another member, like Joshua, to work beside him to see who could plow and furrow the most land. But some mornings he got up late and simply disappeared into his studio.

Woody had hoped to reap a profit from his beautiful stand of maple trees. Initially, other members were equally enthusiastic and helped him weld together an evaporator from rusty car tops. He bought books on maple sugaring, buckets and taps and set an ambitious 300-gallon production quota. He wanted to make enough to recoup the thousands of dollars he'd invested in the community, not because he needed the money, but because of his conviction that communities should be able to pay their own way.

But the others only wanted to make enough for themselves. When the thaw came, Woody was ready to oversee the sugaring. One morning, he hitched up the horses to collect the sap, which was rapidly dripping into buckets scattered over the property. However, that day the others were taking a trip. When he walked into the farmhouse to get help for the sap run, Woody found everyone rolling in a "love heap" on the floor. He left, furious, and collected the sap himself. On his return he stopped the cart in front of the house and slumped forward in the seat, exhausted. He later recalled that one member shouted, "You're just trying to make me feel guilty."

Instead of 300, 45 gallons of syrup were made—a respectable amount. All of it was used for home consumption. Woody wanted to ration it at a gallon a week; it was one of the first rules he had tried to enforce. The others rebelled. Deliberately, Jeff would pour himself a large glass and slowly drink it off—in front of an enraged Woody. The syrup vanished before summer's end.

The more Woody pushed the commune to work and to organize, the more the others rebelled, just as they had against their parents, teachers and the police. Jeff and Dana would taunt Woody by asking him for money and keys to the car: "Come on, Daddy, give us some money. Pop, can I have the car tonight?" Woody retreated to his room and also made extended visits to the library in Hanover.

Partially, the split between Woody and the rest was a rift in consciousness. Woody rarely smoked and never took psychedelics. Sexually, he was prudish compared to the others, who enthusiastically took part in group gropes.

Woody held himself aloof. Once during a long bruising meeting in which he was harshly attacked, one woman sympathetically put an arm around him. He stiffened.

Part of the problem might have been that there was no organized process for getting at the psychological roots of differences. The long after-dinner meetings were discontinued when some members rejected them as artificial "mind-fucking sessions that brought people down." Everything would go smoothly if everyone made love, some argued. Others said vaguely that personal conflicts should be resolved through the natural and spontaneous interplay of feelings. And if that didn't work, then those who didn't get along should leave. One member later observed that the philosophy at Bryn Athyn was to stay high as much of the time as possible. So when quarrels were "bringing them down," some people would just smoke. They couldn't accept the fact that you have to come down sometimes and deal with things.

In the spring of 1969, Woody decided to leave again. He called a meeting at which he analyzed Bryn Athyn's economic failure. The community needed a realistic plan to get the most work and income out of its fifteen members. He announced that he was willing to transfer ownership of the farm to the commune. But they would have to take the initiative, Woody insisted. He wrote a letter outlining the legal steps necessary to effect the transfer. Posting it on the bulletin board, he split.

In late 1969, I began to make one-day visits to Bryn Athyn. At first, I would avoid staying overnight and hasten home to my own family. I wasn't coming up with much "material," discovering that communes would demand from me much greater commitment and a total reaction. So I began to spend two- or three-day stints there; besides, I was beginning to enjoy Bryn Athyn. Most of the time Woody was away. In his absence no one had acted on his offer to transfer the deed. Neither had they attained anything close to his goal of self-sufficiency. The group of fifteen to twenty lived largely off what they grew, raised, cut, bartered for, or bought—usually at wholesale prices. They had a huge garden, a cow, ducks and chickens, several pigs, and a team of horses. Around $400 a month was spent—chiefly for gas, repairs, and Ballantine ale—no mean achievement in communal frugality. "We all wanted to live off the land, but we didn't want to fuck with money," one member said. It was a monthly hassle to scrape up the needed bread. About $150 was contributed by Martha, a thirty-nine-year-old mother of four who'd come to Bryn Athyn after separating from her husband. She received a monthly allotment from her parents. Others contributed around $50, and the balance, as well as payment on outstanding debts, came from odd jobs. The men took turns cleaning stables at a nearby horse-breeding farm.

The garden had been planted in characteristic fashion: "Anyone who felt like planting something did and looked after their own crops." As a result, there were a dozen patches of cucumbers scattered over a two-acre field, yielding far more than the family could preserve. The house was always filled with the smell of smoky fires, as the members hadn't cut their wood in time to let it season. And when no one felt like bringing the cow in at night, it wandered away. The next day, everyone engaged in a wild cow chase. Nevertheless, the commune was muddling through in haphazard style.

Some members, like Mark and Jeff, who had both recently dropped out of college, had had no experience living in a commune or the country. But in general, Bryn Athyn was less serious, romantically idealistic, and self-conscious than Sunrise Hill. The prevailing influence was still anarchistic, but no one was disillusioned by the fact that Bryn Athyn had fallen short of its ideals and in many ways was merely serving as a halfway house for people who'd rejected established society and not yet found their own.

Bryn Athyn's intellectual was Charles Smith, thirty-two, a veteran of Sunrise Hill and Cold Mountain. Charles was seasonally swaddled in layers of clothing: two pair of trousers over long underwear, three or four moth-eaten sweaters and, on the outside, a red wool robe polka-dotted with brown scorchmarks. Flown over the front door, his robe could well have served as Bryn Athyn's flag. He had a full red beard, fierce blue eyes, the bearing of a patriarch and a British accent left over from prep school days. He smoked his hand-rolled cigarettes as if they were joints, holding the smoke in and letting it out in a short series of sucks: "The beats sought to create a countermilieu"—suck-suck—"but what we've done is to *become* it"—suck-suck. "We are a postrevolutionary society."

Charles grew up on Long Island. His father was an aeronautical engineer who believed in behavioral training. When Charles was born, his father anticipated that the baby might interfere with his use of the power tools in the basement. So for the first twenty-four hours Charles spent in the house, his father ran an electric sander to condition the baby to the sound. Charles can still remember its whine.

"During the Depression, my parents' main concern was security. They decided they could only afford the educational opportunities for one child. My mother seemed to live in the past. She was born in England but grew up in the Midwest in a big house set back from the street, surrounded by trees." At an early age, Charles was instructed in the forms of etiquette and was trained to address his mother as "Mrs. Smith." "I can't say I had what you would call a warm family life." He also recalled having an awareness of spiritual presences that he was unable to communicate. He was intellectually precocious and at nineteen was graduated from Swarthmore College, going on to earn a master's in Hebraic studies at Harvard. "The Bible has always been the most influential book in my life—along with Rachel Carson, Wilhelm Reich, *Stranger in a Strange Land*, Edgar Cayce, Tolstoy and Paul Goodman. I guess you'd describe me as a Christian anarchist." After Harvard, he converted to the Russian Othodox Church because "it best retains the mystical elements of original Christianity."

Charles went to New York, lived in a cold-water flat and took odd jobs as a messenger. Through a circle of anarchists, including Bookchin, who then had a small headquarters at 100 Bleecker Street, he met Jefferson Poland and helped him organize the League for Sexual Freedom. "And I had my head bopped a few times in civil-rights demonstrations." After he became interested in the communal movement, he realized he knew nothing about living on a farm. So in 1963, he decided to learn how. He went to northern Ohio, showing up at Malabar Farm, which had been made famous as a model of self-sufficiency through the writings of Louis Bromfield. For almost a year he worked as a farmhand, learning about husbandry, plowing and planting.

The demise of Sunrise Hill and Cold Mountain had not

dampened his faith. The aim of hip community life, Charles wrote in the journal he showed me, was to "revolutionize and raise the levels of consciousness by carefully examining the freightage of the old world which burdens our souls." He spoke of attaining this heightened consciousness through mysticism, drugs, group sex, outdoor fucking and closeness to nature—"the integration of the total person in the seasonal round as an ecological and spiritual unity."

Before dinner, Bryn Athyn's kitchen was a Currier and Ives scene with hip retouchings. A sprig of leaves and herbs hung from low hand-hewn beams. A whine came from the adjoining storeroom where Joshua was using an electric grindstone to sharpen the teeth of a reaper blade. Shriveled bean pods covered the floor, and all the table space was preempted by broken pumps, pipes and tools. Joshua asked if I could stay to help bring in the hay. I said I would.

Julia, eight, came home from school, having walked the last half mile from the school bus stop. The youngest of Martha's four children, she is a pert, bright child, with pigtails and a space between her front teeth. She wore an overlarge hand-knit sweater with ceramic buttons her mother had molded and kiln-glazed.

"How was school today, Julia?" asked Martha.

"We read a book about Little Jonathon who went on this food trip with his mother, and this uptight grocer didn't dig them. They bought a lot of junk food." She noticed a Mason jar of red juice on the table. "What's this shit?"

"It's tomato juice," Martha answered. "We've been canning tomatoes all day."

Martha looks too young to be a mother of teen-agers (her other children are Robby, fifteen, Susan, fourteen, and Davy, twelve). She wore jeans, men's wool checked shirts, and wears her red hair long. Throughout Bryn Athyn's daily crises, she remained amazingly relaxed and even-tempered. The daughter of a physics professor at Antioch College in Yellow Springs,

Ohio, she attended the Antioch School, one of the country's first progressive schools, founded in the thirties and run by Marxists and leaders of the intentional-community movement.* She went to the college for two years, then left for New York City, where she studied the piano and joined the Communist Party. Through her political involvement she met Al, a World War II veteran. They continued working for the party after their marriage, but events of the fifties—the Hungarian uprising and the McCarthy purge—disheartened them. Both wanted to leave the United States, and they thought of joining an Israeli kibbutz or emigrating to New Zealand. Instead, they moved to the suburbs and raised children. "Al became cynical and bitter and decided that the only way left to be free in this society was to make lots of money." He started a building sub-contracting and estimating business. Every night when he called from the station, Martha put a martini in the freezer to chill.

She was discontented and felt cut off, not only from a cause but from other people. She convinced Al to buy a large house in Mount Airy, a well-to-do neighborhood of Philadelphia, and to give rooms to interesting people in order to expand their family. Al went along at first but soon grew to dislike the arrangement—a cross between a boardinghouse and a crash pad. In the evening, he walked into the middle of lively conversations that left him out. He resented it when the others told him he was ignoring his children. Martha had an affair and they separated. Hearing of a commune in Vermont, she packed two of the kids in the car and headed north.

Everyone served himself from pots on the wood stove and sat around the table on benches polished smooth by use. Charles swabbed the juices on his plate with a heel of home-baked brown bread. "Pass the honey, brother," asked Joshua, the most industrious of the men. He wore a headband, rimless glasses

---

* Arthur E. Morgan, president of Antioch and the first chairman of the Tennessee Valley Authority, was one of the main proponents of small decentralized intentional communities during the 1930's.

and seemed angry and self-contained. When he first learned I was a writer, he taunted, "Tell me a story, tell me a story." He and Dana had been through the Southwest together and regarded each other as adopted brothers. Dana was emaciated, grasshopper-like, and his face was almost obscured by dense ringlets of brown curls. He smoked a lot, usually alone, which increased his withdrawal. Most days, he would work for an hour and then quit.

During dinner Charles announced that he'd finished a draft of a letter to a lawyer outlining the legal structure the community proposed for taking over and administering the farm. It meant that the commune members would have to affix their names as trustees of a nonprofit corporation. Moreover, the letter forced them to consider how they were to pay taxes and meet all the other contingencies a lawyer's mind might envision. Charles passed the letter around. It completed the circle unremarked.

No one seemed to care about the opportunity to make the farm independent. Each had problems of his own. Janet's was the baby she would have in two months. Both she and Jeff, her old man, seemed unprepared for parenthood. At twenty she had an emotional block about housework, she explained to Martha, who did most of the kitchen chores. Reared in a middle-class Jewish family, she had been forced by her mother to do housework as a form of punishment. Jeff had flunked out of the University of Pennsylvania. A cloud of gloomy inertia hung over his head. He seemed always to be wringing his hands: "I've got to get a job . . . I've got to get the Volks running."

Another member was Cindy Lou, tan and sultry. She slept with most of the men, never with any one twice in succession—a matter of policy. In moments of "crisis," for example, when she awoke late to find all the yogurt eaten, she exclaimed, "I can't stand living with all these frustrated people."

Though Mark and Joshua agreed to transferring the deed, they were channeling their energies outside the commune. Mark, who worked part time at a brick mill, was saving money to buy *his* own truck and tools. Joshua, who did carpentry, was saving money to buy *his* own land. Later Martha told me, "They [the commune's men] have to go through the masculinity trip—first prove their independence. They're tired of taking from Woody and tired of people taking from them."

Aside from Mark and Joshua, the other men loathed their part-time jobs. They were downers. After one day shoveling manure at the horse farm, Charles would spend the next twenty-four hours recuperating in bed. He wanted the commune to continue; for him Bryn Athyn was the warm, close family he never had; the source of intimacy and acceptance for a person society regarded as eccentric.

Most of the time, the members just barely managed to accomplish the farm's routine chores. Bryn Athyn had no prospects for selling produce or syrup until its members could learn how to work alone as well as with others. Martha would have liked to forget that her allowance was the commune's only steady income. Though she wasn't hung up on money and what it represented, she wondered if it was good for others to be so dependent—whether it be on their parents, Woody, herself or the community. Martha felt she was the surrogate mother for a group of wayward adolescents. What especially discouraged her was the commune's influence—or lack of influence—on Julia, her youngest child. Instead of acting as surrogate parents, the other members related to her children as sibling rivals. Julia talked of returning to live with her father in California.

"Theoretically, anarchism assumes people are independent and can carry their own weight," Martha said. Instead, she continued, Bryn Athyn had attracted young people like Cindy Lou who found that, compared to the city, it was merely a more comfortable place to crash. The commune fulfilled the need which Erik Erikson, the psychologist, described as the "psycho-social moratorium"—time to cope with the "identity crisis." Bryn Athyn seemed to bear out Yaswen's pessimistic observation that communes attracted the neurotic offspring of a neurotic society.

Despite everything, Martha still believed Bryn Athyn would

succeed. The key factor, however, was time. "Most people here are just beginning to find themselves."

It was time to hay the upper field. I helped Joshua harness the two horses to the hay machine, an antique he'd discovered gathering rust and cobwebs in the rear of the barn. He had spent the last two days restoring it, replacing pins, welding a broken bar, and sharpening the cutter blade. It was as good as new (which it had been in 1923). The farm needed to cut eight tons of hay to keep the horses and cows in feed through the winter.

Unofficially, the day had been declared Hay-Cutting Day, toward which all communal energies were to be directed somehow. Joshua set off ahead to the field whose hay Michael, a friend and neighbor, had given to the commune. He bounced on the machine's bucket seat and was pursued by a pack of commune dogs, up the dirt road strewn with the golden leaves and dappled with light. The rest of us ran behind or rode the jeep.

The hayfield seemed to be on top of the world; it was a kind of mountain pasture, part of an old farm, whose main house had been built around 1830. The region's early settlers had taken to the high land. Only after the arrival of the railroads did they come down to the villages of the valleys. They were independent, Jeffersonian upland people, who built graceful Georgian houses that sat alone in the high hills, incomparable.

For miles around, the view was of green-carpeted mountains, the intervening space broken only by the swoop of hawks. The wind sent shimmers and waves of excitement through the lush, tall hay. "The moment of truth," said Charles as Joshua pulled the saw-toothed cutting bar down level with the hay, got back on his seat, and tossed the reins. The machine rattled into life and cut a swath for about twenty feet. We ran behind, disbelieving at first, then picking up the sheared hay in handfuls and throwing it in the air with hurrahs that turned to groans when, *clunk*, the machine struck a rock and clanked to a dead stop, disconnected from the horses. The tongue linking the front and rear axles had splintered. "It was rotten," said Joshua, kicking at the break.

"I think Earl Durkee might have another tongue around his place," Dana suggested. Earl was a farmer who had used horse-drawn machines, a rarity now. I drove Dana and Joshua over to his farm. On the way, they argued about the horses, Dana urging Joshua to give them up, beautiful as they were, for the more practical, though noisier, tractor: "We could borrow someone's tractor and get the hay cut faster than all the hassles it takes to get the machine working."

Johua wouldn't hear of it. He had seen the machine work, and its antique movements had intoxicated him. "I'll have it working before the day's over."

Dana countered, "Meanwhile, everyone's hanging out in the hayfield, and nothing is getting done."

"Nothing gets done anyway."

Earl Durkee was the adopted farmer-father of Bryn Athyn. He was a heavyset man in his late fifties, who hitched his pants high with wide suspenders over a paunch. Behind a trellis of roses, his house was gray, in need of a coat of paint and repairs. He and his wife ran the farm, keeping ten cows and some chickens. Some members of Bryn Athyn occasionally helped with his heavy work. Earl was getting on in years and his sons and daughters had left.

In return for their help, Earl gave the commune calves, scrap lumber from his sawmill, and a lifetime's lore on country matters. We went into the sawmill and poked around for a tongue.

Last week, Earl told us, a realtor had offered to buy his upper fifty acres, but he had refused. He didn't want to see bulldozers plowing down his orchards and backhoes digging sewer lines on the hill and terracing sites for ski chalets and resort homes. "First thing the assessor'd be up here and hike my taxes even higher. That's what happened to all the farmers around here, they can't make the taxes, so they sell out. Maybe I should too, but I don't think I'd like Florida. I had a lot of friends sell out and then come back from Florida."

As he talked, he searched among the rafters and suddenly

pulled free an old tongue. "Don't know that it might be rotten like the other one, but it won't cost you anything to find out."

When we returned, the rest of the family were lying in the shade of a tree, drinking ale. Charles was giving Robby a lecture on hay, in reality a composite of grains: timothy, rye, vetch, clover. Meanwhile, Joshua had shaped the end of the tongue so that it fit snugly into the socket, and he had drilled holes for the bolts. It was ready. We regrouped around him.

The machine worked. Ian and I ran ahead clearing the way of rocks that might frustrate our marvelous antique. Following immediately behind Joshua came Susan, Martha's daughter, home from high school, picking up clumps of hay that clogged the cutter blade. Then came the jeep driven by Dana, towing a rake which he lifted every fifty feet to leave a thatched pile. Then the pitchfork brigade—Martha, Janet, Beverly and Cindy Lou—who pitched the piles on the wagon. Ahead of the procession, Joshua triumphantly rode his hay wagon, as if it were a chariot, his long blond hair blowing like a mane. The pleasant staccato of the machine's clatter had the delicacy and refinement of a Vivaldi harpsichord scherzo. It was working, it was working! We went running over the rises and dips of meadow, looking like a mad, hip version of a Brueghel. When the sun set behind the far mountain and chill fell, we stopped work, reluctantly. Ian and I walked back to the others. "God, I feel like I'd taken a cap of mescaline," he said. His shirt clung to an oval of sweat in the small of his back.

I would like to write that I stayed to see all of the hay cut and hoisted into the barn, but I had decided to leave. Bryn Athyn was too tenuous, too shaky, like the hay machine Joshua had wired together. As a writer, I was looking for a stable commune to study.

In December, 1969, while I was in New York to get an advance for the book, my wife called to tell me that Bryn Athyn had sent out a newsletter. On November 19, Joshua died of hepatitis. Three others came down with it. Four days after Joshua's death, around 3 A.M., Woody Ransom, accompanied by six others he'd met on the West Coast, arrived and announced that they were forming a new work-oriented commune, with him firmly in charge. He gave Bryn Athyn's then-family thirty days' notice to remove themselves—or he would call the state police. The newsletter concluded: "We have a barn full of hay, a cellar full of vegetables, livestock for food, and wood cut and waiting to be taken to the house. We have two children attending school. Then in one month we become a community of a dozen-odd displaced persons with no home and no resources." (A few months later Bryn Athyn experienced more grief. Earl Durkee, after making the agonizing decision to sell his farm, died of a heart attack.)

On the way home, I turned west toward Bryn Athyn and followed winding Route 132 through the snow-covered hills, past the white clapboard houses of the villages, their windows softly lit. Then I hit the dirt road and started skidding on the hard-packed snow.

Woody and his new commune, calling themselves Rockbottom Farm, were living about a mile away in a modern, fully applianced house. I visited it later and found Rockbottom the diametrical opposite of leaderless, ruleless Bryn Athyn. Under Woody's stewardship, everyone worked eight hours a day, six days a week. Visiting hours were set—after dinner and on Sundays only. Woody invested $100,000 in Rockbottom, much of it in machinery, including a bulldozer. Though the horses were kept, the emphasis at Rockbottom was on mechanized efficiency. Woody renounced anarchism entirely, disclaiming he'd ever read Reich. He now talked of behavioral science: of conditioning a generation to work together. In the future, Rockbottom might become a *Walden Two* community. But until it became economically viable, it was under his provisional dictatorship.

The refugees of Bryn Athyn had moved across the river to a house in Lyme, New Hampshire. Dana rode back with me to Lyme and reviewed the month's events and tragedy. Joshua had been working too hard, still trying to save money for his land. He had ignored his sickness at first, treating himself with herbs, refusing to see a doctor. He stopped working only after he became jaundiced. Then he developed pneumonia. The others drove him to the hospital. His heart stopped.

On the radio WABC was playing Blood, Sweat & Tears' song of death and new birth, "And when I die." A week after Joshua's death, Janet had given birth (in a hospital) to a daughter, Sammarah.

The evicted Bryn Athyn family was living in a small house lent them by a liberal Quaker physician. Martha told me that when Woody returned, she alone had resisted his takeover. She ordered him out of "her home." But the others couldn't back her up. Three were in bed with hepatitis. Charles tried to talk rationally to Woody. Characteristically, Dana lit up a joint and sat silent in the corner. Bryn Athyn lacked the will to live.

Nevertheless, Martha said, in the spring they would start looking for their own land. "We're going to do it right. No more living off anybody's largesse." They would try again, this time with more skills, experience and, above all, commitment. Would I join them?

After a year in Vermont, my viewpoint on communes had changed. As a single family, our life in the snowbound cabin was both lonely and impractical. Whenever I left on a trip, I worried about leaving Mary and the kids alone, without a phone or running water. As an isolated family unit, we spent far too much on food, tools, heat. I didn't even have the time to look after chickens. Mary, with two kids of preschool age, couldn't can very much of what we grew. We had to drive Susan to the village to find playmates for her. And then there were those evenings when Mary and I played cards for lack of anything else to do. We would still choose to live in the country and with each other, but weren't there other alternatives?

Theoretically, I could see that a community *could* combine the natural beauty of the country with city sociability; but as yet, the only communes I had observed closely—Oz and Bryn Athyn—hadn't survived due to internal and external stresses. I couldn't reply to Martha's invitation until I'd lived in a commune that had gotten beyond adolescence and realized some of its ideals. Then I'd decide.

Martha understood. After I came back from my trip west, we'd meet again and discuss the structure of the new commune. In his perfect eighteenth-century hand, Charles wrote me a florid letter of introduction to communes throughout the country. "Where do you think you'll go?" he asked. I didn't know—only that I would go west, where the movement had started and was, I hoped, now maturing. But exactly where—I didn't know.

On January 2 I took a jet from Montreal to San Francisco. It was so easy today to make the cross-continental journey. What took the pioneers months and mortal sacrifice I accomplished in the space of a few hours, drinking a martini from a plastic cup and listening over headsets to Peter, Paul and Mary singing, "Leaving on a Jet Plane."

I don't know where I'll be going once the plane sets down. The trail well-beaten by so many Easterners before me leads to Berkeley, the westernmost capital of the country's young and alienated. It is the springboard of the communal movement.

Berkeley . . . Telegraph Avenue . . . the sidewalk cafeteria of culture, where you can select an assortment of causes, art, music and faith to match your individual style and vibrations. A potpourri of smells—incense, grass and doughnuts; a jangle of sound—Hare Krishna chants, tambourines and recorded rock. Everything is for sale—a nickel bag of Acapulco gold, Nepalese black, Panama red; or cosmic consciousness in any number of assorted varieties.

I lunched with Benjamin Zablocki, a former New Yorker (like so many people in Berkeley) and a friend of Charles Smith. They'd been together at Sunrise Hill. Zablocki, a sociologist, teaches a popular course called "Communities" at the university. He sees the communal movement as a reaction against the fragmented confusion of a commercialized culture that peddles every viewpoint but believes in nothing.

Looking back on Sunrise Hill and other false starts, Zablocki observed, "The movement is evolutionary. . . . The first communes started out open-ended, considering all possibilities, but are gravitating toward a firmer definition. . . . It's difficult, when you think of it, for modern man to put together his own culture and come up with one that works—the first time."

Yes, I agreed, I knew too well about the false starts—I'd spent months learning about them. But now I was eager to find a commune that *was* working out, a group of people who'd been together a year and were happy. Could he recommend one?

Zablocki cautioned me that there was no such beast as a prototypical commune. Each one is a unique attempt to blend economics, art, agriculture and the spiritual into the natural round of daily life. The thrust of the movement, he said, was individualistic—part of a worldwide movement in which the hippies, one of many minorities including the French Canadians, the blacks, the Basques, the Chicanos, were asserting their identity as a subculture. In America, the hippies had refused to be submerged in the great melting pot of sameness. Every commune wanted to be—and had to be—unique.

Well, then, I asked, could he recommend a commune that was unique but not untypical? Still cautioning me to put aside the would-be social scientist's preconception, Zablocki steered me to a "together" commune in Oregon, where his ex-wife, Elaine, was living. The group had been together a year. He gave me directions.

The next day, I hitched and bussed my way north to Oregon.

II
Oregon

High Ridge Farm

January 10

I was awakened by a thudding sound near my pillow. It was Reuben doing his matinal yoga, rolled on his back with his long, hairy, spindly legs flung over his ears and his feet about an inch from my head. Incense filled the air. Next to his mattress, the top of a small chest served as an altar—covered with a velvet cloth and small photos of gurus and swamis. So far, we haven't said a word to each other. Yesterday was one of the days he chose not to talk to anyone and instead tried to communicate by notes and sign language.

I lay in my goose-down bag listening to the rain on the roof of the A-frame, which is the communal dormitory for most of the farm's eleven adults. Then Joe and Jean, who sleep in the far corner, began to make turbulent love. I jumped out of the bag and hurriedly dressed, zipping up a slicker borrowed the night before from the box of common rain gear, and sloshed down the hill to the main house.

The farm lies in a river valley bounded by mountains that have been ruthlessly logged and mined. Toward the valley's south end, the peaks of higher mountains are topped by dwindling snowcaps. The muddy path from the A-frame to the main house leads over a brook that runs through about two acres of gardens, past a greenhouse covered with plastic and built for the total cost of $8, and a couple of cold frames where the lettuce and spinach for the dinner salad still thrive despite the gray winter drizzle.

Smoke curled from the stovepipe of the main house, a one-story 30- by 20-foot building covered with particle board, that serves as the commune's central kitchen, living-dining room and kids' dormitory. "Good mornin'," hailed Jack, who was outside splitting wood. In his late twenties, the son of an aeronautical engineer, he spent two years at Berkeley intending to be a math major. He is one of five people here who are separated from their legal spouses; none of them has bothered to get a divorce. Jack's eyes are blue-black and his blondish-red beard is pointed like a billy goat's.

The wood, reddish-grained oak, split easily beneath Jack's double-headed ax. The commune gets it on a permit from the national forest that allows them to cut only dead wood. None would chop down a live tree anyway.

Inside, a pot of oatmeal steamed on the wood stove. I passed it up for brown buttered bread covered with butter and dark organic honey. I've always hated oatmeal, its bland glueyness. Here it is standard breakfast fare, which the kids and adults smother with raisins, yogurt, brewer's yeast, honey and brown sugar.

After breakfast Susan, six, volunteered to take me for a walk. We donned slickers and started out hand in hand through the rain and mud. Like my own five-year-old Susan, she was eager for adult attention. As we walked, I observed the commune's layout. The north side of the main house is sheltered by a grove of tall firs, whose needles make a soft and fairly dry carpet. Clustered close to the main house and connected to it by stone-lined walkways are a lean-to garage, a combination repair shop and food-storage building, a flooded root cellar, a coop occupied by thirty-four chickens, which put out an average of eight eggs a day, and a geodesic, plastic-covered alfresco outhouse known as the crapper. It is stocked with back issues of *The New Yorker* and *Organic Gardening*.

The sixteen-acre farm gently slopes westward up the mountainside. On the edge of the meadows and in the logged clearings crossed with rotting timbers, the branches of small scruffy trees droop with moss, a fantastic landscape out of Tolkien. A few steps away from the brook and the valley, the soil becomes gravelly and red with mineral deposits.

Back at the house, Jean was baking bread with hand-ground whole wheat. Laura was pulverizing eggshells to be mixed with the chicken feed. Jack and Bill sat over their third cup of breakfast tea discussing techniques of identifying *Amanita muscaria*, hallucinogenic mushrooms, from spores. Bluegrass music twanged on the phonograph.

At my request, Jack rang the dinner gong to call a meeting. I wanted the family's approval of my plan to live with them. Everyone grouped around a circular plywood table in a corner of the kitchen. Jean continued her bread making, taking out a dozen pans of rising dough from the warming oven above the stove, then vigorously pulling the dough up and dropping it back in the pan with a wet slap. I introduced myself as a writer, described the book I was researching, and asked if I could spend three weeks with them. I would do a share of the work, I said, and make a cash donation to the communal budget.

There was silence. Maureen looked around the table and after reading the faces of the others, simply said, "For sure." I was a bit let down. I'd come with a walletful of letters of introduction vouching for my identity and good intentions. But all my credentials were unnecessary here. I was accepted not as a writer but as Robert, just another human on his trip through life. How, I thought, did they know I wasn't a Fed? The only question came from Laura: "What sign are you?" Gemini. "Oh, wow, you'll get along very well here."

I talked with Jack as he adjusted the valves on Maureen's truck. Why had I been welcomed so uncritically? I asked. I had expected outrage—the mass media has landed, et cetera. Jack answered that I was accepted as part of the "flow," the natural succession of events you're supposed to groove on rather than resist. I pressed Jack for an explanation of the "flow." He gave one of his high-pitched infectious, giggling laughs. "It means, sorta, sorta, if the vibrations are right, and if there seems to be some sort of destiny about your coming here. You came all the way from Vermont, right? Well, that must mean something. Right?" So far, the commune hasn't turned away anyone, although its members do not agree that the "open" commune is the best policy. There is no decision-making process for resolving such questions. For example, Reuben, who had been asked to leave three previous communes, was told by two other members to split. He refused. "The rest of us felt it was wrong to ask anyone to leave," Jack said, "regardless of how we felt about Reuben personally."

I held the lamp while Jack worked on the motor and gave me a brief history of High Ridge Farm. During the fall of 1966, a series of meetings was held in Berkeley to discuss alternative life-styles. The meetings attracted couples in their mid-twenties, married and unmarried, most of them with college backgrounds. Eventually, they were converted into encounter sessions, some of them nude. The couples began to split apart and find new partners within the group. On weekends there were some group camping trips. Out of the meetings came several communes and a few more separations, including Jack's.

This afternoon Claudia and Laura realized that they had conflicting plans for a pot of hot water simmering on the wood stove. Claudia wanted to make yogurt, Laura, to wash the floor. They flipped a coin and Claudia won. "It's better this way," she explained. "You avoid the situation of one person feeling he has to give in to the other and getting a martyr complex." Laura laughed. "What she *really* means is that Claudia doesn't feel guilty about dominating the kitchen." They both laughed. It was all very "out front."

Before dinner, the gong was rung for meditation—the one consistent group ritual—a period of about twenty minutes, when the family sits or kneels in a circle on the living-room floor to meditate and om together. The children respect the silence and hush anyone who raises his voice above a whisper. I couldn't concentrate; my mind kept drifting off the center. I gave up and let my eyes pan around the house. A supporting wall divides the living room and kitchen from the "children's room." The younger kids sleep on hard shelves which double during the day, cleared of sleeping bags, as play space. The older ones sleep on bunks and in a loft. The adults take turns sleeping in with the kids. Half the wall on the living-room side is a floor-to-ceiling bookcase with neatly labeled sections: do-it-yourself, gardening, medicine, religion, mushrooms, poetry. Beneath the books are boxes for communal clothes: sweaters, socks, shirts, handkerchiefs. Dirty clothes are thrown into a common hamper. On the opposite wall hang guitars and dulcimers. A counter divides the living room from the kitchen. In this corner is a wood stove, above which dangles an array of socks, pants and coats. From the rafters hangs a sloping line of pots, pans and lanterns.

Unlike many communes, High Ridge Farm has gone electric. However, most of the overhead lamps, like some of the furniture, have been made by hand. There is also cold running water —a garden hose connected to the spring.

January 11

Rain continued today. Mist clung to the hip of the mountains. I felt strangely buoyant as I went down to the house for breakfast. This was one of the first times in my life when I had no expectations, schedule, appointments. Like everyone else here, I was free to be. But to be what? Who was Robert? I tried the oatmeal with lots of brown sugar and "commodities" (U.S. surplus) butter. "What time is it, by the way?" I asked. Maureen, wearing an Aussie hat over her short curly hair, answered that she didn't know, since there was no clock in the house. "There's breakfast when you get hungry and bedtime when you feel sleepy."

"I believe it's Monday," volunteered Roland, who is the oldest of the family, thirty-four, a reserved, emotionally controlled

Englishman. He checked the astrological calendar over the kitchen table. "Right, it's Monday and a plus day for Capricorns and a good day for planting. . . ."

The commune has only one schedule, a recent one at that—a chart of who cooks the evening meal. "The trouble was that two people—Joe and Claudia—got into a rut doing the dinner trip," Maureen explained. "They felt overburdened, but they got angry when other people tried to do things in *their* kitchen. Other people felt excluded from cooking." Included on the schedule, in an attempt to do away with sex-defined jobs, are Roland, Reuben and Joe.

Aside from the one meal, all other housework gets done whenever someone feels right. Jack, the early riser, usually makes the morning fires, puts on the cereal, coffee and tea.

Reuben came through the door with a bucket and filled it from the kitchen hose. His thing is to feed the two goats and the chickens, a job he guards almost jealously. A few moments later, he returned with two eggs. "That's all. Chickens must be really fucked up in their new coop."

Roland assured him the chickens would settle down: "They dig stability." Maureen swept the floor. Joe did the dishes, using a nondetergent soap. From the children's dormitory issued the firm commands of Claudia directing the kids to put away sleeping bags and pick up toys. Bill rolled some joints as Crosby, Stills and Nash dropped on the turntable.

Roland and Jack talked about which of the three trucks they would try to get started. "Trouble is there's only one good battery. . . ." They divided up the repair work between them with Bill, adding that his project for the day was to roll up the chicken wire and collect the posts which had supported the beans and peas.

Without the aid of committees, chairmen, quotas, policy or timeclocks, the household chores eventually got done, just as they get done in any other American household—except that the eleven adults and six children of the farm are not a family in the traditional sense. Unrelated by blood, they function like a family, though I'm not sure yet how or why.

Jean was busy making yogurt. She used a long-handled brush to scrub out two big glass jars, then began to mix the powdered milk with water. Along with brown rice, peanut butter and bread, yogurt is a main food staple here. About two gallons are consumed daily, mostly by the kids who have it with honey, jam, and brewer's yeast and slurp it over their oatmeal, steamed vegetables and boiled potatoes. "It's rich in B vitamins, doesn't fuck up your arteries with cholesterol, and keeps you regular," said Jean. First she mixed the powdered milk in the blender, one of the few electric appliances they brought along to the country; then she added hot water and one cup of "starter" per gallon. The yogurt is made economically possible by the free, surplus powdered milk. If whole milk had been used instead a gallon of yogurt would have cost $1. The milk is one of several "commodities" the family receives monthly under the federal surplus (food stamp) program. The farm qualifies as a family of sixteen making less than the minimum income of $4,000. On the first of each month, Bill drives one of the trucks to the county seat and picks up a load of dry milk, butter, lard, cheddar cheese, peanut butter, peaches, and canned beef.

The river valley reportedly contains about two hundred long-hairs living both in communes and as couples. Of the six houses I visited while at the farm, all displayed the silver and black cans of commodities "donated by the U.S. Department of Agriculture—not to be sold" on their food shelves. No count was kept, but during my month on the farm it seemed to me that roughly a third of the food we ate was commodities. Another third was store-bought organic food, including whole grains, brown rice and honey. The remaining third was homegrown. There were huge vegetable stews of potatoes, carrots, onion, turnips and beets, all out of the garden, and on the side, freshly baked corn bread from the dried corn they buy and grind to meal. (They freeze their own corn.) The food mill on the kitchen counter seemed to be perpetually grinding, with people spelling each other; it takes a good half hour to grind five pounds of whole wheat. Thanks to the cold frames and the long growing season, we had exotic salads with Brussels sprouts, kohlrabi and "commodities cheese." ("Store-bought cheese," as well as ice cream, is sometimes brought by guests.) Meat is eaten once or twice a week—"commodities" hash or a curry made from turkeys donated last Thanksgiving by the Welfare Department—and then an alternate vegetable dish is prepared for the three vegetarians, Roland, Jack and Reuben. The rest of the family are occasional meat eaters who prefer mainly a vegetable diet, not for philosophic or religious reasons but out of a common-sense conviction that the all-American menu of sirloin, Cokes and refined starches is unhealthy.

Jean took the jars of hot milk (about 120 degrees), placed them in the Styrofoam chest, covered it, and set it behind the wood stove to incubate. "You can do it a lot more scientifically, you know, keep it at a constant temperature for five hours. This way every jar is slightly different from the others."

She took a break and sat down at the table to roll a cigarette from the Top tobacco can, using Zig-Zag papers. Jean is a robust woman, big-breasted, with dark hair curling over her eyes. She always wears large, loopy earrings in her pierced ears. Like the rest of the women at the farm, her skin is fine, clear and rosy (must be all that yogurt). Jean grew up in New York City, was graduated from the University of Chicago, and met Joe, her old man, while at the University of Washington. "Of course, we're not self-sufficient. Economic self-sufficiency is a myth. We just don't want to be trapped by a system that makes you try to meet a standard of living that's too high; makes you eat food that's too rich; live in a house that's overheated in the winter and air-conditioned in the summer. I like to wear sweaters—this house stays around sixty with the cookstove going. In the summer, it gets up to one hundred, but then you just take your clothes off. It doesn't cost anything."

I asked to see the storeroom where all the cans and frozen foods from their garden are kept. Claudia took me on the tour. We waved to Bill, who was working in the fields, rolling up chicken wire. From behind a half-completed shed came the sound of Roland's hammer. Claudia turned on the overhead light of the storage building, and I made an inventory of the shelves, which had been reduced by half of the goods put up after the harvest: four dozen 2-quart jars of tomatoes; a dozen each of 1-quart peaches, apples, strawberries, cherries, blackberries, and plums. (During the summer they made money picking fruit, and often the farmer gave them some free. But all the berries were locally grown.) Another dozen each of squash and onions; two dozen assorted jars of pickles; several bottles of mushroom catsup; a huge bag of dried mushrooms; bottles of home-brewed root beer and beer; a whole shelf of jams and blackberry syrup.

"Here are the herbs." She opened a bin. All were either homegrown or locally gathered, then dried and ground: savory, marjoram, parsley, basil, spearmint and sage.

Two freezer chests, another inescapable reason for electricity, hummed away. Both were still nearly full of plastic bags of squash, corn, cherry tomatoes, beans and other vegetables. I observed it must have been a busy fall. She described how Roland and Jack pared the vegetables while she, Elaine and Jean sweated over the wood stove, blanching them and boiling and sealing the Mason jars. "It seemed like that's all we did during September and October. If you figured up the hours and multiplied our labor by a dollar sixty an hour, I suppose that economically we didn't come out that far ahead of buying our food. But we're not living this way just to do things cheaply. . . ."

Joe is the keeper of the communal exchequer. That is, he takes care of the farm's checking account and is one of four authorized signers. I gave him $30 in traveler's checks to help cover my stay. The farm runs on a monthly budget that varies from $250 to $400, which is some kind of fiscal miracle, since if you multiply it out for the year, it brings the annual income for a family of sixteen to under $4,800, far below the federal poverty guideline. The fixed-cost item is the monthly mortgage payment of $100. (In August, 1968, four members bought the sixteen acres for $10,000 from a retired gentleman farmer who lives nearby.) Food and electricity tack another $100 onto the monthly outflow, and miscellaneous items like chicken feed, gas, dental bills, and car parts and travel costs for occasional jaunts to the city account for the fluctuating balance.

The income half of the ledger is sketchy. Maureen is the only one of the farm's three women with children by absentee fathers who still collects welfare. The others are Elaine and Claudia. Elaine, the sociologist's wife, receives $40 a month from her husband. From one month's check, she took out $10 to buy some cloth from which she sewed shirts and dresses. Later, she gave them away. The rest was donated to the family account.

The remainder of the farm's income comes from odd jobs, the steadiest source being the garden and landscape projects which Peter, a professional gardener, oversees. The other men alternate as his helpers. On her trips down to the city, Maureen, who is a CPA, will work two or three days as an accountant. While Jean and Joe were in the city on one of their periodic returns, Jean worked for a few weeks as a secretary at the Bank of America. "The miracle is that we've made every mortgage payment so far," said Jack. "It gets close sometimes. The account's down to a few dollars. But something always turns up. The saying around here is: Money manifests." *

Later in the day, Roland, Jack and Peter held a seed-ordering session, which I sat in on to get some idea of how they went about making decisions. The atmosphere was a little tense. Peter had just emerged from a week of fasting and meditation in the solitude of the sauna cabin, located some two hundred yards above the house on the edge of the brook. Above the sauna itself a small room is reserved for whoever in the family needs to escape the constant wear and tear of group life. Peter, tall, and large-boned, has blond hair receding over a prominent forehead and thick, rimless octagonal glasses. I was not certain what kind of problem had arisen between Peter and the rest but felt sure it had something to do with the way Peter tried to organize the garden. (Later he told me he'd made the mistake—a natural one since he knew the most about things agricultural—of trying to direct the garden work in an authoritarian way.)

---

* One month, in lieu of cash which they couldn't scrape up, the farmer accepted five cords of cut oak.

The three of them sat on the floor surrounded by seed catalogs. Jack had called the meeting simply by taping a notice to the back door: "Seed-ordering session this afternoon. Anyone interested in what they want to eat for the next year better attend." Elaine sat on the sofa, knitting. She wanted to be sure flower and herb seeds were included. Decisions were made informally by common assent. "Should we order two varities of peas? Let's see, Harris has a sweet pea for a dollar eighty a packet that will cover one-hundred-foot rows. . . . Here's one that sounds better than that. . . ."

While they ordered, I thumbed through a notebook Peter had compiled about last year's garden. On one page was a diagram of the garden's irrigation system—it was one of the few traces I saw of organization. Had it caused any hassles? I later asked Peter. He said that everyone wanted to be responsible for some crop or portion of the garden. There was no external compulsion to make certain the irrigation got done. "Call it organic organization. We're not against structure, just all the false, unnecessary structures society imposes—like sales quotas, memos, and policies which get so removed from what's real. You know, everyone can understand why you have to water a garden. And so it gets done."

In an hour, they'd completed their order of cool-weather crops for the year: broccoli, spinach, lettuce, peas, kohlrabi and kale. Jack totaled it. "Comes to twenty-three dollars. Do we have any money?" Joe came in from the other room with the checkbook. "Robert gave us thirty dollars today which will cover it."

"That just makes it," said Jack, writing out the checks. Then, turning to me: "If you hadn't come along, we couldn't have got our seeds in on time. You see, you *do* fit into the flow."

January 12

When I came down for breakfast, Claudia was grinding rose hips. She is dark-skinned, with brown eyes that flash equally brilliantly with smiles or anger. Her black kinky hair flares bushlike in all directions. She is the only white woman I've ever known who's been able to wear an Afro.

The rose hips had been hanging over the stove to dry. "We make tea out of them. Elaine likes to make an extract and slip it into the kids' milk. You mix about one cup of rose hips to one and a half cups of water in a crock; boil and mash. Let stand, then return to a second boil. Add two teaspoons lemon juice, can and seal. It's a great natural source of vitamin C."

I have never lived with people more vitamin- and health-conscious than the High Ridge Farm family. On the shelf above the kitchen table are about thirty jars. At least once a day, someone yells, "Acerola time!" and the kids come running for their natural source of vitamin C.

Food is selected and prepared from a nutritional standpoint. It often becomes a subject for dinner table discussion. "Mmmm, this kale is far out. I bet it has more vitamins than spinach. What does Adelle Davis say?" Finally I asked, Who *was* this Adelle Davis? Was she some friend of the family? Everyone laughed. True, she was the family's authority on nutrition, though only known to them through her books. Her cookbook, *Let's Cook It Right,* occupied a position of honor on the kitchen shelf between the soy flour and the brewer's yeast.

Last night was Roland's turn to cook dinner, we had his specialty—steamed vegetables. "The Japanese do all their vegetables this way," he said. "If you cook some vegetables too long, you kill the fragile vitamins." Tonight we had cheese and whole-wheat macaroni; it looks green but, I was told, retains the B vitamins and protein which have been removed from white macaroni and spaghetti.

"The food industry has found out that white products, white sugar and grains, sell better," Claudia remarked, "even though the nutritious elements have been thrown away. Any eggs left over?" She found two and cracked them into the tiger's milk. The daily blending of the tiger's milk is one of the few routines here. Usually Jack makes it before breakfast, following a variation on Adelle Davis' recipe: 1 quart milk; up to $\frac{1}{2}$ cup brewer's yeast (a cheap source of B vitamins); $\frac{1}{4}$ to $\frac{1}{2}$ cup of soy flour (protein, choline, inositol and antistress vitamins); and 1 table-spoon blackstrap molasses. For flavor you can also add orange, apricot, grape juice or fruit such as bananas.

This afternoon the rain let up briefly. Laura said she felt like walking down to the general store and mailbox. I went along with her and the kids, all of us in slickers and rain hats. The children plodded ahead, followed by the dogs—Bear, Coffee and Balzac. A cloud of gray mist hung inside the valley, veiling the upper third of the mountains. The road snaked along the brook, which during the rainy season rushed full and violent within the six-foot-deep gully it had cut in the red earth. The brook had overrun the culvert and now flooded over and around it, washing away part of the road. The three working vehicles (there were about five defunct ones) had to be parked below the washout, a five-minute walk from the house.

Laura began to talk—dreamily, as if I weren't there—about herself and Roland. They had met and married when Laura was fourteen, the daughter of a gardener who worked on the same farm as Roland. "I never went through an adolescence," she said.

Laura wore her black hair in long braids; she had a high rosy complexion and brown eyes flecked with green that seemed brightened by gold-rimmed granny glasses. Her dress was much the same every day: a holey high-necked sweater and a blue denim coat she'd bought for fifty cents from Goodwill and refurbished with patches, embroidery and silver buttons. With her lithe figure, she looked younger than twenty-two. Her mother had died when she was very young, and she had been brought up by her father. For four years, he boarded her with "Mommy Ellen," an older woman. "Roland became a kind of father figure. But I never knew what he was thinking. . . ." Three years after they married, Laura demanded her own room and the freedom to come and go as she pleased. "I didn't want to be divorced. I loved him. I love him now . . . but I needed to grow and it meant I had to love myself first."

After they joined the farm, Maureen, an old friend of Laura's, got together with Roland while Laura was spending the summer by herself on a beach in British Columbia. Laura thought that was fine. "Right now, I don't think I could be a good mother to Roland and Woody [her two children by Roland]. And divorce wouldn't change anything." At present, the kids have both their parents, in addition to Maureen, a divorcee with two children of her own. Now Laura has been able to grow, work through her delayed adolescence, and pick up an education that ended at the tenth grade. She is learning Spanish from library records and has taken up the guitar.

We arrived at the general store. Its corrugated tin roof sloped out over a pair of Chevron pumps. The kids ran into the store to spend their weekly allotment (grandparent money) on candy. On benches beside the doorstep some of the valley's longhairs were waiting for the mail to come in from the next town, over eight miles away. We exchanged brotherly greetings with members of the House of Illusion, another commune in the valley. I sat on the bench and waited with them.

A sleek Jaguar pulled up at the pumps. It was driven by a couple with a child—city hippies up for a few days' vacation. There were smiles, good words, but the distance between us yawned. We were the yokels, their poor country cousins, living off the land and handouts, dressed like scarecrows in jeans with leather patches, checked wool shirts, muddy boots, peasant hats and suspendered overalls. They were in bell-bottoms and silky flowered shirts. "You wouldn't happen to have a joint on you?" asked Charlie, who wore Salvation Army herringbone tweed pants held up by broad khaki suspenders. They smiled no as Andy, proprietor of the general store, returned their credit card, and drove off. "Hope you have a groovy vacation and . . . ," yelled Charlie, pulling out his kazoo and giving them a parting razzmatazz.

Someone bought some oranges and handed them around. Soon, the kids emerged one by one with their candy bars and Popsicles, and we started the trek back home.

Across the road, a hippie hitchhiker with a backpack was picked up by a prosperous-looking gray-haired lady driving a

Chevrolet. Matthew, five, immediately caught the significance. He tugged at Laura's coat and asked, "Why did that straight lady pick up that head?"

Laura explained directly. "Not all straight people in the world dislike hip people. Some of them, some of the time, will help us. There are many good, helpful straight people." Matthew said "uh-huh" and returned his tongue to his Popsicle.

On the way back, Laura talked more about Roland and herself. She made it clear they no longer slept together. They preserved a friendly but distant relationship: "He takes more interest in the children than he did. He and my father are still very close. They write, and Roland stays with him when he's in Berkeley. One of these days I'd like to take an acid trip with Roland and figure us out."

We had no sooner stepped into the house than Susan went to the sink and brushed her teeth with Arm and Hammer baking soda. Claudia quietly nodded to call my attention to her. Susan saw us watching and said, "I don't want to get any cavities." Later, Matthew came into the kitchen asking for "some *good* food, all I had for lunch was a Popsicle." Smiling, Claudia went out to the refrigerator, which stands outside the kitchen door next to the woodbin, and brought him tiger's milk. After he went off, she told me, "We don't lay any trips about food on the kids. But maybe they're picking something up by example. Sometimes I think they'll react by embracing all the plastic crap the American middle class swallows, simply because we deprived them of color TV's and Barbie dolls. And other times, I think they'll live the way we do."

A knock on the door in midafternoon. An exchange of panicked looks. "I wish people wouldn't knock, it make me very uptight," said Claudia, who'd been busted for possession of LSD.

It was Bill, the valley's social worker. A slight man in his middle thirties, he wore a tie, cardigan sweater, and carried a black leather folder. We chatted for a while before he revealed the purpose of his visit. Bill insisted that the county voters and officials did not resent the migration of so many hippies from California to Oregon. (Later in the same year, Governor Tom McCall threatened to raise Oregon state taxes to pay for soaring welfare costs, and public tolerance of the newcomers decreased.) Fortunately for the valley's hippies, Bill is a sympathetic person who personally favors a guaranteed annual wage and patiently works within the system.

The main point of his visit was to determine if Laura had decided to apply for welfare, a question she'd wrestled with all week and still not resolved. On the spot, she decided against it. After Bill left, she explained why: "It was a hassle." Before she could collect welfare, the DA would have had to prosecute Roland for nonsupport, since he was still living under the same roof, though this would take place with the understanding that he would not be penalized. Also, "I didn't want to be any more dependent on the government than I already am."

Claudia took herself off California welfare for philosophic reasons. She believes in neither giving to nor taking from a government that wages war. Maureen, on the other hand, who was in Berkeley to pick up her check, later told me she felt that by accepting welfare and commodities, she and the others were paving the way for more fundamental reforms like the guaranteed annual wage or the negative income tax.

Claudia spooned out some yogurt. "We wouldn't have so much of this without the commodities powered milk. Commodities give us the freedom to do more than just subsist. In a couple of years, we hope we won't need the government's food. . . ."

Roland carried in a pail of muddy beets he'd just pulled from the garden. He washed and trimmed them, leaving the nutritious tap roots. "I don't feel right accepting commodities," he said. Then he proceeded to justify participation in the food-stamp program. "You think of all the surplus the government buys to keep prices up. We might as well nationalize agriculture. We've got to stop thinking of food and everything in terms of prices. It's like charging people to breathe the air. Why, the land doesn't really belong to the farmers. It belongs—to all of us, to God. The Indians didn't have any deeds. If we could do away with private ownership and charging money for food, why, we could cultivate enough land to produce enough food for everybody."

Many straight people, like the county sheriff, regard the local hippies as parasites, living off the affluence of the very system they so loudly deplore. Thus far, I have not found one rural commune that has achieved anything close to economic self-sufficiency. From the viewpoint of the economic individualist, communes are invalid. Even the hippies are confused when they try to rationalize the discrepancies in their simultaneous existence as a revolutionary vanguard and a dependent subculture. Some communitarians gloss over the monthly checks from their parents in Scarsdale, Mill Valley or Winnetka, or the quarterly dividends from inheritances: "What does it matter? It's only happening on a material level. . . ." The more violent revolutionaries argue that the more they take from the system, the more effectively they undermine it. The name of the game is justifiable "ripping off." * For example, two members of a commune in the Southwest returned from a part-time job in a garage with a set of wrenches. Within society, their action was a crime; but within the ethic of their commune, whose members believed that everyone should have access to the means of production, it was an act of revolutionary virtue.

Communes straddle two societies, two moralities and two times: the present, in which every American is expected to pay his own way, and the future, when man will theoretically have learned to share and work together without the barriers of private ownership. Jack, for one, has come to accept welfare as an evolutionary necessity. "We wouldn't be on this earth today without our parents," he said last night. "We can't deny that we have their genes. We can't hate them any more than we hate ourselves. But still we are moving beyond them and beyond ourselves, too. How did we get where we're at? By steps. Everything proceeds by stages."

* The word covers both illegal and immoral theft: whether it be a pound of sirloin shoplifted from Shopright or exploitation of the subculture by using rock music to sell mouthwash. In both cases, the meat and the rock spirit can be said to have been "ripped off."

January 13

Awoke knowing immediately something had changed. The droning rain on the roof that had sunk into my consciousness had stopped. Through narrow windows near the peak of the A-frame, sunlight filtered. The firs swished against one another and birds twittered.

The kids were out playing in the meadow. (How many children have five-acre meadows for their backyard?) Susan, who had become sort of my special kid, ran up and asked to walk on my boots to the main house.

Most people were up already, and a record of the Band was on the phonograph. Everybody was smoking. I had walked into a sunny mood, and I picked up on the rhythm of the morning. It's like belonging to a rock group: You have to follow the beat that's always changing, like rain and sun. Today was an up day. Everything said or seen echoed and glistened with meaning and good humor. Laura, in a rainbow mood, danced the broom around the living room, sweeping into the kitchen to take a toke.

The topic of conversation at breakfast was working at straight jobs. Jean and Joe described working for Boeing in Seattle, Joe as a buyer, Jean as a secretary. Joe has the thin, tall build of so many men on communes—a phenomenon I can't explain. His usually dry humor is couched in a drawl retained from his Texas upbringing. "After Boeing hires you, they give you a form to sign, allowing them automatically to deduct money for U.S. Savings Bonds, which I pointed out were actually war bonds." Joe refused to sign. Although he'd been given the job, he was put under increasing pressure by executives of the corporate hierarchy. Still he refused; he knew they were legally obligated not to fire him. He and Jean worked for a year before they quit. "Corporations have a genius for making work boring."

Felt at loose ends and wanted to do some work. I asked Jack to delegate a chore; but placed in a situation vaguely resembling a position of authority, he hesitated to act. "Laying a trip" on someone else is the cardinal sin of communal life.

Next I tried Roland. He teased his beard for a moment, then said, "Come on." As it turned out, we were merely off for a walk. We passed Claudia doing the wash at a churning machine with a wringer attachment. It went *wrumph-da, wrumph-da, wrumph-da.* Happy and high, she worked standing on a carpet of needles in the grove of fir trees. Roland told me that the farm had salvaged two washing machines from the dump and swapped motor parts to put one of them into working condition. "Everyone just throws away their old washing machines and refrigerators," he said.

The trail led toward the foot of the mountain, through a thicket of second-growth trees. Many of them were madronas, primitive-looking trees that make poor firewood. Their graceful branches reminded me of women's legs in orange panty hose. We picked up rocks glittering with traces of quartz, amethyst and jade.

Roland's hair curls out at his ears. His reddish beard tapers over a rugged chin. His thick eyebrows nearly join over deep-set blue eyes. He expresses himself indirectly, screening his own feelings by using a third person construction: "One feels strange." "Some people believe. . . ." When I tell him he reminds me of an Elizabethan man who ran off to sea as a boy and learned about the world through experience, he replies that he wished he'd run away from home and school earlier than he did. He was raised by a Victorian mother who tried for years to correct the Cockney accent of his stepfather, an easygoing laborer and Communist. Roland hated his secondary school, where he felt inferior for not being able to juggle verbal abstractions. The inherited stiffness of the English which barred them from expressing their true feelings oppressed him. "You keep it all inside. You suppress it for so long that one day you wonder if your own deepest feelings are real."

As a child, Roland read books about organic farming and decided to become a farmer. Because land in England was too expensive, he emigrated to the United States and worked for five years as a farmhand on organic farms in Vermont. He learned about the intentional-community movement by reading *The*

Green Revolution, a periodical published by the School for Living, which is synonymous with Mildred Loomis.* Roland tried to save money to buy his own farm, but in Vermont elderly farmers whose sons had moved to the cities were going out of business. "Unless you have a lot of capital and know-how, it's almost impossible for an individual to operate a farm. You need more than a whole set of skills and a lot of money and labor. It takes a large family or a group like ours to run a farm."

We had climbed the side of the mountain. Barren, deep gullies testified to years of mining for gold and copper, done in the 1920's after the giant sugar pines had already been felled. The soil was red with minerals. We followed the old mining road up a sidewise grade until the trees opened up, giving a view from which Roland said you could see the Pacific, fifty miles away, on a clear day.

Of the men in the commune, Roland is the most consistently industrious. Still, he confessed, there are days when he doesn't feel like working. "But if I had a job in a factory and didn't show up one day, they'd fire me. A lot fewer people would be dropping out of the system if there were more jobs where you could work your own hours. If you could work in one job for one week, another the next week. If you could work a month and take off a month. But the system won't permit that kind of freedom. You're either in it all the way, nine to five, five days a week, fifty weeks a year, or you're a dropout." Suddenly Roland halted, reached down and picked up a deer antler. We took it home to show the kids.

Smoke was curling out of the sauna chimney. We stepped down in back and found Claudia and Jean sitting nude in the doorway, sharing a smoke. They'd hung the family's laundry inside the sauna to dry and while they were at it, had taken a sauna and a dip in the stream.

When we got back to the house, visitors had arrived: a young couple who, along with two other couples, had just bought land

---

* Along with Arthur E. Morgan and Dorothy Day of the *Catholic Worker,* Mildred Loomis is another of the leaders of the intentional-community movement of the thirties.

in the valley to the east. They were paying off the mortgage while building a log house with a chain saw. They had converted an old gas refrigerator into a freezer to preserve salmon and steelhead caught in the spring spawning runs. The group included a chemist and a psychologist with a PhD, who went down to San Francisco once a month to sell *The Berkeley Barb,* an underground newspaper. The one visiting us, a young man dressed in a wool lumberjack shirt and jeans, was also a college graduate. Last month he returned from Santa Cruz, where he'd worked as a riveter in a Ford plant. In twelve weeks, he made $2,200: "I couldn't have done it if I hadn't known that it was for a limited time." The chemist does the same thing—works three weeks in the city and returns to the farm with his paycheck.

After they left, I still felt like working, a hangover from my bourgeois upbringing. So I collected all the scrap lumber scattered in five or six places around the house, hauled it down a slope below the shitter, sorted and stacked it. The weight, feel and smell of the wood pleased my muscles and my senses. I discovered the trick of letting the loaded wheelbarrow roll down the sharp slope, running after and guiding it over a pathway of boards laid end to end over the mud. Internally, I could feel a dialogue unreeling. What drove me or Roland or Jack to work? At the farm there was no compulsion, and during the rainy winter months, little work to do. The need lay inside. Even if the future society became more cybernated and automated and provided guaranteed income, some men would still need to do *real* work.

Jean and Claudia returned with baskets of dry clothes and precipitated a mass scramble like a Macy's basement sale. I came out with two of the four underpants I'd put in and two extra undershirts. I traded off some of my smaller wool socks for a pair of big boot socks. But my green hand-knit wool socks had been swallowed up.

The dinner prepared by Reuben was a disaster: warmed-up lentils that must have been moldering for weeks in the refrigerator and a fish casserole that had the consistency and flavor of moist sawdust. Later, Elaine, sensing the general letdown baked two pecan pies, which kept everyone hovering around the kitchen for hours. Bill, who went through two years of college, talked of his brief career as a longshoreman on the Oakland docks. He looks the part: He's missing one front tooth, and he always wears the same blue-striped jerseys, bell-bottom pants and blue watch cap. He even walks with a nautical swagger. "I could make fifty dollars a day on the docks, working overtime," he said. "The trick is to get a work card." The first step was to get the union's application form. Once a month, the union steward threw them out of a shack near the piers: "I mean, he threw them into the air! You had to know exactly when to be there, and there'd be hundreds of other guys waiting, too, ready to fight to get a card. So you had to stand with your legs spread apart and your hands on your hips—to keep the other guys from getting in front of you—like this," he said, demonstrating the stance. "Man, there were some blacks and motherfuckers in that crowd. Finally, this short guy, with a cigar stuck in his mouth, came out of a shack and tossed the cards in the air like they were chunks of meat. And everyone started to fight over them. The steward screamed, 'Stop acting like a bunch of animals!' and went back into his shack."

The first pecan pie emerged, was sliced up, and immediately devoured. The pan was passed around and licked clean.

Bill's dream was to outfit a school bus as a mobile ecological exhibit and travel with a group across the country, cleaning up riverbanks and staging guerrilla theater forums to bring the ecological message to the hinterland. Bill is twenty-six. Until two years ago, when he packed his bag and rode the freights to California, he lived with his parents. He met Claudia at a commune. They've been together a year now, and she is three months pregnant. Bill is restless and says he needs to climb a mountain—alone. He foresees that he'll have to leave Claudia for a short time to go on his own journey of self-discovery. Claudia understands and encourages him to plan the trip. She

knows he'll return, and in the meantime, she won't be alone—
she has the others in the family.

Maureen and Roland have a similar old-man/old-lady relationship. Joe and Jean are legally married but, like other couples
here, do not prohibit each other from having other sexual relationships. Jack, Laura, Peter, Elaine and Reuben are unpaired,
although Jack and Laura, Peter and Elaine, were once lovers.
Some of them would prefer greater sexual interchange, but most
are content with the present arrangement, which is hard to
describe: It retains some of the stability of monogamy without
its emotional confinement and sexual restrictiveness.

January 15

Yesterday Maureen and the kids returned from the city. Kathy
had had braces put on her teeth.

Spent the morning reading to the kids: *Horton the Elephant*
and *Where the Wild Things Are.* When I tired, Reuben took
over the reading. Some days, it takes a relay team to satiate their
endless demand for stories.

None of the kids was then enrolled in school. Kathy, eight,
had gone to an experimental school in Berkeley, where, she told
me proudly, she'd learned to read and write "a year ahead of
my age." I asked her to spell some words, and she spelled them
phonetically—"SWETTER"—as she'd been taught. Did she want
to go back to school? She thought awhile. "Yeah, I think so.
Both Susan and I want to."

"Why?"

"We want to play with more kids our own age."

It was their choice to make, Maureen said, though she fears
that public school may brainwash them. She hopes that someday
the commune will have its own school, as many others do, but
right now they don't have enough children to warrant one. Jack
and Laura have discussed setting up a Montessori program.
While in Berkeley recently, Jack attended seminars led by a
Montessori disciple. He returned to the farm enthusiastic about
teaching the kids the new math. He hopes that the hippies in

the valley will someday build their own school and get it certified by the state. Generally, throughout the country, truant
officers have not hassled communes that decided to educate their
children at home.

Claudia was grinding more rose hips. The daughter of a
former Undersecretary of the Interior, she had been raised in
the Maryland suburbs of Washington, went to Miami University
in Ohio, did the sorority bit, and soon after graduation married Tony, a graduate student, whom she encouraged to become
an English professor. They turned on, dropped acid, and started
growing apart. "We simply became different people; our heads
were in different places. I once tried to explain why we split up
to Tony's mother. She couldn't understand it. She told me how
she had lived with her husband who drank and beat her up for
years. But she stayed with him for the children's sake." Though
separated, they aren't divorced, and they remain friends, ex-
changing cards, letters and humorous drawings through the
mail. Matthew sees his father off and on, perhaps one weekend
every two months.

Laura cut up orange peels. Later they would be grated and
used to flavor cookies and bread. The farm's motto should be:
Nothing is wasted.

Maureen had put on Crosby, Stills and Nash and was dancing
around the living room. Maureen is Irish and Italian and from
Long Island. She looks as though she could have been a high
school cheerleader: short-cut blond hair, greenish-blue eyes. All
sunny on the surface, full of small talk that seems evasive to me,
she often reveals a hard, unanswerable logic.

From the children's room came provocative taunts of "Matthew's full of bullshit, Matthew's full of bullshit . . . ," then
screams of revenge, a loud crash, silence, then explosive tears
and crying. Susan emerged, sobbing that Matthew had socked
her. Maureen, who assumed that Susan had provoked Matthew
(actually it might have been Kathy or all of them for that matter), shrieked that Susan was a little bitch who got what she
deserved. She pushed her daughter away. Maureen's anger, so

sudden and out of all proportion, was paralyzing. Later, she drove over to visit the House of Illusion to cool off. The kids settled down. Laura, wandering around aimlessly, said, "It really scares me when Maureen gets so mad at the kids. It reminds me of Mommy Ellen."

I spent most of the day playing with the children. They had found some long wooden rods and were engaged in mock swordplay. I watched uneasily, knowing where it would lead. Should I take the sticks away with stern admonitions: "Somebody's going to get hurt"? Or ignore the situation? After all, they weren't *my* kids. But in a commune they *were* my kids, in the sense that at that moment I was fully as involved with them as any other adult. When I visited friends living in suburbs, it was clear to me why I refrained from disciplining their children: In straight society, each child has one set of parents and one set of rules, and you don't confuse children by taking the chance of contradicting what their parents have been pounding into their skulls. Here, there are many parents, few rules and many values. It seems closer to reality.

So I let them learn the inevitable lesson for themselves: Those who play with sticks get hurt with sticks. Roland got hit hard over the head by Kathy. He retaliated with wild thrusts. At this point I intervened, jerked the sticks out of their hands, laid down a moralistic trip about the difference between playing and fighting, and diverted their attention to another game.

The same situation could have been handled in a number of ways. Claudia, generally authoritarian, probably would have headed off the swordplay at the start. Laura might have allowed it to go further than I did, risking injury: "The kids are a community of their own, and they have to learn the same way we do, that if you hurt somebody, he'll hurt you back. . . . I guess I'd stop them if someone was in danger of getting killed. . . ." Elaine might have avoided the situation altogether, for she avoided the children as much as she avoided everybody; when she *did* do something with them, it was on her terms, like driving them to the library to see the weekly travelogue film.

From time to time, Maureen exploded in violence, usually directed at her own children, especially Kathy, toward whom she apparently harbored some deep resentment. On the other hand, Jean was calm and gentle and might have coaxed them into more peaceful play.

Altogether, the kids experienced an uneven, inconsistent upbringing by six daddies and five mommies, each of whom could be counted on to handle the same situation differently. For the kids, the only constant in the communal environment was constant inconsistency.

Claudia told me, "I think it's a mistake to bring up kids with the notion that there's a single code of what's good, bad, manly or feminine. The fact is, we're living in a world where all the absolutes have been broken. Each man finds his own path. So to prepare the kids for that, it's better to give them a lot of examples, a lot of fathers and mothers who are all different personalities and have different values."

Confined by the rain, the kids, bottled up, started to run through the house, slamming doors and barging into each other. Firmly, Roland restrained them because "it makes everyone uptight." He was leveling with them, and the children appreciated it. Commune children dig the word "uptight." It's an accurate description of a feeling central to human behavior. We lay rules on children to cope with our own internal tensions.

If there's anything consistent at all about raising children here, it's honesty. Since you know there are no more absolute rights and wrongs, you tell it like it is: "*I* don't like that," which is really the same as "That makes me uptight." I asked myself, if I honestly believed there was nothing harmful in smoking dope, why not let my own kids smoke? Kathy gets giggly stoned; the smaller kids vie with the adults for the honor of swallowing the roaches. If you believe sex is good, then why hide it in a dark corner? At one time or another, mainly in the summer, most of the kids have observed grown-ups making love. Once Matthew asked Claudia if Bill hurt her. She explained, "No, it looked that way, but really it felt good." That was enough for Matthew.

After lunch, I was comfortably drinking tea and reading Aldous Huxley's *The Doors of Perception* when Susan sat down beside me and asked to be read to. "Don't feel like it right now," I answered. She whined and tried to pull the book out of my hand. I was firm, but she was testing to see *how* firm I would get. She grabbed the book away and laughed. I gave her shoulder a hard push, and she desisted.

That kind of tug-of-war testing of limits goes on all day with all kids, whether in a commune or a single-family ranch house. It's part of the growing-learning process. The drawback of the typical nuclear family is that most of the time preschool children have only one adult to test—Mom. After twelve hours of testing a day, the nuclear mother becomes tired and bitchy. The air of the ranch house is charged with "Don'ts," "If I told you once, I've told you a thousand times . . . ," "Linda McDonald, when your father comes home he's going to give you the licking of your life . . . ," "Will you *ever* learn?" and so on. The abrasive testing that gives many mothers of small children gray hair still occurs within the communal, extended family, but the destructive effect on everybody is spread out among more people. At High Ridge Farm, it seems the kids play more on their own or as a group than other young children I've observed and don't need constant adult supervision. Sure, they fight, but they can always be sent outside to allow their aggressions free rein in the meadows and forests.

It seems the mothers spend more than half their time involved in nonchild-oriented activities. When they *are* looking after the children—putting them to bed, feeding them, giving them baths —they care for them as a group. This gives the mothers more time to themselves. For example, this afternoon Claudia was left with all the kids while the rest of the family went off in various directions. Laura spent a lot of time writing in her self-analytic diary, painting and playing the guitar. Elaine stayed up almost all last night with a C. S. Lewis novel and slept until noon, certain that somebody would be looking after Abraham.

At High Ridge Farm, as elsewhere in American society, the women as a group still bear most of the responsibility for the children. Out in the country there is a natural impetus to revert to traditional roles: Women stay inside, cook, and look after the children, while men plow, chop, and build roads. However, in other communes women are making attempts to counter this traditional tendency by learning to work chain saws and drive tractors, sometimes dumping babies who need to be changed in the laps of their men. In some communes (not here) the women belong to women's liberation groups, but in most, the redefinition of what it means to be a woman and mother is gradually taking place, with little rhetoric and few hassles.

This afternoon, at the kids' demand, Claudia tried to give them a lesson in arithmetic. She started with addition. The lesson disturbed Matthew, who left the table and went into the dormitory room to sulk. "He still finds it hard to accept that I can be a mother or a teacher to all the kids," Claudia told me later. "But he's improving." When she and Bill joined the commune, Matthew refused to sleep with the other children and wouldn't allow anyone but Claudia to dress him or serve him his dinner. Now he dresses himself and puts himself to bed in the kids' dormitory. Said Claudia, "He's getting over all the Oedipal hangups of being strongly attached to one mommy—you know, possessiveness, jealousy, competitiveness."

The experience of communal child rearing seems to confirm the theories of Erik Erikson and others: relax the structures which shape the personality, extend the limits of the family, and then perhaps a generation will be ready for utopia.

Claudia runs a tight ship to compensate for the other mothers' permissiveness. Near the end of the afternoon, she announced clean-up time. She marshaled, cajoled and cowed all the kids— including Woody, the smallest—into clearing their room of toys, paints, and discarded clothes. Somebody protested, giving a lame excuse. Claudia's voice could be heard throughout the house. "Look, I want you to clean up your room without me hanging over you. I don't want to be your master. You should get to the point where you can be your *own* master."

Claudia was trying to inculcate the philosophy of self-rule:

The kids were their own community, this was their room, and they should take care of it as their own. I saw this approach succeed in other communes. In one, I watched slightly older children proceed through their dormitory-playroom in military style, with the larger kids prodding the younger ones into compliance. It was like watching a mini-kibbutz in action.

There are few arguments of the "Roland won't give back *my* doctor set" sort. There aren't many toys, and those there are are kept in a common toy bin. But the concept of "mine" is slow to vanish. Last Christmas, the grown-ups discussed whether to put nametags on the toys or to leave them untagged to signify that they belonged to all the kids. They decided on traditional tagging. But before Christmas they did open the presents from grandparents and redistribute them equally so that each child got the same number.

The children are not unaware of or unattracted by the society which lies beyond the general store and which they glimpse during their jaunts down to Berkeley. They know a hip from a straight and the difference between "commodities" and the more highly prized "store-bought" cheese.

"Do you have lots of dollar bills in your wallet?" Matthew asked me once.

"A few."

"Can I have some?"

Later, I told Claudia about Matthew's interest in material wealth. She laughed and wondered again whether the kids would ultimately accept hip values or reject them "just like we rejected our parents'." In the future "there'll be more alternatives. Right now, you're hip or you're straight. As Ken Kesey says, you're either on the bus or off the bus."

As darkness settled, people began to return home. Roland and Bill had spent the day on either side of a two-man crosscut saw, cutting timbers for a new bridge to span the washed-out section of the road. Jack had been driving around looking for a fuel pump for the Chevy pickup. Maureen returned high from the House of Illusion, Peter emerged from his seclusion and put on a recording of the Prokofiev cello concerto. He squatted next to the speaker. Jean and Claudia cut vegetables for dinner.

When the gong rang, everyone began to take his place in the living room for meditation. Peter was still rapt by the last movement of the concerto, which was rushing toward climax. Insensitive to his passionate involvement with the music, Maureen called, "Could you turn it off? We're going to meditate." Peter implored for one minute more. Maureen waited about a minute, then as the concerto entered the homestretch, she said, "I can't *meditate*."

Peter: "Just one second."

Maureen: "I've waited a minute already. . . ." Peter, exasperated, ripped the needle off the record with a *wwwrrrackkk* and rushed out of the house. Awful silence. I was stunned. It was the first ugly scene I'd witnessed here, and it jolted me out of the illusion that the commune had escaped all contrariness.

After dinner, Jack began talking: "I'm down about Peter. He's drifting away and it kinda reminds me of how John and Carol [two of the six original founders] left. We didn't try to stop them. Don't you think we should make some effort to tell Peter we need him and love him?"

There was little response to Jack's concern. Before the meeting began, I had warned myself to keep quiet during the family powwow, but the inquiring reporter overcame my sensible caution. I broke the silence, asking, "What led up to all this? Surely something else must have happened between Peter and the rest of you besides the record scene?" As the words left my mouth, my mistake became obvious. My question was ignored, and soon the meeting broke up.

Later I lay in my sleeping bag, thinking everyone asleep, furtively taking notes on the day's events by flashlight. Lantern in hand, Elaine entered the A-frame. She saw me and smiled knowingly. Removing her layers of raincoats—so many she looked pregnant—she came and sat down beside me. She is a thin twenty-seven-year-old Jewish girl from New York, who graduated in political science from Swarthmore. She has straight, lustrous brown hair which she brushes over her ears, which stick out slightly. Very thick glasses in oval frames help correct her severe myopia. She always wears the same pair of loose, flowered, pajamalike pants. When she chooses to talk to you, her speech is punctuated with anguished gaps to indicate her extremely careful choice of words. "I've noticed . . . from when you first came here . . . that you've held yourself apart from the family."

I was engulfed by tension. She continued, "You introduced yourself rather formally . . . and you said you wanted to be a member of the family. . . ." That's right, I said.

"But there's something about you . . . I guess it was tonight that I first realized what it was . . . the way you broke in with that question about Peter . . . it was a question that *intruded.* I saw that you weren't thinking of yourself as a member of the family . . . you were a detached observer in disguise . . . taking notes in your head . . . and secretly at night." She smiled and looked down at my pad. I felt caught.

"Have you ever tried *not* observing . . . just experiencing . . . or do you always remain detached from whatever you're doing?" Man, this chick was what you call laying a trip! And of course all she said was true.

She concluded, "To catch the essence of communal life, you should put your notebook away, and then you may decide it is more important to live it than to write it." I thanked her for revealing my foibles, and we said good night.

January 16

This morning, I tried to start a conversation with Jean as she ground some flour (she baked a dozen loaves and they were eaten in two days), but she didn't respond to my openers. Instead she said, "I agree with everything Elaine told you last night," and paused to let it sink in, all the time continuing to grind, smiling and jiggling her earrings. "What you said during the meeting was with the tone of not caring about Peter or any of us. It was the tone of a ruthless curiosity, digging for a fact to fill out the story. It was your ego speaking."

There was more. She ground away. "I get the feeling when you talk that you are holding back. An aloofness. And that you don't dig the *feeling* of words, only their logical sense. And, you ask too many questions."

Wowwww. I shook my head dumbly and mumbled about having to think over what she said and went off to dig a hole for a fruit tree.

Along the big brook, Peter had staked out spots where the fruit trees were to be transplanted. Beneath the topsoil the ground becomes red, gravelly and mixed with large rocks. I picked savagely at the gravel, sparks flying, and sometimes I jumped into the hole, scooping out the larger rocks by hand. I was angry: first, that Jean had overheard the conversation (Big Sister is listening) and angry at my own oversensitive reaction. On another level, I was watching myself being drawn into the interpersonal reality of the commune and away from my past well-practiced roles. It would be impossible to remain detached here and not to invest (and thus expose) my ego in the others. Small talk was out. I was being forced to justify myself. "Why write a book? Isn't it another ego trip? Aren't I using people like material?"

After lunch Peter asked if I'd help transplant the fruit trees. He had been paid in kind for his work at a local greenhouse— cherry, plum and apricot trees.

It was drizzling. Peter turned up the hood of his blue rain jacket. While I held the trees in place, he stood at a distance, like a painter, viewing the shape of the tree; then he stepped closer and pruned a branch until it was symmetrical. I told him about the exchange with Elaine and Jean. He was sympathetic, for we were much alike, both Geminis and intellectual Easterners. "It's impossible to stay here and not go through some heavy changes," he said. "I went through more changes here in five days than I would in five months somewhere else."

Peter was born in Connecticut. He graduated from Goddard, where he was much influenced by Gandhi's ideas of decentralized village democracy. He went to live for an isolated year in the small French-speaking towns of eastern Quebec. "I felt a need to find roots in some culture, but even the French-Canadian towns are being commercialized." He helped found the War Resisters League on the West Coast; earlier, he had been field secretary for a communal peace group living near Voluntown, Connecticut. "But I was running out of steam. How many times do you need to run your head against the wall to learn that society isn't going to change because of political demonstrations? You begin first by changing yourself, then your friends, and working outward. Creating a new life-style that speaks more strongly than political slogans. . . ."

The others had also reached the same point of frustration with society and had dropped out singly in despair. But now they were attempting a collective, more creative withdrawal. More than the five other founders of the commune, Peter insisted on giving it clearer structure by imposing a membership procedure and limiting its size. "From my anthropology course at Goddard I learned that the maximum size for most small groups to function is around twelve people." The rift between Peter and the rest of the group, however, was not due so much to his ideas as to the abstract way he expressed them. At first I couldn't see this because the trait was so much a part of myself. Now I knew one of the reasons why the two women had reacted the way they did.

While Peter held the tree in position, I filled the hole first with bonemeal, then black topsoil, and last the gravelly soil. Gently, as if sensing its vibrations, Peter tamped the soil around the base of the cherry tree.

Elaine wandered by, all bundled up. She had slept late. Peeking at the trees, she paused. "Hummm, I feel torn . . . I *know* the fruit trees will be good . . . but I hate to have the view blocked." She turned and plodded off, hands in her parka, eyes downward on the ground.

Peter leaned on his shovel, watching her walk toward the house. "She can't take any external limits, the kind of structure I need, because she can't set any limits within herself," he said. Again I felt a rush of panic at slipping into a different, more fluid reality, loosening my grasp on my inner handlebars. Through intuitive flashes, Peter had perceived Elaine's carefully guarded self. Why hadn't I noticed Peter's and Elaine's personalities before? Now, set before me, they seemed magnified. The going was getting very heavy.

Back in the house, Elaine had put on Crosby, Stills and Nash again, peeled off her clothes, and was dancing nude to "Judy Blue Eyes." The kids, who'd filled a big pot with popcorn, went about their playing oblivious to her gyrations—she who in the past had been a member of an intellectually elite group called "The Society for Creative Anachronisms," and who had danced topless in seedy San Francisco bars. That was Elaine—all extremes.

Reuben came in and squeezing by her murmured something like, "What a crazy chick." Elaine wheeled on him, her low-slung breasts still in motion, her hair spilling over her face, hissed, "Sometimes, Reuben, I think I could choke you," picked up her clothes, and stomped off. Reuben just stood there in his Robin Hood cap, with a long feather that looked like an antenna, his beetlelike eyes behind glasses even thicker than Elaine's. He just stood there and went uhhhhhhhhhh.

Reuben was the misfit. There's one or two in every commune. Or there should be. Reuben, whose real name was Irving, had been heavily into drugs (he could and did give you the pharmaceutical directions for making cocaine), and now it was yoga and the Eastern spiritual trip. He seemed perpetually on the edge of the family, spending much of his time meditating alone in the A-frame and continually annoying the others by diverting the conversation. Elaine, Peter and Jean disliked him intensely and had told him to leave, but he refused. He was allowed to stay because the rest of the commune was opposed on principle to obstructing the free flow by excluding anyone. But Jack felt that a policy of expelling undesirables was an admission that the community was unable to function naturally. "People should be able to select themselves, tell themselves that they don't belong here. I'd say we've had maybe thirty people who've done that. They stay for a week or two and decide that this isn't the spot or that they haven't any more to learn from the people here. Also, being closed would shut us off from change."

I once asked Peter if he felt communities bore a responsibility to take in some of the disturbed people who might otherwise end up in mental institutions. "Yeah, I dig how the commune is a kind of therapeutic institution. Certainly Reuben's better off here, he's improving a lot." Reuben was looked on as a burden, but he was accepted. His quirks, his oddities, his differences that bordered on schizophrenia, accepted, and for Reuben, that was a crucial step forward.

Peter was considering leaving the farm for a couple of weeks. He planned to go down to Berkeley to work in a greenhouse and, as he characteristically put it, "to reevaluate my role at the farm." Before he left, he heard a rumor that Andy, the owner of the general store, might donate some of his land for the construction of a hip church, meeting hall and school. Peter and I talked about the political problems that might be presented by hips organizing within a straight community. Later, during a conversation with Claudia and Elaine around the circular kitchen table, Peter tried to express his concern, knowing that he might not be around for a family discussion if Andy's proposal materialized. But he expressed himself rather abstractly: "It might be wise to contact a spokesman of the straight community"; and he dropped phrases like "anticipating their objections," "appointing a committee that would embrace a spectrum of society," etc.

Peter made sense to me, but his choice of words angered both Claudia and Elaine.

Claudia screamed, "It's not what you say, it's *how* you say it that makes me so mad."

Then Elaine took over. It was as if she were peeling an onion. "All the time I've known you I've had the notion you were trying to keep things from us . . . as if we were children and you were trying to spare us the pain of knowing all the cares that weighed on your shoulders. . . . It's a kind of insidious paternalism, and you're the leader. You had the foresight to press on and buy the land when everyone else was holding back. But now you try to influence us just by the tone of your voice. . . ." Elaine halted. Silence.

"Go on," said Peter.

Claudia: "Why don't you come out and tell us how you feel? Instead of using all this formal shit. I've very, very rarely seen you express the real *you*. The other night with the record player was one time. You were passionate, angry, frustrated, but it was you."

Peter (meekly): "This has been a very helpful conversation."

Claudia: "Fuck! There you go again. By the very *tone* of the words I can tell it hasn't sunk in."

Bill (who has been reading a how-to book on raising earthworms): "What are you all talking about?"

Peter (angry at last): "Why don't *you* get your head out of the sand? Why don't you ever say anything?"

Claudia and Elaine: "That's more like it."

Elaine (to Peter): "For as long as I've known you, I've thought you were always judging yourself and others. Every time we make music together [she plays the guitar, he the recorder] I can feel you criticizing . . . It destroys it for me. It makes me feel very unhappy. Why don't you throw away the report card you're always keeping? Take a vacation from school and teacher's dirty looks? Once I came into the kitchen when you and Claudia were talking, I don't remember when or about what, but I remember the tone . . . it was like hearing an interview between a social worker and his client. . . ."

Peter: "Well . . . thank you." He tried to say more, but Elaine hushed him with a kiss, and Claudia hugged him.

Elaine played the guitar, singing the melancholy Gordon Lightfoot song, "Early Morning Rain." I could empathize with her, but the gap between us was so great that there seemed no way to tell her that I felt the same way she did. I tried to build intellectual bridges between us. We talked. Of her ambivalence toward men, of Christian ritual, carnal love, community, but I was always driving her into some mind-fucking intellectual corner and she was always dodging me. I still pressed on, boring into her brain to get a photograph of it and match it with mine so that the differences could be analytically reconciled. Finally she became so overcome with inarticulate passion that her lips moved without any words coming out. She took my hand and led me to a beam by the kitchen counter where everyone had posted their favorite aphorisms and lines of poetry. The lines by Thomas Merton, transcribed elegantly in pen, were evidently Elaine's contribution:

... to understand that one has nothing to say is to suddenly become free with a liberty that makes speech and silence equally easy. What one says will be something that probably has been said before. One need not trouble about being heard. The thing that is being said has been heard before ... speech has only served us against the secret terror of not existing. Once the illusion is clear, man is delivered from the necessity of speaking in his own defense and henceforth speaks only for his brother's comfort.

What was there to say? We hugged and it was said. I took a flashlight and leaving Elaine to her guitar, headed up toward the A-frame. After days of rain, the sky had finally cleared and the moon was out. It shimmered on the muddy puddles along the path. The flashlight was unnecessary. The moonlit meadow with moss hanging from the trees looked unearthly. What strange world was I moving through? A reality of reflected light, a house of twelve mirrors, each reflecting twelve images of the self. But which was the real image? Perhaps it was all nothing but reflection, image and fantasy—but to be sure, we were all in it together. There was a part of me in Peter that I could only see through Elaine. All three of us were Geminis. All of us were thwarted by different but similar blindnesses in the others.

January 17

The rain has settled in again, pelting evenly and intently, seemingly endless. I have a cold. My perceptions are as fogged in as the valley. The brook has backed up around the holding dams that were built last year to prevent it from eroding.

After breakfast I felt at loose ends. For the first time here, I craved some escape, like reading a newspaper or watching a movie or even TV, anything to assure myself that the dull, predictable outside world was still there.

The kids were uptight, too. Their unspent tensions and energies boomeranged through the house. The walls seemed to have shrunk. "Little" Roland teased Kathy about her braces. She parried with a "Fuck you" and chased him through the house. Finally she tripped him. He fell and knocked over the kitchen spice shelf.

The kids are a barometer of the general atmosphere. The grown-ups have also grown tense. The group mood could spiral up, attaining a collective high, and we could be Woodstock Nation again; or it could spiral downward into the darkness of Altamont.

This afternoon, Jean straightened and sorted through the shelves in the children's room. Each person has his own shelf for things like toothbrushes, combs, rings, papers and most clothes. Everything else goes into communal boxes and on communal shelves. Then she searched for a hand mirror missing from the common shelf. She found it on Peter's private shelf. He was sitting on a cushion in the main room when she came out, pissed off: "It really annoys me when you put the communal mirror on your shelf." Peter shrugged. Jean continued, "I spent a lot of time looking around for it, and it's happened before."

Trying to brighten the mood, I put on some Vivaldi concertos, but I forgot the unwritten rule that he who puts on a record must also return it to its cover and rack. Peter later discovered his records were left on the spindle, gathering dust, and chewed me out.

The phonograph played all day, but it never struck a common chord. Elaine cut off Vivaldi in midmovement and replaced it with Big Pink. Maureen turned the volume down. Elaine turned it back up.

The day before, Bill had had to go into town and the taillight on the pickup truck wasn't working. So he transferred the one from Maureen's truck (which was always referred to as Maureen's—she kept the keys) to the pickup and drove away. Today Maureen noticed the missing light and confronted Bill: "I could get busted for this, you know. It's not the first time something like this has happened. You're careless and you're. . . ."

Bill: "You get this straight, Maureen. As long as I'm in this commune, what you have is mine. You can't come in and dangle the keys over my head and say that as long as I'm a good boy you'll let me drive your car. I have every right to touch your car."

Maureen (shrilled): "You don't, you don't!"

Bill: "You're trying to push me but I'm not going to run away. Go ahead and hit me if you feel like it, but I'm not going to let you alone. If I see your kids doing something, I'll lay a hand on them."

Maureen: "You mean you'll act irresponsibly with them just the way you acted irresponsibly with my truck. Last summer you threw stones at them. Is that responsible?"

For a while I thought they might really come to blows. Finally, Bill picked up his flute and walked off playing it, into the rainy meadow.

Before dinner, J. D. and Jim, two guitarists from the House of Illusion, arrived to practice some spirituals and other songs for the community church to which we'd been invited by the local Pentecostal Church. We had just begun to get into the songs, which they strummed with a rock beat, *"What a friend we have in Jesus, all our fears and cares to bear,"* when Claudia

stentoriously rang the gong and announced that it was meditation time and that we had to find some other place to sing.

Everyone was embarrassed by Claudia's rudeness. Jack took
her aside to rap in the kitchen. She got angrier. Her face red-
dened. Meditation didn't develop. It wasn't the right day anyway. We were on a communal manic-depressive roller coaster,
and now we were plunging downward with increasing momentum.

January 18

Much brighter and crisper. Elaine and I were talking across
the room, still in our sleeping bags, when fat fluffy snow filled
the bright sky and batted gaily against the windows.

After breakfast, Claudia asked me to help replant the Christmas trees. For sure. The snow came and went, alternating with
a misty rain. A rainbow arched over the valley. The kids
streamed out of the house, running toward it crying "happimiss,
happimiss"—their word for joyous occasions. It originated with
Woody's lisped pronunciation of "happiness."

Instead of following the yule custom of cutting down a tree,
the commune had dug up two small firs, roots and all, and
kept the roots wrapped in canvas while they were decorated.
The true, pagan meaning of Christmas was a celebration of
life's eternal renewal, Claudia explained, signifying that the
winter solstice has been passed. So why kill trees in celebration?

I hefted one fir, its roots heavy with water, into the wheelbarrow and pushed off toward the meadow. Weighted down
with trees, shovel and pick, the wheelbarrow plowed into the
mud. I strained to push through it, puffing great balls of steam
into the chilled air blown off the frozen mountains. At the compost heap, I paused to catch my breath.

The garbage from every meal is scraped into two plastic
peanut butter jars and then emptied on the compost pile. Wood
ash from the stove is sprinkled over it. Nearby is the gas-pow-
ered shredder used to chew the cornstalks into a fine mulch.
From time to time the compost heap is turned over and mixed,

revealing layer upon layer of decomposition and, near the bottom, a mass of pink, slithering worms. Jack loves to turn the pile over with a rake and see "how a corncob breaks back down to its component parts. Everything must break down before it can be reborn."

Claudia joined me. As we stood musing over the compost heap, Roland came toward us, his jeans, quilted with patches at the knees, tucked in his boots. He looked very much the farmer. He was able to answer some of my questions about the principles of organic farming. "After years of using chemical fertilizers, the nitrates seep into one layer of the ground and become deadly. The microorganisms are killed off and the soil loses fertility. Also, the ground gets very hard—it's the dead bodies of the organisms that keep the soil porous. So you have to use machinery to break it up every year.

"There are apple orchards in Washington State that have been so heavily sprayed with copper that they've had to be abandoned." To the organically-minded, the use of chemical fertilizers represents the imposition of man's ruthless will on nature. "You can plant just so much. Every seven years, the land should lie fallow so the natural processes can catch up. The commercial farmer takes far more than he naturally restores, and he tries to make up the difference with chemicals. What does the farmer in Nebraska with a thousand acres in wheat care if the land will be infertile in fifty years? By then he'll have sold out and moved to Florida."

Instead of chemicals, the farm uses lots of chicken shit, free for the hauling; rotten sawdust from any of several lumber yards; and seaweed such as kelp, high in minerals like iodine and potassium and also free for the taking along Oregon's ocean beaches. The farm was also planning a visit to one of the canneries to collect a load of fish scraps.

Roland led us over to the site of a new communal building, built on a gentle slope on the far side of the brook. We looked around for a place to transplant the Christmas trees. Before winter the men had sunk the building's supporting structure and dug a trench to keep the stream from eroding its underpinnings. "Erosion is one of our problems. We're going to plant some grass here to keep the slope from washing away, but it will have to be a special species that will be very tough and resistant to the dry, hot summer weather."

We selected a spot for the trees, a place where in some fifteen years they might be able to protect the front of the house from the torrid sun of August. In the summer the streams become parched gullies and grasshoppers plague the farm. Last summer they chewed away a third of the fruit trees' new growth. The neighboring farmer scattered pesticide-tainted bait over his fields. "We found dead birds around. The irony is, of course, that the birds eat the grasshoppers." Rather than resort to pesticides, the farm decided to meet this year's assault with a natural predator. From a seed company, they ordered five boxes of praying mantises, who gorge themselves on their cousins, the grasshoppers. And to check the aphids, they sent away for an army of ladybugs.

After the holes were dug, we gently lowered the trees in place. "I always feel like saying a prayer after planting a tree," Claudia said.

"Go ahead," Roland urged.

"Grow!" was all she said.

Took a retreat to get my head together. I walked up the mountain to the cabin Laura was building for herself. It was about half finished. The floor was completed, and above it the rafters for the roof were nailed together. I sat on a box and pondered the view. The facing mountains were national forest land that had not been recently lumbered. The mountains had texture and color. In the ravines and hollows, the shaded trees were blue. Five miles away, the jagged spine of the mountain was so sharply etched against the sky that I could pick out the tips of individual trees. Even at this distance from the brook, the air was aroar with rushing water. Nature had pattern, gestalt. Man was beginning to see himself again as a part and passing stage instead of the be-all and end-all of evolution. Was there any kind of social ecology that united man to man as vitally as the aphid was linked to the cabbage and the moth? What was there to keep the people at the commune from going their individual ways? From replaying the old struggle of tooth and claw? Why should a dozen unrelated people remain together? Yesterday I had seen a natural force working in the commune—the antagonistic force of ego. And yet the commune went on. Why?

Methodically, I ticked off what *it* was not. *It* wasn't ideological. The family had left politics and revolution behind in Berkeley. *It* wasn't sexual freedom. They had no Reichian faith in orgasmic potency, no orgies, no group marriage structure. *It* wasn't cooperative economics: outside the communes, hundreds of individuals and couples were surviving in the country by accepting a simpler standard of living—and food stamps.

Intellectually, I knew that *it* couldn't be grasped by man's analytical tools, his ologies: *it* was a consciousness totally different from that of analytical modern man, who always differentiated himself from his subject, categorically dividing Man from Nature, the Self from Society. *It* was a gestalt, a fresh vision, a . . . but my thoughts began to muddle. I was a would-be explorer, locked in a study, piecing together a map of a distant country I had not yet seen.

When Maureen returned from Berkeley, she brought some grass and several tabs of acid—Sunshine, she'd been told. This afternoon, when everyone was in the kitchen, she took one tab and offered the rest to anyone who wanted to trip along. Laura joined her.

"Robert?"

I declined. I wasn't ready yet. Would they mind if I accepted but didn't take it now? I might change my mind. For sure. Maureen gave me a tab wrapped in tinfoil. I put it in the top pocket of my wool shirt.

At the start of my travels, I had resolved not to take acid. I didn't want to lose my objectivity, freak out, return home wearing a hair shirt and having no coherent notes. I was afraid of changing, losing control, becoming submerged. I have never dived into water but have always eased in step by step.

They didn't press me, the conspicuous acid virgin of the group. No one here has the Timothy Leary compulsion to turn everyone on, or the dangerous faith that acid is everybody's cure-all. They respected my caution but clearly doubted that I could write a good book without having tripped. While acid was not the commune's foundation of life, it was a common point of departure. They were trying to live the acid vision without the acid itself.

I am a cautious map reader who must know where I'm going and why. But I was beginning to learn that no trip turns out the way you planned it. Objectivity—philosophical and journalistic—affords only a partial account. Nothing—no person, no atomic particle—exists complete in itself, unaffected by the viewer. This is a fact of both physics and journalism. Reality is relationship.

After dinner we got into a rambling discussion and stumbled onto the topic of electricity. Elaine wanted to cut it off, sever the umbilical cord, secede altogether from the technology whose inevitable by-product was environmental pollution. Everyone agreed it would be good to disconnect. Someone switched off the overhead light and lit a homemade candle. Elaine continued rapping: They should also forsake toilet paper. With all the wastepaper in the world, produced at the cost of millions of trees a year, why not wipe with old newspapers?

Bill: "Where do you draw the line? How can anyone *exist* without taking away from nature? You're reasoning like the Catholic philosophers who argue backward from the existence of the soul to the conclusion that abortion is murder."

Elaine: "Well, it *is* murder."

(A gasp)

Bill: "Don't you believe in contraception?"

Elaine: "It debases women to use the pill. It takes out all the joy when you're trying to keep your own nature under control."

Peter: "But how about all the other women in the world for

whom the pill is an escape from unwanted children? Think of India. Are you speaking of all the women in India too?"

Elaine: "I'm speaking of how *I* feel. And it *is* a non-Western way of feeling. As Westerners, we look at India and see all the squalor and kids with matchstick legs and the dead bodies in the street, and we say that's hell. But the Indians don't. Death is a part of life, a part of the process. Death isn't as horrible for them. They have their children and their bodies and spirits pass on. Nothing is ever lost."

Roland: "It's true our bodies decompose just like corncobs. Unless you get sealed up in a casket where the bacterial action can't get. . . ."

Jack: "Maybe we should join a burial society and get cheap pine boxes for ourselves."

Peter: "Make our own."

Bill: "I read in *Whole Earth Catalogue* that you can make coffins out of papier-mâché."

Elaine: "I'd like to be composted."

Peter (laughing): "I don't know if I could take that every morning, walking past the compost pile and noticing one of Elaine's eyeballs staring up at me."

Everyone laughed, then fell silent. Suddenly Maureen burst through the door with a handful of tan pups with closed eyes. "Coffee's had her puppies!" she announced, and then, "Hey! Why do you have all the lights off?"

January 19

Today we visited another commune, the Onion Farm. We drove the two trucks, heading out late in the afternoon. J. D., the folk singer, came with us. It may have been the clear day and the distant purple mountains which prompted us to break unexpectedly into "America the Beautiful," surprised that we hadn't forgotten the words. We sang, "For purple mountains' majesty above the fruited plain," as we cruised down a canyon of tall firs.

"I sorta like that," said J. D. at the end. The song had once been the national anthem, he said, before the militarists had adopted "The Star-Spangled Banner." "Did you ever listen to those words?" he asked in his Tennessee twang. "Why, there's bombs a-bursting, rockets a-glaring . . . people dying to defend a piece of cloth." He took up his guitar again: "This Land is Your Land. . . ." With Roland at the wheel of the old Dodge decorated with peace symbols, we crested a hill and drove past white water knifing through rock. On the far side of a green valley, we passed a lonely farm. A small boy on the farmhouse porch gave us a V sign as we coasted by. The flag of *our* vision was not a star-spangled, blood-soaked banner but green, the color of grass.

The eighteen of us were arriving unannounced at dinner time, which was the custom among the communes. The Onion Farm's road was even ruttier and muddier than ours. We drove as far as we could and walked the rest of the way. The house looked like a sharecropper's on a *Bonnie and Clyde* set. Chickens roamed freely around the dusty yard.

Miraculously, there was enough food for dinner. We discovered that the farm was in the process of breaking up. One group was heading for British Columbia, and a few other couples were going to find their own houses in the valley.

After dinner J. D. led the singing. In his thirties, J. D. had seen pain. His hair was dirty blond. He wore a black leather jacket and boots. He had played in coffeehouses with Judi Collins and Tom Paxton and had turned down recording offers to go into the Mendocino Forest and compose his own music. He is a modern-day troubadour. The immediate contact live music brings between performer and audience is more fulfilling to him than cutting or listening to a record. Musically, J. D. has moved from acid rock into the heartland of American folk singing. "We've left the electrified mind behind. The country's always been there, but we had to go full circle to find it."

We smoked and sang folk songs. Three others from the Onion Farm joined J. D. and sang numbers like "It Takes A Worried Man To Sing A Worried Song." We stayed very late.

Trying to back down the road, one truck crashed through

the thin sheet of ice over a rut and dug itself axle-deep in mud. Somebody went back to the house to see if we could borrow their four-wheel-drive truck and chain. The scene had been played before in my consciousness: a country road at night, engines racing, wheels spinning, the headlights catching clouds of steam and exhaust. The men crawled under the vehicle to attach chains. The women stood patiently, waiting, waiting, the stars very close overhead, singing to pass the time and soothe the children in their arms.

On the way home, the kids fell asleep in a tumble. Small towns emerged from the darkness, a scattering of houses, a bar and a darkened general store. In the front windows were reflected the pale-blue lights of TV's. The people inside were probably watching the eleven-o'clock news: the newest unemployment figures, casualty reports and Nixon policy statements. Nixon! He hardly mattered; he couldn't touch us. We had slipped away from 1970 and politics altogether. The President might as well be Calvin Coolidge. Let SDS try to change Nixon. We'd begin by changing ourselves, our own families, and then, maybe the valley. The frontier lay somewhere between the farm and the general store, across from which the longhairs might someday build their own church. A simple, plain kind of church based on a fundamental belief in God and man.

Claudia broke the silence. "I wish I'd thought to lay out the sleeping bags for the kids." While I was on a flight of fantasy, Claudia had been thinking ahead to the business of carrying the sleeping children into the dark house and clearing their shelves so they could be put to bed. The children always bring us back to earth, I thought, carrying a sleeping Woody over the washed-out culvert. We can go very far out, to the fringe, and live in the *now*, without schedules or plans, but the children bring us back. And if they don't, they cry. Their cries bring us down to the good earth.

January 21

Today's mail brought more of the typical queries, from college professors and disgruntled suburbanites. A lot send mimeographed questionnaires and form letters. Tacked to the bulletin board, most go unanswered.

Roland thumbed through. "It's disturbing that so many people think we can send them the secret formula for a working commune . . . they don't realize you just have to experience it—including the failure. I guess they really believe the world comes ready-made."

Bill decided to answer one of the form letters asking how to found a community, in a hundred words or less. He wrote:

Principally, I am saying do not be bounded by old-fashioned ideas of success and failure. Do not be afraid of the possibility that your first attempt (or even second) will fall apart. In God's universe, there is no waste. If things do not follow the city-conceived ideas of how they should work, then know that you're not seeing enough. Everything has its place in the organism. Every experience is full of value. Do not be afraid of failing. Take the leap. Do it. Get on with it.

Claudia and I finished a day's accumulation of dishes. Drying and sorting, she stopped to hold a fork up to my attention. Most of the utensils were W. T. Grant's or university-purloined, but the one Claudia singled out was real, though battered, sterling silver. It was monogrammed. "It's from my wedding silver," she said and dropped it in a tin can with the others. Claudia recalled her marriage. The wedding had been conventional: bridesmaids, bouquets, champagne at the country club. She would never get married again. "It's putting all your eggs in one basket. You bank your emotion, hope and security on one other person and expect him to remain just the same, faithfully constant, till death do you part. It doesn't work that way. Everything changes and everything grows. Sometimes I have fantasies about Bill and me having some sort of ceremony, not a marriage ceremony, but something more like a love-in, out in the meadow with just the family. It would be nice to have some kind of ritual. . . ."

David had drifted into the kitchen. Though he and Marlena lived most of the time in Berkeley, they were awarded family status on their visits, due to their long acquaintance with people at the farm. He picked up the end of Claudia's fantasy. "Hip life changes too fast. But that's what we need, a few rituals. Like at Morningstar. After they planted their garden, they held a fertility dance and a fuck-in."

"Groovy, maybe that's what our tomatoes needed this year. Last year they were puny," Jean said.

David proposed a ritual to celebrate the birth of Claudia's child. "I heard that one commune in San Francisco collected the afterbirth in a bowl and passed it around to be drunk, like communion."

Claudia had her own idea. "We could plant a tree." She thought a moment. "A persimmon."

Maureen elaborated on the fantasy. "And while you're in labor, Bill can dig the hole for the tree. Anxious fathers need something to do. Then we can take the placenta and drop it in before we transplant. That way, *nothing* is wasted."

January 23

There was a get-together of the valley's heads to practice for tomorrow's community sing at the Pentecostal Church. Four of us had attended last Sunday's service, and the minister had invited us to bring the rest along for the sing. It was held in the shed behind Morton's house. Morton is a patriarch of the long-hairs, one of the first to settle in the valley. He's a dropped-out economist, who holds a doctorate and now supports his family by cutting firewood and collecting welfare.

Almost sixty heads and about ten local straight people had squeezed into the toolshed heated by a wood stove. John and J. D. and Jim and Steve, from a neighboring commune located on a mining claim, played guitars, banjo and a washtub base. They were joined by two straights, members of the church who sang spirituals and played the electric guitar. An older man in a cowboy hat sawed the electric fiddle. The wives of the church people were sitting around uneasily when the meeting began. There was an unspoken understanding among the hip people that no dope would be passed. Nevertheless, as it turned out, we got very, very high.

First we rehearsed the songs we'd sing the next day at the Four-Square Church: "What a Friend We Have in Jesus," "Heaven Is So High You Can't Get over It," "Get Together" (a contemporary rock song with wide appeal), "We Need a Whole Lot More of Jesus and a Lot Less Rock 'n' Roll," and "Jesus Met a Woman at the Well." There was some anxiety about making a good impression. Some of the straights were fearful that our musical ardor might in some way offend the churchgoers.

Since 1967, when the hip invasion of the valley began, relations between longhairs and local people had become tense. The critical summer, again, was 1968's. For a time, it looked to some of the straight residents as if the hippies were overrunning the valley. Teen-agers drove around taking shots at hippie shacks. Just once, the hippies shot back. In a wire-service story, the deputy sheriff was quoted as saying, "Every hippie is armed with rifles, pistols or knives. Even the girls have knives."

For a time it looked like a repeat of Oz versus Crawford County. A "betterment" association was organized to curb the influx and sponsored a mass meeting at which the association's president asserted that the county had no narcotics problem until the hippies arrived. "We'll get it whipped, and then we'll move in and clean up the rest," he said to loud applause. A Methodist minister who urged tolerance was booed. The sheriff's office began to make raids; the health inspectors made inspections, accompanied by police. On one, the deputy sheriff was knocked unconscious by a hippie defending himself against an illegal search. A manhunt ensued; roads to the area were blocked, but the hippie was not apprehended. The deputy sheriff, called Uncle Hal by the hippies, carried out a vendetta against longhairs, picking up and then busting hitchhikers going to and from the valley. Stores in the nearest town posted signs: WE DO NOT SOLICIT HIPPIE PATRONAGE.

But over the past year, the influx has slightly abated, and as the communes have taken root and made friends among the local people, relations between straights and hips have improved, how much no one here is quite sure. They may find out tomorrow at the community sing. It will be the first time a large group of hippies have met their straight neighbors face to face.

After the repertoire of spirituals had been exhausted, we sang old songs like "She'll Be Coming 'Round the Mountain" and "Oh, the Rock Island Line is a mighty good road. . . ." Clapping and stamping, the girls pulled up their long skirts to dance. Spontaneously, a square dance broke out. We whirled each other, arms locked, spinning around and then flying off to grab others. The fiddler picked it up immediately: "Swing your partner, do-si-do, right and left. . . ." Until then, the fiddler's middle-aged wife had held back. Now she was on her feet, demonstrating the Virginia reel.

We got higher and noisier. Elaine was in a frenzy, turning like a whirling dervish, making inarticulate sounds. People tripped and were caught, embraced and pulled back into the dance. I recalled how the Shakers, another communal sect, had gotten their name from the dances that sent them into ecstacies. We shook with the same frenzy. It came from within, unprompted by drugs, in a bare shed set in a valley of muddy roads, dark woods, prowling coyotes. I looked at the faces. Here were plain, simple folk who had found each other. It was inconceivable we could ever have been apart.

January 24

A perfect day at last. Blue sky feathered with high cirrus clouds. Everyone was excited and tense about the community sing. After breakfast Elaine and Maureen took sponge baths in the kitchen. Next, Roland dropped the kids, two or three at a time, into the washtub. Then Maureen combed their hair over cries of pained protest.

We donned our Sunday best. The kids wore hand-knit woolen sweaters. Kathy and Susan tied ribbons in their hair. Maureen reminded them not to piss on the church lawn. "Maureen, I know that!" Kathy exclaimed indignantly.

Laura put on one dress but felt uncomfortable in it. She finally chose a long red-and-white checked gingham. With her hair wound in a bun, she looked like a young schoolmarm, *circa* 1874. Joe wore deep-blue corduroys and a white tunic, with wide sleeves that Jean had trimmed with embroidery. Roland wore an orange corduroy shirt Elaine had made. Maureen put on an ankle-length gown and headband.

Just as we were all ready to leave, a car drove into the front yard. Two men wearing suits knocked at the door. They were police officers, conducting an investigation for the state attorney general's office into charges filed by the ACLU that the civil liberties of hippies were being violated by the local sheriff. Could they ask a few questions?

They sat on the sofa and took small notebooks out of their jackets. Their shoes were black and spit-shined.

Roland answered a few general questions and called Rueben, who had the most specific complaint. Last week he had been arrested in a nearby city for carrying a concealed weapon— the hunting knife he always carried. "I use it all the time, it's a drag to put it in a sheath," he said, showing them how easily he could pull it out from under his belt. The two officers made a note but added that the arrest seemed to be technically legal.

Maureen recalled the many times her truck had been stopped for license and registration checks. Morton, she said, had gotten seven tickets in three days. Roland told of some friends whose house had been illegally searched.

The officers took note of the search and said they would check it out. They asked about the commune's relations with the townspeople—shopkeepers and so on.

Maureen smiled. "Oh, that's different. We had a little trouble at first when the signs went up. We didn't want to make any trouble because we knew the Betterment Association pressured a lot of the shopowners into it. Like the laundromat. We stayed away for a year, until one day I went in with the kids and asked them—I went out of my way to be polite—if they minded if we washed our clothes there. They said, 'Don't pay any attention to the signs.' Since then we've gotten along real well. Last week the lady bought ice-cream cones for the kids."

Jack: "It's the people we *don't* know who make trouble. Almost everyone who comes out here and sees how we live goes away a lot more friendly. . . . Remember when Carol took the inspectors on a garden tour?" Everyone laughed. The incident occurred in the tense summer of 1968, when all the communes were inspected by health officials, county supervisors, the sheriff and members of the press. "Carol [a former member] blew their minds. She took all the supervisors out into the garden and led them from row to row, explaining how each one had been planted and naturally fertilized . . . and one supervisor, an old geezer who was a farmer himself started giving her advice on how to use low-frequency sound to keep the rabbits out, and she smiled and listened. Later I overheard the supervisor saying, 'Shucks, these are just kids tryin' to farm.' "

The two officers laughed and closed their notebooks. They handed Roland a card and said to call their office with any complaints.

After they'd left, Jack said, "They seemed pretty fair."

Roland added, "It's good to know there are some cops like that around."

By now everyone was dressed and anxious to get on to the church.

First we headed over to the House of Illusion. The dogs followed, cutting across the meadow, running ahead and then falling behind as we gained the hard-top road. I sat in the back of the pickup, looking up at Maureen's profile against the rushing green background. Passing by the shacks along the river where hippies lived, we honked, cheered and whooped. Some of them followed us in their jalopies.

At the House of Illusion, J. D. and John led the way to a grove softly carpeted with needles, which was "down by the riverside." There were about thirty of us standing in a wide circle under tall firs with shafts of sun splintering through. As the guitars were tuned, the smoke went around. In his piercing, almost whining voice, J. D. sang the verses to an old folk song about heaven, while the rest of us did the chorus: "So high, you can't get over it, so low you can't get under it, so wide you can't go 'round it." I watched a girl gather up her long skirt and run along a rocky path slightly uphill from us, her body tilting gracefully from side to side, toward an A-frame.

We arrived at the church early, around fifty of us, exceeding half the church's seating capacity. I was afraid that the presence of the longhairs would be a disaster in public relations. So was Elaine, who talked of walking home. But Maureen was undaunted. "They'll love us. They *have* to love us," she said cheerily—as if our smiling faces, glowing with inward grace, would win them over.

Bob, the clean-shaven minister, arrived wearing a blue suit. He took in our numbers, gulped, and invited us to take seats.

The interior was functional: linoleum floors and white-brick walls. The congregation began to arrive. Men wore cufflinks and monogrammed handkerchiefs in their breast pockets. Their wives, high heels, teased hairdos and penciled eyebrows. They shot us sideways glances. The minister welcomed everyone, including "the bunch from T—" (the town nearest High Ridge Farm). He introduced the ministers from six local churches, who were there for the sing. The congregation from each church sang a hymn. One contained a double chorus. "Praise the Lord!" sang the women, jumping up. "Hallelujah!" answered the men, springing up in turn like jack-in-the-boxes. A girl in nylons and a purple sweater came up to the stage with an accordion. Before playing, she spoke into the microphone, saying that she loved "Jesus Christ more than anything else in the world." Then she began a lugubrious hymn: "Silver was the price they paid to nail him to a tree. . . . He could have sent ten thousand angels to destroy the world." Next an older man played some spirituals on the saxophone. Then two gray-haired sisters in long black dresses sang a duet: "On a hill far away stood an old rugged cross."

It was our turn. There were too many of us to take the stage, so we rose and grouped around J. D. and the others: "Je-sus met the wo-man at the well, ah-el-el. . . ." * It was an old song known to Baptists and heads alike, but we sang it with a new spirit that effused as the song progressed. "He said: Wo-man, wo-man, where is your husband. . . ." Elaine, in her flowered pajamas, glasses off, was doing her bumps and grinds. Reared a Jew, she believed in God but not the revengeful Yahveh who would send ten thousand angels to destroy a recalcitrant world.

"She said: Je-sus, Je-sus, ain't got no husband." Reuben, resplendent in beads, crosses and his Robin Hood hat with the freaky antenna, was shaking a tambourine and finger cymbals. He'd gone all through Meher Baba, Hare Krishna, Maharishi, Krishnamurti.

"And you don't know everything I've ever done."

As the fervor mounted, J. D.'s blond head thrashed from side to side. "He said, Wo-man, wo-man, you've got five husbands, he said. . . ." Maureen's face was radiant. Once she'd been buried nine hours in a mountain snowslide and felt that God had stayed with her, keeping her warm, until she was rescued. "And the one you've got now, he's not your own." Laura had discovered the joy and saving grace through acid. "This man, this man must be a prophet, she said. . . ." They had come to God by many paths. Now moved by a common spirit, not a doctrine but real experience. "Jesus met the wo-man at the

* The spiritual is based on John 4:7–42, a passage that holds special significance for hippies who've converted to Christianity, since it reveals Jesus as a social revolutionary, as well as a mystic. The passage, involving an encounter between Jesus and a Samaritan woman at Jacob's well, has been recast into hip language by Wayout, Box 2329, Hollywood, California, one of many neo-Christian youth groups that developed on the West Coast during the late sixties as the drug-hip subculture began to break down.

well, ah-el-el, oh, yeah, And he told her everything she ever knew. . . ."

Afterward, coffee and cookies were served. Maureen tore chunks off a loaf of fresh bread she'd brought and offered them to the parishioners. Some politely refused. Others accepted. None seemed to understand the symbolism of the act. One prosperously dressed middle-aged man, with a fraternal society pin on his lapel, was grim-facedly engaged in conversation with Bob, the minister, who was apparently defending his decision to invite us. Most of the local people were friendly. The commune kids played with theirs. The church musicians made a date with J. D. for a downcountry music session. An elderly couple struck up a conversation with Laura and asked her to do some housekeeping work for them.

Bob finished his long conversation with the hostile man, who drove off in a Chrysler, and then came over and spoke loudly enough so the whole congregation could hear: "I sure hope you can all come back next week and give us some more of that music." For sure, for sure, everyone answered.

January 28

Each morning I wake up and resolve to leave if nothing "new" happens to provide material for my notebook. Something "new" always does happen, nothing dramatic, small events that slowly deepen my insight into communal life.

I am torn between splitting and staying. The old reporter is anxious to leave, to get on with my cross-country itinerary, to put together a regional balance. A newer voice tells me to stay: One commune is all communes, nothing is "typical"; truth doesn't lie in a regional balance or averages or prototypes but is always here and now.

I've settled on a compromise plan: to go on a brief hitch-hiking sidetrip to three communes north of here, then return to High Ridge Farm and decide not only where to go next but what to do about the acid still rolled in tinfoil in my breast-pocket.

I've begun to ease myself into an acid trip, finishing Huxley's *Doors of Perception* and reading *The Teachings of Don Juan: A Yaqui Way of Knowledge,* by Carlos Castaneda. *Don Juan* is an account of the cosmology and spiritual beliefs of one American Indian who ritualistically took the natural hallucinogens, peyote, Jimson weed and the magic "mushroom." The book is really about Castaneda, who came to accept the existence of the supernatural while conducting his anthropological research.

Last night I sought advice from Jack about acid. We talked in the small alcove reserved for whoever was sleeping in with the kids. Should I take a full tab the first time? Jack was reluctant to advise me. Acid affected everyone differently, he said. For some, a full tab was good to take the first time. "It's better to wipe out all the garbage in your head, otherwise you get stuck halfway." He thought I was too honest to have a bad trip. People who repressed a lot found acid frightening.

The conversation gave me more confidence. I would be tripping among people I trusted. I decided to take the acid after I returned from my sidetrip.

Tonight Elaine was silent and communicated by notes. "I want to go along with you tomorrow," she wrote. "We can take my car."

I decided to leave the acid behind, putting it in a small pill container. With the trench shovel (used at night by people who couldn't make it to the outhouse) I dug a shallow hole and buried it under a fallen log.

III

Oregon

A Digression and a Return

January 29

This afternoon Elaine and I left in her battered Plymouth. Our first destination was Sunny Valley, the Family of the Mystic Arts, one of the first communes to settle in Oregon. Elaine had heard of Jane and Donald, two of the oldest members, and we had both seen the *Life* magazine story on the commune.

As we drove, Elaine reminisced about her last commune-hopping tour with Ben, her husband, who was working on a PhD thesis on communities. At that time there were few communes resembling today's. One was Kerista, a group marriage of mystics then in New York. On the advice of a Ouija board, they emigrated to British Honduras and later disbanded. Ben and Elaine visited them before they left. Ben decided that Kerista was "too far out" for a doctoral thesis. "In those days, mysticism was academically taboo," Elaine said.

Instead, Ben selected the diametric opposite of Kerista, the Bruderhof, a community of Christian Communists who fled to this country from Germany after the Nazi takeover. Known here as the Society of Brothers, they were an authoritarian, austere, monogamous and industrious sect, who built their own school and developed industries. The largest of their three communities is located near Rifton, New York, and manufactures toys.

After their brief experience with Kerista and later with Sunrise Hill, both Ben and Elaine seemed to feel that the most "viable" communities were those that had a solid religious base.

But High Ridge Farm had none, I pointed out. Did she think *it* would last? Elaine wasn't sure. Like me, she'd been educated to doubt and was only recently overcoming her distrust of the mystical. "I think we'll have to find some kind of religion, or something just as strong."

It was dark by the time we got to Sunny Valley. We parked the car on a steep slope and found a path that luckily took us to the commune's main building.

It was an Indian lodge set three feet down into the earth, constructed of hand-cut cedar logs. The main part was in the shape of a hexagon. In the center of a dirt floor was an open rock-enclosed fireplace. Smoke rose through a baffle opening in the roof.

Around the perimeter was a raised platform divided into sleeping spaces. During the winter, the thirty members live and sleep in the lodge. When spring comes, some return to separate tepees and cabins.

Two steps up from the circle was the kitchen, lighted by Coleman lanterns and dominated by a huge wood stove. "We got it out of an old inn that used to cater to the gold prospectors," Jane informed us. In her thirties, she wore a blue bandana over reddish-blond hair streaked with gray. A cross hung from a small chain around her neck. Her forehead was creased, her skin dry and flaky. Her piercing blue eyes were deep-set. Her strong, well-worn beauty evoked the pioneer women who had left the comforts of civilization to go west in covered wagons.

She was, in fact, their modern counterpart. Reared in Westport, Connecticut, she went to Radcliffe, married a graduate of Lehigh, and lived the gracious suburban life for a while. Since we were both renegades from the silent, buttoned-down generation of the fifties, a kinship was immediately established be-

tween us—like two old czarists who meet after the Revolution
and talk of the old days. "I bet you wore Donald's scarf and
went to the Winter Carnival!"

"For sure, for sure," she said, smiling back.

While we stood talking—almost an hour—other things were
happening in the kitchen. A woman took a sponge bath. Someone shouted, "Save some cheese Danishes for the men!" From
time to time, several of Jane's four children, all blond, approached her. A little girl thought she was getting a cold. Had
she tried garlic? Jane asked. No, she hadn't. "Well, try it."

A few years ago, Jane and her family were living in Westport, and Donald was making $20,000 a year as a computer
programmer for a large corporation. Then they left suburbia
for academia, trekking westward in a camper to the University
of California at Irvine. There Donald taught programming
while Jane took the kids to the swimming pool in the faculty
housing development and attended lots of coffee discussion
groups. Out of boredom, as well as commitment, Jane and
Donald became involved in war resistance work.

"I wouldn't be here today unless Johnson had spoken at
Irvine during the 1964 campaign." They joined in the large
antiwar demonstration. "I could tell the police were going to
charge us." Jane's face tensed as she recalled the scene. "I went
to one of the officers and said, 'I can see that you're annoyed
at us and you're going to do something because of it, and we
want you to tell us what we're doing wrong.' He didn't say a
thing. His face was stone. A few minutes later they charged. One
student sat down in the lotus position. I saw a cop bending over
him, swinging his club."

The demonstration capped their slow but steady social disaffection. They had already joined an encounter group and
begun to smoke grass. Donald quit his job. They moved north
to Oregon, as hundreds of other Californians were doing, and
then they met Barclay.

I'd heard about Barclay before. He was fast becoming a
legendary figure in the history of Oregon communes. Jane filled
in some of the details. He was a Los Angeles millionaire busi-

nessman who went to India after being told by his doctor that he had cancer and had only a month to live. There he met his guru, studied astrology and the cosmology of Velikovsky, and probed the dietary secrets of the Hunza, a tribe famous for its health and longevity.

Barclay cured his cancer by eating dried apricot pits, adopted a son, who spoke only in Sanskrit, and computed the date of a holocaust, when the axes of the world would shift and trigger earthquakes and floods. California would break off and sink into the ocean. Among the few places to be spared were the areas 3,000 feet above sea level in southwestern Oregon.

Barclay returned to the United States with a long white beard and predictions of doom. He bought a flatbed trailer in California on which he loaded a four-room house with a kitchen. He headed north, stopping at communities along the way to serve macrobiotic meals and gather converts to start a post-apocalyptic community in southern Oregon. "He had visions of a geodesic dome set on a mountaintop like an ark," Jane said.

After their arrival, when no deluge occurred, Barclay's group disbanded. By this time Donald and Jane were living in a rented log cabin at a crossroads outside Cave Junction. They joined the remnants of Barclay's group for a harsh winter in the national forest. By spring most of their savings were gone and they had no place to live. Donald decided to join the commune being organized at Sunny Valley—the "family." Jane was against it. "I told Donald that this was his trip, that I'd go along, but not because I wanted to."

During the first year Jane went through heavy changes. "I learned that you have to be completely busted and lose everything before you can become new and whole again. Praise the Lord."

Meanwhile, members were taking their sleeping places on the shelf, a kind of circular Pullman divided by draped blankets, shelves and bookcases. Some read and sewed by kerosene light. Others talked quietly. Occasionally, there would be cross-talk: "Nona, bring me some of the raisins."

Elaine, Jane and I sat on a low bench before the fire. "The

hardest thing was to give up all our possessions," said Jane, recalling how quickly their life had changed. They sold their truck, drained their savings account, and canceled Blue Cross. "It took awhile to get used to the kitchen not being my own. I think it was Margaret Mead who said that American society is based on the precept: One woman per kitchen." But the kitchen was only the first thing she had to relinquish.

The next was her intellectual self. "I really think acid has a greater effect on people like you and me, who were brought up to do the academic trip." Acid, she said, did more than give her psychedelic effects. It broke her out of looking at the world intellectually: "It was like making love when you have the first release and think it's all over. Then it happens, you have an orgasm you never expected." She flung her head back and let air escape through her teeth, making a sssssssssssssssssssssss sound, like a great rush of energy. "And then, you're out of yourself for the first time."

Jane no longer takes drugs. "It's like going through a door. Once you've gone through, there's no going back and coming through again."

Quiet fell over the lodge. The fire had been stacked high for the night with three-foot logs. The rough walls flickered in and out of view.

"We've learned how to be naked with one another—like a family." Yes, I realized they called themselves The Family of the Mystic Arts, but what did "mystic arts" mean? Jane smiled and quoted Martin Buber to the effect that man's absurd impulse was to grasp the evanescent butterfly. From their bed Donald added, "There's a spirit that comes and goes. You can't hold onto it."

Jane went to bed. We would talk more in the morning. Elaine and I cleared off a section of the shelf for our sleeping bags. I sat up for a while, feet pointed toward the fire as if it were the center of the world. The fire seemed to symbolize some center of energy, some fulcrum of spirit, which the commune guarded against the dark void outside.

Three men returned late and knocked around. "Where're

the Danishes?" shouted Turtle. From the darkness on the shelf, the tired, patient voice of a woman: "They're in the right compartment of the stove."

The last person to bed dropped large pieces of wood on the fire, sending a shower of sparks up through the opening. My imagination followed them outside, and I could see their orange specks above the low lodge set in relief against the night sky; then falling, dying of light. For twenty uninhabited miles around, no sound. Then for those who were still awake, Donald began the ritual chain of good nights:

"Good night, Turtle," he said.
"Good night, Donald," answered Turtle.
"Good night, Jane."
"Good night, Donald."
"Good night, Ratface."
"Good night, Jane."
"Good night, Michele."
"Good night, Ratface."
"Good night, Evening Star."
"Good night, Michele."
"Good night, Sandoz."
"Good night, Evening Star."
"Good night, Ama."
"Good night, Twig."
"Good night, Sandoz."
"Good night, Jane."
Good night, good night, good night.

January 30

When I woke up, everyone was talking from their bunks. Herman hopped out onto the floor, like a playful bear in long underwear. He went around kissing and tickling the feet of those who were not quite awake and doing an imitation of Detroit spade talk. "Gib me sum of it, mama."

For breakfast, there was applesauce, yogurt, cereal and coffee. Jane served Donald his breakfast in bed—it was their wedding anniversary, I think. I sat next to their bunk, drinking coffee. Donald has a long red beard and a restrained intensity. He told me how a mountain lion had dug up fish entrails they'd buried in the garden, and he described their deer hunts. He was disappointed that the commune was still dependent on "store-bought" food and materials.

"We can't grow our own wheat and grains up here. Impossible to produce corn oil." The problem was that civilization was too close to them. "It's too easy for people to come and go." That morning, for example, a group of ten visitors departed and headed for the Mendocino State Forest in California.

Donald said that some of the members, including himself and Jane, had thought of moving elsewhere—possibly Mexico. "It would be good to spread out the 'heavies,'" he said, meaning members who were spiritually high and had a lot of energy and leadership.

Soon after the *Life* cover story on the commune, they received a letter forwarded from a wealthy Quaker who'd acquired ten thousand acres in Mexico, near the Guatemalan border. He invited them to look over his land as a possible site for expansion.

"The land is jungle. The last frontier—virgin consciousness. Seven days by pack train away from the nearest roads. You can raise twenty-four different kinds of fruit there."

Public schools were another consideration. So far, the Family has managed to keep the kids out of public school, but they were fearful that the state might bring action against them. In Mexico, they'd be far outside the reach of government. "They're not going to send a truant officer out seven days on a mule."

Elaine and I went with Jane to see their little cabin—one of several scattered over the commune's 240-acres of rolling timberland. It had little furniture, a few rugs, no chairs. We sat on the floor in front of a low window, with a view of a cloud-draped mountain. A spot of sun came through the window, striking a prism that slowly twisted from the end of a string, sending diffracted colors over the burlap walls.

Jane told us more of the changes that had brought her to a personal faith in Christ. During the first year in the commune, Donald started sleeping with another woman. Emotionally shattered, Jane went to another community, where she lived in solitude. "Again I had to learn to give up what I loved." After she returned to Sunny Valley, the three of them slept together. "We never made love, but we omed a lot and prayed together." The triangle broke up when the other woman found another man and split. Jane said the pain of losing Donald had driven her to find the greater love of God. During this time she was baptized at a Christian community called Living Springs, a few miles away. The community had attracted and converted many hippies. Unlike some from Sunny Valley who stayed on after being baptized, Jane decided to return to the Family. She doesn't believe in organized religion. Out of intense personal faith she speaks warmly of the "earth mother" and of the mystical Christ revealed in the Gospel according to Saint John, who taught that man should give up possessions and ego. For Jane, Christ is a real spirit who can communicate and intervene. "If people all over the world would invoke Christ's name at the same time, we could stop war."

Jane has an infectious faith that the universe is unfolding as it should, but she admits she is a bit uncertain about Donald's plans to go to the jungle. But if that is God's will, she will follow. "Praise the Lord."

As we walked back to the car, Elaine was very talkative. She chattered about Reuben and why he irritated her. Her words went right through my head. For the first time on this trip, I felt as though something outside myself had taken over. Instead of my making decisions—where to go, how long to stay—I needed only to follow. Jane and Donald had pointed the way ahead, both for me personally and for the movement.

Elaine asked where we were heading next. "Living Springs." "Really," she exclaimed.

I hadn't known the community existed until Jane spoke of it. Elaine felt uneasy about fundamentalists. I persuaded her by promising we would only stay overnight and get on our way in the morning. We were going that way anyhow.

We turned off the interstate onto a smaller road that went past cattle ranches, lumber mills with their huge mounds of orange sawdust, and lifeless stump-covered hills. Living Springs, looking like an ordinary farm, lay in a valley along a small stream.

We entered the one large house and found ourselves in a large cement-floored meeting room that looked like a church basement. There were two long tables, folding chairs and a gas stove. We'd arrived an hour before dinner, and most of the twenty members were assembled. Most were in their early twenties; all were dressed neatly and plainly. They looked very straight.

Elaine was wearing her baggy pajamalike pants and sandals; I was shaggy and newly bearded. The younger members greeted us like long-lost friends who had not yet seen the light. "Before I found Christ, I took every drug I could get and had hair as long as yours," said one young man, pointing to Elaine. Others came on the same way—friendly, but always making comparisons between their past degradation and newfound bliss. Maybe Elaine had been right.

I asked if the farm was connected with any denomination or church. None, they said. Did they have a leader? I was told to see Bill.

We got into the dinner line that wound through a modern kitchen separated by a counter from a dining area, and I sat down next to an older man wearing a sweat shirt. He was Bill, I learned, the founder and father of Living Springs.

In his mid-forties, Bill carried himself like an athlete who'd diligently kept himself in trim. His hair was combed in oily waves and his nose appeared to have been broken. Once a professional wrestler, he had saved his winnings and built a sports coliseum in Los Angeles. He made a lot of money. One night, for amusement, he and some friends went to a revival meeting. Laughing, his friends thrust him forward to the stage to be baptized by Leroy Jenkins, a fundamentalist faith healer. Bill went along with the joke.

Jenkins laid his hands on Bill's head and called on the Holy Spirit. Immediately, Bill began to speak in tongues—glossolalia—a mysterious linguistic pattern that members of Christian cults since Biblical times have been known to utter in moments of spiritual release.*

The experience convinced Bill that Jenkins was no fraud. He attended another meeting, bringing along his son, who'd been born with a club foot. Jenkins baptized the boy and at one touch enabled him to walk without a noticeable limp.

Now a believer, Bill asked the healer what he should do with his life. Jenkins instructed him to sell his business and buy a farm in Oregon. "I asked why, but Jenkins couldn't say." Nevertheless, Bill complied. Afterward, he received illuminating visitations: The farm was to be a hostel for wayward hippies with whom Bill would share the power of the spirit.

He spoke in a low, hoarse voice. "The spirit will put you in tune with God. It is His language. People who speak it can be healed of both the ills of the body and the sicknesses of the mind." He said there was no way to receive the spirit except from direct physical contact with another person—someone in the line of baptismal succession that began with Christ. As he talked, I had a flash that he was not merely explaining but persuading. He did pique my curiosity.

Bill was tired. He had spent the day directing a crew of members who worked under contract for a logger, cutting wood off their own property. Others held jobs as clerks and farmhands in the area. Bill said that most work got done spontaneously, but he and his wife seemed to be in charge of the work and the kitchen, respectively.

* Speaking in tongues is one of the rites of many new pentecostal groups that have sprung up in the last four years as a reaction against liturgical orthodoxy. Beginning as an offshoot of such Protestant sects as the Assemblies of God, Pentecostalism has made an estimated 2,000,000 converts in this country, including many Catholics and ex-hippies. It is regarded by many as the most powerful force that has entered the American religious scene. See Edward B. Fiske, "Catholics Turning to Pentecostalism," New York *Times*, November 3, 1970.

Admission requirements to the farm were vague. "Right now the gate is physically closed," he said, "but it can open to anyone who bears Christ's witness that he is meant to stay here."

After dinner, a girl clapped her hands to announce it was "time for sharing." Everyone went into the cement-floored room and took a seat around the long narrow tables. On the way in, I found Elaine and asked her how she was getting along. OK, she said weakly. Her eyes were dots of panic.

Within the community, "sharing" had a special meaning. When anyone related his deeds, he "shared" his past. If God spoke to a member in a dream, he shared that experience. If a member was given insight into another's hangup, he shared his insight out of love.

"Sharing" was also the name of the general meeting during which such experiences and revelations were exchanged. The time was also used for group glossolalia, if they were so moved, and to cure members' minor ailments—rashes, wounds and infections.

Tonight one girl sobbed out the "before" of her case history. After running away from home, she had gone to Haight-Ashbury, where she first sold god's eyes—a "heathen idol"—and then herself to support her drug addiction.

An almost-bald older man told how yesterday he had fallen into a dreamlike trance in which he witnessed events that actually happened today. In discussing his experience, members spoke of positive and negative vibrations and the shifting of consciousness from one "space" to another.

Near the end, two members got into some gentle interpersonal criticism. A middle-aged woman told Warren, who appeared to be in his mid-forties, "I don't think your facial expressions, which seem so hard to me at times, convey the love inside you." Her words did not seem to sting. After the meeting, individual members approached me and told me their own before-and-after case histories. My longest discussion was with Ted, a young man, with pale skin and several scars on his face, who talked in a monotone, as if he'd just come out of shell shock.

A year ago he'd taken drugs in an attempt to cure his fits of apparent schizophrenia. One night he was found unconscious under a bridge in Trenton, New Jersey, and woke up in a mental institution not knowing who he was. After electric shock therapy, he was released.

"I hit bottom. My mind was blown out." He took up drugs again to counteract his severe paranoia. "On the night of the moon landing people were shooting off guns in the neighborhood, and I felt sure they were shooting at me." He contemplated suicide. Then he heard of Living Springs from his brother, who had passed through. He got on a plane and flew directly to Portland.

After his baptism, Ted still had moments of madness, but Bill helped him through. "One day I felt the old paranoia coming back, and Bill told me to go outside and run around. I did . . . and while I ran, I prayed and spoke in tongues. When I closed my eyes, I had a picture of the earth as just one speck among the planets and stars; I felt how insignificant it was, how insignificant I was." Ted attested that the love of Christ had filled the void inside him. "Praise the Lord."

Randy joined the conversation. He told how Leroy Jenkins had refused to baptize him until he "cut his hair for Jesus." Randy obeyed and returned to be baptized. When Jenkins touched him, Randy said, it was "like connecting with a high-tension wire." He was knocked unconscious.

A member who had served time in jail came over. He was able to unburden "all the shit inside me" to Christ.

Since I was an attentive listener, they must have assumed that I was also interested in receiving the baptism. Bill could do it now, Randy suggested. I backed off. I was writing a book, you see. . . .

Ted said, "It wasn't an accident you came here."

Warren, the older member, added darkly, "Time's running out. When God sends His Son again, He'll come down with the angels of destruction for those who haven't listened."

The farm was prepared for the Second Coming. They had stocked the barn with canned food, had an auxiliary tank containing a year's supply of butane, and a waterwheel that could be hooked up to generate electricity.

I was surrounded by five members, all intent on conversion. Sensing my discomfort, a young woman member, Joany, took me aside for a low-keyed pitch of her own. Once an intellectual herself, she had sensed my skepticism. While at Sunny Valley, she had tried yoga and meditation, "but they didn't work." Following an acid trip at the commune, she fell into a catatonic state. No one at Sunny Valley could reach her. She was brought to Living Springs. Talking in tongues freed her. "It opens up your soul the way acid opens up your senses but allows your soul to speak because it bypasses connections to your fucked-up mind."

I was interested, I told her, but would like to sleep on it. That seemed to appease everyone. Ted showed Elaine and me to the pine-paneled lounge upstairs where we could sleep on two couches. There was a TV in the corner and down the hall, a bathroom. When we were alone, Elaine asked me if we could leave as early as possible in the morning. "I don't like to be pushed," she said. First thing, I agreed. Living Springs didn't hold much allure: It was too therapeutic, too detached from nature.

Elaine asked if I were going to be baptized. I hadn't decided. Part of me was cynically in favor of it. Not as an act of faith, more as reportorial opportunism: It was an experience that would pay off in good copy, lend a first-person touch to the visit, and so on. What was there to lose? I cited Pascal's wager: If there was just one chance in a million of salvation, wasn't it worth taking the leap of faith? Elaine couldn't regard it that lightly. "I won't be forced into anything. I'm not ready for it." She turned over and went to sleep.

I lay awake for a while. I had to admit I was frightened by the possibility that Bill *did* have the power of the Holy Spirit at his fingertips. It was a power to be feared many times more than the 500 milligrams of LSD I was prepared to take. Why not first be baptized in the name of God and thus bless my forthcoming acid trip? Intuitively I felt a chain of events had led me here and that it was wise not to try to pull myself out of the flow.

January 31

Pancakes were on the grill when I came downstairs. Joany, who was cooking, took my order for two. I poured coffee and sat opposite Bill. I've decided to receive the spirit, I told him. He looked surprised, as if he'd already written me off. "Good, good! Do you want to receive it now?" and he seemed to move closer.

Couldn't we wait till I finished my pancakes? As soon as the words were out, I realized how ludicrous it was to postpone the eternal gift of the spirit for two paltry pancakes. But they did taste good.

While I ate, Bill nabbed members on their way through the kitchen to outside jobs and chores. "Robert has chosen to receive the spirit," he told them. Gradually, they formed a circle around us. Before the baptism, Bill asked about my religious background and spiritual experiences.

I was raised an Episcopalian and sang in the church choir for many years. I thought briefly about being a minister, but after a year in college I enrolled in a premedical program. For a while —the year I spent in medical school—I was an atheist; afterward, an agnostic who didn't think of God except in moments of severe distress. Once I lost the key to a sports car on a beach and found it after invoking the name of Christ. That was the only spiritual experience I could recall. I believed the Bible was interesting literature and wisdom but not literal truth. Most of the time, I didn't think about God.

Bill's hands came across the table and took mine. The others piled their hands on my head and shoulders—plugging me in spiritually, I supposed. Bill said, "Don't be afraid to speak, keep your mind in neutral." Meanwhile, I heard a low mumble from the others. I was still a listener.

It sounded like a far-off wail of sirens heard late at night in bed, a gurgle of tongues and indistinguishable words. Gradually it increased, as if approaching from some great distance, a very gradual crescendo that seemed beamed into my inner ear.

"Go ahead," urged Bill. "Try it."

"Try what?"

"Try making sounds, any sound. Don't be ashamed."

I balked—something deep inside inhibited me from babbling. Perhaps it was the pride of ego that paralyzed my lips. I forced myself to blather for two or three seconds, then stopped. "Go on," Bill urged.

I tried again while an amused self looked on. Oh, well, be a fool. Blather, blather. Then suddenly it seemed that someone had turned up the volume and intensity. I felt an electric sensation from the concerted pressure of hands on my head and thought, "This must be like wearing one of those electrode helmets they use in shock therapy. . . ."

Then I began to speak. Involuntarily the words rolled off my tongue. Something else had taken control of my nervous system. Meantime, another part of self continued to listen passively. It sounded like Greek and was very rich in vowel sounds and inflections. My speech began to blend with the others' and to lift upward until I (that distant removed listener in me) hovered in the vault of a Byzantine church around the fifth century, hearing the cast-up prayers and chants of the worshipers below. The words rolled on. Bill smiled at me. His hands were warm and pleasant. I continued speaking until whoever was using my tongue came to a closing line that he repeated five times. I did not know for sure what any of it meant, but the last line, I felt certain, was "Praise the Lord, Praise the Lord."

After it was over, I sat in my seat, numb. Bill and the members went off to work. Elaine stood nearby, itching to leave. Bill's wife sat down beside me and asked why I had come to Living Springs. I had set out to write a book about communes but was getting a little off the subject, I said. At moments I wasn't exactly sure what my subject was.

"Why do you doubt?" she asked. "God sent you here for some purpose. Perhaps He is telling you what kind of book to write. The best books in the world are those written out of personal experience." But I didn't want to write about myself, I objected. "You don't write about yourself!" she said. "You let the spirit in you write the book. It just comes out of you."

We had driven for about an hour in silence through the fogged-in river valley before Elaine obliquely asked if I wanted to tell her about the experience.

I didn't mind. It *did* happen—that was a fact. It had happened to lots of people and was a mystical phenomenon mentioned by William James in *The Varieties of Religious Experience*. I couldn't intellectualize it away.

"Do you feel any different?"

I felt blank. I had the sense of a void inside that could not be filled by ideas or sensations.

Bill had said that immediately after receiving the spirit, I would not feel changed. "But a seed has been planted. In time it will grow."

We continued our sidetrip, winding into the Willamette valley, past orchards, sawmills, trailers, through the misty gray of Oregon in January. We headed for Crow, a commune a few miles west of Eugene.

Elaine talked about sexual love. She used to think that it could bring two people into closer emotional and spiritual union. "But sometimes, sex just closes me off from another person."

We stopped at the crossroads in Veneta to buy cheese and fruit and ask directions to Crow. I'd known about the commune for a year. One of its ex-members, Tom Moore, was among those who returned to Vermont with Woody Ransom and helped him evict Bryn Athyn. Crow had inspired Woody to try Rockbottom Farm, Bryn Athyn's opposite: well organized, solvent, decisive, industrious.

Crow turned out to be all that and more. Two rather conventional houses came with the eighty acres of property the commune had bought. They had later acquired a third house for use as a free school. It had been certified by the state and was attended by about a dozen kids, half from outside the commune.

Its full name was Crow Research Organization. However, when I visited, the only research being done was by a mathematician who worked under contract for a nearby research institute and turned $1,000 a month over to the commune. The membership varied from twenty to thirty and was an odd mix of itinerant hippies and college dropouts who had solid science backgrounds. Some of the latter talked of obtaining a contract to do oceanography research.

Crow had no money problems. The largest of several enterprises was their beef cattle business. Women members with children received Welfare (ADC) payments and commodities. Accepting government aid was acknowledged to be a "rip-off," but not felt to contradict the commune's ideals.

Comparatively, Crow's level of material comfort was high. The houses were connected by intercoms and had a full range of electric appliances, a washer and dryer, hot water and flush toilets. One of the houses, a split-level with wall-to-wall carpeting, was dubbed Bloomingdale, after the well-to-do suburb of Minneapolis. Most of Crow's founders came from the Twin Cities.

In other ways, life at Crow seemed harsh and turbulent. One of the first people Elaine and I met was Torgensen, a tall, rangy ex-Marine who had long blond hair, a rugged chin and clear blue eyes. He was capable of withering sarcasm and used the word "hippie" to denote his contempt: "You're nothin' but a soft, spoiled hippie. Just what your middle-class parents deserved," he said mockingly of Irish, another member. Irish wasn't offended. Torgensen's comments seemed typical of the normal abrasiveness at Crow.

Impressions of the main room before dinner: Curley says he's going into Eugene to shoot pool. Torgensen is sarcastic. "Why doesn't he save the money he always loses and spend it on a pool table for the whole commune?" Two toddlers are wailing. "Shut up or I'll break your head!" someone yells. They stop crying. The telephone rings. They have a chance to score on a big shipment. A woman loses her temper, saying they should save their money to buy more beef cattle. Someone else objects.

The radio on top of the refrigerator is tuned to a rock station at the University of Oregon. Four women, making dinner, each work independently on four separate courses. The phone rings again: a man calling to order a cord of wood. (As another sideline, Crow cuts and sells wood from its own property.) Phone dangles while someone locates the order list. Luke teases a prepubescent girl about her budding breasts and chases her around the kitchen. Meanwhile, a guy is putting the make on Elaine, who has backed into a corner. Poor Elaine. First I dragged her to Living Springs, where she was spiritually raped, and now . . .

Sexually, Crow was very turned on. There were several triads going on—unsuccessfully, I was told. Some of the members were bisexual, and there was a lot of daytime dalliance, *i.e.*, members who fooled around during the day but returned at night to the side of their old man or lady.

Some favored establishing a formal group marriage. One was Tina, who was in her late twenties and had a young daughter. She had tired of sleeping with two men at once. "It was impossible. If I gave a favor to one, the other would insist on equal treatment." She'd like a group marriage that would include all the members and permit homosexual relations. "When you have sex with a lot of people, it strips your ego down and you find out who you really are." The main obstacle to group marriage was the other women, said Tina, who were much more conservative, sexually and socially, than the men. "Some of them are romantics who think they need the security of one man."

February 1

This morning Elaine drove home. She was homesick for her own family. Crow's turmoil had unnerved her, and she didn't want to spend another night fending off the men.

The second day Crow seemed less turbulent to me. Every commune has its unique consciousness, and Crow's was a tough individualism. "We've attracted a lot of high-energy people who are into making communes work," said Luke Carpenter. He is the brother of Michael Carpenter, whom I'd met the previous fall (which now seemed light-years ago) at Johnson's Pastures in Vermont. Their mother had bought the land used by Michael's commune.

Crow lacked Johnson's Pastures' organic, mystical quality. Ruthlessly, Crow fattened its cattle on chemically fertilized grain. The garden was small and neglected. Economically, they were making it. Luke estimated the farm's capitalization at more than $50,000.

In the afternoon I hitchhiked back to High Ridge Farm. In Eugene, the manager of a rock group, who drove a microbus, picked me up and played tapes all the way to my exit. There I got a ride with two high school seniors on their way to the Coast. One of them was seeing a shrink, who had prescribed reading Tom Wolfe and visiting communes. They dropped me at the general store.

Walking up the road to the farm, I felt I was coming home. Emily hugged me. Roland wrapped his arms around me and his beard brushed my face—the first time it felt natural to embrace another man. "You came back!" said Laura.

"Of course he did. He can't leave us," Maureen said.

Two days before my return, Jerry had shown up at the farm. He had left his parents' house in Pasadena and hitched up the coast. A tall seventeen-year-old, who parted his blond hair down the center, he was engaging and overeager for acceptance. Tonight, for example, Jerry washed his underclothes in the big kettle customarily used for brewing tea. It was the kind of blunder new members always made. Claudia chewed him out. Downcast, he scoured and dried the kettle. The rest of the evening he repeatedly apologized to Claudia and doggedly went out of his way to please—which only irritated her more.

"Look, do you think I'm your mother?" she said. "You don't have to please me, you know. Why don't you look into yourself and do what you think is right, what pleases you?"

February 2

An after-dinner meeting was called to rap about Maureen and Bill's differences. Everyone sat silently and tensely on the floor for about five minutes. Finally, Elaine spoke. "Why don't each of you tell us how you feel right now."

Softly crying and barely audible, Maureen said she felt insecurity, incompleteness, an anxiety partly arising from her relationship with Roland but which went all the way back to her mother. It was a rare thing to hear Maureen speak from her insides, anguished and broken. She had always been so cheery and superficial.

Bill: "What annoys me is that you're never here—you're always going down to Berkeley or over to the other communes. And you think of your kids as yours and your truck as yours."

Maureen: "They're security. I only get possessive when I feel other things slipping away. . . ." Claudia said she felt uncomfortable working in the kitchen with her because "I can't tell whether you want my help or just to be left alone. I wish you would come out frankly and say, 'Look, I want to make my own mistakes, so just let me do my own thing.' " Bill said Maureen's small talk annoyed him: "You come in bubbling about something that happened and it's like you don't care about me—you just bubble on . . . I feel like you don't recognize my existence, so I do things to hurt you. When I make you mad, you can't ignore me."

Roland, turning to Bill: "You mean you don't exist unless people recognize you? That's your problem, not Maureen's."

The meeting ended without any clear-cut resolution. The tensions, however, were more out front now. The meeting had been different from the usual encounter session, where people turn the candor on, only to turn it off again outside. At the commune, you couldn't change roles behind doors. Potentially, every minute was an encounter. There was no retreat. Your mumblings in your sleep could be overheard. Every little habit and personal idiosyncrasy was exposed. Everyone knew that Elaine loved to nibble sweets because her mother had deprived her of candy as a child. Every time we saw her furtively spooning brown sugar we would tell her she was an anxiety eater and that what she really needed was affection, not confection.

February 3

I woke deciding to drop the acid. It hadn't decomposed under the log. I walked down to the main building. People from the Bear Gulch commune had come to borrow the drill press. Some of them were retired dope dealers who'd put their savings into land.

After all the visitors had left, I asked if anyone wanted to share my half tab of acid, or else trip along. Laura said she'd trip if Roland did, but Roland was in a hard-work mood. Jerry asked the others if he should drop now or wait until he felt more at home. No one told him yes or no.

All the while, my heart was beating rapidly. I'd put the one tab on the table. It was orange and about the size of saccharine. I lost patience. With one gulp of coffee I washed it down, crumpled the tinfoil into a ball, and threw it across the room. "He took it!" Cheers, applause.

I paced around grimly, like a father outside the delivery room. Nothing happened. I talked to Roland and to Bill. A half hour elapsed. Life in the room went on as usual. I stared out the window at the garden and the meadow, checking my perceptions for any sign of a change. At the garden's edge, jays and wrens hopped and stalked. Their existence suddenly seemed important.

I went to the bookcase and began flipping through an anthology of poems, but before I found the line I was searching for, it came to my lips: "The world is charged with the glory of God." As soon as I uttered it, a frightening wave of energy rushed through me. It was too much like drowning. Immediately I went over to Claudia and put my arms around her. She seemed the most stable and immediate point in the universe. The earthy smell of her sweat shirt was comforting. It was real. I asked her to stick around the kitchen. She understood.

I went to the sink and tried to look out the steamed-over window. I rubbed the condensation away, but it blurred and steamed up again. Laughing at my idiocy, I unlatched the window. The meadow was wet and glistening and colorful and charged with glory. Bending over the sink, I cried into the dishwater. What a convenient place to crack up! But between the sobs, the pain of breaking felt good. Death must be the same.

Jerry had put on a Simon and Garfunkel album and one line stuck in my head: "Blessed are the meek, for they shall inherit. . . ."

Somebody had made popcorn. It was celestially white. I took a handful, laid my head down on the circular table, and began to pulverize the popcorn with the heel of my hand, grinding it down into a mixture of tears, sweat and Mazola. I wiped my face with toilet paper, dying for the sins of the world, all the time grinding the popcorn. Everything must be reduced to its components.

Laura overheard my babblings: "This is a delivery ward." She and Gary split a tab. I wouldn't let Claudia out of the room. I could feel the new life in her and that was consolation, since I was dying, breaking down.

Under the counter the dogs lapped from their bowls. I had an impulse to join them on the floor and eat their food. When I looked at Claudia's face, it enlarged and assumed frightening power. Suddenly it revealed all the anger, love, passion and compassion she was capable of. I asked her if she believed in God.

In answer, she opened the door of the wood stove. Two or three pieces of wood burned over a bed of red coals. Wood changing to coals to heat, altering form but not dying. "I am God. You are God." Like the meadow, her face became too awesomely powerful and beautiful for me to behold. I dropped my head to the greasy pile of pulverized popcorn.

The dying took about an hour. Near the end, I gasped and shuddered and clung to the table. It subsided and was over. I—the ego, the self—had been busted.

I announced my intention to go outside. Would they let me go alone? No one seemed worried about my safety, so I went. Outdoors, I had to adjust myself to new dimensions of space and depth. The little bridge over the brook seemed like a high footbridge over the Himalayas. I knelt on it, an altar, and thanked God. My vision was sharp, stereoscopic. Fir trees, rising one above the other on the mountain, each had a definite position in space. Everything was alive and moving. The wood planks of the bridge crawled. From now on, I wouldn't tread so heavily on it.

Jerry came down from the meadow. He had begun his trip and had seen monsters in the upper meadow. We calmly compared our trips, then returned to the house, agreeing that nature was too powerful.

Laura was tripping, too. She'd begun to paint the inside window frames bright yellow—the color of Van Gogh and Blake's sunflowers. By now, the sun had gone down, and the yellow seemed to have a light all its own.

Claudia, exhausted from delivering both Jerry and me through the throes of acid, lay snoring on the couch. Laura talked—to me, to herself—about her father and the absurdity of calling anything yours. "We don't possess anything." I watched her paint. A dab of blue paint was on her cheek, the color seeming to bleed over the rest of her face and her glasses. I told her she was beautiful. Upset and on the verge of tears, she gathered her paints and brushes and was going to leave the room. I implored her to stay and offered to leave instead. She understood how utterly alone I felt and remained.

We were on radically different trips, But that was always true. We were planets spinning in separate orbits. And all our orbits seemed to have a common center.

"I want someone to play with me," Laura said. We sat together and talked, alternating between intimate communication and utter aloneness.

"I wish," she said, "that there was some ritual we could perform now. I imagine us holding hands around a fire, chanting." Her description reminded me of the Druids. "Yes, a tribe," she said. She expanded the fantasy: After the cataclysm had destroyed the cities, the only survivors would live in tribes. "There will be mountain tribes, river tribes, valley tribes, and each of them will have their own customs and gods."

During Laura's trip, something clicked inside her that helped her concentrate her boundless energy. In a flash of insight, she chalked an aphorism on the blackboard that hung by the back kitchen door:

> FOR WAITING TO DO IT PERFECT,
> IT NEVER GETS DONE.

Then she took her paints into the children's room and began painting the walls and floor—artistically now. I stood apart and watched her, a butterfly that couldn't be grasped. Sometimes she'd step back from her work and appraise it from a distance, completely absorbed, looking, smiling and talking to herself. "That's how I see it," she said once. "That's what life looks like to me."

During the trip, I felt the futility of verbal communication. We send words across the great stellar distances, like radio signals between galaxies. By the time the messages are received the original meaning is lost. Better to use fewer words and suggest more.

Thumbtacked to the bookshelf was a postcard I had looked at many times without seeing. It was a reproduction of a painting, a Brueghel, that showed a boy up a tree, attempting to catch a bird. Under the trees walked a stout, stupid peasant carrying a hunting piece over his shoulder. He pointed at the boy, the expression on his face seeming to say, *"What a fool the boy is to try to catch a bird."* He being as much a fool as the boy; and I, the viewer, as much a fool as the peasant.

The dinner of potatoes and vegetables was delicious. I used no salt or pepper, grooving instead on the essential taste of the potatoes. I grunted and slurped with gusto. What difference did it make? I took a sip of tea from Bill's cup. He didn't mind. His tea was my tea was our tea.

After dinner someone put on the first album of the Incredible String Band, an English group who use Jew's harps, whistles and hammer dulcimers to re-create tribal man's animistic vision. I had looked at the album cover before, a photograph of a freak family. Before they had looked weird. Now they were beautiful and no longer strange.

Then, I put on the first movement of Beethoven's Ninth Symphony and listened ear-up against the speaker. The beginning phrase was the most fundamental proposition of life: All must break down, down, all must die. The cadence of a dirge elevated to the cosmic scale; a rush of energy that stretched musical form to its limit. How could he have done that—to hear, and more, to capture the rush of the universe?

Jerry and I made a pact to stay up until dawn. I listened to the rest of the Ninth. Jerry did his macramé and talked of his parents, who deprecated everything he tried. He wanted to be reassured that he was having the right kind of trip and went into long descriptions of his thoughts and hallucinations. I could understand and listen, but I couldn't reassure him. We were together but apart. The roosters crowed through the night, and we kept going outside to check for the dawn. Finally, the sky brightened. We lighted a lantern and started up the hill to the A-frame, being careful not to fall into gullies or awaken Jerry's meadow monsters.

February 4

When Jerry and I got down to the house, it was late in the afternoon. Betty told us the others had gone to buy a calf. A former member, now at Berkeley doing a PhD on Jean Cocteau, she had arrived last night. The three of us walked over to see Alice, a friend of Jerry's who lived a mile away across the valley. For once I didn't feel like initiating conversation. Alice was outside splitting wood when we arrived. Her old man was in Hawaii. We stayed for an hour and listened to a Carl Oglesby album that belonged to Betty.

When we got back to the farm, a sauna had begun on the hillside. It was just three steps down from the sauna to the brook. When I opened the door my lungs were sucked out by the hot, dry air, and I gasped. A fifty-gallon oil drum had been converted into a stove by blowtorching a door and a hole for the stovepipe. It was glowing red. I took off my clothes and hung them up in the dressing area on the same level as the stove. Then I stepped up to the hottest part of the sauna, under the low, sloping roof. A kerosene lamp hung from a rafter. It continually flared and then subsided, strobelike. About ten people were in the sauna. I squeezed into a space on the low bench.

Periodically, someone would toss water on the red-hot drum top. As it hit, it would vaporize with an explosive hiss. No one spoke. We sat separately stewing in our sweat. Our bodies seemed to have one skin of the same honey color. Yet our bodies were all different. Breasts had different tilts. Kneecaps could be smooth, chubby, or knobby.

Laura and I took turns rubbing backs. She spoke again of her tribal fantasies and of finding rituals "to get us all into the same space." I told her acid had suggested to me that unity of consciousness which she sought through ritual depended on some intermediary, a third being or presence.

Simultaneously we reached the unbearable point of heat and sweat. We opened the door and blinked at the light. In previous saunas, I had held myself back from immersing myself in the stream's deep current. But holding back enhanced the shock. This time I went under. Millions of open, relaxed sweat glands went wowwwwwww! and snapped shut. I bolted up. Laura lay in the streambed, buttocks and breasts rolling and twisting in the current. Then, seated on the pebbly bottom, she bubbled and spurted water like a naiad. With both hands she sleeked her wet-plastered hair back from her forehead.

We returned inside for another round. Jack began to om, softly at first, growing louder. We sweated and ommmmmmed. Silence—the rush of the stream. The lantern flickered.

Laura went to the water bucket, knelt and washed her hair, which had dried crisp. Maureen knelt beside her, and Laura cupped water and poured it over her head. Laura withdrew. Peter knelt down and Maureen washed his hair. Then Maureen fell into the intuitive sequence that had proceeded from the oming. No one spoke, yet we knew who the next to step forward would be. Jean washed my hair, and because I was the last, Laura returned to be washed by me, completing the circle.

We sat, drying on a tarpaulin spread out in the meadow. The sky was a dusky blue. A faint blush above the mountains. A slight scallop of a moon appeared, the eyelid of God. Against the music of the water, someone played strange improvisations on a flute. It was preharmonic music that evoked Druids worshiping at Stonehenge and the animistic world of gods and mystery; all the unity that had been lost on the way. We had to travel back in time, which was no time at all, to put the pieces back together, to put man back together, and to retrieve the original harmony.

Elaine, who'd been in seclusion all day, came down from the A-frame and we walked barefoot through the mud to the main house. A stew simmered on the stove. The Incredible String Band was on the phonograph singing their "Very Cellular Song." The last refrain bespeaks the vision of commonplace divinity infused into every particle of creation which only the very meek or the very stoned can see. It had been enshrined in crayoned letters on a wall of the commune.

February 5

It was early in the morning when I said good-bye to Maureen and Laura, who had driven me to the highway. No sooner had I laid my pack down and stuck out my thumb than a jeep braked to a stop. Good-bye, Oregon.

The driver was a thirty-eight-year-old former high school football coach on his way to Eureka, California, where he owned a Colonel Sanders Kentucky Fried Chicken restaurant. He wore a cowboy hat and a red-checked lumberjack shirt. We drove through cathedrallike groves of redwoods and past a herd of elk browsing at the edge of the woods. He slowed down, reminded of the elk he'd shot last fall in Montana and of his dream: early retirement to a ranch there. He had just bought an airplane and three more Colonel Sanders franchises in Arizona. In a few years he would subcontract all the restaurants and with the profit buy the ranch and spend the rest of his life killing elk, deer and ducks and driving his jeep around Marlboro Country. Like everyone else, he wanted to be free.

After learning that I'd just come from a commune, he began firing questions. How could the commune support itself? When I explained how their meager income was supplemented by food stamps, he said, "Oh, you mean *Welfare*. . . . Don't you realize that we're all paying for that? What kind of freedom is that?"

As we traveled on the cliffs above the Pacific, I had no intention of blowing the ride by insulting the driver; so I didn't question *his* vision of freedom.

Like so many who picked me up, he just couldn't believe that hippies have found their freedom so easily and simply. He suspected that at the bottom of their free and easy life lay fraud and dishonesty. That's the way it was.

Bought the San Francisco *Examiner:* The conviction of the lawyers for the Chicago 7 on contempt charges had set off riots in Berkeley; a police station in San Francisco was bombed, killing one cop.

Between the headlines, America was splitting apart or, more accurately, was being driven apart by the wedge action of its violent fringe groups. Set in the bold letters of Hearstian America, the headlines themselves seemed to distort and compound the misunderstanding. Like a spit of land under the tide, the country's middle ground was disappearing.

Halfway down the coast, at Willits, I checked into the only hotel in town, interrupting the clerk in mid-crossword puzzle to give me the key to a $4 room. She struck up a conversation about hippies, on which she had firm opinions. "It's no wonder they all come down with"—she whispered so as not to offend the denizens of the lobby engrossed in Merv Griffin—"with—social diseases."

What gave her that idea?

"Why, haven't you been keeping up with the Manson family?"

On the way down to Berkeley, staying overnight at cheap hotels, I reread the New Testament, courtesy of the Gideon Bible Society. As Bill had predicted at Living Springs, a seed had been planted—a seed of simple curiosity. I wondered if any of the early Christians had spoken in tongues; scholarlike, I went searching for references among Acts, the early Christians' chronicle of the revolutionary days when they were being hounded by the Pharisees. The narrative sucked me in: stories of the apostles hitchhiking through the small towns of Galilee, getting busted and thrown in dungeons, then God's energy opening up the walls and freeing them. The stories weren't all exaggeration. Too many details—accidental and irrelevant—stood out.

In Santa Rosa, I acted on the impulse to take a detour and see if Lou Gottlieb was still at Morningstar. It meant renting a car and taking a long chance of finding him, but I had a hunch I would.

Given the poorest directions to the ranch, out in exurban Sonoma County, I found it without a wrong turn. I parked the car just off the highway and walked in to the ranch. The path led to a small house. Sitting in front, nude and sunning himself in a yoga position, was Gottlieb. Rena, his pregnant wife, lay on her side.

Beside Lou was a Bible. Written on the front wall of the house was a saying: Disquietude is always vanity because it serves no good—Saint John of the Cross.

Feeling that I had come into the presence of a guru, I sat down and accepted a smoke. Gottlieb is tall and has a high forehead. Behind thick horn-rimmed glasses, his eyes move quickly. He mixes the spade lingo of his jazz days with mystical

allusions and parables. "It's simple, baby, we gotta stop divvy-
ing up the breast of our earth mother."

It was difficult to ask the questions I'd planned: about open-
land philosophy and the local harassment that had destroyed
Morningstar and was now threatening its successor, Wheeler
Ranch. Did he think the commune, which had become such a
visible target for the foes of drugs and social and political radicalism, could survive against militant middle America? But
Gottlieb was no longer on that plane of consciousness. He *had*
been when he campaigned for Wallace—"that's HENRY Wallace, baby." That was the other Gottlieb, jazz player, musicolo-
gist, beat, brilliant, opportunistic Jew, who bought the ranch
as a "scam," an investment which he intended to subdivide.
Now he was Gottlieb the holy man, a mystical Henry George,
the prophet of open land—all-embracing solution to social discontent and racial strife, and the path to enlightenment. "Once
you deed your land over to God," Gottlieb said persuasively,
"you'll start living in His kingdom."

Gottlieb sees himself as the embodiment of the spiritual
movement toward synthesis of East and West. "You know what
the German roots of Gottlieb are—God and love, like the
Greek, Theophilus."

He was born a double Libra, son of a Jewish physician and
a Roman Catholic mother. "All his life my father believed that
he had been Greek Orthodox during a past existence." He
draws on many spiritual disciplines and traditions, from Hinduism to Zen; bends your mind with paradoxes: "Can you
imagine the sound of one hand clapping?" or "If everything
were reduced to one, what could you reduce one to?"; and
doesn't believe in organized religion, churches, or even spiritual communities. He believes that Wheeler Ranch, which lives
according to the doctrine of voluntary primitivism (see Book
Eight), is developing "a liturgy of life" that has broken down
the artificial distinction between life and religion. Shitting in
the garden, for example, he said, is a spiritual act, as well as a
constitutional right. One of the health violations used to justify
the country's closure of Morningstar was its members' disre-

gard of flush toilets. Gottlieb insisted it was ecologically sound. Equating god with a pantheistic respect for nature, he maintained that shitting in the garden was protected under the First Amendment to the Constitution which bars governmental interference with the "free exercise" of religion.

One of the major spiritual influences in Gottlieb's life has been the New Testament. He thumbed through the Bible by his side and read the parable of the centurion and the prodigal son. Then he gave a modern and mystical exegesis. The gospel of Saint John was a mystic's handbook, he said, handing me the Bible, marked by his fingernail at John 14:6. I read it aloud: "Jesus saith unto him, I am the way and the truth and the life: no man cometh unto the father, but by me."

"Read it again." I did. "You see—it's a mantra." (A short prayer which, repeatedly chanted, can induce a spiritual high.) He read the passage himself, once in English, once in Greek. Between readings he did an imitation of a film producer: "That's fine, Lou, but not great. Let's take it again." Despite his guru-like characteristics, Gottlieb doesn't take himself seriously.

Suddenly, an unmuffled engine snorted up the hill and a lone motorcyclist sped past, leaving a dusty jet stream, his bent, white helmet humping and bounding along like a beetle. Gottlieb, refusing to acknowledge the intrusion, read on: "I am the way and the truth. . . ."

Engaging, lucid, convincing, Gottlieb is one of the most remarkable people I have met. When I told him I owned land in Vermont and was mildly interested in forming a community, he entreated me to deed the land to God, as he had done. He promised no less than miracles. "Your sex life will get better, you'll be healthier than ever."

Really?

He cited as evidence a modern parable. One day, a Brooklyn Jewish doctor, Emmanuel Bomse, came to his door seeking his son. The mother and son had had a generational falling out, and the son had left home and dropped out of sight. After a year elapsed, the doctor wanted to heal the breach. His only lead was that a friend of the boy's had said he was living on a commune in the Southwest.

Gottlieb didn't know the boy, but he offered the doctor advice on how he might find him: As an act of faith, buy land and deed it to God. The doctor pledged he would go to New Mexico and do what Gottlieb asked. But just before leaving, he was stricken by a heart attack. While he was in a hospital, the long-lost son called up Gottlieb, who put him in touch with his father. Dr. Bomse recovered "in a few days—it was a miracle." The father and son went to New Mexico together, where the doctor made good on his promise, buying a tract of land near Guadalupita and not only deeding it to God but naming it The Kingdom of God.

When I said I was going to New Mexico, Gottlieb wrote a short letter of intrduction for me to carry to Morningstar East. The card bore the Morningstar emblem, a heart enclosed by an overlay that suggests a synthesis of the Star of David and a cross:

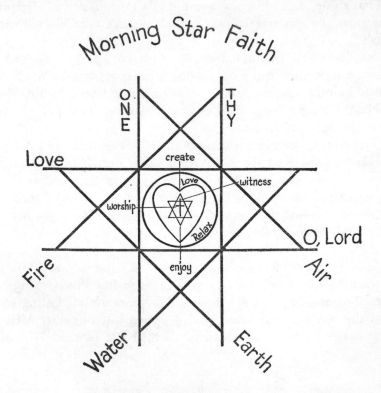

"When you get back to Vermont, put it in your window," he suggested.

February 12

After a month in the country, Berkeley seems even more unreal. Here, as elsewhere in the cities, the voices of reconciliation are being drowned out.

I located an old friend, Rocky, the reporter whose long hair had led to both our departures from the newspaper and the establishment. Now he is one of Berkeley's street people, attending lectures and rallies and swimming at noon in the university pool. Rocky tried to resist the political violence to which so many street people have lately turned. When window breaking started in Berkeley after the Chicago 7 lawyers were sentenced, he and a few others tried to stop it. "It was senseless . . . I can see how the Bank of America and the chain supermarkets had something coming to them, but not the small shopowners. They were caught in the middle. A lot of them used to give out food to longhairs."

I sat with Rocky at the table he and a few friends had set up in Sproul Plaza to raise money to reimburse the merchants for the damage. "We've got to stop this cycle we're into: more violence, more repression, more violence."

"Help the small shopowners!" he cried to the passing crowd of students. "We all broke the windows. Help fix them."

An SDS worker came toward us and sneered, "Don't be sentimental about the petty bourgeois."

A girl in buckskin and headband joined the discussion. "You can't change people by violence. I don't know what we're all trying to prove in Berkeley." She was almost crying. "People's Park should have been enough. I mean, violence doesn't change anything. The only way to change them is to change ourselves. Clean up our own community." She dropped a dollar bill in the box.

In a week, Rocky and his group, the New American Dream,

raised and distributed $600 to the victims of the windowbreaking.

I visited People's Park. A few blocks off Telegraph Avenue, it is still a drab, fence-enclosed parking lot patrolled by a lone campus guard.

In the spring of 1968, street people and students took it out of the hands of its owner, the university, under whose stewardship it had been allowed to become another bottle-littered vacant lot. Its new proprietors swept up the broken glass, hauled away the wrecked cars, planted flowers, laid down sod, and put in swings, slides and play sculptures. They declared it "the people's park," the property not of the university which had abused it, but of those who used it—the people of Berkeley. Understanding the ramifications, university officials reacted cautiously but firmly by erecting a fence. Enraged street people ripped it down. Then the administration called in the police, and when the first contingent was overrun, more police, until all Telegraph Avenue was engulfed in mass uprising. I had seen the photographs which later appeared in *Ramparts*, depicting a scene resembling Czechoslovakia: young people backing up, throwing bricks at lines of helmeted police. In the fighting one man was killed by police buckshot fired at close range. The park fell.

People's Park was yet another futile cause that made many radicals reconsider their attempt to carve a free community within the established structure's web of power and ownership. It had come down to force; and the police—who used helicopters to spray tear gas—had maintained the upper hand.

Now many Berkeley veterans were leaving. The exodus took two main directions. One was north to Oregon, Washington and British Columbia. The other route was toward the Southwest, principally to Taos. So heavy was the rush to the Southwest that some of the hip press were predicting that New Mexico might become the first state to secede from the Union. This migration gained greater momentum with the announcement that Earth People's Park was planning to acquire a 100,-000-acre section of the state for a hippie preserve.

Headed by a psychiatrist who went by the name Dr. Bill, the organizers of EPP were drawn from the *Who's Who* of the hip-entertainment-capitalist complex. The coordinating chairman was Milan Melvin, a pop record producer. Others were Stewart Brand, publisher of the *Whole Earth Catalogue,* Paul Krassner of *The Realist,* and Wavy Gravy, formerly Hugh Romney of Hog Farm.

EPP started off as a "media shuck" frankly designed to capitalize on "Woodstock consciousness." One organizer explained, "We can play the media hype better than anyone, and since it seems necessary to do a media shuck to rip off that much land, we'll do it." The goal was to raise $1,000,000 in small donations from those who had either attended Woodstock (around half a million) or wished they had. After buying land, EPP would hold an "earth warming," or mammoth rock festival, on the site.

Beyond the financing, plans for the park were vague. A team of ecologists would select and lay out a site. A maximum population of twenty thousand was suggested, although it would be, like Wheeler and Morningstar, liberated land—to access denied no one. The park would be able to adopt creative, dramatic uses of technology.

After the campaign was launched in the hip press early in 1970, the letters and money rolled in. Then the objections and criticism followed.

The revolutionaries resented EPP's use of the name People's Park and opposed EPP because it would drain energy and attention from the *real* battleground—the cities. Moreover, it smacked of corporate capitalism. The grassroots critics—hippies throughout the country—claimed that EPP involved too much money, too large a site, overuse of the mass media, and too centralized an organization.

Good Times, the underground San Francisco paper, wrote: "What Earth People's Park is creating is the falsified (media) version of everything that's part of our real life: our everyday communal existence and our vision of revolution and new culture. They sell us to the media (along with the movie rights, record rights, book rights) and make a mockery of everything that's essential to the successful existence of our culture in a hostile environment."

Others, like Marty Jezer, writing for *Win*, the Socialist periodical, argued that a commune preserve would be neither ecologically sound—in the arid Southwest there would not be enough water to support such a large population—nor free. So many speed freaks and crazies would move onto the tract that it would create a Haight-Ashbury in the desert and bring down the forces of external bureaucracy and control, or else force the EPP to create its own police force and regulations.

The loudest outcry came from New Mexico, where a land office had been opened. New Mexico's communes were already battling for survival in a region of little water and hostile Chicanos. For months, the beleaguered frontier outpost of communalism had been imploring hippies, *Don't come here.* Hip New Mexicans saw that the added presence of EPP would intensify the tension already caused by thousands of immigrating hippies who, for the most part, were like the stereotypical American tourist in Europe—intolerant of local customs.

One of the many "Please don't comes" was written by Elizabeth Martinez and published in *The Village Voice* of June 12, 1969:

Think about the fact that there is a wave of repression, which includes indiscriminate busting of anybody with long hair; frequent pot busts and frame-ups; infiltration of hippie groups by hippies who got busted and then let off in exchange for agenting to find grass and drugs; a hate campaign whipped up by the Anglo and Chicano power structures, to which some hippie groups are responding with equally hate-filled racism and violence. There is rape, murder and arson. . . .

Think about the fact that, much as you reject your middle-class Anglo society and its values, you are still Anglo. Think about the twelve-year-old struggle by poor Chicanos and the even older struggle by Indians to get back millions of acres of land stolen from them by Anglo ranchers with their Anglo lawyer buddies. Think about what it means for a new influx of Anglos—no matter how well meaning—to come in and buy up land that the local people feel to be theirs and cannot afford to buy back themselves.

When I visited the EPP offices on Grant Street in San Francisco, the organization had just adopted a plan: Instead of one huge preserve, they would liberate several smaller sites throughout the country. The glamor and money and media involvement were fading from the EPP. Branches had opened all over the country. EPP had responded to the feedback from the far-flung hip community, radiating from San Francisco into the hinterlands. It had taken on the shape of the movement: It was now highly decentralized and made up primarily of small groups who shunned the media and were becoming conscious that their first task in returning to the land was to become good neighbors with the people who already lived there.

Despite the warnings, I've decided to head for New Mexico, the homeland adopted by the earliest communes. A question foremost in my mind is whether Taos County's Spanish, Indian and Anglo subgroups *can* accept yet another—the hippies. There is also the reverse question of whether the hippies can adjust their "Woodstock Nation" to fit the history and customs of their adopted homeland.

In 1970, it could go either way. With the apprehension of a correspondent assigned to a war zone, I boarded a jet for New Mexico.

IV
New Mexico

New Buffalo

For the 70 miles between Albuquerque and Santa Fe, as the elevation rose to 1,000 feet, the bus groaned in low gear. The sun rose behind the jagged backbone of a mountain range. Again the sensation of journeying backward in time. New Mexico is like Troy, or Greece, where the ruins lie in open view. New Mexico is the Aquarian Holy Land, an ancient country, vast and enduring. The mountains, eroded by wind and rain, worn down to their primeval bones, testify that they have and will always survey the seas of sand inhospitable to man. The Interstate slices into the sides of the mountains, through igneous rocks that date to the beginning of the world. After the asphalt has crumbled and heaved and cracked and been drifted over by sand, and after the snake-weed and mesquite and sage have taken root again, the mountains will endure. Robinson Jeffers would approve.

The bus stopped at small clustered villages of squat adobe houses, TV antennae protruding through flat roofs. A few Indian women, talking, talking, mounted the bus. They were on their way to sell beads and baubles to the tourists on the Plaza at Santa Fe. We passed historical markers at side roads leading to the ruins of pueblos.

Santa Fe—streets wide enough for a pair of burros. The high altitude and clear light intoxicate. Santa Fe is still the end of the trail; now, in place of the fur traders, hippies fill its streets and restaurants. At the Army-Navy store and the health-food shop they outfit themselves before plunging into the back country.

At a Spanish luncheonette run by a family—a waitress, a cook and a cashier—another writer and I ordered some tacos. The only other customer, a drunken Indian, came over to introduce himself. "I am Lupe Lopeka, the first American." His breath reeked of alcohol. He had a barrel chest and a large head. His nose appeared to have been flattened—recently, from the beads of blood dripping from one nostril. In a mixture of Indian, Spanish and broken English, he told us that he lived at the Santo Domingo pueblo (one of the few inhabited pueblos left in the state). That much we could understand. The rest was stream of consciousness, but within the stream I could decipher a poem of injustice, of how the white man had ripped off the Indian's land, his game, his religion, and how the white man spat at the Indian, laughed at the Indian, beat him like a dog. But someday the Indian would arise. The Indian was a corn plant that would keep on growing "higher and higher, when it will stand tall over all the land." And with every other sentence, as if to remind himself, and us, of the essential theme, he'd repeat, "I am Lupe Lopeka, the first American," until we'd agreed that indeed he was the first. You couldn't take that away. We left him still talking to the empty tables and the snickering waitress, a lost man in an alien city on a Saturday night swept by the evil red light of wailing police cars, that he was Lupe Lopeka, the first American.

March 15

I waited for the Continental bus to leave for Arroyo Hondo, north of Taos, which the travel ads might one day dub "the heart of the commune country." There are about twenty communes trying to scratch a living out of the dry soil of northern New Mexico alone. I'd decided on New Buffalo, now the oldest and still going through upheavals. I knew it was overcrowded with visitors whom the old settlers wanted to pare down; I might not be welcome, or even admitted. But New Buffalo had survived for three years, and I had a hunch I should go there.

March 19—New Buffalo

For the last four nights I've slept on the floor of Tonio's room. It's dusty but not entirely uncomfortable, one of twelve in the pueblo. All are about 10 by 12 feet. They have dirt floors and flat roofs of heaped earth supported by peeled log beams, called *vertigas,* and smaller pieces of aspen, *lotillas.* The rooms, all spoken for, are referred to as Chuck's, Mary's, Aquarius Paul's, etc., a form of private ownership, if you will, within the commune. However, every room is jammed right now, some with visitors, others with members and their kids. There are about a dozen new arrivals in Bob's room, and five in Mary's.

I was the first to get up. Tonio, under a tousle of black hair, was snoring away in his famous hanging bed suspended by chains from the *vertigas.* Three feet off the floor, it is kept warm in the winter by heat rising from the wood stove, and it stays dry in the spring. In the other corner, under a pile of surplus Army blankets, lay Doug. During the day he acts like a hood, but asleep, he looks like a nice seventeen-year-old kid. I blew out the small Turkish lamp set on a shelf below a huge mandala of the Lord's Prayer. Then I noticed the water.

It had seeped below the planked door and was menacingly trickling toward my sleeping bag. The door to the plaza opened with a scrape. Blinding whiteness stunned me. Overnight three inches of snow had covered the pueblo. Under a bright sun, it was melting, quickly. Next door George and his son, Chris, were digging a trench to keep the water from running into their room. Others were shoveling off the flat roofs before the snow could melt and seep through. Chris, who is twelve, threw a snowball. I reciprocated. Some visitors were flailing axes at the woodpile. I hoped they wouldn't break any more ax handles, which, like so many things here, from eggs to kerosene, are running out. I looked for a shovel.

Around the plaza—an open space enclosed on three sides by the wings of the pueblo—the free-roaming chickens and turkeys had left their initials in the snow. Big David, an ex-Hell's Angel, who measures 6 feet 8 and is the commune's unofficial bouncer, met me as I crossed the plaza. "Hey, man, how long you think you'll be staying?"

I answered evasively, "Maybe a day or two. Don't worry, I'll be splitting; I'm a writer and I have my own family." And I reminded him of the can of honey in the kitchen that had been my donation.

"Groovy," he said. "Stay a while."

That's how it goes here. The commune is apolitical, but you play politics in order to keep from being expelled.

I arrived four days ago during a blizzard. After walking two miles from the highway, bent forward into the wind-driven snow, I came up the long driveway looking like a live snowman. As I approached, the low, bunkerlike outline of the pueblo came into dim view through the snow. Only one man, splitting wood, was outside—George, one of the commune's six founders. Snow clung to his curly black hair and his thick beard. He wore glasses with clear plastic frames that would have been more appropriate for a graduate student in physics than a hippie. He reminded me of a plain-dressed young Amish, solid, hard-working, individualistic.

I introduced myself as a writer, unaware that was the worst possible opener. George launched into a tirade against the "media" which had wrecked the communal scene in New Mexico by romanticizing it. The stories, George went on, had attracted hordes of trippers, drifters, parasites, and criminals who had, in turn, aroused the local Chicanos to violence against all hippies. The media had made New Mexico a dangerous place to raise a family and were forcing hip pioneers like himself to go elsewhere. "If you respect what we're trying to do here, you'll split," and he swung his ax at the knotty length of piñon. I turned to go back down the road to the highway. "Hey, you can stay tonight," George yelled. I still don't know why he changed his mind.

A clear view this morning of the commune and surrounding country: The pueblo lies at the base of a gently rising hill spotted with small, scrubby piñons looking slightly hunched under the snow's fluffy weight. The courtyard opens toward the west on fields soon to be planted with corn and beans. Beyond the fields, the land slopes to the brink of a deep gorge, which a small stream, the Arroyo Hondo ("deep brook"), has whittled from soft red sandstone over the years. New Mexico bears the wounds of geologic history. Against the backdrop of mountains, I cannot forget that man is part of an evolutionary stage—perhaps a transient form, the future shape of a new fossil. Here in Taos County (population 17,500, 3,880 square miles) man has again regained his role as a widely spaced species.

Against the western sky the Sangre de Cristo Mountains, rock peaks of blazing snow, glazed rock, and wispy cloud, rise to 13,000 feet. At their base squats the village of Arroyo Hondo—a gas station, Celso's Bar, and a scattering of small houses.

Two wings of New Buffalo's pueblo each contain three rooms; the main wing holds six rooms, plus the common room, or "circle," and communal kitchen. The pueblo blends into the land: its adobe walls, made of sun-dried brick, are of the same yellow as the parched earth. The projecting butt ends of the round *vertigas* follow the architectural style of the fifteenth-century Spanish conquistadors. Visually, the pueblo's only anachronisms are the jaunty black tin stovepipes that protrude at odd angles from its windows. Next to me, George paused in his trench digging. "Adobe is the most organic building material. Leave the place for two years and the wind and rain and snow would wash it away. It'd look as if we'd never been here."

Together we scanned the mountains, which seemed closer now that they were totally blanketed with white. "Are you going to stay awhile?" he asked. "If it's all right with you," I answered, feeling my way. I added that Chuck, for whom I was buying wine, was happy with the arrangement.

George shrugged. "If it's OK with Tonio, you might as well stay. Everyone else does."

I finished trenching the room and headed for the kitchen, by way of the circle, passing through its swinging oak doors, one inlaid with a buffalo head in relief. Designed after the kiva, the ceremonial chamber of the Indians of the Southwest—where the tribe carried on its religious rituals in accordance with the changing seasons—the circle is sunk four feet into the ground. You must humbly step down to enter. Four massive beams thrusting upward toward a triangular skylight support the circle's high ceiling. Shafts of sunlight slant through to the dirt floor.

On a shelf dug in the circle's rim, the day's visitors sat and waited for the next meal. Walter, the commune's only black, a wiry, defensive guy wearing a cap, improvised blues on the flute. Whenever visitors entered the circle, Walter would say, "Hey, man, got a smoke on ya?" If they didn't, he'd look offended and ask if they had a cigarette—tailor-mades?

I went into the crowded kitchen, hoping some coffee was left. Mary, a sturdy English girl, tried to bake some corn bread while holding Nancy, her six-month-old. She was constantly jostled. "Please, please," she pleaded politely, "could some of you who aren't cooking remove yourselves so we can move about?" Hurriedly, I rinsed a battered tin cup, poured the last of the coffee and grounds into it, and returned to the circle.

It was a depressing, discouraging day. I had come with high hopes. New Buffalo had the reputation of being a hardworking commune that followed the diet and traditions of the Indians, including peyote meetings. But now New Buffalo was no longer a tribe. Under the crush of visitors, the older members—George and Joyce, Justin and Joanna, Ira and Maureen, Mary—had retreated behind the doors of their rooms and may soon leave. This would pass stewardship to a group of ten or so who have been here for a year or less. They will also inherit the problem of the visitors, the modern counterpart of the Apaches who descended from the plains to raid New Mexico's pueblos centuries ago. These modern Apaches outnumber everyone, making up approximately thirty of the fifty people here. Over the last two weeks, they've come up the road at the rate of five a day. Since the commune is powerless to expel anyone, they've camped out in the kitchen, in junked buses, in the fields, in tepees. Bob's room, containing twelve to fifteen "Apaches," resembles a scene out of Gorki's *The Lower Depths.*

Under these conditions the senior members are barely approachable. I tried to strike up a conversation with Ira as he fed the animals. Someone had "ripped off the eggs" from the chicken coop. "If you don't get out here by dawn, forget it," he said bitterly. He answered a curt yes and no to questions I posed about the animals, probably the same ones hundreds of others had asked him before me.

By contrast, the visitors were eager to talk. There was Tim, a short-haired Army deserter on his way to Canada via the "underground railroad" of communes; furtive Leonard, who had hitchhiked in with his five-year-old daughter, Tracy; Burt, a middle-aged, philosophical bum, who tramped around the country accompanied by his small dog and only appeared after dinner to collect the leftovers and return to his room; Paul, a mystical version of a young Henry Fonda, who walked around barefoot in the snow, wearing a thin sweater, hands clasped upward in prayer. And there's Anne, a quiet girl, with a cross around her neck, who arrived two days ago and has taken over the kitchen duties.

I helped Anne wash the lunch dishes. After dropping out of college, Anne had lived in an urban commune on the edge of the black ghetto in Portland, Oregon. Her father, a retired Air Force officer and a Roman Catholic, threw her out of the house one day after she had declared that Christ would come to earth today as a hippie. Nevertheless, she sends letters home and signs them "in Christ." She's still trying to convince her parents that the hippies constitute a new social and spiritual movement. Anne came to New Buffalo to become part of this new movement, as well as to attempt a new life-style. "You can't find the way back to God in the cities anymore." Most of the more recent arrivals have simply stumbled into New Buffalo seeking the home they never had; others are looking for another scene, a Haight-Ashbury in the desert.

Tonio and I made a wine sortie down to Celso's. I wouldn't mind buying the wine so much if it didn't actually harm Tonio. But as the commune dissolves, he escapes to the bottle. His father was a Mexican drug dealer who died in prison, and he thinks his mother, an alcoholic, is also dead.

At Celso's, a young Chicano yanked off Tonio's wide-brimmed hat—an invitation to combat. We were outnumbered by a barroom full. I stuttered a few *buenas noches, amigos,* humbly took the hat—*gracias, gracias*—and backing to the door, turned to flee in the Volkswagen. As I drove, Tonio guzzled. "I used to go in there and buy drinks along with everybody else. . . . I'm a Latin American. Got Mexican blood in me. But to them, now, I'm another hippie. Like the ones who get off the bus and treat Celso like some stupid spic, not like the honorable bartender he is. Celso wouldn't lift his hand to save my life."

Before dinner is served, the custom is to form a circle of silent prayer. There were so many of us that when we joined hands, we formed a snaking line that wound in and around the beams, up the stairs, into the kitchen. It was no longer a circle in which anyone could see the family's faces. Two minutes passed before George spoke, "Thank you, God, for this day. Thank you for the snow. It will give us water for our crops. Thank you for the food to feed all the people who come to us." Silence again, finally broken by a squeeze and a "Let's eat." I fell into the end of the queue that had all the cheer of a Salvation Army soup line. When I reached the kitchen a half hour later, the utensils and plates were gone. I stood waiting until someone dropped a plate and fork into the sink, rinsed them, and ate a mass of warmed-over lentils, brown rice and groats. Most of the commune members were eating in their rooms. The appetizing smell of frying onions came from one room, where George, Joyce and their three kids ate by kerosene light around a small table.

March 17

Sunny and clear, with a wind that comes prechilled over the snowcapped mountains. In less than a day, all trace of snow has disappeared, and the eternally thirsty ground has sucked up the moisture. This morning, I looked around for some activity, but the tractor stood idle, the fields empty—not even the sound of a hammer. The mood is listless, dispirited. With none of the older generation to initiate it, nobody works. The pueblo looks like a hip resort. Backs against the adobe walls, eyes closed under the warm Southwest sun, the visitors bask the morning away. Some rap quietly about their peregrinations from one hip watering hole to another—Big Sur, Mount Shasta, Mendocino, Boulder. Taos is on the summer season circuit. "When it gets cold, I'll split for LA, deal for a month or two, and head for Mexico," one seasoned traveler told me.

Near the repair shed, George bent over his pickup, a six-cylinder '52 Chevrolet. He wore gray coveralls and a this-is-all-absurd smile. George and I were on good terms now, possibly because he had recognized me as a fellow conservative, or at least skeptic, who agreed that communes needed form and structure more durable than the flower-children fantasies. "This is my getaway truck," he said, wiping the valves. Where was he heading? He didn't know exactly, but for sure, George, Joyce and their four kids were leaving New Buffalo. After three years it had become increasingly unstable, aimless and dangerous. Not only had the commune changed, but George was quite different from when he arrived.

A few years ago he rode the Staten Island Ferry every morning and evening, to and from his job in a Wall Street brokerage house. At night he attended business school. After he dropped out, they sold the house on Staten Island and rented a loft in Lower Manhattan. He struggled for a time to make it as an artist, gave up, and embarked with his first wife and kids in a camper bus. "We wanted to find a better, simpler life." They covered Wyoming, Oregon, and Mexico and, finally, Berkeley. There, George met a group of six others who were looking for some alternative to working nine-to-five in a city, some purpose to existence other than making money.

One evening they conducted a ritual of the Native American Church, an experience that introduced them, as through a dream or *déjà vu,* to a vanished way of life. "We recognized ourselves as a lost tribe who had forgotten, maybe for two or three generations, how to live—to plant, dance, sing, raise children—and how to die." And so they set out to revive almost extinct wisdom and lore by buying land in northern New Mexico. They named their commune after the buffalo, which had once supplied food, clothing, fuel and shelter—all the elements of an integrated life—to the Indians of the plains. The name was suggested by one of the founders, Max Finstein, a poet of the New York beat scene, then married to Joyce.

Fortunately one of them, Rick, had $50,000 to underwrite their venture. (After the first year he left and now lives twenty miles to the north.) Half of Rick's money went for the land; more bought the tractor, freezer, refrigerator, pump and building supplies. "The rest, we just blew," George said. The six of the original founders incorporated and named themselves officers of the corporation. Of the six officers, only George and Justin remain.

The first summer they lived in tepees, cooked in an open-air kitchen, and carried their drinking water from the arroyos. After the corn was planted, they invited Indians from the nearby Taos pueblo to come and teach them how to do the ritual corn dance. Under a relentless sun, they built their pueblo, mixing earth and water with straw and pouring the mixture into molds left to bake in the sun for ten to fourteen days. Then the bricks were cracked out and simply laid end to end in a foot-deep trench—hardly a foundation. On top of each row, mortar was slapped. When the wall reached seven feet, a piece of planed lumber was laid across it; over this were lifted the *vertigas;* across them was nailed a thin, silver matting of aspen *lotillas.* All the wood was freestanding dead lumber that the men cut and hauled on endless wood runs from Kit Carson National

Forest. The planed lumber was the main building supply purchased. Total cost of the pueblo—$200.

The commune's diet was traditionally Indian: corn, beans
and, occasionally, a poached deer. The first year, they plowed
and cultivated fifteen acres and gained a local reputation for
industry. They got up before dawn, had a light breakfast, and
were out in the fields by 8 A.M. "In the middle of the morning
one of the women would lug a big blackened pot of coffee out
to the fields," recalled George fondly. "In those days, the hard
work brought us together."

At first, the work was divided traditionally into men's and
women's. None of the women that first year wanted to be liberated, the nineteenth-century image of aproned, long-skirted
womanhood appealed to them.

Then one day a new woman arrived and joined the others for
a solid day's work in the windowless kitchen. She ground flour
by hand, sorted beans, and washed endless sinkfuls of dishes.
By the end of her first three days on the commune, longing to
get outside, she volunteered to work in the brickyard with the
men. The men ignored her offer. The other women brought
her back into the kitchen. A similar example of sexual chauvinism involved a hip cowboy who rode in one morning and started
slicing carrots at the kitchen table. The women shooed him
outside to work with the men.

There was a lot of sexual reshuffling among the tribe during
that first year. They found themselves in a desert-island situation, the only Anglos in a sparsely populated corner of Spanish-
speaking New Mexico.

As usual, in the first twelve months of a commune, there were
some breakups. George's wife left him and the commune with
another member. Joyce left Max and joined up with George.
Mary left her husband, came to New Buffalo, and lived with Ira,
before he moved in with Maureen. Since the re-pairing occurred
within the tribe, so to speak, it was accompanied by less than the
expected animosity. "The first year we all believed we could
love one another freely without guilt," said Mary.

In their closeness to the seasons and following the example of the Taos Indians, New Buffalo's early settlers developed ritual celebrations to coincide with the equinox, solstice or full moon. In this tradition a wedding was held on the full moon of September of 1969. The ceremony took place in a field. Hundreds of area hippies encircled the couple. Justin, acting as chief, simply asked them: "Well, if you're willing to stand out here before your friends and promise to walk the road of life together, you're already married." The couple then shared a taste of roasted cornmeal and water—sacraments of the Native American Church—which were later passed around to the guests.

The feast included barbecued meat from a freshly slaughtered goat, an electric punch, and a rock band performing from the incomplete roof of the circle. Below, the circle itself was booming with conga drums, handmade from hollow logs and stretched skins. Women danced around the fire. The others raised whoop after ear-splitting war whoop. In that first year, New Buffalo had always enjoyed hosting such orgiastic festivities. The growing number of hippies seemed cause then for celebration rather than a danger sign. However, near the year's end, more and more visitors arrived and stayed. Their mounting numbers and influence began to split the commune into two camps: those who wanted a closed community and those who wanted to keep it open to anyone and everyone. The split has not healed over.

As George recapped New Buffalo history, Joyce approached, holding their fourteen-month-old son, Cedar, named after one of the sacraments of Native America Church ritual. "Will you hold him while I take down the wash?" She walked away, taking long strides, her back straight. Joyce has a thin, wiry body and wears her hair in a long braid. She conveys mental toughness and detachment. We watched as she passed the root cellar and descended the path toward the clothesline, where every day some fifty diapers flap in the mountain breezes. About the same moment, we caught the approach of two figures carrying packs —two more visitors. They walked straight up to us, and after a ritual "Hi, man." George launched rapid-fire into the same rap he'd given so many times it had begun to sound like a 33-rpm record played at 78 rpm: "Look, this is marginal land. That means a man, wife and four kids can barely hack it by farming every inch, saving every drip of water that comes down the irrigation ditches, assuming you get an average rainfall. We were overdoing it with twenty-five people. Now we've got fifty here. We don't have enough work, food or space. With twenty-five it's just barely possible, with luck and five years' hard work, to be self-sufficient. But not with fifty. We can't keep ourselves together. If you respect what we're trying to do, you'll leave." The newcomers listened restlessly, their eyes darting between us, sizing us up, all the time agreeing, "Yeah, man, I can dig that, etc." After walking away from us, they bumped into Jim, who was filling a pan from the faucet at the end of the main wing. The three of them ducked into Jim's room. By dinner gong, they'd joined the line—along with the ten others who arrived today.

During the first year, secluded, industrious New Buffalo had attracted few visitors. Now deluged by refugees of the Haight, the commune was caught on the horns of a philosophical dilemma. The open commune draws on the Rousseauian vision of the earth as it had once been: wilderness over which tribes of men freely roamed, killing no more than they could eat. Man was a member of nature's communal household. As Lou Gottlieb maintained, when man began to subdivide the earth and spill blood over his fences, walls, corridors of influence, Maginot Lines, he fell from paradise.

The commune symbolized the return to unowned, undivided Mother Earth, a neoromantic gesture of defiance against the great asphalt-roller urban society. Closing the commune violated its impelling vision. How could a commune, by definition, draw a perimeter of private property around itself? Inside the perimeter they were brothers and sisters who shared the last of the Bugler tobacco and the last sheet of toilet paper; but what did brotherhood and love mean if confined to twenty-five people? Expand the perimeter, though, and how could they possibly befriend, shelter and feed everyone who came up the road? If the gate wasn't closed soon, though, they'd sink like twenty-five men in a small rowboat.

The spokesman for the open commune, as well as for the philosophy of all-inclusive love and brotherhood, had been Bob. A short, forty-five-year-old ex-junkie, Bob always wore cowboy boots and had eyes that radiated a warm, what-I-have-is-yours feeling. Whenever George told visitors to leave, Bob would extend a brotherly hand, some dope, food and a sleeping space on the floor of his room. Soon all the floor space was covered with bodies—from twelve to twenty at a time. When everyone else was working in the cornfield, the people in Bob's room were smoking, eating Spam, and drinking Hawaiian Punch while the Led Zeppelin blared on the stereo. (Electricity had been used only for the pump, freezer and sewing machine until one night someone surreptitiously ran a wire from the power pole to Bob's room.) Two months ago, Bob died of tuberculosis, but his death did not end the division. "It's left the wound open," remarked Justin. Bob willed his stereo, his room and his open-commune philosophy to Jim, one of the many newcomers he'd befriended.

Dinner was meager—rice, lentils, squash and, if you were first in line, a few tortillas. As I sat in the circle forcing down the lentils and thinking what a good source of protein they were, Chuck sidled over and whispered that there were some Swedish meatballs in his room. First he left the circle, and after waiting a moment, I followed. Sure enough, on the wood stove, stewing in their sweet synthetic sauce, were Swedish meatballs Doug had copped from a secret stash in the pantry. As I learned, others were doing likewise. We had become a commune of hoarders. Doug and I went out to the repair shed and drained the last of the kerosene to have a reserve supply for our lamp. Others were copping the eggs right out from under the chickens. Mothers had to fill their milk jars almost directly from the cow's udder; otherwise all would be drunk by those who disregarded the notice on the milk pitcher: "For kids, pregnant ladies, and lactating mothers." The custom was to smoke together in the circle, an occasion to which everyone was summoned by a gong. But now, everyone smoked in his room or in small groups. Hoarding was a crucial index of communal decline.

When I returned to the room tonight, I found a motorcyclist sacked out on *my* dusty spot on the floor. I was furious. What right did he have? But then I thought, what right did I? New Buffalo's devolution was depressing me. Maybe I'll split tomorrow, I thought. But the writer-observer said, cool it, stick and see what happens, it could be an interesting devolution. No matter if the floor *is* dusty, and the lentils tasteless—if New Buffalo portends the end of the American youth commune, I'll write the autopsy. But another voice in me, the more involved self, couldn't believe that the second generation of people, who stood to inherit the commune after the founders left, would let it go down.

March 18

So far I've watched Jim, Bob's heir, from a distance. This morning in Aquarius Paul's room, Jim entered with a pan of freshly plucked leaves, and placed it on a beam to dry under a skylight. Jim is an earnest, young, blond flower child, a Billy Budd. While Jim talked of Bob, Aquarius Paul sat silently on the bed, wearing his white tunic, which always stayed spotlessly clean. "The most beautiful cat I've ever known," Jim said of Bob. From him Jim had learned that every man was God and that love could reconcile all human differences. New Buffalo could shelter even more people, if present members would recognize that a closed commune was a surrender to fear and insecurity. "Man, at Woodstock hundreds of thousands of people lived together peacefully on less than we have here! They fed themselves, took care of their sick and. . . ."

"That's acid fantasy, Jim," Aquarius Paul interrupted. "Sure, if we were stoned all the time we'd get along for three or four days, which is as long as Woodstock lasted. But you can't stay high all the time."

By then the leaves had dried; Jim brought them down. I walked out with him, talking of Bob's death. Jim offered to show me the burial spot on the edge of an arroyo. Standing on the loose stones and dirt, which were the grave's only markers, Jim recalled the last days of Bob, the cosmic cowboy. When the coughing began, Bob treated it like any other ailment—with massive doses of dope. "I think he knew he was going to die, but it didn't frighten him. One day we were walking around up here. 'When I die,' he said, pointing to an arroyo, 'just throw me in and let me decay. And no bullshit. I don't want no eulogies.' "

A few days later Bob coughed up so much blood that Jim decided to drive him to a hospital; on the way he lost consciousness and was given mouth-to-mouth resuscitation in the back seat. About twelve hours later in the hospital, he died. His friends collected his body, took off the white hospital gown and plastic wristband, and redressed him in his own duds—boots, jeans, headband, beads and a shirt that was like a florist's shop seen through a psychedelic lens.

About two hundred showed up for the funeral—if you could call it that. It was very natural. First, the funeral party got high; then four of his young friends bore Bob up to the grave, each one lifting an arm or a leg. The funeral party grouped around the grave, which overlooked the commune: the repair shed; chicken coop and cow stall; the goat pen, next to the shaft of a broken windmill; and moving east, a hump marking the root cellar; the underground springhouse; a hexagonal log house and three tepees. On the other side of the fence, a patchwork of fields enclosed by more fences; orchards and sagebrush stretching to the mountains. Toward the west, flat fields that had just been plowed over; two more tepees, a Union Jack flying from one; another kiva-like house; and then fields of short corn stubble running to the road that skirted the canyon's edge.

"We lifted him down into the hole. I said he didn't want any bullshit, and they started shoveling." Jim jumped into the grave and gently covered the face of his friend with dirt. The shovels cut into the ground making metallic sounds that set a dirge rhythm against the duller sounds of the loose earth thudding into the grave.

Jim left me there to wonder about a man I'd never met but felt I knew. Jim had said Bob believed that what feels good is good; anything was legal and every man was a god. It was a bleak existential faith—a loner's code—and not one on which to base a community. I wondered if Bob's explicit prohibition of ritual at the funeral had been his final act of secession from community.

This evening Mary came into the kitchen to get some pots and hot water that were needed to milk Chloe, the goat. I volunteered to help. Mary wore a bulky hand-knit sweater over a blue gown that broke on the black leather of her high-topped boots. The sun had slid into the western canyon, and in the opposite direction a light show was playing on a titanic movie screen of mountains. A tint of orange deepening to red crept up the mountainside. Standing there, holding the pails, Mary and I didn't need to say that the goat would have to wait until the show was over. Below the mountain, the huge flat-topped mesa was already sunk in light shadow, but still had in this twilight a color softer than usual, a pastel greenish-blue. The sun had fallen and the wave of color had almost scaled the highest peak. For the few seconds, when the sun struck a particularly acute angle below the horizon, the mountain's snow-cap bathed in ethereal pink. "*Sangre de Cristo,* the blood of Christ," Mary murmured. "Sometimes I feel as if I am in this world but not of it." She was beautiful: her smooth black hair parted down the middle, a slight space between her upper front teeth, and serious blue eyes deep set in the fine bone structure that is indomitably English. I looked at her face for a moment, and when my eyes returned to the mountain screen, it had faded to lifeless gray.

Chloe and her two billies were baaing hungrily. Mary washed

the swollen teats of the mother goat, who munched shovel-sized mouthfuls of alfalfa. Born and educated in Britain, Mary has retained both her accent and characteristic English courtesy —a rare trait on a commune these days. "Rawbert," she would say, "would you mind please cahsting a few cupfuls of grain into the feed can?" Mary has the sturdiness of a charming milkmaid and the reserve said to be typical of a double Virgo. She left home and came to New York, where she wrote for *Win* and attended the Art Students' League. She married another artist. When he developed a bad case of bronchitis, they left New York and headed for the clear, clean climate of the South-west. After running out of money, they stumbled into a commune. When they separated, he took their four-year-old son, and Mary came on to New Buffalo. That was three years ago.

The first pulses of milk squirted *zing!* into the open pail. "It's about time for me to leave the commune," she said cryptically, for her reasons are less obvious than the others'. I hesitated to ask why. Against the evening's dusky-blue afterglow, the three of us, Chloe in the lead, jogged back across the field to the goat pen, where the two young billies were bawling for their mother's return.

After dinner, a debate developed in the kitchen over food stamps. Until a week ago, there were altogether twenty-five people at New Buffalo using the stamps under two arrangements. Around ten (the number varied wildly with the population) individually collected the stamps; they simply went to Taos, the county seat, applied, and collected stamps worth $28 in food by paying 50 cents. This group included the individual families who'd begun to cook their meals separately. The other fifteen members—for the most part singles without kids—collected stamps as a single-family unit (the regulations vary from state to state, but in New Mexico it was possible for a group un-related by blood to qualify as a family). These stamps were used to supply food for the communal kitchen.

A week ago, the people who were running the kitchen decided not to use any more stamps. Partially this decision was brought about by the county's discovery of food-stamp fraud, as well as the rising cost of administering the program, which is subsidized by the federal government. Hippies were collecting stamps under different names in more than one county. Administrators of the welfare program cracked down and enforced a requirement that all members of communal families produce identification and proof of financial need. If one member proved ineligible, the entire family was disqualified. Because some of the fifteen who were using the communal kitchen did not want to make their identities public, the decision was made to drop out of the stamp program. (However, some of those who had formerly eaten in the kitchen reapplied individually for food stamps and began to cook and eat in their rooms.)

Another reason for the kitchen's decision to forgo stamps was to bring the commune closer together by weeding out drifters. By reverting to a more Spartan diet, they hoped to starve out the less committed souls and stomachs—those who couldn't survive without a diet of meat and carbohydrates. Diet became an index of communal loyalty.

A few have gone, perhaps, but the dinner line is still long; and the Apaches can still plunk down their 50 cents for enough stamps to keep them in Spam and Dinty Moore beef stew for a solid month. But no one protests the stamps very strongly. The families here depend on the program to balance their diet.

I estimate that, unlike more self-sufficient High Ridge Farm, about two-thirds of New Buffalo's food is attributable to stamps. A year ago, members say, it was only a third; and two years ago, the commune existed entirely on what they grew, supplemented by the last of Rick's legacy. "Someone would come back with thirty pounds of hamburger from the store, and in two days it would be gone," recalled Aquarius Paul. It took near malnutrition to force some of New Buffalo's members into the stamp program, for taking them was tantamount to acknowledging their economic defeat. Once a well-meaning visitor brought presents of food, including bags of grain. The food was refused. "They pretended that they didn't need any," the visitor told me. "But the kids were hungry." Finally the members relented, deciding that the risk of depriving their young of nutrients outweighed the ideal of self-sufficiency. Thus New Buffalo's first generation made its compromise with the system. Now a new generation, primarily singles without kids, has to wrestle once again with the same issue.

For a few minutes I listened in on the debate. It pitted Cave David against one of the visitors, a girl in a blue nylon windbreaker, who insisted that taking stamps was one of her "rights." During the debate, Crazy Jim, said to be an escapee from a mental institution, stood to one side of the stove and laughed sporadically. Whether he laughed at something that eluded our too-sane perceptions I could never tell. Finally, I became so angry at the girl's defense of the stamps—of such callous disregard of the commune's objectives—that I left rather than explode.

Outside in the high night air, the teeming galaxy of stars seemed to press their brilliancies closer to earth. Down in the valley a dog barked, was silent, and then barked again. New Buffalo floated in time and out of time, caught in the backwash of present society, and riding the crest of the future. To be open or closed; to accept or reject food stamps; all seemed strands of the same riddle. Somehow its members were getting tripped up by their visions. They were like acidheads who'd lost their time sense. Behind the doors, small groups rapped through the night about the crisis brought on by the swarms of visitors.

Dust and tasteless lentils notwithstanding, I'm going to stay. New Buffalo is being forced into a decision.

March 19

Today, while Cave David and I were at the kitchen table, we simultaneously noticed a stranger, a short-haired young man in a blue collegiate blazer. He stood frozen like a bird dog, staring at a spot on the adobe wall. Cave David tapped him on the shoulder. "Are you bad-tripping?" Obviously, he was. We led

him to a quiet room and told him to relax. He spoke of hallucinations and said his name was Dennis.

"Where did *he* come from?" Cave David asked on the way
back to the kitchen. "He looks as freaked out as I was when I
got here." His body covered with staph infections, David had
come to New Buffalo after hermiting for three months in one
of the mesa's caves; thus his name. Prior to the cave, he had
dropped out of the University of Chicago, become an active
member of Old Town, Chicago's hip-radical community, and
been beaten up during the Democratic convention. Saying
good-bye to politics, he went to the University of Washington
and was hired to tend the Botany Department's experimental
garden. He loved the job and the plants, so much that he refused to apply inorganic fertilizers and pesticides. The university fired him. Meanwhile, his old lady left him. David came
to New Mexico and went into the cave, meditating and sub-
sisting on herbs and weeds.

Since joining New Buffalo, Cave David has broken out of his
psychological isolation. His interest in "vibrational biology"
has been revived. Dressed in the same trenchcoat and plaid
scarf he'd worn for a week, he talked for hours about experimental proof that plants emit emotional vibrations. "If you
even *talk* about burning a philodendron in its presence, it will
register peak shock waves at the exact moment you say the
word 'burning.'" Yesterday, Cave David moved his sleeping
bag, books and a lamp into the greenhouse to be in constant
touch with his plants. This summer he plans to build a combination greenhouse-laboratory and conduct experiments to prove
that plant vibrations are more than acid fantasy; that leaves,
trees and roots have their own consciousness and a sensitivity
exceeding man's. Every day is a new opportunity and inner
struggle for Cave David—to gather his energy, take the first
step, break out of self-absorption.

In a commune, it's difficult *not* to be moved by other people.
There are fewer walls to withdraw behind and to prevent people from bouncing off one another. The interplay provides

natural therapy. For example, I am not the only one to be annoyed by Cave David's indecision. Though he can see both sides of the visitor issue, he rambles on and on about both pros and cons, never deciding, never acting. Yesterday I told him bluntly, "Stop breast-beating like Hamlet. You know what's right for New Buffalo." Others give him the same feedback, he admits. Consequently, he's trying to be more assertive.

Cave David, Henry, Tonio, Larry, Marilyn, Torah, Doug—all belong to New Buffalo's second generation of settlers. Conceivably, there will be a third: the newly arrived and often most fucked up. Like Crazy Jim and Dennis, they come here suffering from various degrees of urban sickness. Some will leave again after a few weeks; others will stay and possibly be cured. In this sense, communes are therapeutic. In fact, one of the mottoes of Morningstar, California, had been: Morningstar is remedy. The second wave, people like Cave David, have been here a year or less—long enough to undo the severest hangups.

The first wave of senior communitarians are ready to move on, wanting greater privacy and surer purpose. On the surface, New Buffalo looks transient, but its surface mobility masks the underlying growth of the people who have come and gone. Cave David theorizes that people, like plants, give off healing vibrations to each other and that when people live close to nature, they grow. "The plants are trying to tell us something."

I poked my head in the greenhouse and found Henry bending over his cabbage sets. He looked up as if I were an intruder. Henry is still withdrawn and mutters to himself, but much less than when he arrived. His friends recall that in those days he rarely spoke to others, worked or showed emotion. He has brooding brown eyes and an elegant reddish beard that he teases thoughtfully. Henry dropped out of college after taking on a heavy science program. Before coming to New Buffalo, he'd been shooting up Methedrine three times a day in San Francisco. Here he has found outlets for his natural inventiveness. His first project was to build a windmill generator out of scrap auto parts: a transmission served as the shaft, cut-out car tops as the blades, and generators and batteries hooked up in series that could have stored 500 amps. But the gear ratio of the transmission was too heavy, Henry discovered, so only a rare, strong wind could rotate the arms. Henry has given up the windmill for the time being. "The first priority of community has to be agriculture—the machine drove men off the land and into the cities and we lost our natural sensitivity. We've forgotten that the land is the only true basis for the economy. The only basis for . . . man." As he talked, Henry gently lifted the small seedlings out of their flats and replanted them in larger containers. They must be watered, weeded, set in the sunlight, fed and pruned. In a way, they are his children: "No matter how fucked up I feel in the morning, the plants have to be watered. They tie me into an outside rhythm and they force me to get my shit together."

The imminent departure of New Buffalo's chiefs (the first wave) has disturbed those who will succeed them. For the last three years, George and Justin have led by example. Usually they were first up in the morning, first in the fields, first to decide. Now it will be up to the next generation, they say, to make or break the commune.

This morning, I helped plant strawberry sets in the lower field. It turned out that I knew no less about strawberries than the six or seven others. The only one who *surely* knew what he was up to was Henry, but he muttered to himself, dropped his hoe, and walked away, disgusted about something. Were we leaving too many stones or spacing the mounds too far apart? For almost twenty minutes after Henry left, we stood there directionless. Finally, I suggested that Cave David direct the transplanting, but he refused: "Look, this is Henry's baby, don't ask me." The waste of manpower grated on me, so I continued pestering him. Reluctantly, he began to lead. We resumed planting.

At lunchtime so many people, including a lot of hungry, crying kids, had crammed the kitchen that Mary threw up her hands. "How can we get anything done if you all crowd in here?" And later, "I'm going to call a meeting!"

The unwritten bylaw of New Buffalo is that anyone can call a meeting anytime. It's been a month since the last. Before the influx of people, New Buffalo got along with few and very informal meetings. As the population increased, the meetings became less and less effective: "When you get over twenty people in the circle, it's too disorganized, everyone trying to talk at once." However, a meeting may be the only way to prod the second generation into action—to make them define the commune they want, beginning with the crucial decision of whether to be open or closed. Like the other senior members, Mary had once favored an open commune, but now she's uncertain. "A commune that admits this many people is like bringing children into the world you can't feed." Though she called the meeting, Mary, like the other seniors, intends to stay clear of the discussion and not attempt to affect its outcome.

The second wave is divided but leans toward closing. The newcomers sense a purge in the air and are busily making alliances or checking out the road maps for their next destination.

Some visitors, particularly the women, have assured their position in the commune by diligent work. Like a frontier town of the wild west, New Buffalo has almost two men to each woman. By taking up the thankless kitchen work, Anne and Marilyn have automatically secured quasi-membership. Marilyn's standing is even firmer since she moved in with Larry, who has been here a year. But for most of the men visitors, there is no work or place. As for my status, I've let everyone know that I have no intention of staying. I've contributed to the communal kitchen, given money for gas, and bought Tonio's wine. "As long as we've got wine, you've got a room," Tonio guarantees.

Fell into conversation with Justin about the state of the cosmos. More specifically, it had something to do with how the yin and yang forces of history would eventually culminate

(the apex of Piscean duality) and woooooosh! usher us apoca-
lyptically into the Aquarian Age of Oneness. I think we were
high. As we talked outside the room, Joanna began to fry vegetables. Justin invited me in for dinner. Justin, Joanna, Milan,
two, and Michael, two months, occupy a 12-by-10-foot room
furnished with a wood stove, a plain table, and a cradle suspended from the ceiling. Mary was napping in the one bed.
She had converted her own room into a sick ward for visitors
who had come down with dysentery and had no place to sleep.
Justin and Joanna's room is a composite of styles, "with a little
of plastic Americana mixed in," quipped Joanna, nursing
Michael (who had been born with a harelip). She pointed out
the metal Sears & Roebuck high chair, a Hopi papoose carrier,
and a Spanish sarape. "But I think of myself as an American,"
she said. Joanna was reared in Stimpson Beach, a middle-class
section of San Francisco. In college, she was influenced by
Sartre's negative existentialism and made the Venice, California,
beat scene. "The beats rejected America outright—and so did
we when we came here. How can you get any further from
white middle-class America than trying to live like an Indian?"
But the experience of the last three years has moderated her
and Justin's philosophy. They accept some features of American
life, "like the fact that my baby's harelip can be fixed surgi-
cally." The operation will cost money and will bring them back
into the system, for Justin plans to get a job, his first in ten
years. In a number of other ways, they've come full circle.

Justin, tall, tanned, pins his long black hair under a blue
stocking cap. He's in his early thirties. His beard is carefully
trimmed over a long angular jaw. For the last week he has lived
in jeans and a red zippered jacket. When I looked at him—perhaps it was an optical illusion created by the dimness of their
room—two faces seemed to flash off and on: one the face of a
restless outlaw, the other the face of a resigned holy man.

Justin said he was born in Colorado, the last in a family line
of gamblers, bank robbers, deer poachers—lawless frontiermen.
Four years ago he was down and out, living in a San Francisco

hotel room. He jogged around the city, writing notes to himself that would remind him to eat. He served time. When he got out of jail, he and Joanna headed for New Mexico, where they heard land had been sold for a commune. I get flashes of the old Justin—the outlaw, the con man—but the main impression is of a man who has found inner peace. He moves, thinks and talks as though our most trivial concerns were steps in some slow upward movement. "It's all getting better. We can't see how, our egos interfere . . . but we're all going to make it." I would like to know how he's reached such equanimity.

Joanna rocked Michael in his cradle, and Justin threw handfuls of wood chips into the firebox. Due to overpopulation, the woodpile had been nearly exhausted. "There are enough chips to last a year, though. . . . That's one good thing." Like Frost's philosophic ovenbird, Justin can make the most of a diminished thing.

"At first we felt bitter about leaving New Buffalo. We resented all the people who'd crowded in. But now we see the truth: We *should* leave and give others a chance."

Like many communes, New Buffalo started out as one big unstratified tribe, everyone was under thirty, had few possessions and kids. The commune seemed immune from straight society's social divisions which tended to segregate young people into cities, young marrieds into suburbs, and old people into retirement homes. Now a split has developed between the generations.

One of the senior members' complaints is that the dinner gong can ring anytime from 5 to 8 P.M. "Adults can take irregular meals, but a late dinner can knock out a child, and a mother too," said Joanna. Justin and Joanna live next to Jim, and the wall between their rooms often resonates to rock "which is groovy, except at night. If you don't get enough sleep, your kids are still going to wake up at dawn."

They've been cooking their own dinners now for two months. "I simply got tired of trying to satisfy the tastes of forty different people. For a while we were into macrobiotics * and didn't feel like eating spaghetti and Safeway hamburger."

Food stamps were another reason for their decision to leave the communal kitchen. "I'd take a job now rather than food stamps. Once I make enough money, I can always quit my job, but the stamps are demoralizing and addictive."

Their immediate plans are to build an addition to Michael Duncan's house on the mesa (Michael Duncan is the owner of an entire mesa, four miles to the west of New Buffalo, where Morningstar and Reality are located). "We'll have a two-family house with a common room in the middle for peyote meetings. . . . It won't exactly be a community, but we need some time to digest all the changes New Buffalo's put us through."

Dropped into George and Joyce's. I helped them sort the rocks from a bowl of beans, one of New Buffalo's customary chores. They are leaving for many of the same reasons: irregular meals, overcrowding, and the threat of attack by Chicanos. Last week they withdrew their kids from the public school rather than endanger them during their two-mile walk to and from the commune. Two years ago their kids roamed freely. Now they've had to pull in the parental reins. "I don't want other people giving alcohol and candy bars to my kids." Another reason for dropping out of the communal kitchen was to bring their own family closer. "For me the evening meal is a lovely, close time to talk. . . . I believe that you have to spend time with your kids. . . . I don't believe in the Summerhillian bullshit that children can grow up to be happy and creative without a mother and father of their own."

George described himself as a conservative and no longer a hippie. "When we came to New Buffalo, we questioned why

---

* The macrobiotic diet, limited to rice and other grains, doesn't seem to have held up on the commune. After a few months, Justin and Joanna discontinued the diet, feeling that it was nutritionally deficient. In general, vegetarianism was yet another ism that fell by the wayside after hippies moved to the commune.

society has laws and customs—like monogamy. Now I know why and I dig it."

March 20

Today I sought out Big David. If it comes to a purge, Big David will be a figure to contend with, and a formidable one at that: a lean 6 feet 8, dressed in black—black pants, a black wooly vest and furry black astrakhan hat. Around his neck hangs a Hermetic cross.

"After I tripped, I left the Angels," but not before losing two upper teeth in a biker's war. During the summer of 1968, he was one of the prime movers of the People's Park project in Berkeley. "One day I was out on Telegraph Avenue throwing rocks at cops who were just aching to shoot somebody's head off, and I stopped and said, 'Man, this is insane.' " Was the city really *worth* liberating? Many, including David, thought not and headed for the Southwest to reclaim what land in the United States was still worth reclaiming.

Barbara, his old lady, is two months pregnant and has lent a domestic touch to their room: curtains, a swept floor, a neatly made bed. I had the feeling that Big David was also being domesticated. "With the baby coming, I don't want New Buffalo to become some sort of freak-out ward. It's gonna be our home."

In Berkeley, he fought to liberate land; now, in New Mexico, David uncomfortably finds himself fighting for a closed commune, to keep his new home from being overrun by urban refugees. The contradiction eats at him. "We all came here as visitors. I don't have any right to tell anyone they can't stay."

During the conversation, I brought up my uncertain status as a visitor, explaining that I wanted to stick around for a few more days and would then split. If a purge ensued from tonight's meeting, could I be spared? Big David looked pained. "Look, I don't want to be the heavy—sure you can stay." For most of his life, he'd been "warring with the pigs." Now, the roles were reversed. Being the commune's unofficial lieutenant weighs heavily. "I had a dream the other night that me and Barbara had been hitchhiking and were tired and lost. And we found this commune and walked up a long road. At the end this guy blocks the way and tells us to split. The guy . . . looked like me."

The impending showdown has freaked Tonio out. He knocked off several bottles of wine this afternoon. Drunk, he accosted Walter in the kitchen and accused him of using his blackness to camouflage personal inadequacies. "You go around whispering how everyone discriminates against you when you know that the chicks won't ball you because you're just a jive-ass punk. It's not because you're black, I'm sorta dark myself, its just because you're a jive-assed punk," Tonio repeated.

For a while, it looked as if the meeting weren't going to come off. A house divided cannot get a meeting together unless someone pushes. And no one was. Big David, losing heart, was whispering for an adjournment. Mary, who called the meeting, was standing clear: "It's for the new people."

From a few years of covering council meetings and legislatures, I had learned something of political timing; if the meeting weren't held *that* night, the handful of members who wanted to stay and work for New Buffalo would leave. By default the commune would become just one more hip watering place. Drunk as he was, Tonio seemed the only one who could get the meeting going. I told him that. His black eyes, which seemed to have been floating, fixed on mine; he scratched his head, wrapped his sarape close, and staggered off to rout people out of their rooms. His sidekick, Doug, followed. I could hear Tonio bellowing, "Dammit, *tonight,* Jim. And you're coming if I have to drag you. . . ." In a short time, the circle had filled. Six kerosene lights had been placed one by one in the center. Doug rang the gong.

The first to speak was Big David. Standing in the center, he cast a gargantuan shadow on the cavelike walls. "Look, I'm a desperate man. There's a problem here. Too many people. Now this place can handle about twenty-five. Few of us did anything to build New Buffalo. People like myself who came last fall and helped with the harvest—we don't want to kick anybody out. That's the scene we left. You're all brothers and sisters. But all of us *can't* live here. And you have as much right here as me. But there's not enough food, not enough space on the floor. So how do we decide? I've been on the run all my life. I've never had a home. I've lived on street corners, in a different pad every night. This is the first place I've wanted to call home. And now I see it being destroyed. My old lady and I have been out on the highway, and we know what it's like. We're going to have a kid, and I don't want to have to leave. But unless some of you people split, you're going to force us to go back on that highway. That's why I'm a desperate man."

Silence as Big David's eyes moved around the circle, coming to rest on Crazy Jim, who wore his usually vacant smile. Big David's long arm shot out, grabbed Crazy Jim's shoulder, and pinned him to the wall, "Do you understand what I'm saying now?" A chorus of voices: "Let him go, he's freaked out." Confusion. To maintain order, someone proposed they select a chairman to recognize speakers one at a time. Ira, a senior member, was unanimously chosen. Mary, beside me, whispered, "That's the most we've accomplished in three years."

Next, Justin spoke. "The danger is as much outside as inside. This used to be a working farm. The Chicanos saw us driving down the road in a truck loaded high with *lotillas*. They saw us out plowing, working the irrigation ditches. But now they see hippies out in front of the general store eating sardines out of cans and bumming change off anyone who comes by. They know that it was a visitor from here who ran into that old couple's house." (Last month, a visitor on a bad acid trip took off his clothes and ran out into the night. No one gave it a thought. However, he ran to the nearby house of an elderly Chicano and his wife, breaking in while the couple was watching TV and smashing their furniture and TV set before disappearing into the night. Later, members of the commune raised money to cover the damages, but the worst damage—to neighborly relations—was irreparable.)

A major argument advanced by most of the people who spoke against a wide-open commune was ecological: The land could not support fifty people. "We're the last on the irrigation ditch. When the rainfall is light, we'll be the first to go dry." They pointed out that the commune could grow no more than the rainfall allowed. Nature imposed a natural limit on its population. Others spoke of the negative vibrational environment created by too many people in too small a space. They were no longer a family that could fit comfortably into the circle before dinner. George observed that most of those in favor of the open commune were at that moment getting stoned in Jim's room. As long as they didn't participate, it made little difference *what* the rest decided. "If there's just one person here who takes it on himself to tell a newcomer, 'Stick around, nobody can force you to leave,' we don't have consensus. Someday somebody's going to walk up that road who's going to say, 'Stick a gun in my back and tell me to get off of *your* property.' He'd force us to use violence and then where would we be at?"

Finally Jim spoke. A closed commune was a surrender to the fears and anxieties of straight society. Again he cited Woodstock. "When we were thirty people, some said we were too big. Now we're fifty, and everybody's being fed, everybody has a place to sleep. If we only have trust and faith, there'll be enough. What are we, some kind of country club? Don't you know that people are freaking out in the cities?"

George: "There's all kinds of land in the United States. If people are really interested in community, they'll do it on their own. The thing is to discover it yourself, if it means starting your own commune, not by moving into a room with twelve other people and a stereo. . . ."

Jim: "We could have five hundred people on this farm. As long as we had love. The food would take care of itself."

George (sarcastically): "You mean food stamps would take care of the food."

Jim: "It's all subjective. There are some people who *can* adapt themselves to living twelve in a room."

Mary: "Then why did Candy, at the first opportunity, move

out of your room to get into the tepee? She wanted to be alone."

Tonio accused Jim of turning New Buffalo into a hippie ghetto. "You want us to start building high rises out of adobe?"

Jim (resentfully): "This isn't accomplishing anything. You're not able to love very much."

Mary: "You're the one who can't love. You don't have anything to do with us. You stay in your room all day with your own group. If you really loved the rest of us, we wouldn't have to drag you out to the meeting."

Justin: "I think I understand a little how Jim feels. Three years ago, I was on the side of the group who kept the commune open, though I didn't agree with Bob all the time, and I wasn't as conservative as George, who wanted to keep us closed. I still believe in an open community, but now it's more as an ideal to reach for, not something we can do today or tomorrow. We have to wait till a lot more people in this world begin thinking of the earth as the *whole* earth. We have to grow, and so does the rest of the world. We can't change the whole world. That's why we left politics behind. Getting just twelve people on the same wavelength is difficult enough. Surrounded by miles of sagebrush, it's easy to forget the rest of the world hasn't evolved as fast as we have. We have to accept where the Chicanos and the cops and the rest of the world are at. But being aware and accepting doesn't mean we're copping out or allowing ourselves to be stamped out. We can't import all of Haight-Ashbury to New Mexico and still serve as a model. Yet we can't cut ourselves off—we need new people. And we still have to believe the world can be changed for the better. But we start with ourselves."

Silent acceptance followed Justin's speech. He hadn't seen the issue as an either/or choice of mutually exclusive options, an open or closed commune. After a long pause, the next to speak was a newcomer from Berkeley. Her voice had an academic ring. She had heard "a great catharsis of emotions," that had not produced any consistent policy or screening process for new members. She was angrily shouted at. When the meeting settled down, George tried to explain to her, "Can't you see that until some of you leave, we can't get it together as a family to make any *kind* of decision? You have to leave first."

Big David circled the room like a caged panther. "Who's going to leave?"

I got up: "I'm going to leave" (in a few days, true). Slowly, about twenty-five others got up, leaving about twenty seated.

Big David was astonished. "I'm really happy, people. Thank you very much. You good people have just saved my home." The meeting adjourned, happily.

Over the next two days, about thirty visitors departed, including the leader of the open-commune faction, Jim, who headed back to California in a Volkswagen filled with boxes of Bob's records. Big David nailed a sign high on a pole outside the gate: NO VISITORS, UNLESS ON BUSINESS.* To my surprise, New Buffalo had pulled itself together.

March 21

Overnight the harsh northeast wind has died. The day is warm and still. With the visitors gone, there are just twenty-five here now, a comfortable number. The older members have emerged from their sanctuaries. I am getting to know them. Joanna has brought Michael outside into the sun and is feeding him an Indian "formula" of rice, groats and wheat, the consistency of porridge. Joyce seems more relaxed. She spent part of the morning in the kitchen with Marilyn, the two of them singing as they cooked, alternately filling the lines of folk songs: "When I first came to this land, I was not a wealthy man. . . . So I got myself a wife. . . ."

Larry returned from the post office and called the mail. An overdue notice from the liquid-gas company was read aloud. "We need to make some money," someone said.

In the kitchen, much roomier now, Richard was grinding flour and Mary was diapering Nancy, who lay placidly on the

---

* Characteristically, the "unless on business" loophole allowed for a great deal of flexibility, but the long-range effect was a significant reduction in the volume of visitors.

kitchen table. The kitchen floor—dirt like all the rest—needed raking. First I doused it with water to keep down the dust and then simply raked it, gathering a large pile of butts, wrappers and other trash discarded by the now-vanished visitors.

At the table Cave David observed, "Overnight the vibrations in this place—woooooooowwwww. The level has gone down." He let fall his hand as if it were a barometric gauge of the commune's vibrations. They were once more a tribe. The place had regained its easygoing pace, the natural rhythm of a large family.

The unmuffled sputtering of the tractor signaled that field work preparatory to spring planting had begun, however belatedly. One by one we went out and volunteered. The tractor was being warmed up by Larry, one of the second wave. Until now, he's been uncertain about staying, but because of Marilyn, he might stick—good for the commune if he does, since he's one of the few who can operate, as well as repair, the tractor.

From his high perch on the green and white John Deere 1020, Larry explained that he wanted to spread the huge mound of compost manure over the fields. We leaned on our shovels and watched as the teeth of the tractor's hydraulic scoop dug under the compost heap, lifted, swung around, and dumped its load on the flatbed cart. When the pile had risen to about three feet, Larry motioned us onto the cart. We rocked and bumped our way to the field. Before our slow, rattling advance, prairie dogs scurried for cover to the entrance of their holes, where they paused and periscoped their little brown necks at us, then darted out of sight.

For years, the prairie dogs had been the only residents of the land, which was then a stretch of eroded gullies and arid soil that could only support sagebrush, snake-grass and piñon. The last owner, a rancher, had overgrazed it. Sheep and cattle had clipped the grass to the ground; as the grass withered, the soil lost its water-holding capacity. Soon the topsoil washed away. "Before the white man came to the Southwest," said Henry, who was sitting on the cart beside me, "can you believe that there were trees and grass all around here?"

The land's new stewards were reversing the cycle of poor land management. They had filled in the gullies with stone and gravel. Through careful irrigation, plowing and terracing, they had returned twenty acres of once-unproductive land to cultivation, which last year yielded hundreds of bushels of corn, beans, wheat and a great variety of vegetables. They had renewed the land and the land had renewed them.

We began broadcasting the compost onto the field. My shovel overturned the ghosts of the compost pile, a winter's garbage. Shoveling alongside me was Doug, who shared Tonio's room. He came here on his third escape from a Michigan reform school to which he'd been committed for car theft, armed robbery, breaking and entering, and drug possession. "My psychologist told me I was incorrigible," said Doug, laughing and flipping the hair out of his eyes. In reform school, he learned how to blow safes and hot-wire cars. At New Buffalo, Doug has turned his ingenuity to better purposes. He has repaired some of the trucks and done leathercraft and yoga. He is violently loyal to his new home. Yesterday two "Apaches" were contesting the new restriction on visitors. Doug picked up a tire iron and threatened them. They split.

Riding back on the cart, I asked Henry if the composting restored enough nutrients to counterbalance those removed by cultivation. He was certain the land was gaining each year in fertility as the commune's collective shit was plowed back into it: the droppings of the farm's ten goats, two cows, three horses, twenty-eight chickens and six turkeys. In addition, they plan to compost shit from an old outhouse. "It's safe if you let it stand for two years. The Hopi and the Japanese use human shit as their main source of fertilization." He and Cave David are designing a biodynamic compost pile. Cave David explained: "First, you have to grow herbs and plants like yarrow, oak bark, stinging nettle, and dandelion. Compost them, add earthworms, then an enzymatic mixture that catalyzes the decomposition. There are several on the market. In a short time, you've made a rich compost pile that's forty percent higher in nitrogen and trace minerals."

Communes like New Buffalo are discovering cheaper and safer substitutes for chemical fertilizers. They have also tested natural substitutes for pesticides. One is simply following a live-and-let-live policy toward pests like the prairie dogs, consistent with the communal philosophy of reducing man's control over nature: Like other animals, man should take only his share from nature and return something, too. Unlike the local farmers, New Buffalo doesn't shoot or poison prairie dogs because they feed on the corn. "Sure, they destroy some, but we have a lot of corn to go around," said Henry. Their neighbors dust their apple orchards with DDT. The New Buffalo people simply eat their apples, worms and all.

In the case of one predator, the Mexican bean beetle, the hip farmers, like those of High Ridge Farm, had to devise natural forms of extermination or risk their entire bean crop. During a tribal meeting on the problem, Rodney proposed spraying rotenone, a relatively mild pesticide. Unable to think of natural controls which would succeed, George proposed plowing the crop under and replanting. Henry pleaded for a day to devise an ecological insecticide for the thousands of inch-long yellow bugs. He rigged up a hand-pump sprayer and tried dusting the beans with a mixture of ground onions and wood ashes. Undisturbed by the mixture, the bugs kept munching away on the juicy bean leaves. At his wit's end, Henry proposed the only other alternative: to pick them off by hand, one by one. It took the entire commune a week. "You had to kneel down and pick each bug off every leaf and crush it between your fingers. Everybody came in for dinner with yellow hands." But they saved the beans.

The wind carried the sound of the lunch gong to us. After a morning of hard work, even lentils would taste good. We tramped through the back kitchen door and lined up at the sink to wash. "You all smell like shit," said Joyce, who was at the sewing machine.

"Anyone want a bath?" Joanna rose gleaming and unembarrassed from the tub. "The water's still warm," she said. The utility room, partitioned from the kitchen by a wall of vertical *lotillas*, houses the one bathtub, a hot water heater, a galvanized washtub, and the sewing machine.

"If nobody claims it, I'll take it," Tonio answered. "Do you come with it?" Joanna shook her wet hair no and strolled outside to dry in the sunlight. Taking baths at New Buffalo has to be casual. When there were sixty people around, few used the tub. Now that they're down to twenty-five everyone wants to.

After lunch there was a siesta and relaxation hour. In the kitchen, Henry decanted homemade beer by sucking on a plastic tube. A few spoonfuls were tasted and pronounced groovy—Al. To celebrate the return of New Buffalo's good vibes, the domestic beer would be broken out tonight.

I sat against the sun-warmed adobe wall reading Frank Waters' *Book of the Hopi*, one of the books that had inspired the first generation to move to New Mexico. New Buffalo was beginning to look like a tribe again. Under the hot sun, some had taken off their clothes and moved around easily.

George emerged grease-covered from the viscera of his truck. He, too, was less uptight now that the hordes had gone, and he was less pessimistic that the second wave would blow it. Momentarily, he admitted, the ship of fools had righted itself. "The truth is, the older people like me are standing in the way of the younger people learning how to farm." When Indian tribes went through similar divisions, he said, two groups, or clans, just split up and moved peacefully away. It was a form of natural spacing.

George swallowed the last of the coffee and flipped the grounds into the yard. First one sharp-eyed chicken spotted the scattered godsend and came pecking. Then a second, third, finally a dozen wobbled toward us like a flock of old ladies chasing a bus. They pecked away sociably at first, but as the supply dwindled feathers flew. The stronger hens, wings upraised in rage, chased the weaker away from the last few grounds. The pecking order had taken over.

Sputter, sputter: The tractor announced the end of siesta. The shit-shoveling crew reassembled. We shoveled steadily for the afternoon, but working as a group was efficient and sometimes fun. Leonard told a long story of how he'd taken an overdose of Jimson weed in jail and nearly died.

The work seemed naturally synchronized. Standing at the top of the heap, Leonard used his hoe to push the compost toward the cart, where my shovel caught it and swept it over the field. Each of us performed a different job, like the individual members of some gigantic manure-spreader organism. Synergy is the word that explains why it was more than six times as efficient for the six of us to do the job. Justin recalled that in the brickyard, when the pueblo was being built, five men could easily produce five-hundred bricks a day, but one man working alone "would have to break his balls to make seventy-five."

The kids hopped aboard the cart. Chris, ten, George's oldest son, rode behind Larry, eager to learn how to drive the tractor. Maureen's daughter Andrea, nine, hung onto my belt for fear of falling off. Michael, eight, swung his legs off the rear. They began to cheer: "Hip, hip, hippy!" Like most kids reared on communes, they were caught in the cultural crossfire. They were proud to be the children of hippies, and yet when they went to public school, the boys had cut their hair and Andrea dressed conservatively.

On our last run out to the fields, as we bumped toward the sun hanging low over the gorge, each strand of Andrea's hair seemed to stand out as if on fire. Chris was operating the tractor alone now. Larry detached the cart, and we walked back toward the pueblo, the day's work done, in the chill of dusk. The sun struck flatly against the rough adobe walls. The muddled pieces of straw shone like gold.

It was the evening hour. Each day at this time, the men gathered outside the greenhouse to watch the last minutes of the sun's slow descent. The talk and laughter were subdued. From the open kitchen door wafted the smell of frying vegetables and the clatter of women preparing dinner. Out in the field, the tractor groaned. Chris was plowing the fresh compost into the expectant earth. George was proud. He kidded Larry: "I hope you taught him how to stop it." Henry suggested that tomorrow we had better get the peppers sown in cold frames. There was quiet assent. It was about time.

In the gathering dusk, the new moon, a baby's curl, had appeared. Beneath it, Venus seemed to wobble like a pearl set in blue gel. Larry's high-pitched voice sounded quaint, a parody of a homespun farmer's: "Think the moon's in Cancer. Should be good for plantin'."

There was plenty of room for us to form a circle before dinner. We could see one another's faces, and no one had to stand behind a beam. "Thank you, Lord, for this day," prayed George. "It has been the day we came together again, Lord. Thank you for the work which brings us together. Thank you for the good earth ready to receive our seeds. Bless all the people who left here, Lord. May they travel safely and find their dream of the good life. May they have the strength to build their own community. . . ."

Even the food seemed tastier (or was it the heavy work?): tortillas, chili sauce, squash, beans, and for dessert, apple pie. Afterward the homemade beer. Now that the crowd had gone, the smoke circulated freely and the gong announced smoking in the circle. Even the lamps which had been hoarded were brought out. Late into the night, ghost stories were told. When the Bugler can ran dry, someone tried rolling dried spearmint leaves: "Not bad, better than a Kool." The beer was drunk to the last yeasty drop.

March 22

Sometime after dawn, the gong rang in the new regime. The night before there had been a meeting of second-wave people— Henry, Dave, David, Torah and Tom. They had decided on an early rising and a breakfast of eggs served in the fields to promote group planning and work. Today, I couldn't make it to the dawn breakfast. A mean wind whipped across the plaza, and I walked backward against biting clouds of dust. Alas, no food for late risers. The group was down in the lower field planting strawberries. I joined them. Walter wandered by, playing at being straw boss. "What you-all doin'? . . . Why, that's not how. None of you was raised on a farm." He was ignored. No comebacks—because that was exactly what he wanted. No one complained that he was the most idle and obnoxious person on the commune. Like Reuben at High Ridge Farm, Walter was New Buffalo's cross to bear. Finally he walked away. Although the commune would not expel him, a natural form of exclusion was at work.

George came down to help with the strawberries. It was too windy for him to work on the engine. George and his group would never have thought of planting strawberries, which weren't among the staples of the Indians: corn, beans and squash. The second-wave people were more diversified, and in more areas than agriculture. Generally they are less uptight about men performing so-called women's work. They are willing to make do with less technology; they've considered selling the tractor to pay off debts, and instead of the chain saws, they prefer to use two-man crosscut saws. While some of them have severe hangups, they are less burdened by the romanticism of the commune's founders. They have learned from the mistakes of their predecessors. There are no handbooks to follow. From day to day they are working it out by trial and error and evolving their own traditions, policies and precedents.

Dietetically, the emphasis was off corn. There was a new demand for greater nutritional variety. Though they had subsisted on a diet of corn, beans, and brown rice for two years, George suspected that the children were lacking some important nutrients. Despite an otherwise healthy environment, they were plagued by too much unexplained illness. Michael had birth defects; Cedar had been premature; and Mary suffered from a series of ailments. "We had the Navahos' diet," said George, "but the Navahos were resigned to a forty per cent child mortality. It was a population control. Our cultural conditioning puts more importance on the life of the individual than the tribe, and it's hard for us to accept the death of a child."

In the kitchen I offered to spell Joyce, who was operating the kernel-stripping machine. She declined, saying she enjoyed the task. The first year, the women spent hours shelling the purple and white Indian corn as squaws had done for centuries, tediously scraping one ear over the other above an earthen pot. Again, they were determined to follow Indian tradition. But after five months of this tedium, when somebody located a hand-operated machine that could shell ten ears in the time it took to do one by hand, there was no argument about purchasing it.

Joyce put four cobs into the machine's throat. She cranked the handle and *woooosh*, the cobs were pressed through a gullet of small metal teeth that stripped off the kernels. They fell into a compartment below. The cobs were tossed into a brown crock marked "organic."

Joyce asked me to grind some cornmeal. I used both hands to grind the large dried kernels into a meal of soft purple dust. Mary tested it. "Too coarse," she said, and so I ground it again. Later she rewarded my efforts with a plate of cornmeal roasted in peanut oil. Freshly ground, freshly roasted, its sweetness and pleasantly grainy texture surpassed anything General Foods could package. Mary listed the other corn dishes on the commune's menu, including tortillas and posole, a chicken dish served with cooked corn that has been bleached white with wood ashes.

At New Buffalo and communes everywhere, a lot of effort, thought and discussion go into the preparation of food, not only because it's a common need, like clothes or housing, but also because food can be a direct vital expression of man's relationship to the whole life cycle. Significantly, George had once proposed that the commune be named Corn.

On the stove, a pot of a steaming, opaque solution bubbled. Henry was making the commune's first batch of corn syrup. I dipped a finger in. The mixture was getting faintly sweet. Henry was also developing a method of extracting oil from peanuts and sunflower seeds. He'd read about making corn oil but concluded it was too industrial a process. I went outside with Mary and her baby to bring in the laundry, holding Nancy while Mary took down the diapers. She has an appealing Mother Courage quality. She said she was going up on the mesa to build a hogan. "It's time for me to be alone." I couldn't understand why. She was too beautiful and alive to become a hermit at twenty-five. Wouldn't she miss the community? "No, I shall have Nancy, Chloe and some chickens." Had community life worn her down? "No, I just don't need other people so much anymore."

We had filled the basket. The smell of rain blew in on the wind as we hurried back. I am too much of this world, and she is prematurely of the next, I thought.

Again a lunch of warmed-over lentils. For once my taste buds, conditioned by my early years of eating Snickers Bars, rebelled against what my mind knew was nutritious. So I headed for the village, ostensibly to use the pay phone at Celso's. Tonio and Suzanne came along. We walked down the rocky hill and past a farmhouse, where Chicano kids were dribbling a basketball in among the chickens on a dusty court. As we passed, they stopped playing to jeer, "Hip-pee, hip-pee." Last night they threw rocks at the Volkswagen I was driving down to Celso's.

The road wound with the gurgling Arroyo Hondo. The little stream was now cresting with the water which comes off the snowcaps and is eventually carried by the brook into the Rio Grande. Its banks were lush with watercress. Sandpipers leaped and tweeted. Halfway to the village, we passed a wide, flat area that serves as the local car wash. A Chicano was washing his big Camaro with brook water. He took a draft from a can of Coors and stared at us.

Celso's is the local tavern, carry-out store, bus stop and phone booth. We were early enough in the afternoon to avoid a lynching. Six men from Morningstar thronged the bar, drinking shots and chasers like Pittsburgh steel workers. Celso, the proprietor and bartender, has managed to turn a profit from both

Chicanos and hippies. During the morning and afternoon, hippies patronize the bar; but from five to closing, it's Chicano turf. Even the jukebox is culturally partitioned: to the left, all rock music; to the right, Spanish.

We didn't stay long. The three of us were in the midst of a passion for zu-zus. (Zu-zus are plastic food, high in carbohydrates and preservatives, *e.g.*, Fritos.) On the way to the general store, we confessed to each other our ugliest repressed desires. Suzanne craved sherbet, cold and sweet; Tonio a salami and cheese sandwich. I wanted a Snickers Bar. And so—who would ever know?—we bought a loaf of bread baked from *bleached* white flour; a salami containing goodies like sodium nitrate; a package of American cheese, each slice wrapped in a plastic slip of its own (only in America); a jar of gooky sandwich spread; a half dozen Snickers Bars; and a pint of sickly sweet pineapple sherbet.

Stealthily we took our bag of zu-zus across the road to the brook and down out of sight beneath an embankment. We didn't care about the Chicanos; it was the disapproval of our communal peers we were desperate to avoid. Tonio swabbed great gobs of the spread on the cheese and salami. After weeks of dietary celibacy we fell lustily from grace, the all-American zu-zu way. God, it was great.

Guiltily we stole back to the commune, passing the sherbet among us. "What I really like the best," Suzanne said, giggling, are those little bits of synthetic pineapple."

Back at the commune, we guardedly doled out the Snickers Bars to the other zu-zu freaks. I slipped one to Maureen who immediately pocketed it. Later, I spied her leaning up against an adobe wall, out of sight, nibbling away. It was not long ago that we were all guileless suburban children of the Pepsi generation, who ran Pavlov-like to the tinkle of the Mister Frostee bell. It takes us some time to break the cord.

Time for some penitential work. I helped Cave David construct a new bin for the compost. We dug down a foot, then covered the floor of the hole with a layer of moldering sawdust and wood chips. Then we sank posts in the corners and began nailing boards across. "If we don't enclose it, the chickens and goats will scatter it everywhere," Cave David said. There was plenty of scrap lumber, but nails were scarce. However, some of the boards still contained rusty, twisted nails. We set up a nail-recovery operation. I used a crowbar to pull and pry; Torah, a blonde, buck-toothed girl from Vermont, hammered them straight. "Probably enough nails in dumps to keep all the carpenters in America busy for years," she remarked. "Except straightening isn't profitable."

"It's more profitable to use up all the iron and metal resources and let the iron foundries pollute the air and streams," said Cave David, who hitchhiked to Taos on Wednesdays, the day of the garbage pickup, to rummage through the cans from supermarkets and return with bags of wilted lettuce, bruised apples and soft bananas. I told the others of an Oregon commune I'd briefly visited that supported itself by operating a junkyard. The members earned most of their money by reselling auto parts and by salvaging copper, brass and other valuable materials. In addition, they put together their own fleet of cars and trucks and outfitted themselves with refrigerators, furniture and baby carriages—all rescued and then repaired from tons of junk which others virtually dumped at their doorstep. "Unless we start recycling our junk," said Cave David, "Buckminster Fuller estimates that the United States alone will exhaust the world's resources in twenty years."

We were watching the sunset light show when the Volks sputtered up the hill. George, who'd gone into Taos to pick up some truck parts, was at the wheel. He alighted hastily, leaving the car door ajar. "They dynamited the Hog Farm," he shouted, breaking the evening's gentle spell. About forty miles east of us, the Hog Farm is one of the country's oldest communes, renowned for its mobile troupe, who travel from coast to coast in buses, staging happenings, feeding rock festival crowds, and ministering to bad-trippers. Two nights ago, around 2 A.M., a bus had exploded and burned in the commune's yard. The explosion embedded pieces of metal on the side of an adobe building where people were sleeping. But that was just the lead item in George's report of violence: In nearby Penasco, a house rented by hippies had been set on fire, and a sports car bombed; luckily no one had been hurt. And an old footbridge spanning the Rio Grande, to connect a hip farm with the highway, had been burned down. At the Ponce de Leon hot springs some longhairs had been shot at, and one wounded in the leg, by snipers who were apparently using .30–.30 rifles with telescopic sights.

Not all the violence had been Chicano against hippie, George continued. There had been an intracommunal brawl among two hip groups at Lorien Retreat, a commune near Questa. The patron of the commune was Chick Lonsdale, the wealthy head who'd endowed his own foundation, Lorien Enterprises. The foundation owns and manages three facilities in Taos: a free clinic, the Taos General Store, where organic foods can be bought at the lowest possible prices, and an Information Service to direct thousands of itinerant hippies to food, and shelter.*

When Chick left the commune to go on a vacation, he put its management and $5,000 in the hands of a deputy, Skip. Then a group of malcontents who'd left the commune a year ago returned. They didn't dig Skip, with his new money and power. One day they demanded he hand over the money to buy forty fruit trees. Skip said that the sum was too large—fruit trees planted last year had died of neglect—so how about enough for twenty? No, they answered, and began lobbing furniture through the farmhouse windows. Rounding up the women of the commune (the other men were away), Skip tried to flee with them in a car. He pulled a rifle to cover their flight. The malcontents wrenched the rifle away from him and were stomping him to a pulp when the men returned and pulled them off. Skip was hospitalized. His attackers, under the threat of criminal assault charges, left the state.

---

* Later one night, someone riddled the windows of the Information Service with bullet holes. The windows were left that way—riddled—as an ominous greeting to any more hip newcomers.

The sun had disappeared by the time George had finished his account, and a solemn chill fell over us. "Man, the shit's really coming down," someone said in the twilight.

Someone else replied, "Yeah, from all sides."

March 23

Toward noon a couple trotted up the hill, dropped their bags on the plaza, and reported they'd just been attacked down the road by a gang of drunken Chicanos. They had gone for his girl, the man told us, and yelled something about draft dodgers and welfare. While the girl made her escape through a field, he had exchanged blows with them and then followed her. The Chicanos threw rocks and struck the girl on the arm. She showed us the purple bruise. "If I can find their car, I'll blow it up," the man threatened.

"That's all we need," Justin answered softly.

Told that the commune was closed and given a knife for self-protection, they headed back to the main highway on a seldom-used road. Soon members of the commune returned from town with similar reports. Leonard had walked to the post office to see if his relief check had been forwarded from California. On the way back, a car had forced him off the road. Jill, who makes a regular morning trip to the general store, was pelted with rocks from a passing car. Open season on hippies has begun, someone said darkly. From the corner of the pueblo, Tonio yelled that cars were massing at the gate. Sure enough, a line of six had stopped at the foot of the commune's road, two hundred yards away down a slight rise. They stayed there a minute or two, honking their horns. Then they slowly drove off toward the gorge. "They might be planning a surprise attack from the ditch road," Tonio said and went off to alert the others.

George was unperturbed. "They won't hit us in the daytime. They know they'd get their heads blown off."

Like most communes in New Mexico, New Buffalo had a small stock of weapons—three or four shotguns, some .22's, and revolvers. No one dreamed they'd be used for anything but hunting, until recently when the hip subculture's deteriorating relations with its Chicano neighbors reached the flash point.*

Instead of enjoying tonight's sunset, everyone was tense and kept glancing nervously down the road. Tonio had distributed the guns. Big David asked, "Do you ever have the feeling the Arabs are out there ready to attack our kibbutz?"

During the circle prayer, George said, "Dear Lord, we're having trouble in this valley. Help us, Lord, to keep it cool."

March 24

Now that the scores of visitors and drifters have left, some members were beginning to voice their discomfort about living inside a closed commune. Last week, Cave David had carped about city visitors' "speedy vibrations"; now it was the "negative vibrations" generated by exclusion. "Maybe I should go back to Morningstar," he pondered aloud.

Enforcement of the "no visitors" rule depressed Big David, too. This morning, while working on the new compost bin, I looked up and realized I was being photographed. The visitor had simply disregarded the sign. Soon he was informed by Big David that he had to split. "But, brother," he pleaded, "I've come all the way from New York."

"OK," said Big David wearily, "take a few shots, stay for

---

* Generally, the problem was not the commune's making, rather that of the hundreds of hip drifters who pissed on the streets of villages, shoplifted from small stores, and defied both health and traditionally modest Spanish morality by bathing nude in streams used for drinking. After leaving New Buffalo, I discussed the rising hip-Chicano conflict with Norman Feldman, director of the state division of community development in Santa Fe. He traced the violence to the extant tradition of the lawless West, the "authoritarian" personality of the Anglo and Spanish businessmen and politicians who seemed to be condoning the attacks on the hippies, and the breakdown of the *patrón* system—the large family farms. "The young Chicano doesn't care about inheriting a piece of the family land and scratching out a living. He doesn't listen anymore to his father, the *patrón*. His girlfriend tells him they can't get married unless they have enough money for a concrete block house, a color TV and a washer-dryer. And so he gets on the first bus to Albuquerque. When he comes back, if he does at all, he's no longer Spanish. To the older Chicano, who sees his sons and daughters drifting away, the hippie is a symbol of cultural change, a terrible acceleration of it, a rejection of all tradition. . . ."

lunch, and split." When the photographer went the other way, he added, "I'm getting mighty tired of making the speech . . . I wish other people would help out." But most members avoided the duty of routing the visitors. No one wanted to close the gates —all the way. Despite the sign, they remained half open.

This afternoon we planted peppers in cold frames. I kept running between the greenhouse and kitchen to fill a five-gallon can with water. Suddenly, Joyce ran by, skirts lifted: "Heat's coming! Heat's coming!" Up the driveway came two big white cars bearing state emblems and wagging long antennae. Henry scurried around the greenhouse to cover the seedlings, and others shot off in all directions to batten down the hatches. The cars parked in front of the kitchen. Out of one stepped a tall bearded man in jeans. "Cool it, it's only Van Arsdale," someone said. Officially, he was Minor Van Arsdale, a caseworker for New Mexico's Health and Services department: in practice, the state's token hippie bureaucrat paid to advise the state government on New Mexico's growing minority population of longhairs.

In April, 1970, the U.S. Census Bureau identified 3,314 hippies in New Mexico, half of them in Taos County. Of that, the bureau isolated 1,000 living in communes, a high estimate, I think. No one in state government knew how the Census Bureau arrived at its definition of a hippie. Of the total hip population, there were some 52 welfare cases—or 4 percent, compared to a 5.2 percent case rate for the general population.

Van Arsdale was here as a guide for a delegation of building and health officials making an inspection of communes. George led them on the tour. One by one they went into the six-hole outhouse, pushing open the door in which a folksy crescent moon had been cut. Van Arsdale, who was already familiar with the commune, stayed behind.

He is around forty, has a full red beard, a high furrowed forehead and sports a Meher Baba button. I first met him while in Santa Fe at the state offices of the Health and Services department. It hadn't been difficult to figure out which of the desks on the floor was his. He had hung a large Sagittarius poster on the wall. The side of the desk bore a sign: REVOLUTION, the *R* covered by an X to spell EVOLUTION—the key to Van's newfound spiritualism.

Ten years ago Van Arsdale was doing graduate work and teaching anthropology at the University of Colorado, from which he'd received his AB. From there, he went to Berkeley, taught at a free university, and was one of the first to drop acid: "In those days [1962] it was pure Owsley acid. It was like any new revolution. We wanted to turn on the world." But Van has since given up drugs and looks back on the flower-children years as an acid fantasy. When the fantasy popped, the flower children gave way to sick kids who'd been seduced into a treacherous hedonism. "If all that feels good is right," said Van Arsdale, "then why not spear a Vietnamese child on the end of a bayonet?" Van compared the drug experience to being launched on a vast uncharted sea of sensation. "You're sailing out there on a sea of all-possibility, where everything can be pleasurable and nothing right or wrong. If the devil is groovier than God, you worship the devil."

After he converted to the philosophy of the Eastern mystic Meher Baba he renounced the "polymorphous perversity" of drug-intensified sexuality. "My wife [his third] and I hope gradually to become celibate. But it will take time."

Van believes communities are making a parallel conversion from drugs to spiritualism, and from loose and anarchistic forms to greater organization and purpose. "You can't sustain a community on the drug vision—it's too sensual and leads off in too many different directions. Only by getting beyond the ego and the senses can we find a common basis."

Van planned to quit his job and devote all his energies to building a spiritual "biotechnic" community. Meanwhile, his main concern was the rising vigilanteism, which he believed was being triggered by itinerant gangs of hippies he compared to the Manson family. One gang of longhairs called themselves the Black Banditos and hid out at the Ponce de Leon hot springs, indiscriminately robbing tourists and fellow hippies. They were the group that George had told us about in his violence report, unaware that the Chicanos fired "with some justification," ac-

cording to Van. Another gang of so-called hippies had raped a
Chicano girl in Taos. "If this keeps up," he said, running his
fingers through thinning hair, "*I* may even get a haircut."

Meanwhile, a small crowd had formed around George, who'd
locked horns with the head of the state contractors board, a
chunky man in plaid pants and large sunglasses. They were
arguing about the outhouse. The state was going to require
communes to install flush toilets. George was incensed: "In
this country, where water is gold, that's just stupid; man, every
flush wastes three gallons . . . are you going to require migrant
labor camps to install flush toilets, too?"

"No, they're farms."

"Well, we're a farm."

The big sunglassed head shook negatively. "You're a multiple
residential use," he said.

Walter drifted by. "Hey, man, you sound like some California health inspector; you know, don't you, that's how they're
getting rid of all the communes in Mendocino."

A more conciliatory inspector intervened: "Except for your
outhouse, we're not worried about you people. You're hard-
working and peaceful. But I can't say that about all the other
thousands of young people coming into New Mexico and who
will be building shacks and other substandard—"

"What's substandard?"

The inspector explained that under the "national building
code," which the state legislature had ratified a year ago and
which his agency had just begun to enforce, new buildings
would be required to provide 90 square feet of space for each
resident, and a certain number of windows and doors, ventila-
tion shafts, flush toilets and foundations 4 feet deep.

"Foundations!" exploded George. "You don't need foundations in this country, the frost never goes that deep. Why, the
Taos Pueblo was built without foundations and it's been standing for centuries."

The president of the state contractors board shook his head
again, saying, "We don't make the laws, we just enforce them,"
and climbed into his air-conditioned car.

March 25

This morning the truck from Reality was parked at the faucet filling its five water barrels. I wanted to visit both Reality and Morningstar, two communes that occupy opposite geographical and philosophical ends of the mesa to the east, so I hitched a ride. In the front rode Jasper, from Reality, and Michael Duncan, who owns the mesa. I bounced in the back among the water barrels.

Two years ago Duncan liberated the land and invited members of Lou Gottlieb's besieged Morningstar in California to come to the mesa and carry on their "open land" primitivism. The second year a band of young revolutionaries arrived, recruited in New York and San Francisco by Max Finstein, who'd been disgusted by New Buffalo's apolitical, spiritual atmosphere. They called themselves Reality. Nowhere had I found such diametrically different communes so close together. On the north end was Morningstar: mystics, winos, runaways and hermits. At the south was Reality: Weathermen and outlaws who warned visitors away with rifleshot. The two communes represented the extremes with which the movement had begun: the political revolutionaries who'd gone through communes like Bryn Athyn, and the children of faith and fantasy like the family of Oz.

The truck whined in low gear as it climbed the road Michael Duncan had blasted up the side of the mesa at a cost of thousands of dollars. We passed through several gates, the last padlocked. Finally we crawled over the edge onto the great table. Nothing in the immediate perspective distracted the eye from the 360-degree vista: On one side, the mountains hung over us, immense and wooded; on the other, the placid, quiltlike valley; and beyond, the vast stretches of desert, blocked by a few buttes, trailing off into the dusty horizon.

Michael Duncan, his wife and child live between the two communes in a round house, which had been built by Taos Indians he hired. It is thatched and adobe-plastered, set on a jutting piece of land over a deep ravine and looking as if it had been transported from Tibet. After delivering Michael's water,

Jasper and I drove over to Reality. At first glance, it appeared more orderly than New Buffalo. No junked cars; wood stacked neatly in piles. Even the adobe bricks of its pueblo walls—one long building of ten rooms and a single communal kitchen and dining area—stood out in clearly defined rectangles. Jasper connected the barrels in the truck by hose to the empty barrels inside the kitchen. While the water ran from one barrel to another, we talked of Reality's brief history.

Max had led them to this mesa, convinced the Fascist-police state that was about to take over America would surely exterminate all its young radicals. Here they could safely resist and launch liberating forays into the surrounding country. They called themselves the Reality Construction Company. The first summer they worked with the zeal of a revolutionary cadre to move 85 tons of earth, from which they mixed, molded, and baked bricks for their own use and for sale. They plowed, terraced, built goatpens, workshops, garages, raised chickens and goats, and made continual wood runs into the national forest. In one great leap forward, the commune was built. But the revolution didn't come. Nixon wasn't overthrown by the Joint Chiefs of Staff. Moreover, they were rebuffed by local Chicano members of the Alianza Federal de Mercedes, the revolutionary movement intent on reclaiming thousands of acres of federal land in New Mexico, who assert that the land belonged to their ancestors before the Mexican War of 1846–48.* In the face of this, Max decided to split to Israel, where he hoped to find a truly revolutionary movement in the kibbutzim. "American youth are too soft," he later told me at his going-away party. "They're not prepared to make the necessary sacrifices."

Inside Reality's kitchen a young man in a University of Wisconsin sweat shirt looked at a plate of beans and moaned, "We're never going to get out of this place. Nixon is going to keep com-

---

* Paralleling the communitarians, a half dozen farmers in the Tierra Amarilla vicinity formed a cooperative and began to farm three hundred acres communally. It is one of several cooperatives being tried by Chicanos throughout the Southwest.

promising while we sit up here eating *beans,*" and he shoved the plate away. Then he brightened. "Can I have one of those eggs up on the shelf?" Jasper's old lady, Chris, turned from slicing dates into a bowl. "No, those are for the fruit bread." Without food stamps, she observed, they wouldn't even have the dates.

That brought a snarl from David, an angry young man, who lacked front teeth. "We should get off those fucking stamps; they just tie us into the system."

The sweatshirt: "Not until I get used to beans for breakfast, for lunch and for dinner. I go farting around all day as it is. Isn't there a spice you can add to take out the gas . . . ?"

"Coriander," said Chris, adding, "You're right, David, we got to get down and scratch a living off this land."

"We can't do it overnight," said Jasper. "We spent a childhood eating plastic food. First we have to overcome that. Then we need some protein. But before we can increase the goat herd we got to get alfalfa growing, and a barn built."

By maintaining a strict closed-door policy, Reality has held membership to around twenty-five, two-thirds of them men. They have even expelled some members. Last month, they expelled a self-styled Chicano revolutionary, actually a mixed-up Puerto Rican junkie from New York, who shot up New Buffalo and raped two college girls who came to study the life-style at Morningstar. The first year Reality got a reputation for advocating violence. "But we don't feel as angry as when we first came up here," said Jasper, a poet, who'd fled criminal charges in Minneapolis. "We're a strange bunch. Most of us are outlaws. But the whole West was settled by outlaws. We're strong individuals. And the less political we get, the more our anger gets turned against one another."

With a few exceptions, political communes have been short-lived. Partly, it's the nature of politics. An SDS commune in East Lansing, Michigan, was split into bickering factions, one pledged to the Peace and Labor Party controlled by militant blacks; the other more traditionally New Left. A revolutionary commune in Canjilon, an isolated hill town forty miles to the northwest, was set up by several ex-Motherfuckers, some of whom had passed through Bryn Athyn. They'd settled in the heart of Chicano country, hoping to ally themselves with the leaders of Raz, the revolutionary land-reform movement. But the Raz leadership distrusted the Motherfuckers, as they would all other middle-class Anglos. After six months the Mother-fuckers disbanded, some of them vowing never again to pack a gun. The country had pacified them.

I left Reality and set out for Morningstar, walking across fields that until recently had been farmed in common by the two communes. Reality and Morningstar were now feuding. Where Reality kept a steady population, Morningstar's had climbed to around eighty. No boundary separated them; legally, all the land was Michael Duncan's. The original understanding was that Reality and Morningstar would cooperatively farm the land. Last summer, when Morningstar didn't get around to planting its side, Reality appropriated it. Later in the season, Morningstar people began to rip off Reality's corn, and Reality reacted by driving off poachers with rifle fire aimed a few inches above the corn silk. Reality accused Morningstar of wasting water from the common irrigation ditch and of needlessly cutting down the mesa's few piñon trees for firewood. Reality gathered its wood from the national forest to preserve the trees on the mesa for The Revolution. Jasper explained, "When we don't have any gas to get out, that's when we'll need the piñon to stay alive."

Thrown up helter-skelter over Morningstar's side of the mesa are tents, hogans, tree houses, and junked buses. The one central pueblo contains about a dozen rooms. The land is open, and people can live anywhere, anyhow. That the rooms in the pueblo have been claimed and occupied as private is not seen as a contradiction to open-land philosophy. The human animal, like other animals, must stake out his own territory.

Lou Gottlieb once said, "The land selects the people." Consequently, this Morningstar includes a random assortment. There is the "Professor" and his sidekick, Tim, who spend the greater part of the day guzzling diet drinks—they insist the cyclamates get them high. Jason, who wore an embroidered robe, had just returned from Texas with a supply of peyote. "I stood very quietly and listened for Mescalito (the messenger of Peyote) to guide me to it." He is a folk singer, who once performed at Fillmore West in San Francisco. Today, he sat strumming Blake poems he'd set to music: "Little Lamb Who Made Thee?" and talked of leaving Morningstar. "Every man must find his own religion . . . it means going off alone." There were a lot of young girls with kids. The atmosphere was happily chaotic. Kathy bore a black eye. Her old man, Joe, had beaten her up, again. "He drinks too much . . . I should leave him, but I can't."

The commune's spiritual mentor is Byron, a soft-spoken man in his forties, who was once a high-paid science consultant. Now he is a leader of the local Native American Church. He wore gold-rimmed glasses, Indian moccasins and a beaded deerskin vest over a button-down shirt, and invited me to have soup in the kiva. On the way we stopped at his room, which he currently shared with ten others. "Everything here happens seemingly by accident, you see, but it's *supposed* to happen that way. . . . Today, two visitors showed up and laid enough money on us to buy a truck. They said, 'God bless you,' and split. We're not uptight about visitors. Most of them go away without being told. Some can't hack living out here"—he motioned to the panorama —"where there's no corner drugstore. Only those who have a real reason stick."

We entered the kiva by ladder from the top. The ladder's five rungs represented the stages of the world in the Hopi cosmology. A solid ring of people were inside, surrounding a huge pot of steaming soup. Most of the smoke rose through the hole in the roof. "You've heard that Morningstar is open," quipped Byron. "Well, here's our wide-open spot." There was a middle-aged man who in an effeminate voice talked to the group of starting a commune in a bomb shelter on his land in Missouri. A girl, very black and wearing a shaggy muskrat coat, passed around a box of Zonkers. Her old man, who was white, kept repeating, "Does anyone feel like getting some wine?" as if the bottle might descend through the hole in the kiva in answer to his wish. Several beardless teen-agers looked scared. A very young girl wore a Girl Scout uniform bearing the emblem of a Mill Valley, California, troop.

When I got back to New Buffalo, George asked me what I thought of the two communes. I hadn't spent enough time at either to make a good comparison, I said, but from what I did see, Reality would be the one to survive, if indeed a holocaust came. Overall, Morningstar's joy and disorder appealed to me only slightly more than Reality's grim paranoia. It wasn't much of a choice, I told George. Hopefully communes will find some middle ground between the two extremes of surviving and aspiring—the delicate balance for which New Buffalo groped—coexisting *in* the world but not totally *of* it.

Tonight I was restless. I read some Robert Frost, and for the first time on this trip, I wished myself back in Vermont. All the rooms were dark except for a dull yellow light in Mary's window. "Come in," she answered my tentative knock. She was also reading late. Beside her on the bed, wrapped in blankets, Nancy slept. "Would you like some hot water?" She went to the stove. "I've given up tea . . . I find that hot water is enough to keep my throat from getting dry at night."

Mary didn't care for Frost. "I guess it's because I'm less involved with the material world." In the last year, Mary had detached herself from the community, material possessions and human love. She had become too dependent on men, she said. In the first year of the commune, she had several lovers, one of them Ira (now with Maureen), Nancy's father. "The first year, we all believed that we could love more than one person. It's true, but loving just one person requires great selflessness . . . and sometimes I think human love isn't enough."

She spoke again of her plan to build a hogan and support herself and Nancy by baking bread and selling it to the Taos General Store. Her retreat from the world, I told her, was an unnatural, unhealthy denial of her own beauty and capacity for love. She answered, "I want a love that transcends man. I need human love so much that the only way to get beyond it is to do without it. I want to learn to love God. When I do, I'll come back."

She found a passage of the book she'd been reading, a collection of poems by the Indian poet Rabindranath Tagore:

> Comrade of the Road,
> Here are my traveler's greetings to thee,
> O lord of my broken heart, of my leave-taking
> And dawn, of the gray silence of the day fall,
> My greetings of a ruined house to thee,
> My guide
> I am a wayfarer of an endless road,
> My greetings of a wanderer to thee.

I walked for a while under the stars thinking about George, Joyce, Justin, Joanna and Mary and why they were giving up the community into which they'd poured their sweat and blood. They were not leaving, I began to see; they were going beyond, heading down the road to spiritual discovery. Mary had said that the single most important thing that had changed her life at New Buffalo were the Indian rituals, "and I can't tell you any more than that. You don't talk about it."

March 28, the day before Easter

Left New Buffalo with a friend to attend a peyote meeting at another commune. As we drove he spoke of the first peyote meetings he'd attended. "We were ignorant of the ritual. Everyone just went off on their own trips." Indians from the Taos Pueblo began attending the hip meetings and instructing them. The Indians were members of the incorporated Native American Church, which has claimed constitutional protection for its use of peyote as a religious sacrament.*

---

* Though the religious use of peyote can be traced to the Aztecs, the Native American Church (NAC) dates from the late nineteenth century, when cultists banded together as protection against legal harassment by Indian agents and Christian missionaries. Estimates of its membership vary radically, from 30,000 to 250,000. Some anthropologists and psychologists have asserted that religion has its origin in the mystical experiences of small groups, similar to NAC,

It was a clear night. We stumbled around the mesa looking for the meeting place. We found it at around ten o'clock. Homer was outside the tepee gathering cedar for the ceremonial fire. Inside some twenty people were seated in a circle all swaddled in blankets; they parted to give us kneeling room. Sprays of cedar boughs hung from the tent poles. Homer was acting as "Fire Man," a position of honor and responsibility. His duty was to keep the fire burning with pieces of cedar, within a crescent-shaped ridge of sand. A furrow ran from one end of the ridge to the other, as if someone had run his fingertip through the sand. This furrowed ridge symbolized the road of life.

The service began with a prayer smoke performed with strict obedience to ritualistic detail. The only tobacco that was permitted by the church's peyote tradition was Bull Durham rolled in Cornhuskers. Bayard was the first to roll. He presided over the meeting and was respectfully referred to as the "Road Man"; his word was fiat. He took several deep drags, raised his head, and exhaled the smoke upward to rise toward heaven with his prayers. Next to smoke were the two other officers of the meeting, Homer and Crowley, who was the "Cedar Man." The bag of Bull Durham and Cornhuskers went slowly around, followed by the charred end of a cedar log. Homer blew on the log until it glowed red and each of us lighted our smokes from it.

The Bull Durham tasted strong. I prayed for a good trip in this life and the next. After the smoke, sprigs of sage were passed. Like the others, I broke off a piece, mashed it between

who ritually took natural hallucinogens including *Amanita muscaria*, a mushroom. In *Chemical Ecstasy: Psychedelic Drugs and Religion* (New York, Sheen & Ward, 1969) Dr. Walter H. Clark compares the characteristics of the NAC to religious separatists throughout the ages—the early Christians, Francis and his followers, the Albigenses, Waldenses, the early Quakers and the Sufi movement: ". . . All, in one way or another, have discovered within themselves that universal river of ecstasy from which flowed the energy, power and refreshment to revive religious bodies tired out by too much intellectualism, moralism and institutionalism. An integral part of the cultic ecstasy of the peyote Indians and an unmistakable evidence of an intense religious life is their willingness to defy the law and to endure harassment and persecution rather than give up what to them is central in their religious practices." (p. 87.)

my fingers, and rubbed its fragrance over my neck and face. My friend whispered that I should take an extra piece; it was good to sniff in case of nausea.

After the prayer smoke was finished, Bayard spoke: "All conversation must be through me. No one can leave the tepee unless I say so. I hope you can all wait until midnight water. It's important that we keep the circle unbroken. If we loosen one link, the chain of energy is weakened. Everything must be passed clockwise. No drugs are to be used. There is an old saying of the peyote masters: 'Be very careful, be very careful.' "

Bayard gave Homer detailed directions on how to build up the fire, instructing him to rake the glowing coals into a smaller crescent within the sand. Now and then, Bayard would turn to Crowley and ask him to perform his function. Crowley would rise, wrap his blanket around him, and sprinkle water on the fire. As the steam rose, he took a handful of cedar berries from a pouch and tossed them on the flames. An aromatic smell of cedar permeated the tepee.

Homer carefully collected the butts of our prayer smokes and buried them in the ridge of sand. Bayard brought forth an earthen bowl containing the peyote. Eyes closed, he began to eat small pieces of diced peyote, consuming in the course of a quarter hour about fifteen of them, the equivalent of two and a half buttons. Peyote is a small cactus that grows throughout northern Mexico and in parts of Texas. The small buttons of the cactus, fleshy protuberances about the size of a quarter, contain a hallucinogenic compound from which organic mescaline can be synthesized. According to Indian belief, peyote's effect is the work of Mescalito, a spiritual messenger of enlightenment sent by God, comparable to the Holy Ghost of Christianity.

Homer raised the bowl and prayed. After he had eaten, he fell forward and prayed some more. Then the bowl made the circle. I ate about ten pieces. They had the consistency of soggy cucumbers and tasted bitter. I had to force the last three down. When the bowl had made its first round, we began to sing the chantlike songs that would last the night.

In his left hand the Road Man grasped a staff topped by eagle feathers. Whoever held the staff received the mystical power of Mescalito. In his right, he held a rattle, which he shook in time to the rapid beat of the Cedar Man's small, tightly stretched drum. The peyote songs, passed on by oral tradition, are composed of meaningless sounds. At first, I could hear no pattern, melody or grace in them, but as the night went on and the drug took effect, the high whining chants sung to the same insistent beat assumed a hypnotic beauty. A few of the songs were in English. One, sung in a plaintive manner, went:

> We are so tiny,
> We are so small,
> We're hardly anything, anything at all.
> Fish in the ocean,
> A grain of sand,
> We're all God's children,
> Come and hold his hand.

Another was sung in the rousing spirit of a hallelujah:

> I wanta thank ya, Lord, Thank ya, Lord, Thank ya, Lord,
> Thank ya for the pey-o-te way . . .
> I wanta thank ya. . . .

Bayard went outside and brewed a tea of the peyote juice. He returned, drank some, and passed it around. I gulped three cups, careful to do as instructed and keep the handle turned away from my mouth, toward the center of the tepee. The tea left a resiny taste. Close to midnight, I felt a revolution brewing in my stomach. Since childhood, I'd fought the natural reflex of vomiting, as if it were death. Others had already vomited, calling for Homer to bring them the "puke can," a half-gallon tin that still bore an Imperial Peas label decorated with fleur-de-lis. Across from me, Lois fell on all fours, head over the can. She retched and heaved, giving up a greenish opaque liquid that was strangely beautiful in the firelight.

I was the last. By now I had realized that vomiting was an act of faith, as well as humiliation, a relinquishing of the will, a yea-saying to death, a graceful letting-go, a small crucifixion. Our small shared suffering was the first step on our journey together:

We would reach the same ultimate place by different routes that intersected at points of suffering.

Afterward I felt purged. I realized that the others were experiencing the same new sense of inner cleanliness. We were closing the circle; our trips were coming together. Someone asked Bayard if he could read from the Bible, but the rest of us said we felt the reading would be inappropriate. We all knew what the Bible said and meant. We had no need to hear the words anymore because we were living the Biblical experience.

I closed my eyes for a moment. Aztec designs danced on the walls of my retinas. Like the news board above Times Square, a thousand bulbs lighted up in succession. But when I opened my eyes, all the psychedelic effects disappeared. In the darkened tent, the pulsing coals and licking tongues of the fire commanded all our visual attention. As I kneeled and chanted, the upper half of my body swayed involuntarily. Though a draft of cold night air blew in below the flap behind me, I experienced no chill.

Bayard halted the songs. Before midnight water, it is customary for a man to give a prayer. Bayard selected Homer, who retold the story of the Crucifixion.

". . . And they made Him carry the cross up the hill. And there they took nails and drove them through His arms." In the firelight, Homer's face contorted with remembered pain. "Oh, God, how could you let them do it? How could you have let them take your Son and hammer nails through his legs and his hands?" Sobbing and cries filled the tent. Someone cried, "Oh, Christ, we killed you!" Homer continued, "You didn't have to send your Son down here to die, but we kept asking for a miracle. We wouldn't believe, and He hung up there suffering to show us that we all are to be reborn." Some of his listeners wept convulsively. Others simply gave affirmative grunts—ugggggggh, Indian style.

It was time for midnight water. A pail and dipper traveled around. It was the appointed time to go outside to piss. One by one we asked Bayard for permission to leave. I wondered why he kept such careful track of how long each person was outside:

"Homer, check on Parker, he's been out too long." After I had gone outside, I understood. The stars closed down over my head, a canopy that drew me in every direction at once. I took a few steps—ah, the night of infinite wonders and sensations. I could wander forever on this high altar under the stars . . . suddenly the insistent beat of the drum caught me up short, and I remembered the Road Man's ancient warning to initiates: "Be very careful, be very careful. . . ." The drum called me back to the center, the fire which cast long shadows on the skin screen of the tepee and unfurled orange sparks against the blackness. I hurried back, too frightened to linger any longer, fearing I'd wander off in some unknown direction, perhaps to plummet down some dark ravine. And so it is with all our trips, on or off drugs. We speed outward from the center, like centrifugal particles propelled from the primal bang of creation.

The night seemed to pass quickly, praying, chanting, smoking. I had entered the tepee a stranger to most of the people there. Now I seemed able to read each individual's emotions and thoughts. We became solicitous of one another's comfort. Without asking, I could tell that the young man beside me was cold. I put the spare blanket over his shoulders and he accepted it, unsurprised. Our songs became more harmonious and sychronized. There seemed to be a third presence in the tepee, who kept our beats together. When I tapped the drum for Homer, I knew precisely when he had come to the end of his song, "Who Am I?". We stopped on the same beat.

Our prayers became more personal and confessional. Lois prayed to have a child, to be worthy of a child; she had been a poor wife to John, she said. She had been unfaithful, and she had been unforgiving of his drinking. But Christ would forgive her. . . .

More than I had expected, Christ entered into our thoughts and prayers. No other prophets were mentioned by name—not Krishna, Buddha, Mohammed. Only Christ. It was not surprising, since many of us had been reared as Christians, though we had rejected most of the Church's creed and morality.

We prayed for the children of the commune: "May they

grow up in a better world, Lord, may they grow to be strong."
Pam prayed for greater patience and tolerance for newcomers.
"I have been too self-centered and possessive, Lord. Open my
heart to all the new people. Teach me that I have nothing to
hold onto." John asked forgiveness for hitting Lois and for
drinking.

The night seemed charged with symbols. Bayard asked me to
look outside for any sign of dawn. I couldn't believe my eyes:
Over the hump of mountains edged with powder blue sailed a
comet, trailing blue and pink strands. It was in a direct line
with the opening of the tepee, the fire, and Bayard. I reported
the sighting. Bayard restrained his surprise: "It is a good sign."
But he forbade any others from going out to see the comet.

As dawn approached, Homer raked the ashes into a shape
directed by Bayard. In the distance, an owl hooted. "It's Mescalito coming to speak to us," whispered Homer, kneeling, his
head cocked. He raked the ashes into the shape of a dove, its
wings unfolded, plummeting down: "The mourning dove, the
dove of Christ." Through the smoke hole of the tepee, we could
see that the sky had now lightened. It was time for morning
water. Ritual prescribed that a woman should offer a prayer.
Bayard selected Lois. She knelt and prayed: "In the morning,
the women came to the tomb where they had laid him. And
found the door open. But He was gone, and an angel appeared
and told them that the Lord is risen." The folds of Lois' blue
dress glowed in the morning light, and her face was suffused
with suffering and beauty. She was the bringer of water, the
renewer of life. She was to be counted among the women who
had come back from the tomb and brought the good news.

The fire was dead. The sky was light. Outside, we heard the
low tones of the commune's women and children, who were
waiting to enter with the morning feast. Bayard told them to be
admitted. The young mothers, madonnas of the morning, carried in the children who awoke and rubbed their eyes. None of
them cried. The mothers were those who would bring a new
generation to carry on life, those who had always carried on life,
no matter how long the night of history. They brought food—

roasted cornmeal and fruit served in paper cups. Reverently, I ate the fine, purplish cornmeal.

After breakfast there were some last prayers before the meeting ended. The first to leave, I raised the flap and took a step out into the world, then lifted my head to the east, toward the mountains and the sun rising above them. I was blinded and stunned. In my blindness, I shook with sobs. I took a few tentative steps to adjust my senses. Why, the world had been created again! Another day. The sun again had risen. Lois and I embraced. We had emerged from the long night of our past and our sins. Our outer and inner vision had been purified and cleared. So this was *real!* Like the others, I knelt toward the sun, which burned gigantic crosses across the sky. "The Lord He is risen indeed." Then I wandered through the mesa's high grass. About a half mile away, across a ravine, a girl was hanging sheets on a clothesline. They fluttered in the wind. It was Easter morning.

March 31

The Volks crested the hill. Someone yelled, "Look at Ira!" He had cut his hair. "If I'm going to get shot at because of hair, it's not worth it," he said. He, Maureen and Andrea, nine, were leaving to manage a ranch in southern New Mexico. Ira seemed more relaxed. Yesterday he told me that Ira (after IRA, the Irish Republican Army) was a name he'd assumed when he was into revolutionary activities. "Call me Sol, that's my real name, that's who I am," he said.

It was a day of leave-takings and haircuts. Last night Marilyn had sheared Anne's hair. She looked like Joan of Arc. She had decided to hitchhike to the Coast, get a short-term job, and pay off the $300 she felt she owed her parents for college tuition. "Then I'll be free of them." Joyce had cut George's hair. Dressed in his grease-splotched overalls, he looked like the local Shell station mechanic. "The hippie movement is over," he said. "When you have Charles Mansons walking around calling themselves hippies, it's time you cut your hair. It's just an external thing."

The day recalled the Beatles' advice to Jo-Jo: to get back, to where he once belonged. Were they going straight—cutting hair, getting jobs, raising kids? Were they following predictable patterns of the young rebels who returned to the fold after reaching the mellow age of thirty? It looked as though their lives had come full circle. But George, for one, had not come back to the same point. He was not the same hardheaded, embittered atheist who'd abandoned New York City three years ago. An old friend said of him, "George feels things more deeply. He's compassionate and a lot more tolerant."

Justin described the pattern of his life not as a full circle but as an upturned spiral. "It must look from the outside like Joanna and I are going back to the kind of conventional life our parents had. But inside us we're two different people now." He said that the hippie movement appeared to be going back to the nineteenth century. "That's only because we've come around to this point of the spiral"—he moved one hand in a spiral over the other—"that is directly above the nineteenth century. And so we look like the past, but we've been transformed by spirit."

I think New Buffalo's second wave people will make it. For a week now, they've kept up their schedule of early risings. The planting is beginning to catch up with the season. Today they held a meeting in the greenhouse. Cave David had made a map dividing the fields into sections, each labeled for a crop. Three acres of beans and corn, companion crops, were to be planted together row by row. "The corn has long roots, the beans short roots," Henry explained. The beans restore the nitrogen the corn uses up.

The only discussion of the planting plan concerned its grid design. "Why can't we plant in circles?" someone suggested. The idea intrigued Cave David. "You're right, nature works in circles," he said vaguely and went off. In a few minutes, he returned with his black, loose-leafed notebook that contained his diary and selected readings. He called for attention and began to read a passage that he had copied from *Black Elk Speaks,* the reflections of a Sioux:

You have noticed that everything an Indian does is in a circle, and that is because the power of the world always works in a circle and everything has to be round. In the old days, when we were a strong happy people, all our power came to us from the sacred hoop of nature, and so long as the hoop was not broken, the people flourished. The flowering tree was the living center of the hoop. . . .

Everything the power of the world does is done in a circle. The sky is round, and I have heard that the earth is round like a ball, and so are all the stars. The wind, in its greatest power, whirls. Birds make their nests in circles, for theirs is the same religion as ours. The sun comes forth and goes down again in a circle. The moon does the same, and both are round. Even the seasons form a great circle in their changing and always come back again to where they were. The life of a man is a circle, from childhood to childhood, and so is always set in a circle, nature's hoop. The nest of many nests where the great spirit waits for us to hatch our children.

But the Wasichus [white man, foreigners] have put us in their square boxes. Our power is gone and we are dying . . . you can look at our boys and see how it is with us. When we were living by the power of the circle . . . boys were men at 12 or 13. . . .

"Okay, let's plant some of the corn in circles," said Henry, persuaded.

George needed some help taking down the tepees, which he said were a standing invitation to attack. "It'd be easy for the Chicanos to take shots at them from the ditch road or douse them with gasoline and set them on fire." The tepees were a visual reminder of the commune's tribal beginnings. After the first wave moved into the pueblo, the tents stayed up and were used by new arrivals, who in turn moved into the pueblo. Now the tepees were going with the old families and would help them start new lives elsewhere.

The four of us who volunteered to help George walked up the slope toward the tepees. Some were still occupied by visitors who'd managed to avoid the purge. They grumbled when

George told them they had to move out. We pulled the stakes out of the ground, withdrew the tent poles, and unlaced the overlapping folds of canvas. It took all of us on tiptoe to keep the heavy canvas from being whipped around by the wind. We folded each one into a bundle. I carried George's to his room. "I'm looking forward to living in a tepee again," Joyce said as I laid the bundle in a corner. "You have to adjust the smoke flap to the wind and the rain. If you don't, you'll freeze or you'll choke, but it makes you feel closer to the earth. Besides, we've accumulated too many things here," and she motioned to the room's furnishings: handmade benches, a table and a cook stove, and a few books, including *Back to Eden,* a book about herbal medicine. "You feel very free when you don't own anything. I can't wait to get rid of this wood stove."

George came back. He still hadn't decided where they were headed, but he was determined to leave New Mexico, its surplus hippies, vigilantes and building codes. Perhaps they would go to sparsely populated northern Idaho, where there was rich soil and ample water. There, George thought, he might trade in the truck for a team of horses. When George came to New Buffalo, he was the one who proposed using a tractor. Now he preferred the idea of a horse-drawn plow. During one of our long debates about technology, which he thought was inherently depersonalizing and I felt was neutral, George said, "There's an Aztec legend that at the peak of their civilization, they discovered the concept of the wheel. But they suppressed it. They never made a wheel, even though they knew how. They foresaw what it would lead to, that it would be disastrous."

This afternoon Anne and I climbed down the side of the gorge to gather watercress along the banks of the arroyo. I helped her step across the slippery chain of rocks and a green log that was wedged lengthwise across the current. Through the gorge came the same low moan of the wind that Indian hunters must have heard as they waited on the cliffs to ambush deer. They'd left their marks on the canyon walls. I spotted the petroglyphs nearly obscured by a curtain of brambles. It felt as though an electrifying spark had flown across the arc of time. Since 1200 A.D. the Hopi, Zuñi and Pueblo Indians had wandered the Southwest. Wherever they went, they left behind symbolic records of their migrations and spiritual progress laboriously chipped in boulders and the walls of canyons and caves. Ignoring the brambles, we hopped from rock to rock to get a close look. We could make out the figure of a man, arm and spear cocked, and before him a fleeing deer. We also saw several of the ubiquitous migration symbols: a spiral unwinding from its center in ever-widening circles.

We sat on the rocks and pondered the inscriptions above us. The Hopi had seen themselves on a great journey as individual hunters, as migrating tribes, as part of an ongoing natural process. Anne took a small stone and scraped her own symbol into the rockface: a Greek hieroglyph, she explained, that meant "Christ lives."

Springs trickling from the sides of the gorge had channeled out tiny rivers choked with green watercress. The best way to gather it was by tugging the top of one plant at a time so that the thin, hairy roots were pulled free of mud and slime. It took only a few minutes before both our burlap bags bulged with enough for a commune-sized salad. We sat down on a large boulder, where the brook slowed into a deep pool. Anne covered her eyes with one hand and went to sleep.

I watched the pool for trout rises and thought that the notion of permanence was illusory. "But communes never last, do they?" was one of the first questions straights asked me. True, the Oneida Colony had only lasted thirty years, but what could be called permanent in America? Certainly not Manhattan Island, or places like Willingboro, New Jersey, where one can spot a moving van on every other street. Man insisted on building his cities on foundations of steel and concrete, as if they should endure for years. I could see why some men could prefer to live in a community of adobe that could be disposed of naturally; and after the community had become a useless form, to go elsewhere.

We reforded the stream, climbed the gorge, and found the

old entrance to the commune. Barbed wire had been strung over the gate. Beside it was a huge boulder on which the settlers of New Buffalo, imitating the Indians, had left their own migration symbols in white paint and these few words: "Thank you, Lord, for this way."

When we got back, the circle was shaking with drumbeats. Inside we found three Indians: Twin Oaks and two young men, his two sons. All wore blue denim jackets, drank from a bottle of orange juice and vodka, and were eager to teach us Indian songs. It was well to learn the songs, Twin Oaks said. Their magical powers could dispel sadness, evil, and enemies. He and his sons had come to cheer up their "hippie friends," having heard of the commune's troubles with their Chicano neighbors. "Songs and dances bring all people peace," said Twin Oaks, who led us into a winding snake dance, lifting his feet high and throwing his head backward.

People are splitting. Tonight I learned that Crazy Jim had left this afternoon after telling a few people in the kitchen he was off to buy land and farm alone. "He said 'Peace' and left," recounted Mary. "I don't think he's crazy anymore." Walter had also left without a good-bye to anyone. Leonard had taken his little girl, Tracy, hitchhiking back to LA. "There's something telling me I've got to go back there," he said to me the night before. "I don't want to leave here, but I have to." This evening a bus pulled into the commune, EARTH LIGHT painted on its side. It was a mobile theater group on their way back to San Francisco. Anne decided she'd go with them. "Maybe I'll show up someday in Vermont," she said and left.

The after-dinner discussion in the kitchen was about where to go next. How about Hawaii? "There's Banana Patch [a commune], but I hear they're already crowded." How about British Columbia? "You can get landed-immigrant status if you don't have a record" (which disqualified half the people in the room). "Oh, well, don't feel so bad. I hear British Columbia's getting to be another California." Rodney and Travis, two older members who had left the commune, had returned for a vacation before going back to New York City. They planned to stay in New York only as long as it took them to make enough money —through jobs and welfare—to buy land in Alaska. "It's just about the last frontier," Rodney said.

Someone else brought up South America, but Justin warned, "Trouble is, you'd be the only white man and the first to lose your head when the revolution comes down . . . You might as well stay in this country."

Cave David talked of returning to graduate school after the crops were harvested in the fall. He'd discovered that he lacked the basic scientific knowledge—biology and physics—to be able to conduct his vibrational experiments. He would work his way through school. He'd worked before. He'd cut his hair and go straight, take what he needed, and then return and build his laboratory.

After the dinner gong, I joined hands in my last prayer circle. Minutes passed silently before Larry spoke: "Thank you for this day. Bless all the people who are leaving us, Lord. Bless George and Joyce, Justin and Joanna, Sol and Maureen and Mary and little Nancy. Help them find a new life. Bless all those who left us today, help Anne on her way and bring her back to us. We need her. Help Jim find what he is looking for. We pray that you keep his head straight. Help all of them to find peace. And bless those who are going to stay and carry on the way of New Buffalo. We have a lot to learn. Whether some of us stay or some of us go, help us perfect our circle, and may it go unbroken."

Minutes of silence. Then the parting squeeze, "Let's eat," traveled around the circle of our hands, which parted—for a time.

April 1

Today I left New Buffalo. I would return for a short time after making a tour of other communes. Carrying my backpack and sleeping bag across the plaza, I met Cave David and Dennis, lugging water cans that had just been filled at the faucet. Cave David had taken the freaked-out Dennis under his wing and lent him a pair of jeans and an old wool shirt. Without his blue blazer, Dennis had begun to look as if he belonged. He carried his can off to water the seeds germinating in the cold frames, while Cave David and I said our farewells. The commune had unconsciously accepted Dennis—the first of many exceptions to the "no visitors" rule—in the same spirit in which it had accepted Crazy Jim. Both needed to be here. I told Cave David that Dennis was looking less spaced out. "He's coming out of it," said Cave David. "I've seen others in worse shape. He's going to make it."

Yes, I agreed, recalling Justin's cosmic optimism: "We're all going to make it." We embraced. And I started off again down the road.

V
Colorado

Technology, Power, Art and Synthesis, Libre

After New Buffalo I reached a midpoint in my journey. The first half had been spent in the hip communes, where the movement had begun in the middle sixties. Now I was moving outward from this center, following the general trend toward more defined communities.

Until now, I've used commune and community almost interchangeably, but at this point a general distinction must be drawn to understand the evolution of the movement. Typically, communes were made up fairly uniformly of young people who identified with the hip subculture of drugs, rock and voluntary poverty. Their structure was open-ended. Money was to manifest. Work was to do your own thing. Decisions were made spontaneously or by long, drawn-out consensus. Communes weren't established for any one purpose: Their members didn't want to divide the experience of life into narrow purposes and goals; rather, they wanted to restore its wholeness by attaining a group consciousness. Generally, communes involve much sharing and close interaction. During the first years, they resembled tribes—often bunched together in one room, dome or circle of tepees.

By contrast, the community embraced a greater diversity of people, not just the hip and young. Where communes left finances, work and decision to the fickle will of group consciousness, communities leaned more heavily on definite structures: work systems, treasurers, and corporations. Generally, communities were more specific in purpose. Many were united around a single craft or art. Some focused on a Summerhillian school or an Esalen-like institute. Many were limited to a spiritual purpose and organized around a definite body of faith and ritual, or around the authority of a single guru or master. The physical, as well as emotional, distance was greater in a community than in a commune. Traditionally, a community was made up of separate houses rather than a large common dwelling.

The most objective index of this shift from commune to community was the appearance of hundreds of new experiments organized for any number of specific purposes: group marriages such as Harrad West (Book Six), *Walden Two* experiments like Twin Oaks (Book Seven) and a plethora of spiritual communities—ashrams, orders, cults—such as those briefly covered in Book Eight. Another pointer was the many communes that broke up after their first or second year. Significantly, their members did *not* desert the communal movement; rather, they found their way into other communes and forms of community.

I've set up an arbitrary distinction—which, like most, is constantly tempered by life. Harrad West, the group marriage, had the intimacy of a commune but also the ideological, work and financial structures of a community. Wheeler Ranch embraced the open-land mysticism found in many communes and the one-family-per-dwelling pattern of the community.

The distinction is further blurred by a convergence effect that occurred toward the end of the 1965–70 period. A few communities became less formally structured and ideological as they were joined by younger people. However, by far the stronger, more dramatic trend was demonstrated by the communes that evolved toward community structures.

One of the oldest, still thriving experiments, Tolstoy Farm—which began in 1963 as an anarchist-style commune—took the commune-to-community road. Hew Williams, its twenty-year-old founder, declared that eighty acres of land in a wooded canyon near Davenport, Washington, were open for anyone to settle. It was an experiment in anarchism, he said, to prove that man could live noncompetitively without private ownership and the external compulsion of laws. Hew, who as a young man had been influenced by reading Tolstoy and Gandhi, had promised himself never to become attached to material possessions after he lost his prized books and stamp collection in a fire that destroyed his family's home. Later he became a conscientious objector and went on peace marches. Disillusioned as many others were by the political movement, he left the University of Washington to start the farm.

The first summer fifty others joined him, and they all lived under the one roof of an old homestead called the Hart House. Then, around 1966, they felt the impact of the drug revolution. Speed freaks, runaways, bikers and crazies from all over the West Coast heard about the farm. Hundreds descended on the canyon. Hew moved out of the main house and built his own cabin for himself and Sylvia, a girl he met the first summer and later married. The other "settled" members followed suit until the Hart House was abandoned to the crashers and crazies. The most popular version of what is now legend is that the "settled" residents, Hew included, set fire to Hart House and stood around and sang merrily while it burned to the ground. After the transients left, the farm found its present form as a community of separate houses and families, who looked after their own gardens.

Hew amended his anarchist philosophy, acknowledging that the land should be the comunity's determinant.

"Anyone can still camp or live on the land if they find a place," Hew wrote me. "We just don't try to feed and shelter everybody, and we don't hesitate to tell people how we feel about the way they treat the land—fire, garbage, woodcutting, overcrowding, etc. These conditions seem to be pretty effective for selecting responsible people in the long run. The people who don't belong here eliminate themselves voluntarily." At present some twenty-four adults are living on the farm. So far, their main common enterprise is a free school that's attended, off and on, by the community's fifteen children.

Another instance of the trend away from the commune was the Merry Pranksters, one of the earliest and most legendary communal bands. During the flower-children days of the early sixties the Pranksters rallied around Ken Kesey, the novelist, and what they saw as the altruistic cause of dispensing free acid. After making the madcap cross-country bus trip celebrated in Tom Wolfe's *Electric Kool-Aid Acid Test,* they settled down to a communal existence on Kesey's eighty-acre dairy farm outside Springfield, Oregon.

By 1969 Kesey no longer dug the communal arrangement of some sixty crashers and ex-Pranksters living on the farm. "I started developing this thing I called a Communal Lie," he said in a taped interview.*

"There was just a lie in the air. It was not *about* anything, it was just a lie in terms of our existence." In theory, the commune was to be self-sufficient. But Kesey said: "I haven't seen a commune make it on its own terms, where it's making it off its own piece of stuff and it's not having to draw from outside." Another myth he'd seen disproved was communal sharing and cooperation. "What made me mad was that one day I looked for a crescent wrench, and I knew they were here on this farm, but George had his toolbox nicely locked up, Gordon had his toolbox, Babbs had his toolbox, Page had his toolbox, but the farm didn't have no fuckin' toolbox. . . ." Kesey said they'd been unable to overcome their cultural conditioning. In times of stress they all reverted to being like rats who'd been "raised hungry" to selfish behavior: stashing their food and fighting among themselves, instead of facing up to the real source of their tension.

Kesey implied that the real source of stress was spatial. "Like when you're driving on the freeway, somebody'll come up real close behind you and you know it as soon as they're there. When they violate that sense of space, you know it immediately. When people are pressed together for a long time like that, it like

* Michael Goodwin, "The Ken Kesey Movie," *Rolling Stone* (March 7, 1970).

homogenizes them, it breaks down that sense of space. Without that, we don't know what we are. We're into each other's drawers, we're stumbling over each other, and it's like a pad between us . . . and the worse thing about it is that it's with your best friends."

One day, just before the Woodstock Music Festival, Kesey decided he'd had enough. "I'm just gonna kick everybody off, except me and Faye [his wife] and the kids." The crashers went by bus to Woodstock, and never came back. However, some of the original Pranksters—Babbs, Page and Hagen—returned to the Springfield area to resettle in separate houses. Zodiac was the only one to continue living with Kesey and family.

Now Kesey thinks a more conventional community, where heads and straights live side by side, is healthier. It "does something to the people around you. Like they say to themselves, 'Humm, they're just like we are.' " To back up his change of heart, Kesey cited Babbs' "great statement": "We don't want a commune, we want a community."

Communes are born, turn over rapidly, and die. Within the communal movement, the main strand of continuity is the lives of the members, particularly those who leave the commune. The restless ones shuttle from commune to commune. Some go straight—completely and return to society. Others—like the Pranksters and New Buffalo's first wave—resettled in the vicinity of the mother commune, thus establishing yet another kind of community.

An example taken from Book One: Remember the group who threw the I Ching and left Bryn Athyn in Vermont to head for New Mexico? They settled at the Domes, a commune built around three interconnected zomes. They were later joined by the New York chapter of the Motherfuckers. A period of chaos ensued. Finally, the commune was closed down by one couple, who picked up the mortgage payments and bushels of broken glass, moldering glass and human shit. The Motherfuckers went to a house in Canjilon to be in the heart of Alianza country. The others, now paired as couples (many had split up and repaired), moved together into the nearby village of Placitas, taking separate adobe houses and forming a hip community within the framework of a traditional one.

Elsewhere, hippies were moving into nearly deserted towns in Vermont (whose populations had been decreasing since the Erie Canal had opened) and into villages in New York's Hudson Valley, between New Paltz and Woodstock. In California there were prospects of a hip suburbia—the prime candidate being Canyon, a town taken over by hundreds of longhairs and artists.

Possibly, the clearest example of the commune-to-community shift was Libre. It was to be my next destination after leaving New Buffalo. Though I spent only two days there, Libre left a strong impression that later shaped my own plans for a community and deepened my insight into the cultural synthesis toward which all communes were moving. Before resuming my journal with Libre, however, I want to draw together some observations and conclusions that may suggest the general line of the communal movement's evolution.

The first phase of the movement was *implosive,* that is, an escape from the all-pervasive influences of a plastic, fragmented mass society and a return to the primal center of being and man. In the classical utopian tradition, the commune was an island, a free space, a cultural vacuum. It was the ideal situation for spiritual revelation—for regaining the vision of a simpler, unified life and the pristine consciousness of uncomplicated, tribal man. But unlike the desert island, the communes were not naturally surrounded by an ocean to keep the "outside" society at bay. Exiles in their own country, they had to erect psychological defenses against the "outside" by drawing a "we/ they" dichotomy that often verged on paranoia. Erik Erikson, the psychologist, has remarked that American youth needs a cooling-off period, needs to go through a phase of being left alone, free from the competitive pressures of education and career—a kind of decompression chamber. In *Future Shock,* Alvin Toffler observed: "No society racing through the turbu-

lence of the next several decades will be able to do without
[some] form of future-shock absorber: specialized centers in
which the rate of change is artificially depressed. . . . In such
slow-paced communities, individuals who needed or wanted a
more relaxed, less stimulating existence could find it." But
often, the "outside world" of rapid technological change would
not leave the new communes and communities alone; moreover, the umbilical cord linking them with the outside economy
and culture, so easy to ignore in acid vision, proved tough to
sever.

Recurring problems such as food stamps, visitors and technology challenged the communes' view of themselves as islands
divorced from the straight culture. Gradually they had to transcend the "we/they" dichotomy and establish some rough system of priorities balancing other conflicts as well: the need for
privacy versus group unity, feeling versus reason, spontaneous
joy versus order, individual freedom versus group stability.
They had to evolve a value system. Through this slow process,
the open-ended communes moved toward firmer definition of
purpose and identity.

An elementary step in the process was deciding how to make
a group decision.

A main characteristic of the political system the communes had
rejected was the tyrannical nature of the massive majority. In the
decentralized rural society of the early Republic, they felt,
democracy had been possible. Now a mass society of vast metro-
politan corridors had made participatory democracy a matter of
financial and psychological manipulation. Mass advertising, entrenched parties and vested interests were, they believed, gradually alienating the single voter from his role in making most
public decisions. The majoritarian process submerged the
voices and needs of minorities and subcultures and ironed out
shades of political and social dissent into uniform national
choices. Numerical pluralities were satisfied, but few individuals were.

As an alternative to majoritarian rule, the open-ended communes adopted a process of decision making based on consensus

on every issue. Adoption of the consensus method grew out of their sense of political futility, although it was not a consciously political act. It reflected the highest priority of communal life: maintaining group consciousness through the kind of intense, constant communication that occurs in small, close families. In some communes, the consensus, as well as the consciousness, shattered (or never jelled); in others, it worked miraculously well.

Larry Kanevsky, who did the photographs for this book, spent a week with the people of Mullein Hill, a Vermont commune, as they looked around for a farmhouse to rent for the winter. They had spent two summers in tents and tepees, dispersing before the previous winter to cities and small Vermont towns. Now they had made the decision to rent as a family. After looking over each building and barn, the twelve would hunker in a circle and quietly rap until a tribal decision was reached. They kept at it until a farmhouse was found that satisfied everybody.

Other communes failed to reach a consensus that could reconcile extreme differences in temperament. And so people left and new people arrived until a compatible group had formed and a group consciousness could emerge.

As communes matured, they found that the consensus method of decision consumed too much time and energy. However, they did not want to revert to the conventional organization of managers, schedules, rules and committees that would specialize functions and disrupt full and equal participation. A compromise evolved: The group retained ultimate authority and still based long-range policies on consensus, but everyday decisions and responsibilities began to be entrusted to individuals.

For example, one commune spent an evening discussing the problem of how and where to stash the dope (grass and a very few psychedelics). Although no clear-cut decision was reached on the crucial issue of whether or not individuals should maintain private stashes, the long meeting made everyone sensitive to the dangers involved, and it was agreed to appoint a stash master. Some individuals still kept private stashes but now looked after them with greater care. Appointment of a stash master insured that someone would act quickly and effectively in an emergency. The outcome was characteristic: Faced with an either/or decision, the commune elected to have it both ways.

Another example of collective decision making is furnished by the communes that publish weekly newspapers. At first, they tried to make all editorial decisions collectively; secretaries, typists and reporters had equal jurisdiction over headline sizes and story lengths. As the communes learned, deadline pressures sometimes made this impractical. Without forgoing consensus, they came up with alternatives that integrated their decision-making ideal with publishing realities. The branch of Liberation News Service that migrated from New York to Montague, Massachusetts, in 1968 alternated editors every week: One week Marshall Bloom played the tyrant; the next week, the mantle passed to Steve Diamond. Thus the leadership was rotated among the staff, the way ducks take turns flying lead in their V-formation.

Whatever arrangement was devised, it remained subject to change and to the collective will. Communal decision making was flexible; a rule made one week might be abolished the next.

One commune with a kitchen problem posted a sign above the sink, which usually overbrimmed with dirty dishes: WASH YOUR OWN—AND ONE MORE. Soon everyone did it automatically, and the sign was taken down. The rule had been internalized, had entered the group consciousness.

No matter how trivial, the discussions that communes held revealed the larger issues at stake. Consensus forced everyone, as individuals and as a group, to sort through the hodgepodge of contemporary values, beliefs and ideals and out of this chaos to patch together a coherent system of values.

I had just seen how New Buffalo had wrestled with the issue of whether to be closed or open; and how it arrived at a decision —semiclosure—after establishing ecological balance as a communal priority of the highest order.

Similarly, Maureen wrote me that eventually High Ridge Farm had come to grips with the question of food stamps and the related issues: the Vietnam war and involvement with the capitalist economy. They decided against accepting food stamps and faced the fact that without them they would have to earn more cash from outside jobs to buy the necessities they couldn't produce. They elected, however, to take jobs, like gardening, that didn't conflict with their ecological beliefs. Thus the net decision was consonant with two communal ideals: self-sufficiency and enlightened ecology. It compromised them in only one way: Jobs would involve them peripherally with an "outside" economy.

Initially, diet—specifically the meat issue—posed yet another either/or conflict. As people moved to the country, they disregarded the vegetarian's credo. Many were finding through experience that meat was not only a good source of protein, but could be easily produced. Many communes had small herds of beef cattle, goats, in addition to chickens and domestic rabbits. Nevertheless, some members remained vegetarians. The solution was easy enough and reveals some of the communal tendency to resolve conflicts by bridging them: The diet was simply arranged to satisfy vegetarians and meat-eaters alike. When stew was made, two pots were served, one with, the other without, meat.

Another good illustration of this process is furnished by the tools and materials—the technology—that communes selected. In itself, a tool is a symbol that bespeaks its user's attitude toward nature. Technology at once attracted and repelled the young, who looked on themselves as the first mass-produced generation. Technology gave them television and stereophonic rock—nonverbal forms of communication that tied them together in Marshall McLuhan's "global village." Technology also whetted their imaginations by giving them the hope, articulated by one of their mentors, Buckminster Fuller, that a humanized science could ultimately save the world's life-support systems and bring about utopia by insuring food and shelter for all.

The same technology that produced "Better living through chemistry" also inadvertently gave them LSD. Thus biochemistry provided a visionary escape from the cave and speeded their revolt against the whole technological "illusion."

But they had a victim's knowledge of the harm a dehumanized

technology could cause. They had gone to multiversities that had communicated through punched cards and corporate procedures. They had lived in high-rise dormitories like those at Michigan State, which loom above the plains of East Lansing like Kafka's great beehives. They had seen the Los Angeles Freeway at sunset, ribbons of taillights curling over ramps and overpasses, as the sun died into the Pacific through a filter of exhaust. Young people who had grown up in such a nightmare revolted more from the viscera than the mind.

Those who sought exile in communes initially rejected technology *in toto,* making little discrimination between the tools that liberated and those that enslaved. They went back to the past for tools.

This technological reversion upset one of the major expectations I'd entertained at the outset of my journey. From reading Edward Bellamy, Fuller and Murray Bookchin (who called for a synthesis of "liberating technology" and anarchism), I had expected to encounter far-out, creative adaptions of modern technology: solar heaters, hydroponic gardens, steam-powered tractors—in short, the "synergetics" Fuller foretold. Instead, I walked into communes that looked like antique shops. The open-ended communes used cider presses, flour grinders, earthenware crocks, looms, scythes, wood stoves, kerosene lanterns, treadle sewing machines, washboards, Fels Naphtha soap, potter's wheels, kilns, candle molds, double-barreled shotguns, bicycles and two-man saws. The furnishings recalled Goodwill stores and took me back to the funky Bols period of American taste: overstuffed armchairs, scuffed linoleum, electrified gas fixtures, '42 Fords, wringer washers.

I found a widespread, sometimes irrational distrust of technology. At a conclave of communes in northern Vermont, one group was the Videofreaks, a New York-based commune using video tapes to promote the communal cause. They'd gone from commune to commune filming building and craft techniques; at each one, they replayed their collection of films, disseminating knowledge many communes in their isolation could only gain by painful trial and error. When they started to film the conclave, they were asked to leave or keep their equipment outside. The Videofreaks complied. Someone said of them, "We know the Videofreaks are movement people. It's just that the cameras have a way of ruining the experience."

Perhaps no one else in the communal movement is more aware of its antitechnological temper than Steve Baer. After I left New Buffalo, I drove down to Albuquerque to talk with him. At thirty-two, Baer is the president of Zomeworks Corporation, a company he and others set up two years ago to manufacture the zomes and domes they sell for children's jungle gyms. In the future, Baer hopes Zomeworks will produce dome parts for communes and possibly sun trackers (recently developed solar heaters). For now, Zomeworks is biding its time.

Baer is a tall, preoccupied genius, who dropped out of Amherst and studied physics and math at Stanford and Zurich. He went through a period of revelation and insight and broke away from the technological conventions epitomized by the "cube." In his *Dome Cookbook,* published in 1968, Baer wrote:

The cube assumes a significance that goes beyond the geometric properties it enjoys, for it has imposed itself upon us. Perhaps any geometric system would end by imposing itself on man. They start as forms which answer a need but end by answering even when they are not called. People are trained for the construction of the form, special tools are designed and manufactured, a language grows with the workers, finally the relationship between need and form capsizes and instead of forms being thrown out because they don't fullfill the needs, just the opposite occurs.*

In the late 1960's, he traveled throughout the Southwest, where communes were just organizing and, like an itinerant Johnny Appleseed, helped build zomes—a name coined by a friend, Steve Durkee. He designed and helped build the zomes at Drop City, outside Trinidad, Colorado, and several at Libre, near Gardner, Colorado. Baer collaborated with Durkee to design the magnificent central complex of the Lama Foundation,

* Steve Baer, *Dome Cookbook,* published by Lama Cookbook Fund, Box 422, Corrales, New Mexico. Price is $1.

near San Cristobal, New Mexico. But Baer never settled in any of the communes he helped build. "I decided I was a person who got a lot of satisfaction playing with technology . . . and communes weren't ready yet for sophisticated applications."

The experience, however, provided material for the *Cookbook*, which has become standard commune reading. It is a clear, personal manual on how to erect anything from an exploded rhombic dodecahedron to a simple zonahedron. The *Cookbook's* humble, sometimes self-effacing tone contrasts with Fuller's obsessive technocratic fervor. Baer is more restrained than Fuller (and Fuller's "world game" disciples) and doubts that simply transferring power from politicians to technocrats will remedy all. Instead, Baer regards as the proper role of technology and scientists the relinquishing of control over nature, allowing it once again to take its course. As he says in the *Cookbook:*

> Today you hear people who are said to be ahead of their time say, "The world is a huge spaceship." I suppose that it is sometimes useful to think of the planet this way—the trouble is that spaceships are built by men, but this planet was not built by men—man evolved on and from this planet. There seems to be a huge urge to take over and completely control every variable of our environment—to in fact reform our planet into a giant spaceship—a living machine. I see this as the work of small-time ingrates; why not leave this place alone.

Like many others who were into technology, Baer left rural communal life. For three years he tried to make domes and solar heaters out of junk parts, as no money was available for even the basic materials. "If I wanted to accomplish anything, I realized it meant going back into the system and making enough money to buy the materials. All this talk about a self-contained counter-culture—can you imagine us freaks trying to manufacture plastic, pipe and glass?"

However, Baer is not without hope that someday communes will become comfortable with technology. This will involve arriving at some point of reconciliation with the "outside system." "I've learned that if you want to get to point C, you have to go through A and B," Baer says.

Slowly, communes are moving toward greater trust and use of technology through a process of sorting out priorities.

For example, the decision to use or not to use a chain saw involves a welter of overlapping issues. Sure, a chain saw is efficient, but it also means procuring money from the system to pay for the gas and broken chains. Many communes which began by using chain saws later abandoned them. For instance, at New Buffalo, George told me, "We used to take the chain saw out and cut down twenty or thirty trees in one morning, but it made so much fucking noise and fumes, I felt I was working in a factory." Like New Buffalo, many communes have reverted to two-man saws. "It takes a little more time," said George, "but it gives you a better feeling, and it doesn't drive the animals away. Justin and I have been out in the forest cutting with the two-man saw and seen deer come into the clearing."

On my travels I overheard endless debates about whether or not to use electricity from outside sources: electrical connection meant becoming party to the national electrical network and being indirectly responsible for helping perpetuate a power system that poisoned the air with pollutants and strip-mined farmlands. Some communes that had started out using electricity decided to do without it, even though this meant reading by dull kerosene light and hauling water. Others who'd begun without electricity concluded that the plusses outweighed the minuses and plugged in, but most limited electrical use to essentials: freezers, pumps and, in some cases, stereos. The net shift was away from electricity.

The rationale that emerged was to adopt only those limited segments of modern technology that fit in with a number of other communal ideals, such as self-sufficiency and craftsmanship: e.g., electricity to heat a kiln or run a sewing machine.

While other farmers had discontinued sugaring and were cutting down their stands of maples, New England communes were reviving the industry. They saw it as one of the few rural industries that worked with and not against nature. Still, the hip sugarers were faced with a problem: Should they use plastic pipe instead of the old buckets that were now so scarce that they were selling for $5 apiece at roadside stands? Should they use chain saws to cut the enormous quantities of wood necessary to boil down the syrup? Or instead of wood, use fuel oil? And to haul the sap, should they use a tractor instead of a team of horses?

A major technological problem confronting the communes was how to retrieve knowledge of the almost-forgotten arts of self-sufficiency now dying with the older farmers. It doesn't take much skill to plant a garden (though most communes over-planted in their enthusiasm the first year), but a greater challenge is the preservation of what had been so easily sown: how to make sauerkraut; how to can, pickle, salt, dry and otherwise preserve a host of crops without spoilage. Throughout my journey I found cellars full of rotting vegetables.

Marty Jezer, a Vermont friend, who alternates between the New York office of *Win* and the Packer Corner Farm in Guilford, wrote that his commune wanted to use draft horses for its sugaring operation this spring. "The trouble is that there *are* no draft horses up for sale." Likewise, "we had a surplus of corn and wanted to dry it and then to grind it to cornmeal, but we could not get information anywhere on drying. Storage is a lost art."

Technologically, open-ended communes were headed for a synthesis of nineteenth-century skills with a scrupulous selection of modern tools, methods and materials. Many open-ended communes started off like the nineteenth-century Brook Farm, in a burst of romantic resolution "to live off the land." When this proved not altogether practical, they developed crafts to earn the money for the few necessities they could not provide for themselves. They made candles, dulcimers, guitars, pottery, leather belts, handbags, clothing, shoes, tie-dyes and roach clips out of silverware. This way they combined the crafsmanship of the past with the tools and materials of the present: electric sewing machines, propane-heated kilns, welding torches. Most important, they transported their wares to market in vehicles like microbuses, on interstate highways. Thus it was possible for a craft commune like Mad Brook in northern Vermont to reach sales outlets in Boston in a matter of five hours. Slowly, the open-ended communes were bridging the self-imposed gap between city and country, between "us" and "them."

During my talk with Lou Gottlieb, back in February at Morningstar Ranch, he'd toyed with a small hand mirror that sent spots of sunlight into the garden and the pines on the edge of a hill. "It must be so simple," he said, "that we can't see it." Gottlieb was talking about the problem of converting energy from "father" sun into electricity that man could use. He regularly sits and plays with the mirror, hoping that God will reveal the answer.

"We've got to stop robbing the mother earth and start taking from the father," he said.

All over the country communes talked enthusiastically of finding such new pollution-free sources of energy; they resurrected yellowed manuals of companies that had manufactured windmills in the 1920's, like the Le-Jay Corporation; they sent away for the designs of Pelton Wheels to harness water power; they read in *Mother Earth News* of how the methane in animal dung can be used to run electrical generators.

Despite all the talk and plans, I found only one commune that had actually put into operation an alternate energy source: the solar heater at Drop City, which during the winter of 1969 had supplied 75 percent of the heating needs for one large zome.

Distrust is only one explanation for the communes' technological lag. On the whole, communes attract more English majors than students of physics, and they have little money to spend on developing new energy sources. However, one such alternative may soon become economically feasible. It is the sun tracker being developed by Day Charoudi at Zomeworks, under a grant from Lorien Enterprises.

The principle by which the sun tracker follows the sun

through the sky, trapping its energy, is elegantly simple. It looks and behaves like a sunflower. Its head is a concave mirror, five feet in diameter, laid over a fiber glass dish; its eye an automobile thermostat that functions through a system of weighted bags to keep the mirror automatically trained on the sun. Heat trapped and intensified by the mirror is conducted and stored by a stream of oil. Thus one day's sunlight, stored in a tank of superheated oil, can be used to heat a house, pump water, or even refrigerate.

It cost $400 in materials to develop the sun tracker, Charoudi estimated. Mass production, he hoped, would lower costs to $100 and bring it within the grasp of most communes, but like Baer, Charoudi was not overly optimistic that the "synergetics" needed to make communities viable and nonpolluting could be developed in isolation from the greater economy. "Take windmills, for example," he told me. "The technical problem has never been generating power, but finding some way of storing it. Right now, there are cadmium zinc batteries on the market that can store tremendous amounts of power for future use. The only thing is that they cost hundreds of dollars. . . . The only way that the cost can be brought down so communes can use them is through mass production . . . and that means keeping some parts of the system intact."

When I left New Buffalo, George gave me directions to Libre. Many of New Buffalo's first wave had considered making the changeover from open-ended commune life to a more traditional kind of community. If he had still been into art, George said, he would have moved his family to Libre. He liked the concept of community Libre embodied. Instead of living in one house or complex, Libre scattered its houses over a large tract. "I'd like to find another community like that, but they just don't exist."

I grabbed a ride with Susan and Ron, who were going into Taos. I'd met Susan in 1968, when she was a shy graduate student in English literature, idling away the summer in Baltimore. By accident, I'd met her again at New Buffalo, hardly recognizing her. She and Ron, another ex-Hell's Angel, had been living in Canjilon with the Motherfuckers. But after that group disbanded, they set out in their Scout to look for another place to live. Susan was pregnant, and they were searching for a community that offered greater peace and stability.

They dropped me at a good hitching place on Route 3, north of Taos. I thanked them and suggested they check out Vermont. I told them that the members of Bryn Athyn and I were planning some kind of community. Its shape wasn't clear yet, but I had a hunch it might resemble Libre.

A salesman dropped me off the Interstate north of Walsenburg, and I followed George's directions, hitching and walking about 20 miles west toward Farisita. There I began my ascent up the dirt road into the mountains. "On a clear day," George had told me, "you can see the domes. Follow the forks that go toward them. It's about five miles." When I started off, at around 3 P.M., it was clear, but clouds, rain and, finally, snow set in. By the time I'd taken all the wrong forks, the distance was closer to 15 miles.

At around 7,000 feet, a cold rain clotted the clay in the road, and huge lumps like fresh cement formed around my boots; at 9,000 feet, snow swept down Greenhorn Mountain into my face. Every 200 yards, I had to stop, adjust the pack on my shoulders, and let the blood recirculate. Darkness fell. Only one car passed me. I couldn't be sure it wasn't the wind until I saw its headlights bouncing through the snow. The driver opened the passenger door wide enough to see my face, hair and ice-caked beard, shouted, "Don't pick up hippies," and pulled away, zigzagging up the incline. I listened until the sound of the motor was again buried under the wind.

It must have been around ten when the lights of Libre appeared, faded, and appeared again through a shifting veil of snow. I came to the door of a small house that had a sharp steep roof, its eaves trimmed with daggerlike icicles. The window half of the door was beautifully frozen and danced with the refraction of many colors. Feeling intoxicated, I stared at it a full minute before knocking.

Jim, a tall young man, let me in. I stamped my feet and stammered an apology for throwing myself on their mercy at so late an hour. Sandy, who didn't have any clothes on, poured me a bowl of warm vegetable soup that had been simmering on the wood stove. Boots off, I curled up on the makeshift sofa of strewn pillows, wolfed the soup, and drank cup after cup of spring water.

Jim and Sandy were accustomed to sheltering visitors to Libre. The road to the community ended nearest their house. However, Libre had fewer visitors than most communes, due to their isolation—which had been an important consideration in selecting the site. "We are not a commune," they told me emphatically. "We are a community."

Sandy and Jim had briefly lived at Drop City, which had gone through the same open-ended commune cycle I had just witnessed at New Buffalo and had been deluged with visitors, speed freaks and junkies. Drop City's founders—artists, writers and designers—wanted greater privacy and isolation, so they dropped out of Drop City and moved 60 miles away, as the crow flies, across the Sangre de Cristo Mountains to form Libre (Spanish for "free") on a 400-acre tract.

"The rhythm of life is different here than at Drop City," said Sandy, who had the soft accent of an expatriate Texan. "Most of us spend a lot of time painting . . . I've found I really don't need so many people to feel complete, and you don't need to live in the same house as your friends."

Libre is set up as a nonprofit corporation of six people. In 1970 it was composed of seven houses situated so that no one house is visible from another. It's a very American tradition," said Jim, who is also an ex-Texan. "It's like what the history books told us about Daniel Boone, who kept moving west every time he saw the smoke from his neighbor's fire."

Unlike Morningstar and Wheeler Ranch, Libre is not open land where anyone can move in and build. New members and house sites must be unanimously approved by the present membership (now around twenty, including children). "In a while we're going to run out of room. We don't want to overtax the land."

My sensation on arriving at Libre (it might have been my exhaustion or the altitude) was a dizzy fantasy of having climbed the magic mountain to the top of the world and being ushered into a chalet containing the finest distillation of the world's culture. "Four months of the year, we're snowbound," said Sandy. "It feels comfy." The community owns in common and maintains one four-wheel-drive vehicle that makes daily trips to Walsenburg.

Electrically, they are still connected (at low REA rates of $5 a month per house) to the outside world. Because of their high altitude, their stereo receivers can pick up Denver FM stations. Socially, they don't feel isolated. "I'd rather get to know six people really well," said Sandy, "than sixty on a casual basis." At Libre, degree of isolation is a matter of choice. Because each couple has its own house and kitchen, the community has the crucial advantage of built-in retreats.

At Drop City, Sandy recalled, they had gone through a period of enforced togetherness—most people lived in homes with five to twelve others. "We tried a few orgies but couldn't make it as a group marriage." At Libre, she said, "we've gone back more into our own egos. By having more time to myself, I've learned how to be more confident with other people." Libre has reversed the typical patterns of communes that start with one central building and work outward toward individual houses. Though it has no common buildings, there are plans in the works to construct a meeting place for religious services.

Like most of the members, Jim is an artist and his paintings hang on the rough pine-studded walls of the chalet. Since coming to Libre, though, he's done less painting. "I find that I'm satisfied by just living. The greatest creative experience of my life was building this house."

Jim built it for under $100, using scrap lumber and mill ends. He collected rubble from a wrecked house—a mixture of adobe bricks and wood—to insulate the walls. He has heard of another

hip builder who insulated his house using the empty glass for-
maldehyde bottles discarded by a mortician.

The window that had appeared psychedelically frosted to me
was a smashed windshield Jim had salvaged and smeared with
epoxy glue, in which he'd embedded pieces of stained glass.

As a whole, the house was a carefully selected collage. Jim had
built it in the shape of a right-angle triangle, its hypotenuse the
sharply descending roof that gave me the sensation of standing
in the nave of a church. The upper half of the house was an
open sleeping loft reached by a cedar log, to which blocks had
been nailed as footholds. Even on nights when the temperature
plummeted to 30 below, the loft stayed warm from the heat
rising from the coals of the single heat source, a small wood
cookstove.

The bottom room was undivided. Near the back door, there
was the wood stove, a few food shelves and a spice rack hand
carved and decorated with designs in bright enamel. On the
floor was the water supply: a pail of water, with a ladle that had
once been blue but was now scratched silver by use. There was
a small handmade table built of mill ends, smoothly sanded
and stained dark. Although electric, the light in the room was
an amber color that brought out the honey grains of the pine
walls and roof and was reflected in a line of copper-bottom pots
that hung from a two-by-four over the stove. The pots had been
sent them by Sandy's mother while she was in France. "They're
our most expensive possession," Sandy said.

Jim was the first down in the morning and started a fire in the
stove. Needing more wood, he got dressed and put on his hat—
his most remarkable hat. It reminded me of a British admiral's:
shaped like a man-of-war, it had a prow and stern, a deck of
velvet, with a railing of beads, and for a mast, a sprig of feathers.
In all the world, there was no other hat like Jim's.

I began my tour of Libre by following Jim's directions to
Peter Rabbit's house. A trail of footprints through a pine grove
suddenly brought me into a clearing and face-to-face with the
house—hardly the sandbank at the base of a fir tree of the chil-

dren's tale, but a "four-fused exploded rhombic dodecahedron."

Smoke and steam fanned out of two stovepipes springing from the zome's multifaceted roof, which looked metallic but, I later learned, was made of wood panels painted gray. For a few minutes I warily circled the house, as if it were a spaceship some advanced civilization had arbitrarily dropped overnight into this clearing. I kept my eyes on the zomes. The structure consisted of four interconnected twelve-sided figures that seemed to rotate as I circled them, passing through permutations of form. With every step I took, the arcs of the zomes seemed to roll, and their intersecting angles constantly changed and overlapped. Whatever angle I took, the zomes expressed a different set of relationships, yet the same unity of interlocked stress and tension. I could see why Steve Baer had suggested that the shape of the zome was that of the "new society—load sharing, intelligently put together, one that will someday reveal the load-bearing pillars of today's arrangement as totally unnecessary."

When I finally went inside, Peter Rabbit was making a breakfast of pancakes for his two wives and two overnight guests. The interior of the house was sleek and modern. One wall, which partitioned off the main room from two smaller bedrooms, was a huge shelf of paperbacks. There was a plastic bubble chair, a stereo, indirect illumination from the skylights, and a kitchen that contained two refrigerators, a gas range and a bottle of Courvoisier.

Peter appeared to be in his thirties, with graying sandy hair, freckles and blue eyes. He is an ex-New York journalist and PR man, a published writer, who was then working on a book chronicling the ups and downs of his years as a foundling member of Drop City. Both his wives had the day off from cooking; besides, men could cook artfully, too, he said, sprinkling sunflower seeds into the pancake batter.

Besides writing, cooking and other duties, Peter Rabbit is the community's appointed deer hunter. When he surprises a number of deer, he "talks"—telepathically—to them, swearing to them that the flesh of the deer to be "sacrificed" will be used for Libre's constructive purposes. According to Peter, one deer will move away from the others and remain still until shot.

Libre had its members' ESP powers tested at the Maimonides Medical Center in Brooklyn, New York.* The experiments were done while the group was on a "cultural tour" of the country in 1969. Though it started as an artists' retreat, Libre has become more involved with the outside world—on its own terms. Some members still go to the cities to sell and exhibit their art, and the group produced a film of the community, which they've shown at colleges throughout the country.

I continued my walk. I didn't spend much time talking; I had come here to see and be shown, as one visits an art museum or goes on a house tour. Libre was an artistic statement, and the medium through which it conveyed its image of the future was architecture. It embodied a synthesis of old and new materials, styles and technologies.

The community's few vehicles were parked together at the end of the road, near Jim and Sandy's. The houses were linked by small trails. At a main junction, I came upon a collection of pipes and metal bars suspended by piano wire from a wood frame, a sort of xylophone. With a rock I tapped each bar, producing pure tones that the clear air carried off into space. Few eyes would see this sculpture, few ears hear its music. It had not been created for an audience. Overhead, a jet from the Air Force Academy boomed and left a thin streak across the sky.

Along the trail, I began to notice large semicircles of wood painted blue, red and yellow, set upright, and aligned to create perspectives that led off into the woods. Soon I came to another house. It had been built from railroad ties stacked one on top

---

* A summary of the experiments was published by Dr. Stanley Krippner, director of the center's dream laboratory, in *Modern Utopia*, spring issue, 1970: Six of the Libre adults and two of the children went into the laboratory's soundproof room while a laboratory assistant attempted to send an image by telepathic means. The assistant entered an office, noticed an electric calculator, and concentrated upon it for five minutes. When the subjects in the soundproof room were queried, it was discovered that a "group image" had emerged of a "machine" on which there were "buttons."

of another, as you would build a house of matchsticks, but it gave an effect of weight and durability. From its center rose a clear bubble dome.

My knock unanswered, I opened the door and peeked in. The floor was of bricks arranged in a herringbone design. Off the small kitchen, the floor went down a few steps to a larger room illuminated by the light from the dome. It looked like a courtyard, with adobe walls and Spanish fireplaces at both ends. It had an Eastern meditative quality. From what I could see of their house, with its blend of the practical, traditional and Oriental, I wished I could have met the family.

The trail led on through the woods to another home. I knocked on the metal door, which gave off a hollow, resonant boom. "Come in," I heard a woman's voice say. I walked into an unpartitioned daylit zome, whose interior was made up of triangular panels edged with multicolored ribbons of glass. A gas heater hissed. A formica counter separated a compact, modern-applianced kitchen from the rest of the zome, in whose center, before a full-sized handloom, sat a girl in a long dress. She told me her name was Marilyn, and she was weaving her first rug. Her mother had bought her the loom; her husband, Tony, had assembled it.

Tony appeared in a few minutes. "It would have taken me years to make the parts," he said. "As it was, it took weeks to put them together." He is an abstract painter, who occasionally sells a painting. Marilyn hopes to market her rugs at the many tourist shops located around Colorado's ski slopes. Most other Libre members earn small amounts by selling pottery, leathercraft and paintings.

The rug was almost finished. It had taken Marilyn eight days to weave it, working five hours a day. When she divided her share of the probable sale price by the number of hours she'd devoted to the work, she was not dismayed by the low hourly wage rate. "I'd work for a penny an hour if I dug what I was doing."

A neighbor, Dallas, came over to visit, and the two of us went back to his house, a hogan, for tea. Suddenly I was transported from the twenty-first century to the fifteenth. The hogan was built into the earth. It had a dirt floor and adobe walls. Stephanie, Dallas' woman, was looking after the two children of neighbors who were away for the weekend. Dallas didn't care for zomes himself. They were too imposing and dominated nature. Like the people of New Buffalo, he felt adobe blended organically into the earth. That was the quality missing at Libre, he said; it wasn't close enough to the earth. There were no gardens, partly because the soil was rocky and the water supply limited. Though a stream runs through the land, its water rights are retained by an unfriendly neighbor.

"The people at Libre are mountain people, closer to the air than to the earth," said Dallas. "They have a different kind of consciousness than people who live in the valley." Since they can't grow crops, they purchase most of their food with stamps and by bartering with the nearby communes of Morningstar, New Buffalo and Lama in return for services and crafts. However, a couple from Cambridge, Massachusetts, who recently bought a large tract nearby, has agreed to allow Libre to farm part of it.

Libre also plans to build a "grow hole." This simple device for raising vegetables during the winter was developed by the Lama Foundation, a spiritual community located 50 miles to the south, in San Cristobal, New Mexico. The grow hole is dug into a southerly slope at a recommended angle of 25 degrees. A wood frame constructed of four-by-eights is covered with a membrane of .016 inch vinyl. The membrane and the earth sides of the hole trap heat from the sun. On clear days, when the temperature is 20, it is 65 degrees inside the grow hole. Moisture condenses on the roof and drips back onto the vegetables, creating a miniature tropical rain forest. Warm air from a house can be conducted to the grow hole as supplementary heat.

The grow hole and solar heaters were in the future; for the time being, the community survived by selecting out the liberated aspects of the system. No one seemed conscience-stricken about taking food stamps or using a chain saw to cut wood. "If it weren't for the chain saw, I'd spend all my time and energy on the chopping block," said Jim. "The saw frees me to do more creative things."

My house tour included one of Libre's outhouses. The roof sloped upward toward the rear, creating an updraft for the two vent pipes. I lifted the wooden latch and entered. There were two windows. One, to the side, framed a zome; the other, directly in front of the single seat, looked down the mountain into the valley. A clump of sage hanging from the ceiling gave off a pleasant smell. Reading material included back issues of *Art Canada.*

Almost every commune I visited had gone to special lengths to make its outhouse unique and artful. The seat holes at Lama were covered by paddles attached at the back by rope. Georgeville's contained a junk sculpture composed of circular saw blades, driftwood, and blue telephone-wire insulators. Another had a candelabra for nighttime reading.

I returned to Jim and Sandy's for a dinner of pinto beans and hot sauce. There I met Steve, another member and artist who'd been exhibited in New York but had tired of going to openings and kissing prospective patronesses on their middle-aged cheeks. Steve thought that the general direction of art in this country was away from urban commercialism. "I'm not concerned with selling my work. My art is going into a reductionist period. The trend now is toward the 'useful arts.' I think a cider press is a work of art because it fuses craft with the natural. The other artists here and I are trying to reintegrate our art with life and nature. In a few years, art won't be something restricted to museums and divorced from life. It will be an inseparable part of the process of living."

The others talked of an impending court case. It involved the neighbor who retained the water rights to the stream that ran through Libre. Originally friendly, he had sold them part of his cattle ranch. Soon after, he became the community's greatest antagonist. (Libre had friendly relations with its few other neighbors.) At the stream one day, according to the members, he shot a just-filled water jug out of one of their hands. Libre filed assault charges. "What angers him is that he realizes he's wasted his life," said Dallas. According to Dallas, the neighbor came from a long line of poor Chicano farmers. Unlike his forefathers, he rose above poverty: took out bank loans, bought machinery and a large herd of cattle, and built an aluminum house. "Now he's got a hundred head of cattle and he can't afford to buy hamburger at the supermarket. He's got a color TV and that's all."

Another visitor, a graduate student in urban planning at Harvard, dropped by. In a few years, he predicted, communes and communities would emerge as a major form of American social life, not just for the young and hip but for suburbanites looking for a way out of mounting inflation, pollution and psychological isolation. He could foresee that the federal government might even finance some of the more offbeat plans for new communities.

Libre had already been approached by officials of the U.S. Department of Health, Education, and Welfare and offered a $40,000 grant to host a conference on communal life. On one hand, Libre *was* a decompression chamber, a retreat from the fast pace of change in the plastic society. But it was also a model, an artistic collage, that pointed ahead to a synthesis of man, art, technology. As Peter Rabbit had said the day before, "We live in the future."

The next morning, Sandy made cheese and tomato sandwiches of home-baked brown bread for me to carry on my twelve-mile descent. I left Libre on a clear, dry day and descended in a quarter of the time it had taken me to cover the same distance at night in snow. Three cars passed me but did not stop.

Near a side road I took a rest and ate my sandwiches. After my lunch, I strolled up the road and found that it led to a knoll and an old cemetery. The graves were grouped by families— the Medinas, the Trujillos, and the Vailpandos. They were distinctly divided into older and newer sections. The old graves of the first Chicano pioneers were marked by gray wooden crosses that had tilted in the wind and were almost covered with grass; in the newer section were commercially cut stones. From a distance it looked as if flowers had been planted among the new rows, but something about them struck me as false. I walked closer to check and went by a whole row before realizing that all the flowers that rocked in the wind in this wildest of mountain cemeteries were plastic.

VI
California

Harrad West: A Group Marriage

After leaving Libre, I reviewed my growing list of communities. Should I head north to British Columbia and live in the ashram founded there by the late Frederick (Fritz) Perls, the renowned gestalt therapist? Or spend a week with Cynergia, near Cerrillos, New Mexico, a communal dramatic troupe, who grow their own food, make their own costumes, write their own plays, and share a common faith in the cosmic evolutionary philosophy of Gurdjieff? Should I check out reports that a group of scientists from the University of California at Davis had purchased an enormous tract in upper New York State and were going to establish a research community to be known as Silent Steam (new applications for steam power as one of their projects)?

The new communities exhibited an astounding and perplexing diversity of purposes, structures, and people. These were a new brand of dropout, the middle-class corporate dropouts, with children and college degrees, who'd chucked $50,000 homes in the suburbs and their professions and careers. The communal movement was expanding in scope, as well as numbers, as the contagion spread from the younger generation to the parent.

John Koehne, for example, had been a highly paid analyst for the CIA. All three of his teen-agers whom he'd sent to one of

the best boarding schools in Washington, D.C., had dropped
out one by one.

"I had to stop and look and begin to understand what was
happening. I wasn't the sort of parent who said, 'You're going
to have my values or get out.' And as soon as I tried to understand the kids, questions began to come up about myself." *

Until 1967 Koehne's life had followed the conventional
route: private schools, Yale and twenty years during which he
rose through the ranks. Then, the CIA sent him to an encounter group. The experience changed his total view of himself. He stopped "laying heavy judgments" and began to "open
up to myself and others."

In turn, these personal changes precipitated an agonizing
sense of conflict with the values of the system which he as a
CIA man protected and furthered. In the spring of 1969 he
quit. With $20,000 in severance pay, he and his wife bought
a camper truck, decorated it with peace symbols, and began
scouting the country—the Blue Ridge Mountains, Oregon,
northern California and British Columbia—for the site of a
community. With eight close friends Koehne and his family
were planning to set up a "growth center" based on yoga principles.

Industrial engineers, corporate executives, research scientists,
vice-presidents of advertising agencies—others of this stripe were
joining the movement toward country and community. They
shared a dissatisfaction with jobs repeatedly described as "meaningless," "abstract," and "boring"; and a thwarted yearning to
return to a simpler rural existence. They could no longer tolerate commuting, the inflexibility of nine-to-five schedules, and
the deteriorating quality and increasing cost of urban life.

The escape route varied. In response to skyrocketing inflation, some families pooled their resources and bought brown-
stones in the city centers. They didn't want to flee to the suburbs, and they wanted to keep their jobs. Many were teachers,

---

* Koehne and other specific references to "corporate dropouts" are taken from
a series of two stories that appeared in the *Wall Street Journal*, February 19
and February 22, 1971.

social workers and architects who were dedicated to making the city livable and humane.

They set up comfortable, cooperative-style houses, sharing the rent or mortgage payments, freezer space and baby-sitters. Though numerous—more than twenty-five in Washington, D.C., alone—these urban co-ops and communes lacked the commitment and solidarity of their rural counterparts. The pattern seemed to be: After the first year, the groups of young professionals who set up the co-ops began to talk, plan and finally move to the country by stages. At first, a country farm served as a weekend retreat. Then, as more dropped out, the farm became the commune's main base. Often, groups kept their house in the city, but the prevailing thrust was toward the land.

Some of the corporate dropouts took an individual path, finding low-paying but rewarding country jobs: as ski instructors, private school teachers and caretakers. A fifty-two-year-old former head of a research company quit his $50,000 job and began to till a cranberry bog in Wisconsin. A dentist abandoned his lucrative practice in a Detroit suburb to buy a 100-ton freighter in which he stashed his family, possessions (including a 1932 Rolls-Royce), and embarked on a voyage around the world. When his money ran out, he said, he'd go back to drilling teeth.

Others, like the former CIA man, began to organize and join communities—some of them conspicuously well planned. Questers is an organization that advertises itself as the clearinghouse primarily for middle-class dropouts looking for a well-structured, economically sound community. With a headquarters in Cathedral City, California, Questers uses a computer to assemble complementary populations for communities from the long application forms people send in. Regional committees of Questers were appointed to do careful "land search" studies in Canada, the Ozarks and Central America. Before you can get the smallest bit of information on the organization, you must buy a $4 book, complete the "priority registration" at the back of the book, and eventually pay a registration fee. Questers' approach is a marked departure from the desperate, haphazard formation of the hip communes; it is, in a sense, a continuation of the older format of the "intentional communities."

Another point of difference was that some of the new communities did not close themselves off from the system, its economy, technology and problems. Many were, in fact, established specifically to meet unfilled social services. A number, located both in cities and in the country, were modeled after Synanon. It was the first community successfully to treat drug addiction by allowing addicts to manage their own living environment— a naturally therapeutic alternative to drab, impersonal institutions. Among the other therapeutic communities are Camp Hill Village in Copake, New York, and Gould Farm in Great Barrington, Massachusetts. They respectively treat mentally handicapped and mentally disturbed persons by involving them in maintaining their own community in close contact with the earth.

In contrast to the commune's tendency to reject psychology and other behavioral sciences as dispiriting, some of the new communities were organized around the group encounter techniques pioneered by the Esalen Institute near Big Sur, California. The staff and residents of these "growth centers" became self-supporting by sponsoring workshops, weekend retreats and seminars in group therapy, psychodrama, massage and Oriental philosophy, at a cost within reach of the many people who needed psychological help but could not afford expensive, prolonged individual treatment.

In general, many of the new communities took a stance midway between the establishment rat race and the anarchism of the hip communes which initially rejected all structure and sought a new consciousness. By comparison, many of the new communities were less engrossed in changing consciousness through drugs and the occult; rather, they took the environmentalist approach and sought to change the social structures that conditioned individual consciousness. One of the prime concerns of the middle-class dropouts, especially those who had been married for long, was the structure of society's fundamental unit—

the nuclear family. While many talked of all that was wrong with American marriage and family, few dared to experiment with alternatives.

No one knows exactly how many group marriages there are in the United States. By 1970, the only attempt at a comprehensive study of "multilateral experiments" was the one made by Larry and Joan Constantine, a young couple from Acton, Massachusetts. Doing independent research,* they hitched a trailer to their car and went around the country, locating thirty-three groups and studying sixteen of these.

Their working definition of a group marriage (they prefer the term "multilateral" to group) was broad: A family grouping of three or more persons based on "deep affective bonds, genuine intimacy and interpersonal commitment." The sixteen groups they studied included sixty-four persons and ranged from triads to eight members. The most common arrangement was the four-member marriage, usually the union of two couples.

Because group marriage is so new and untested (the eldest only five years), the Constantines hesitate to generalize; however, most of the groups they observed were in urban areas and included non-hip, employed, middle-class men and women varying in age from twenty-three to fifty-nine. (Generally, hippies avoid the structure group marriage entails and prefer the freedom and simplicity of the old man-old lady relationship in combination with outside liaisons, group gropes and seasonal orgies.)

One reason why the Constantines hesitate to generalize is the mercurial pace of group and individual change characteristic of "multilateral" marriage. When they returned to do follow-up interviews with some groups, Joan said, they were often greeted with "Oh, we broke up a month ago!" Nearly half the sixteen groups they studied failed to survive their first year. They dissolved into smaller regroupings, new combinations of couples and triads. The triad was proving a durable arrangement, said Joan, especially the ones involving two women and

* Monographs of their research can be obtained by writing Multilateral Relations Study Project, 23 Mohegan Rd., Acton, Mass. 01720.

a man. This she traced to the "socially conditioned rivalry between American men." Women feel less jealous, she explained,
and more easily accept the bisexual consequences of a threesome.

Though they note the upsurge of group marriage experiments in the past three years, the Constantines are wary of
sweeping predictions. "Sexuality is a great variable that differs
from person to person," Joan said. By temperament some people are monogamous, she observed. "Others have a kind of
sixty-forty makeup and are satisfied having a spouse for most of
the time and a lover for some of the time." A few can handle
three sexual relationships at once. Given this variability, she
said, it's absurd to limit relationships to a single combination,
any more than you'd expect everyone to follow the same diet.

The Constantines do not foresee that group marriage will
supplant monogamy in the near future; rather, it will become
one of many accepted alternatives "to the sexual restrictiveness
and social isolation of the nuclear family."

One of the longest-lined experiments was Harrad West, a
six-member marriage in Berkeley, California. For just over a
year, the six marriage partners were together. It was a period
of turbulent and constant encounter that ended in breakup.
Though Harrad West still exists in name and place, its new
members think less idealistically and self-consciously of themselves as a group marriage. One member said, "It isn't exactly
what we planned, but it's us."

On and off during March and May, I visited Harrad West.
The experience was comparable to being plunged into the middle of a psychodrama or soap opera. I had missed the group's
honeymoon (if there ever *was* one) and come in on the days of
its dissolution.

The group began with Bud and Daphne, who'd been married for seventeen years. High school sweethearts in Iowa, they
married young and had three children in quick succession. Bud
recalled, "We wanted a close family, a kind of oasis of warmth
in a cold world." During the summers they packed the kids in
the car and went on long camping and hiking trips. Their

family—like so many in our day and age—was rootless. Bud, a commercial artist, changed jobs several times, and they moved around the Midwest. Then they settled in Concord, California, a newish suburb of tract houses, north of San Francisco. Bud became a scoutmaster. They joined a Unitarian Church.

Through the church fellowship, they met another couple; and one sunny afternoon, they swapped and went to bed with each other's spouses. For several months, the two couples spent every weekend together. Initially, the arrangement revealed corners of themselves that hadn't found expression in their marriages. Bud discovered and satisfied a craving for emotional intensity. Daphne, who sometimes felt smothered by Bud's demands, was relieved to have a cooler, low-keyed relationship. The two shared the new insights they were gaining. "We were honest with each other," Bud said. "There wasn't a time when we ever thought about splitting up. If two people can satisfy two-thirds of each others' need, that's a pretty good marriage."

But the arrangement had the reverse effect on the other couple and acted as a wedge driving them forever apart. When they were divorced, Bud and Daphne were set adrift. "We didn't know what to do," Bud said. But they did agree on what they *didn't* want. Having affairs separately, on the sly, was out. Besides being impossible for Daphne, stuck with children in the suburbs where few people know each other, separate affairs were too secretive, guilt-ridden and threatening. "If your wife gets involved with someone you don't know, you can't help feeling that the other guy might take her away."

Like thousands of couples, they briefly investigated "swinging"—dating and swapping sexual partners on weekends. The practice is so widespread in California that swingers advertise in the back pages of the Los Angeles *Free Press* and the *Berkeley Barb*.

For Bud and Daphne swinging was a good experience, but its impersonality was profoundly unsatisfying. "We'd have to drive all the way down to San Jose to meet this one other couple we both liked." They wanted a closer relationship with the other couple. "When we asked if we could all get together during the week, they turned us down," Bud said. "Most swingers are scared—scared that their children, or neighbors or bosses will find out. All they want is to add a little spice to their marriage. They're afraid if they add too much spice, the marriage will break up. That's why they don't want to get emotionally involved."

Bud persuaded Daphne that the ideal arrangement was complete sexual and emotional involvement with another couple who would live under the same roof, sharing bed, board and responsibility for the children. In 1967 when Bud began seriously considering such an alternative, he scarcely knew what to call it. "I thought we were the only couple in the world who felt that way." During this period Bud read a lot, trying to find some basis for the expanded family he'd envisioned. The books that gave him the most direct encouragement were those of Robert H. Rimmer—especially his novel *The Harrad Experiment.*

Many others read it too. Published in paperback, *Harrad* went through eighteen printings and sold more than 1,500,000 copies. Briefly, it is a utopian novel that follows six students through the curriculum and life at Harrad College. As entering freshmen, each is assigned a roommate of the opposite sex, taught birth control and sexual technique. The curriculum is geared toward the indoctrination of a new sexual and social ethic, based mainly on the humanist school of psychology. Students at Harrad read the works of Erich Fromm, Albert Ellis and Abraham Maslow, the theoretical father of Esalen and group encounter technique. One of Maslow's premises is that the capacity to love can be taught. Rimmer carries the Maslow assumption one step further. Perhaps man can also be taught to love more than one person at a time.

Rimmer assumes that young, healthy and intelligent people, when removed from the repressive puritan morality of society and given psychological guidance, will naturally develop lasting, multilateral sexual relationships, free of jealousy and guilt.

For Rimmer, learning to enjoy and handle sexual relationships with more than one other person (one in a bed at a time—

no group sex) is the first step toward attaining full humanness: at once a sense of individual uniqueness and multiplicity of self. In the modern world, Rimmer says, sex is the last frontier of mystery and wonder, the natural means of achieving the transcendent moments of "peak experience," which Maslow found to be one of the common characteristics of the happiest, "most fully human individuals."

Through one of his characters, Rimmer declares: "Television, movies, novels, biographies, alcohol, sex, drugs like marijuana and LSD, even concerts, spectator sports, aimless automobile driving, all the myriad forms of escapism added up to a lot more than proof of boredom. They were symptomatic of a world where no one was ever taught to step out of his own skin and find mystery and wonder and adventure in another person. So human beings used all these other means of indirect contact. They touched each other like carom shots in billiards, an indirect attempt to impel someone in the direction you wished, because most men and woman were afraid to reveal their poor little egos to each other in any other way."

In addition to opening up the individual psyche, multilateral sex also serves as the basis for Rimmer's expanded family form. At Harrad's conclusion, the six students (the "in-six") have formed a group marriage in a big mansion in Philadelphia. In *Proposition 31,* a later novel, Rimmer shows how the Herndons and Sheas, two suburban couples and next-door neighbors, emerge from the stereotypical crisscrossed adultery situation to form a "corporate marriage." By combining the first syllables of their last names, they take the hybrid name of Hershe, merge their bank accounts, and build a plush circular house, a two-family communal compound. At the novel's end, they have launched a nationwide campaign to legalize group marriage, which, they believe, will cure the world of alienation and impersonality and become the basis for a new moral and social order.

Rimmer's sales pitch—a combination of the new psychology and sexual liberation within the traditional confines of the family—was convincing. So persuasive that hundreds of couples, like the two in Louisville, Kentucky—who now go by the communal name of Bridges—were directly inspired to carry out their own real-life experiments. So were Bud and Daphne.

They sold their suburban house and moved into a big, old house in Berkeley's posh highlands. When they moved in, the house was a commune of intellectuals and hippies and the center for weekly discussions about intentional communities. After most of the commune members had moved to the country, Bud eased out the last of the hippie boarders, picked up the lease, and changed the subject of the weekly meetings from communities to group marriage. He called the house Harrad West. Harrad had become at once catchword and rallying cry.

Two of the people who attended the meetings were Herb and Alice, an unmarried couple, who called themselves a "pair bond." They had been together for a year. Herb, thirty-two, combined an intellectual background with the disposition of a swinger. Alice, twenty-eight, came from a conservative St. Louis family and was a virgin until three years before. At Herb's urging, and not without some reluctance, she agreed to join the experiment. They moved in.

At first, they complemented one another. Herb and Daphne were detached, more reflective and emotionally independent; Bud and Alice more impulsive, "gut-level" people who needed to be needed. During a honeymoon period, Herb proposed they add another couple. They had two empty rooms and plenty of expenses to divide. Six could live as cheaply and harmoniously as four—and give the marriage more sexual variety, as well as stability.

Though he had different feelings about the group, Bud agreed. He wanted a large family, like the clans he recalled from his Missouri childhood, when all his nephews and uncles and aunts congregated for the summer on the family homestead. Bud felt confident that the bond between himself and Daphne would be strengthened rather than weakened by the new relationships. Bud shared Rimmer's belief that sexual love within a social structure would bridge most misunderstandings.

Next to join was Moishe, sixty. Daphne liked him. Bud considered him the older brother he'd been looking for. Only Alice had misgivings—about his age. But the others convinced her the intimacy, augmented by psychological support, would bridge age and other differences. Before joining Harrad, Moishe was a friend of Gloria, forty-five. Like Moishe, she'd gone through several marriages and divorces. At his invitation, she visited Harrad, made a good impression, and was quickly asked to join. On first meeting, she had impressed the group as very attractive and self-aware, a woman who'd overcome great handicaps—mainly alcoholism—and was now embarked on a new path of life. How could they reject Gloria or anybody who had marital problems and neuroses; weren't they, underneath it all, just as hung up? After all, who in America, growing up in the same sexually crippling conditions, could claim to have emerged unscathed?

From the day Gloria arrived—completing Rimmer's ideal hexagon—the marathon encounter was on. The day Moishe helped Gloria move her furniture and luggage into the house, he discovered she had two Siamese cats. Why hadn't she told him? He hated cats, couldn't live with cats. Oh, hadn't she? Gloria answered innocently. She thought he knew. Moishe stormed and stormed—the cats were evidence of Gloria's duplicity; she had gained entry into the marriage by using him, just as other women had used him. Gloria refused to sleep with Moishe (and never did). Moishe avoided sitting next to Gloria at dinner.

The others remained calm. Sexually, Gloria and Bud were compatible. For a time, their mutual passion masked deeper differences. Gloria was looking for a dark, handsome hero-lover. But Bud wanted more than sexual love; he wanted sympathy and the warm, friendly love of a family. Gradually, Bud and Gloria grew emotionally apart, even though they still slept together. After two months they broke off all relations.

When I arrived at Harrad in the spring of 1970 I found this configuration: Gloria was intimate only with Herb in a casual, almost brother-sister relationship. Both Alice and Daphne were becoming more independent of the roles they had played in the past with Herb and Bud, respectively. Herb actually welcomed Alice's new independence. However Daphne's self-assertion deeply disturbed Bud and forced him to find a separate identity. Bud keenly felt the lack of a brotherly tie with Moishe and Herb. Most of the lines of stress in the group marriage seemed to have converged on Bud.

March 3

Their eight-bedroom Tudor house blends in with the neighborhood—the hills of upper-middle-class Berkeley, where gleaming Mercedes sit in front of landscaped, redwood-beamed homes. Yet it is still Berkeley, where hardly anyone can quite believe Ronald Reagan is governor and where there is tacit toleration for almost anything under the California sun.

Alice showed me to my room. She has a longish face, curly brown hair, gray eyes and a very straightforward manner. When I asked her if I could live at Harrad for a week, she asked me if I would agree to a "contract" of $5 a day that would include meals and an exemption from house chores.

Before I could move in, she'd had to obtain unanimous approval of the other five. Like most communes and ordinary families, Harrad West operated on consensus.

On the way upstairs I caught glimpses of the interior: darkly stained paneling, bright throw rugs on wooden floors and extension phones everywhere. Bud and Daphne share a bedroom and enclosed porch. The rest have separate rooms. Alice opened the door of hers. It had a small tabletop refrigerator, TV, stereo, and a red satin bedcover with matching pillows. A DO NOT DISTURB sign hung from the inside door handle. "You've got to have a place to escape to and close the door."

She left me in my attic room overlooking a large backyard and vegetable garden. "This is my night to cook," she said. "You'll hear the dinner bell a little before six."

At its sound I came downstairs. The living room was furnished in a mixture of styles. A picture of the Beatles hung above the fireplace. A doughnut-shaped coffee table, painted an atrocious pink, had been made out of a salvaged telephone cable spindle. On it were copies of the San Francisco *Chronicle*, *Psychology Today* and a quarterly issue of *The Sexual Freedom League*. In a horseshoe grouping around the doughnut table were deep, comfortable sofas. Below a stereo system was a mixed collection of records, everything from Pete Seeger to the Jefferson Airplane.

Bud poured me a glass of sauterne. He has short black hair, a goatee and black expressive eyes, which dartingly searched mine for response. He remembers and likes to use people's first names. Very openly, without much prodding, he launched into a frank account of his own boyhood.

He nostalgically recalled the summers on the family farm when he and his cousins skinny-dipped, milked cows, and worked the fields. "It was like a big family camp." However, his own family wasn't as close as that. His father, who did engineering work on the dams along the Mississippi, was a distant martinet who spent more time at work and on the golf course than at home. Bud grew closest to his mother, who had allied the children to her side against his father.

At the time he founded Harrad, Bud had been employed as the manager of a photography agency. He was the right-hand man to the owner, whom he regarded as a father figure. "I had a lot of ego involvement in the job—I was breaking my balls to be number one."

After a few months at Harrad, the psychological strain between the competitive nature of his job and the "ego-involvement" with the group tore Bud apart. On the verge of a nervous breakdown, he quit. He collected workman's compensation while developing a free-lance art business and further supplemented his income as a children's entertainer, making up to $90 an appearance. Now Bud feels his family life and work are more closely integrated and is sure he couldn't have made the conversion without the emotional support of the other members.

Daphne came into the room and began sweeping the ashes into the fireplace—a job delegated to her by the house's labor credit system. Daphne, thirty-seven, wears her long auburn hair loose and dresses in slacks. She has a large-boned body and an air of detached independence like a tree that knows it can stand alone.

Underlying her surface coolness, I sensed a solitary strength. Quietly, efficiently, she looked after most of the house's business, doing the accounting and making the bulk purchases of foods at wholesale prices. At first Daphne was cool to me. I was another person who had come to observe their marriage—as if they were all fish in a bowl.

Alice, wearing an apron, came into the living room and asked, "Where's Iris?" (Bud and Daphne's thirteen-year-old daughter). "The table's not set." Iris' task was marked for all to see on the huge plastic schedule posted in the pantry.

"I dunno," said Bud.

"What do you mean, you don't know," retorted Alice in feigned outrage, poking Bud in the ribs. "She's *your* kid."

"She's not *my* kid—she's just as much yours," Bud snarled like a panther and pulled Alice, tussling and squealing, into an armchair. All the while, Daphne went about her pickup duties, unperturbed. A few moments later Iris slammed through the front door. Willowy and self-assured, she told us about her day in school, using dramatic sweeps of hand and exaggerated facial expressions. For added emphasis she swung a baseball bat over Bud's head (she called him Buddy, never Father) until Bud asked, "Would you mind putting that bat down? It makes me uptight. It's one of those hangups you'll have to live with." She complied, finished her recitation, and went off to set the table.

Gloria came home from work. She was a psychiatric caseworker specializing in alcoholism. Gloria had kept herself shapely, trim and seductively attractive. Her peppered gray hair was cut pageboy fashion. She came over to the edge of the sofa, smiled one of her mysterious, noncommittal smiles, and disappeared to her room. "She looks tired," Alice remarked as the click of Gloria's heels receded up the stairs.

"That's because she has too goddamned much going on the outside," Bud said, his voice edged with resentment.

At which Alice teased, "But, Buddy, we can't all devote as much energy to the house as you do."

Dinner was served buffet style on an old-fashioned sideboard. From the parquet ceiling of the dining room hung the petaled fixture of a gaslight era, a nonelectrified lamp. We ate around a ping-pong table covered by a tablecloth. "We couldn't find a table large enough," said Daphne. "They don't make them for large families anymore."

Meals at Harrad West were always on time, and all the household work, from cooking to cleaning, appeared on the surface to get done effortlessly. In this respect the group marriage revealed the impersonal efficiency of a student co-op. Unlike a commune, where all income is automatically pooled, the members of Harrad West retain separate incomes and checking accounts and are individually assessed for the rent, food, utilities and telephone. Running subtotals of food expenses are kept in open view on bulletin boards. Over coffee the month's telephone bill was sent around the table, and each person initialed his long-distance calls. The bill returned to Daphne, who added the phone calls to each person's monthly assessment—an average of $90 per adult. This, in inflation-plagued Berkeley, where tiny apartments begin renting at $200, is reason enough to live communally.

Two of the group, Herb and Moishe, were still at work. As in most American households, the dinner-table conversation was spurred by the kids, Bud and Daphne's children: Iris, Nigel, eleven, and Courtney, nine, who seemed generally unimpressed by their biological parents' mixed sexual life, but who have learned to be discreetly evasive when questioned by prying mothers of friends. They know that Harrad is morally okay, but nevertheless illegal. (Ironically, in California the law condones adultery committed on a sporadic basis—for instance, weekend swinging. But within the institution of an expanded family multiple sex is technically illegal.) Harrad's problems, however, are not with snooping neighbors or puritanical law officers. Like most communes, Harrad's host of problems are intramural.

Herb got home at about nine. He worked as a messenger for a data-processing company and spent most of his working hours driving a Volkswagen around the Bay Area. Though he has a master's in social work, Herb found that, like Bud, he lacked the emotional stamina for both the group marriage and a demanding profession. "I need a job that will charge up my batteries." Energies that might have gone into a profession Herb devotes to the marriage, which he views as a "showcase and model of a sexually liberated community."

Herb had the air of a dropped-out Unitarian minister. When he came home, he wore a turtleneck sweater, a black one that matched the heavy plastic frames of his glasses. His hair looked as if it had been carefully combed forward, to mask a bald patch. He showered and changed into a silk bathrobe and tucked an ascot around his neck.

Herb is Harrad West's social theorist—the counterpart, in this respect only, to Horace of Rimmer's Hershe family. When he spoke in his deep resonant voice, I couldn't tell if he were veiling his feelings behind theory. Like Rimmer, Herb acknowledged his intellectual debt to Maslow, Ellis and B. F. Skinner, the behavioral psychologist. For a time, he was associated with Walden House, a Washington-based group interested in forming a labor-credit, behavioralist community patterned after Skinner's novel, *Walden Two*. Ultimately, Herb decided against joining their move to a farm in Virginia. "I'm a city person; civilization has always been the product of an urban environment." Also, he was convinced that sex, not economics, was the key to reforming society. Like Rimmer, he considers multilateral sex to be a nonverbal mode of communication, a valuable adjunct to psychological encounter, and in the behavioralist terminology, the most powerful conditioner and reinforcer imaginable.

Alice had saved a plate for him, and while he ate he talked. "Anyone can drive down to Esalen and have a good encounter, drive back to the city, and revert to their old behavior. The trouble is carry-over. Around here, you can't escape to your old games. You get *called*." Furthermore, Harrad's sexual interchange added a deeper, more intimate dimension to encounter. "Most groups, even the marathons, get hungup because of unstated, unresolved sexual tensions. Joe feels tense with Joan because he wants to screw her, and Joan responds with the usual set of female defenses. It sometimes takes a group months to bring it out into the open, and once you do, there's no way for Joe and Joan to get it out of the way. . . . In this society there's so many inhibitions laid on people about love and sex it's almost impossible for men and women to communicate through words."

Dressed in robe and slippers, Gloria came into the kitchen and poured herself a glass of milk. Nonchalantly, she massaged the back of Herb's neck. Alice emptied the dishes from the machine. The phone rang. It was for Herb. When he returned, he explained that they'd all been invited to the SFL (Sexual Freedom League) party that Saturday night and that Pam, who was still on the line, wanted to know how many from Harrad could be expected. Gloria counted on her fingers: "Wednesday, Thursday, Friday, hmmm, that's my night. Alice stopped and also counted: "Wednesday, Moishe; Thursday, Herb; Friday, Bud—but he doesn't like SFL parties . . . maybe we could go as a threesome." For a moment, Gloria hesitated but then said "Sure" and went upstairs.

Later I found Alice on the second floor studying something behind the linen closet door. She turned around, startled. "Well, you might as well know about The Chart," she said. It was a multicolored chart covered by the kind of clear plastic that can be marked on, erased, and used again. Along the vertical axes were the days, a two-week span. Along the horizontal were six letters, each keyed to one of the six marriage members.

"In the beginning we tried to do without a chart, but we found that we spent the whole day mousing around, trying to figure out who was going to sleep with whom that night. It's just easier this way. And it's fair; no one is *supposed* to get jealous." The Chart, she said, had gone through various editions as the group evolved. At first, they'd allotted twice as many nights to the "primary pair bonds" (*i.e.*, Bud-Daphne, Herb-Alice, and Moishe-Gloria). But when the pair bonds began to weaken, the allotment became more evenly distributed. Also, they set aside some nights as "free" (marked F on the chart) when no one was obligated to sleep with anyone else. "The sleeping chart puts a lot of people off," said Alice. "But there's really no other way to do it if you have six people. Mostly it's a matter of convenience. Someday, I hope, we won't need it."

On paper, Alice's background would seem to make her an unlikely candidate for group marriage. The family background that seems common to most members of Harrad and other group marriages is that of the WASPish, God-fearing parents who ride out unhappy marriages for their children's sake and social appearances. Alice's parents are conservative Methodists who have no idea that their daughter—whom they sent off to finishing school—is now part of a group marriage. "I was taught that you saved your virginity and all your love for your husband," she said. Alice went to college for a year. "I'm not an intellectual." She also has trouble making chitchat—one of the premarital arts at which girls in America grow deft. While in St. Louis, she dated young men, buttoned-down types, whose endless conversational patter seemed culled direct from the columns of *Time*.

"Even talking to a guy made me uncomfortable—I mean, I couldn't let a man *touch* me." She went to Washington, D.C., got a job as a dental assistant, and there had her first affair. She thought she loved him, but after he slept with her once, he didn't call back. "So at twenty-five, I became a middle-aged spinster." She shared an apartment with another girl and her cocker spaniel, overate, went to air-conditioned movies, and read detective stories.

Then she met Herb. Instead of one deep durable relationship, she said, Herb preferred many diverse, short-term ones.

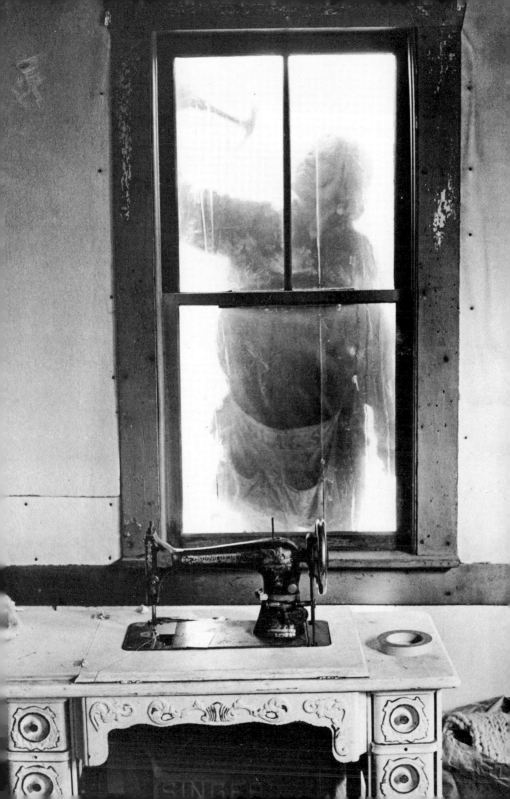

Nevertheless, they stayed together, even after Herb insisted they join Harrad, because, Alice said, "We were both shy people; we used each other as a crutch." Of the six, Alice adjusted most slowly to the chart, due to her conditioned belief that affection should precede sex and not the reverse. "But it turns out that I'm a person who takes a long time to warm up." Sexual intimacy helped teach her how to love in different ways. At first she detested the schedule. For weeks, on nights when Alice and Bud were together, they simply talked in bed, until Alice felt comfortable enough to make love. "Without The Chart, I don't think I would have overcome my general uptightness; at least, not as fast as I did." The multilateral sex enforced by The Chart also broke down Alice's possessiveness and finally her dependency. Some nights, when she knew Herb was sleeping across the hall with Daphne, she would weep in Bud's arms, until their own relationship developed its own warmth and love.

When Moishe joined the group, it took Alice even longer two months—to accept him as lover. But when she did, she unlocked yet a third side of the multiple self, the cast of three Alices. With Moishe, she could be playful, Alice the giving; with Bud, passionate, understanding, able to meet his endless need for reassurance and affection; and with Herb, who had never demanded deep affection, she could still be loyal but no longer dependent.

During the first year, Alice pleaded many times for changes in The Chart to allow her to spend the night with Herb—nights when she felt particularly low. But the others gently refused. Behind her tears and pleadings they saw her coy possessiveness. If they didn't hold to The Chart, anyone could use sex as a powerful lever of recrimination. Without the schedule, it would be easy for one person to feel left out or be bitten by the old serpent of sexual jealousy. "Just because I'm scheduled to sleep with Moishe tonight doesn't mean I have to make love to him," Alice explained. "We spend some nights together listening to music, but The Chart makes it certain that I spend an equal amount of concern and time with Moishe, as much

as I do with Bud and Herb." Still, Alice concedes, if she were
to write her own schedule to match her temperament and sex-
ual-emotional needs, she wouldn't apportion her nights equally.
After a year of conditioning, she retains a greater need to be
with Herb than the other two men, even though she feels less
dependent on him. "None of the alternatives are perfect," she
said philosophically, "but I think our way is better than monogamy—which really *is* inflexible."

Read and wrote late. It must have been around 1 A.M. when
I got up to get a drink. Behind the closed doors on the second
floor came sounds of music and conversation. By habit, everyone
at Harrad seems to keep late hours and to get up late in the
morning. Moishe was in the kitchen. He is a slight, elusive man
in his middle fifties, who buckles his belt on the last notch
and has gray hair cut in boyish locks. During the day, he teaches
ballet at a free university. At night, he earns money by doing
janitorial work in a school. He slammed the refrigerator door.
Earlier in the week, he'd bought some liver; now it had vanished. Did I know where? No, I didn't I answered, lying. I'd
seen Gloria feed it to her cats.

When I came down this morning, Moishe was still fuming,
stomping and muttering—to no one in particular—that the
oven had been wastefully left burning. But what really bugged
him was that he'd learned the fate of the liver. Alice apologized
for the oven: "Moishe, Moishe, you're such a grouch. Get mad
at me if you want, but don't go around making those funny
irritated sounds." She wrapped her arms around him sooth-
ingly, then held his face in her hands.

Moishe had been married and divorced twice. His wives had
been strong, motherly types. One had been a Jungian psychoanalyst who indulgently treated him like a disturbed son.
Through psychotherapy, Moishe realized, he told me later, that
his marital problems stemmed from his mother, a strong, ex-
acting and energetic woman, who, besides keeping her large
brood in line, labored from dawn to dusk in a sweatshop. "Psychotherapy can tell you what's wrong with you," he said, "but

it doesn't offer you any way of testing new roles." At Harrad, Moishe had to love and understand younger women, who were able to relax his compulsive crankiness.

The clear sunlight of an unsmogged morning filtered through the cedars outside the front bay window. Among the yellowed winter grass of the front yard, new light green spears appeared. Delicately, spring comes to California. From the street, the drone of morning traffic. No one at Harrad rushed off to work, nor did they need to. The mood of Harrad West is that of a self-contained world that holds all the intensity and adventure anyone could possibly need or absorb.

Harrad's members are on an uncharted voyage, and for all the perils and pain it entails, no one seems ready to jump ship. To an outside observer, the group would appear quite conventional. Unlike Lewd, a hip-style group marriage in Cambridge, Massachusetts, they don't find it necessary to breakfast in the nude, though they do take nude sunbaths on the sun porch, shimmying along the floor so as not to offend the neighbors. A few of them smoke grass on the weekends. Gloria has tripped a few times. But in place of drugs, sex has become Harrad's means of expanding individual consciousness, as well as deepening their psychological involvement with one another. Psychically and emotionally, they have come to know one another's every tender and vulnerable spot. Moishe knows that Gloria is terrified of growing old and seeing her body sag; Gloria knows that Bud is deathly afraid of being left alone at night; Alice knows about Moishe's domineering, destructive mother and the reason why he tears himself apart with self-criticism. But I wonder, with such naked knowledge constantly probing one another's exposed egos, how they can live from day to day. There's something almost masochistic about their strange attraction-repulsion for one another, their seemingly tacit, almost unconscious agreement that they must lash one another to sensitize long-numbed nerve ends; the inevitability that they must work out their pain, as if they were actors in a play that must be played out, even though it is cruel and tragic.

But a playwright would find little dramatic action to write

about. Twice a week they encounter; once a week they have a business meeting. On Wednesday, they host an open house—a discussion group on marriage open to the public. The purpose is to encourage others to try. "Lord knows, we don't want to be the only one in Berkeley," Herb said.

There are few hours when all are together, partly because no one can stand the house's highly charged atmosphere for long. When they do get together, it's like a scene from *Who's Afraid of Virginia Woolf* plus two. This morning Gloria mentioned she'd encouraged a certain couple (Bill and Andrea) to resume coming to the Wednesday night discussions. Suddenly, we were not eating English muffins with marmalade and reading the morning paper—but encountering. Herb led the charge against Gloria: Bill's "cynical and negative" attitudes toward social change dampened the meetings. Bud suggested the couple shouldn't be encouraged to come. At this Gloria snapped, "Am I supposed to tell them that they've been disinvited?"

Bud: "We're not asking you to do that."

Gloria (ripping out a cigarette): "I can see that you're trying to isolate me from my friends. I'll call and tell them they're not welcome."

Bud: "You're playing games again. . . ."

Gloria: "I'm not playing a game. I'm angry; is it okay to be angry? Can't you take anger from a woman, Bud?"

I tried to go back to my muffins and marmalade, repressing an urge to defend Gloria. I didn't feel she was playing games. But then, I hadn't been in on the start.

Alice breezed through the living room, dressed in a bright serape, on her way out to do some shopping. "Don't forget to get the film developed," she reminded Bud.

"I thought Herb was going to do it."

No, Alice answered, he was too busy.

"He's always too busy to do anything for this house," Bud retorted. "I do all the nitty gritty and he takes all the credit."

Of the fourteen possible two-person relationships among the six members of Harrad, the one that seemed to contain the highest emotional charge was between Herb and Bud. The two could share without jealousy the sexual favors of Alice and Daphne, but there cooperation ended. "Bud's looking for a brotherly kind of love that Herb can't give," Alice said. "Herb gets along much better with women than with men." Like Rupert Birken, in D. H. Lawrence's *Women in Love,* Bud wanted love of both kinds. He was always urging the others to *do* something together: plant the garden, do carpentry, go camping or hiking in the country. He dreamed about buying a seventy-acre ranch in Mendocino County, where they would have plenty to do besides encountering, but Herb dismissed country communes as impractical and escapist. Instead, he conceived of Harrad as the basis for a larger community of sexually liberated individuals. The concept, which he called "linear marriage," had been suggested to Herb by Robert Heinlein's novel, *The Moon Is a Harsh Mistress.* Harrad would be one hexagonal unit in a honeycomb network of group marriages throughout Berkeley. This interlocking structure would give individuals greater mobility, sexual variety and emotional freedom. (To a degree, the house had already established a limited "swinging" relationship with an approved "inner circle" of friends.)

Bud didn't openly condemn swinging and sex outside the group; nevertheless, the others sensed that he disapproved of extramural sexual ties that would undermine the "primary loyalties" which Bud wanted to reserve within the house. From the start, Bud and Herb's conflicting concepts of family loyalty and individual freedom created a polar tension. Later, as Gloria and finally Daphne took Herb's position and asserted their sexual independence, Bud's tension imperiled the experiment.

Around five, Gloria invited me to share a predinner toke from her little brass waterpipe. On her bedside table, she kept Panama Red in a baggie, along with other sundries—salted soybean seeds, calcium and vitamin-B-complex pills, nose spray and a drug to suppress the craving for alcohol. She lighted the pipe. Her long fingernails were painted silver.

Gloria's psychotherapist had prescribed the marijuana as a less harmful alternative to alcohol; and the cure had worked. In fact, her case history of victory over alcoholism had been published in a medical journal. Harrad West helped her, in an equally unorthodox way, to become aware of her sexual hang-ups and to undo some of them. Gloria inherited a set of sexual fears from her mother. "When I first menstruated, my mother said, 'Oh, you poor dear, now your troubles have begun.' " And the day before her sister's marriage, she overheard her mother warn her sister that her new husband would probably wound her on their wedding night. Partly as a result of her upbringing, Gloria was unable to enjoy sex very fully with any of her three husbands. She loved them but was driven to find physical satisfaction in a string of extramarital affairs. "It seemed like one compartment was reserved for love and tenderness and another for sex and pleasure. . . . Part of me was this life-sized doll that men liked to play with, a mechanical doll." She realized this at Harrad, she said, when Herb, Bud and Moishe refused to play her manipulative game. "I had to look into myself."

"I've learned how to love, though I can't tell you how. I feel I'm eighteen again and ready to fall in love for the first time." Gloria had no qualms about seeking a love-life outside Harrad West, since she was sleeping with only Herb. She refused to go to bed with Moishe "because it was too forced. I wanted to get to know him first. We never did." As for Bud, she said, "he couldn't accept that an older woman could be sexy—he's got some Victorian image of women in his head. . . . He wants Harrad to be some kind of in-grown, cozy family, sitting around the fireplace roasting chestnuts. He's shocked that I have friends of my own."

Despite Bud's disapproval, she and Herb have kept going to the Sexual Freedom League parties where one room is reserved for those who want to make it en masse, bisexually or in any conceivable combination. By comparison, Gloria said, Harrad was as sexually reactionary as Rimmer's books in which sex is a one-couple behind-closed-doors affair, prudish, if not dull.

Iris tapped on the door, then breezed in to borrow Gloria's recording of *Hair*, which they'd seen together. They were pals who went shopping together, gave mutual rubdowns, and discussed their newest boyfriends. "What are you talking about?" Iris asked offhandedly, going through the records.

"Love and sex," answered Gloria, smiling at me.

"Doesn't anybody ever talk about anything else?" Iris teased, having found the record, and was off.

Later that evening I caught a flash of Bud's resentment of Gloria's outside liaisons. The phone rang. It was "Another guy for Gloria," he muttered, going to the foot of the stairs to call her. "The trouble is she's a forty-year-old woman who feels like she's sixteen." Herb, more tolerant, viewed Gloria as going through the healthy sexual adolescence that had been denied her. If Harrad could help her unsnarl old hangups, he said, then it was serving a good purpose.

March 4

Alice was going out on some errands and asked if I'd like to go along. We headed off in her Volkswagen. For all the other kinds of sharing that go on here, cars remain in the private sector. They're borrowed a lot but are still referred to as Alice's Volks and Bud and Daphne's bus.

"I've got to pick up a course catalog. It's part of my contract," Alice told me. At the last encounter, the others had told her she was going stale for lack of interests outside Harrad. To comply, she agreed to develop some extracurricular activity.

Everyone at Harrad West had their "contracts" to fulfill. The making of interpersonal contracts was one example of their increasing use of behavioral techniques. Originally, their orientation was dual—combining elements of behavioral and gestalt psychology. But as the marriage was wracked by interpersonal crises, it leaned ever more heavily on behavioral crutches. "The emphasis went from individual growth techniques to finding practical ways of making us get along," said Herb, the strongest advocate of behavioral therapy.

The "contract" was an impersonal, constant reinforcer of new behavior patterns, applicable to Harrad West or any group living together, who at any time could "blow the whistle" on one another. Such gentle Skinnerian reminders as "Daphne, remember your contract" ruffled few ego feathers. Bud's contract was to be less talkative and digressive; Moishe's to be more tolerant of individual differences; Gloria's to relate nonseductively to men.

Last night in the kitchen, I overheard Alice say to Daphne, "Remember your contract," (which was to be more assertive) when Iris had given some excuse not to do the dishes. Reminded, Daphne took a firmer stand and insisted Iris had time to do her chore before going to the pajama party.

As we drove, I asked Alice what would happen if she hadn't complied—would they drive matches under her fingernails?

"No, but they might make you *it*," said Alice, as if *it* were some nameless horror. What did she mean by *it*? "Well, it's like everyone gangs up on you for the entire two hours. It's enough to make you want to meet all your contracts."

Alice made one contract when the group complained she tended to shift her eyes away from a direct gaze while talking. Reminded of it repeatedly, by five people seven days a week, she broke the habit.

I left Harrad the next day. Almost two months elapsed while I was in the Southwest. On May 2, when I returned to Berkeley and called the house, Alice answered. They were still together, she replied to my anxious questioning, but I couldn't stay in the attic. A computer programmer who'd separated from his wife was boarding there. Since I'd written ahead that I might be coming back, Alice had arranged for me to stay at the McAllans, a hybrid name adopted by two couples who had a group marriage a few blocks away.

That was fine. I knew them already and had been wondering how their own experiment was working out. I'd sat next to Judy at one of Harrad's Wednesday night meetings. She was there to meet couples who might be interested in merging households with her and her husband, Bob. Like Bud and Daphne, they had tired of swinging and wanted a more encompassing arrangement similar to the Hershes' of *Proposition 31*. At the meeting she was introduced to Lynn and Jim, a younger couple. Two weeks later I had dinner with them, just after Lynn and Jim had moved in with Judy, Bob and their two children. At the time, everything seemed to be working out. The merger had reduced both couples' monthly expenses to $150. Jim had gone back to college to become an ecologist, and Judy and Bob paid off some past debts and still had some money left over to go out to dinner—without worrying about a babysitter. Lynn, who couldn't have children of her own because of a kidney ailment, was looking forward to being a surrogate mother. During the dinner, I remember, the four of them had exchanged tender glances. They were going through a honeymoon, Judy had apologized, adding that I should come back in a month when they'd come down to earth.

I did. Almost two months later and stayed with them while making daily visits to Harrad.

I took a bus to the McAllans' bungalow. Judy made coffee and filled me in on changes of the last months: The honeymoon was over and they were entering a "period of adjustment." The kids were getting on Lynn's nerves and she had fallen passionately in love with Bob, Judy's husband, and wanted to spend all her time with him and none with Jim, her own. Judy and the two men wanted a more balanced relationship, but every time they tried to explain this to Lynn, "she freaked out." The trials of adjustment drained Lynn, and when she came home from her job in the evening, she had no energy left to do her half of the housework. She began to feel it was Judy's house, not hers.

After much discussion and testing they'd agreed upon a schedule of alternating partners every three nights. "And the pattern seems to be that women maintain their own beds while the men shuttle."

The next morning as I sat in the kitchen while Judy baked, Lynn came in. Outside the kitchen window chubby robins stalked worms through the green grass. The fuchsia tree was budding. Lynn wrung her hands. Tears welled in her eyes. She'd wanted more love than Jim could give her; he had been her whole life; what he thought, she believed. When he became an atheist, so did she. When they moved in with Bob and Judy, she thought Bob's love added to Jim's would fulfill her, but Bob, she found, could be as distant as Jim. "I don't like to be alone," she said tearfully.

Bob came into the kitchen, crisp in a fresh shirt and tie. He kissed Lynn and Judy and went off to work on his bicycle. "Maybe your problem doesn't have anything to do with lack of love," Judy suggested.

Lynn shook her head from side to side. "If it's not love we're living for, what is it?"

As I walked up to Harrad West, a passage of *Women in Love*, which I'd read on the plane, came into my mind. Later I found it. Gudrun declares:

"You above everybody can't get away from the fact that love, for instance, is the supreme thing, in space as well as on earth." "No, it isn't," said Ursula. "Love is too *human* and little. I believe in something inhuman of which love is only a little part. I believe what we must fulfill comes out of the unknown to us. And it is something infinitely more. It isn't so merely *human*." [author's italics]

Alice filled me in on the newest convulsions. Emotionally, Bud was on the rampage. When he demanded that the group "divorce" Gloria, Herb had threatened to leave if Gloria did. Meanwhile, like Gloria, Daphne had asserted her sexual independence from both the house and Bud, and was continuing a relationship with Dick, a married man whom Bud said he detested. When Daphne refused to stop seeing him, Bud said they were pulling out of Harrad West. But Daphne refused— she wasn't his puppet anymore. Bud had slugged her.

Alice, who wanted to get away to play some tennis, drove through traffic as if the external world didn't exist. She narrowly missed two pedestrians. Had she ever thought of taking up yoga? I suggested. How could she, she replied, when all her energy was needed to keep constantly adjusted to five other egos? That was just the point, I said. Perhaps she should take a vacation from Harrad West to discover who the real Alice was. She'd thought of going to England in the summer to visit her sister, she said, "But I'm afraid I'll miss something."

Daphne was packing, emptying out drawers and sorting her clothes from Bud's. She had decided to move in with Dick and his wife (later, they formed a bisexual triad). To become financially independent, she had taken a job.

In every way, Daphne has fulfilled her contract to establish an identity apart from what Bud and the others had termed her "neurotic dependency." Bud had always encouraged her, she said, "to relate openly and freely and lovingly to other men, as well as to himself. And then as I did this and really grooved to some of the things that were happening to me, he got scared and jealous and threatened by Herb, Moishe and especially by Dick. The more I liked Dick, the more Bud disliked him. He kept saying that Dick and I were out to destroy him." One night, when Dick came by to pick her up, Bud provoked a fist fight.

"All of his talk about group marriage has been a head trip. I mean, down in his guts, he's very possessive. He can't even look at that part of himself."

The new Daphne is more "open and can express anger and feelings. I'm not afraid of bisexuality or of loving a number of people without getting dependent. I've realized that there's no security in marriage with one person. All you really have is being responsible for yourself. It's scary. But that's how it is."

If Bud had grown and changed along with her, the group marriage might have turned out differently, she said. "But he just sees the old me—the earth mother with children suckling at her breast and total allegiance to her man. I wonder if he ever knew me?"

She plans to keep in contact with Harrad West by returning for the encounters, for meetings and to see her kids—who seem generally unperturbed by the marital crisis.

May 3

Today, they had an encounter. After breakfast, the six braced themselves for the two-hour ordeal. The sessions are led by a psychologist who's paid $45 a meeting. Gloria chain-smoked, Bud paced. After it got underway, I went upstairs and intercepted phone calls.

Around noon they broke up and each fled the living room and the house. Alice begged me to play tennis again. "I've got to get out of here. I can't stand it."

While at Harrad West, I had to repress the impulse to say that instead of encountering, they should take up charades, monopoly, bridge, or listen to the *Grand Ol' Opry*. You shouldn't play group therapy too often, I would have told them; moreover, you shouldn't play it with people you have to live with from day to day. Maybe that's the whole problem with group marriage.

As the marriage began to break up, the group leaned more heavily on outside therapy. In addition to the two regular encounters, some of them attended nude encounters sponsored by the SFL. Bud and Daphne began to see individual psychotherapists.

Last night Bud relaxed on Alice's bed, eyes closed while she droned like a hypnotist, "Imagine yourself on a deserted beach at sunset. The soft lappings of waves . . . now relax your feet . . . your back . . . your neck." Having utterly relaxed Bud, Alice then proceeded to read, one at a time, the names of twenty people Bud had listed. She began at the top of the list with those most comfortable to Bud and continued in order of increasing discomfort. When she read a name that made him uptight, he raised a finger. Back to the top of the list. The theory is that through repetition, reinforcement and desensitization, anyone can overcome his irrational hatreds and dislikes: As Maslow suggests and Rimmer concludes, love *can* be taught. Herb is a believer. "If you keep at auto-suggestion and go over the list two thousand times a month, the positive associations begin to carry over to your negative ones."

All the Harrad members also do desensitization exercises designed to give a clearer perception of reality by overcoming verbal defensiveness. For example, in one exercise a partner can make no reply other than "Okay, you're right" to the other's criticism.

Daphne: "You're too demanding."

Bud: "Okay, you're right."

Daphne: "You talk too much about your anxieties. You're always saying, 'You know I love you a lot.' "

Bud: "Okay, you're right."

Moishe had misgivings about the self-flagellating nature of the encounters but went along with the group's joint efforts as a show of faith. He wished there were some other faith to keep them together.

Moishe was the member who always seemed to be standing on the fringe—smiling and smoking his pipe. He was intimate with Alice and Daphne but rarely gave outward signs of affection. He had little to say or do with Herb and Bud, a source of frustration to both of them. I'd been in the house several days before we exchanged more than a passing nod. This morning in the kitchen, he told me something of his past. As a child, he had been the youngest and frailest of many brothers and sisters in a Jewish household. He still remembers being beaten up by larger boys in his Brooklyn neighborhood. "I've had to struggle with a deep inferiority." Although psychotherapy helped make him aware of it, the group provided a new role. Daphne was the first woman with whom he's had a fully satisfying relationship. However, Harrad has not been able to overcome his inability to relate to other men. "There's a lot of competition going on here," he said, "under the surface. If you'd sit in on one of our encounters, you'd see what I mean."

He didn't mean sexual competition. "It's competition to see who can be the least jealous. Who has the well-adjusted ego. It gets to be very punishing."

Moishe wished that Harrad could pattern itself more after his communal ideal—the Oneida Community. Over the years, he has filled an album with photostatic copies of Oneida documents. Located in upstate New York, Oneida flourished between

1844 and 1879. It practiced a form of group marriage—"complex marriage"—based on the "perfectionist" theology of its founder, John Humphrey Noyes. From his reading of the New Testament, Noyes equated monogamy with hoarding. At Oneida, any consenting two couples could cohabit, but if they became too attached and possessive, the group encouraged them to take other partners. The men practiced *coitus reservatus,* a form of contraception, and tantric yoga. They called their encounters "mutual criticism meetings."

"They were a lot kinder than ours," said Moishe, finding me an example of Oneida criticism in his album: "He is warmhearted and a man of tender sensibilities. He is governed by the spirit of truth more than most men, but his mind and manners do not represent his heart."

May 4

Paging through the morning paper, I stopped to check my horoscope and then asked Herb what the others' sun signs were. He didn't know; moreover, he mocked, "You don't believe in that stuff, do you?" Well, I answered, it was as plausible an explanation for behavior as any. But not to Herb or the others. That is one thing they do share: an association of the supernatural and spiritual with the puritanical religious training of their past.

Herb is an atheist. One night, while on the subject of religion, he referred to primitive cults who tore off their genitals in sacrifice to the gods. Harrad's disinterest in things spiritual was one reason one couple decided not to join. "They were followers of Krishnamurti," Herb recalled. "The girl told me that she regarded sexuality as one of the urges she had to satisfy before reaching the godhead. I got the impression that her goal was celibacy."

This general attitude of rational humanism, so skeptical of the supernatural, is shared by several other group marriages. Notable exceptions are Kerista, a hip-style, mystical group in San Francisco, and the American Landuist Society, a Dionysianlike cult devoted to worship of a twelfth-century god, Apu Landu. Seventeen times a year the society reportedly holds orgies at its one-hundred-acre estate outside Los Angeles.

Morally, Herb doesn't disapprove of orgies, but building a stable group marriage is another proposition demanding firmer, more rational structure. Like Rimmer, he believes the human mind and sexuality are the actual source of the mysteries that religion mistakenly placed outside man. "It's exhilarating that man can keep pushing back the barriers of his mind. There's no limit to what he learns about himself."

While Herb spoke, Alice listened on the bed. Suddenly, she said, "Do you mean that you could know everything—well, most everything there is to know about—say—*me?*"

Herb smiled. "I already know everything about you."

That angered her. "You think you know, but you're wrong!"

May 5

They held their regular business meeting this afternoon. It began with the reading of a behavioral text that was passed around the group. One person read a passage aloud, and the person to his left filled in the blank. Herb read, "If a child is not positively reinforced by other children, he feels (blank) in a crowded room." After a moment's thought, Daphne provided the missing word "anxious." The exercise was a behavioral technique of learning behaviorism.

The next order of business was the totaling of the week's labor credits. Herb, who was the manager of the system, read off the credits and the final total. But when he came to Gloria's work, which included the cleaning of the third-floor bathroom, the operation once again became encounter. "I've never seen such encrusted dirt," declared Daphne, challenging Gloria's claim of 1.5 credit. "And the smell from the cat boxes is disgusting." Gloria waived the credit, but insisted she should get more credit if she were to do a thorough cleaning. She refused to move the boxes. "Damned if I'll put them in my room."

Next they discussed the Wednesday night forums. Attendance

had fallen off to around five, sometimes none. Herb was disappointed so few people in the San Francisco area were interested in group marriage. The few who did come were from out of town. Worse, some Harrad members had lost interest in the meetings. Daphne had become irritated by strangers who pointed up the discrepancy between group marriage as depicted by Rimmer and Harrad West. They decided to suspend the meetings. Bud suggested, "If anyone writes in, we'll invite them over for the evening."

The main topic, though, was the auto-suggestion exercise. The group was drifting apart, despite the exercises. Herb said the reason was that some members weren't faithfully performing their hour a day. He proposed doubling the exercise time and allotting labor credits as a means of reinforcement. (A Harrad member must contribute to the common treasury if he fails to meet that week's labor credit minimum.)

Moishe exploded: "You can't treat me like a Pavlovian dog. I'm too old to be brainwashed into thinking I can love someone when I can't!"

Herb appealed, "We've got to go all the way with this program. That's been our trouble. We don't stick to any structure. Why, at Mendocino State, the program had wonderful results. . . ."

Moishe: "But that's a state hospital! You can't cut off my food and water if I don't do my exercises."

Herb gave up and proposed setting aside an exercise hour when everyone would be at home. Alice suggested the mornings. Gloria objected, "You know that I can't be here because of my job—you're deliberately trying to exclude me." Like the marriage, the meeting teetered on dissolution.

Alice admitted misgivings, but for the sake of house morale and to show she was 100 percent committed to keeping the marriage together, she agreed to an established hour. Bud followed suit. As he spoke, his hands shook. "Herb could be right. We haven't given it a chance. If we do it regularly for a month, then we'll know one way or the other." What could Moishe do but go along? They also decided to drive up to Mendocino State that weekend and watch the program in action.

Bud seemed shattered, broken. He sank into a sofa and talked, talked—like a stuck record—of old remorse and dreams. Herb had let him down again. He had supported Herb, for what? He'd thought Herb was a brother. But Herb was too busy, too self-concerned. He rambled on about his grandfather's farm, where the whole family had gone on Fourth of July picnics. *They* were concerned about each other's welfare. Alice put her arms around Bud. "Honey, you never had a happy family. All this talk about the farm is a dream that never came true. We're not your old family. You can't take us all back to Missouri."

Bud exclaimed, "Why not? We could all go up to Mendocino County and buy a farm, grow our own crops, work side by side. We wouldn't have any energy left for our neuroses."

Alice didn't need to reply. They'd been through this before. And after all, what did they know about farming?

After the meeting I talked with Bud in his room. He seemed to have reached rockbottom. During his marriage to Daphne, he thought he'd been happy. But that was an illusion. He had mistaken neurotic dependency for love. Daphne had been a crutch for him, and he'd been a crutch for her—two monkeys scratching each other's backs.

After they became less dependent on each other, Bud had turned to the others for "strokes" (a term he uses for psychological reinforcement or, simply, love). Alice loved him, but that wasn't enough. She and the others had their own ego problems. So he was thrown back on himself. And how could he love himself? He felt only despair—but at least that was real and intense.

"If I feel real low now, maybe someday I'll be able to feel the high highs." He turned to me for a sign I agreed—some assurance that even though the path he'd chosen had led to crack-up, it would ultimately bring him to full realization of his humanity.

Iris swirled into the room. She wore a black armband in mourning for the Kent State students who'd been shot to death by the Ohio National Guard. She told Bud of the window breaking that occurred at her high school in protest. She had walked away from the violence.

After she left, Bud's spirit seemed to revive. "Iris is turning out okay. We may all be too old for group marriage—too many ingrained hangups. If we don't make it, then at least we've given our kids a chance to be free."

That afternoon I asked Iris if she would ever join a group marriage. She thought a moment, smearing peanut butter on a piece of bread. Not right away, she answered. First, she'd like to have a close one-to-one relationship, not necessarily a legal marriage. She wasn't opposed to group marriage, but loving one other person was enough to start with.

May 6

Alice drove me to the airport. It was a clear, sunny morning. Whitecaps glittered against the turquoise of San Francisco Bay. We put the top of the Volks down before getting on the freeway. We basked in the light, the rush of wind and on the radio: "Here Comes the Sun"—the heady sense of freedom peculiar to Americans cruising at 60 mph on a freeway.

Alice was developing a taste for a life apart from Harrad and Herb. A year ago, when Herb used to go off to weekend SFL parties, Alice had moped around the house. Now she picks up the phone and makes her own dates.

We parked on Broadway and walked past the row of bars that advertise their topless waitresses and fly SEX pennants. We found a table outside at Enrico's and had corned beef sandwiches and gin and tonics. I was catching a flight to Santa Fe. Alice gave me the name and address of Lloyd who might know about communes. He was an old boyfriend. "Have you ever wished you could go back and relive a portion of your life? If I ever met Lloyd again, I thought I'd tell him: 'What a waste that we never got to know each other; that we never made love five years ago . . .' but I couldn't be so easy about it, then."

As she grew less dependent, Alice came to the realization that "love is something inside. It doesn't have to be all tied up with one other person. It doesn't have to be earth-moving. Love can be friendly, love can be fun. Take you," she said. "If you stayed with us longer, I'd want to sleep with you just to know and enjoy you."

Back on the freeway, we passed flocks of ducks bobbling close to the bay's rocky inlets. In the airport lounge, another pair of gin and tonics and a dash to the gate. The plane was boarding.

"I feel like going along," she bubbled. "Maybe it's the gin, but I feel very free . . . don't forget to look up Lloyd for me."

"Should I tell him how you feel—that you wished you and he could go back five years?"

"No, I don't want to go back," she answered and gave me a companionable kiss. And so we parted, after another kiss, friends.

During the summer, I got several letters from members of Harrad. They anatomized their disintegration. As Daphne spent more time away from the house, Bud became desperate and, finally, violent. One night he chased Herb around the house, angered that "I had invested everything [in the experiment] and that lazy son of a bitch had done nothing." He hurled a perfume bottle at him, lacerating his forehead. That night, Alice got Bud admitted to a psychiatric ward. Herb moved out, concluding that the experiment in group marriage had failed.

He sent me his analysis:

I regard my year and a half's participation in a group marriage community as an intense learning experience. In fact, one of my purposes in being there was to try to find out the reason why group marriages prove so unstable, generally. My feeling was that there could be many more operating successfully if people could know the problems to watch out for. The main problem is that no one can relate equally and so some feel left out. They then try to force the others to spend more time with them, thus creating obligations which are resented. If they would seek their further friendships outside the small group the marriage could work. But few people are this emotionally mature and so they resort to destructive behavior outside the group. . . . Therefore my conclusion is that

group marriages composed of a small number are extremely hazard-
ous. I wouldn't bet on anything lasting more than six months.

Herb added that he was helping organize a residence club of
150 people who specifically believe in "sexual freedom." It
would be managed by a corporation and business manager and
would rent out rooms at $150 a month. "There would be ample
privacy," Herb wrote. "And when you want companionship,
you can find it instantly in the public rooms and dining areas.
If you choose your companions from a hundred and fifty people
instead of six, your chances of compatibility are greatly enhanced . . . The principles that would make the club a success
are: freedom of interrelationship; emotional self-determination
—if a person feels he has a jealousy or possessiveness problem, he
may decide to join a growth program (encounter groups sponsored by the corporation); the right to individual privacy and
heterosexuality and bisexuality."

Gloria also moved out after falling in love with a man twenty
years younger. They were living together, she wrote. "At this
point monogamy is for me . . . though it's possible in the future
that I might become involved in another group marriage."
Alice flew to England and spent the summer with her sister. She
returned—but not to Herb. She went back to Harrad to live
with Bud, his three kids, and two boarders, an eighteen-year-old
girl who worked as a student teacher, and a sixteen-year-old girl
who was attending a Summerhillian school in Berkeley. They
were no longer a group marriage, Bud wrote, nevertheless, "We
function as a family: joyful, angry, helpful, turned on, turned
off. Our children are cared for, we care for each other."

At about the same time, the McAllan marriage broke up. Judy
wrote that Lynn began "freaking out three times a week." She
still clung to Bob. The kids had begun to bug her. She had
nothing in common with Judy except the two men. Once, at
around 3 A.M., she woke Judy and Jim with screams that Jim
had dragged her into marriage. In August, Lynn and Jim moved
out.

Bob and Judy did not abandon hope for an expanded family.

But if they marry again, Judy wrote, they will find a larger house. "This doesn't necessarily mean a separate house, but just one structured to allow for complete privacy. A second need is a more natural way of getting to know one another before deciding on a group. I want to be close friends with both the female and male in a relationship. Third, we won't try to program the relationship the way we did. . . . I may be insane, but in my insanity I feel that there still exists the possibility of group marriage. I just don't have all the answers."

Yet another experiment began, made up of ex-members from Harrad West and the McAllan marriage. Moishe joined Daphne, Dick, and his wife. Later, Jim and Lynn moved in. "It's very different from Harrad West," Daphne told me over the phone. "Nobody asks who's been sleeping with whom—in or outside the house. We don't have any schedule and we've been getting into group sex. We don't struggle to live up to any high ideal. That was the trouble with Harrad—you felt guilty if you didn't love everybody. Here, we have our own friends, jobs and activities. There are three kitchens in the house so it's a lot freer— more like a community."

The actual Harrad experiment had turned out far differently from the novel. The obvious difference was the one between fiction and reality—between Rimmer's characters, who are so objective and good-humored they seem already to have undergone intensive therapy, and real flesh-and-blood people who hadn't gone to Harrad College and been imbued with a new social and sexual ethic. Instead, they had grown up in America and hadn't emerged unscathed.

The experiment didn't fail because the six were all psychological cripples; on the contrary, they seemed to me to have the normal degree and variety of hangups, no more or less than most people of their age and background. But unlike most, they had joined a group marriage. And the intensity of the experience brought everything to the surface: Daphne's thwarted independence, and bisexuality; Bud's compulsive need for external approval, and possessiveness; Gloria's unconscious separation of sexuality from tenderness.

But much of the conflict was derived not from individual neuroses but from hangups common to the whole of American society and culture. The inability of men to communicate, cooperate and to love each other, nonsexually, as brothers; and the overemphasis on love and sex as an escape from the hollowness and aloneness of the innermost self.

However, Harrad West was more than good therapy. For the first time in her life, Gloria learned how to love with both her body and her emotions. For Alice and Daphne, Harrad erased the imprint of an old sexual and social code, freed them from the restraining roles and allowed them to love in a number of ways—to be fuller people. But for Bud, the Harrad experience— particularly Daphne's new independent identity—triggered a deep self-questioning. Again and again, the others had told Bud that he had to learn how to love in a different way. First he had to accept and love himself. But who was Bud? he asked. For a time he heard only echoes of his own question. The others couldn't help find the answer. Like Bud, they had also come to the point where they must grow alone. So, like the characters in the book, the six didn't live happily ever after—at least not together.

These were only hunches as to why the real Harrad experiment fell short of the fictional one. Later in the year, I interviewed Robert Rimmer in Boston to get his explanation. We met at the offices of his family-owned printing business, located in a grimy old Victorian building that had a modern facing. At fifty-three, Rimmer looks like F. Scott Fitzgerald in his stocky middle years. He has broad shoulders, a wide smile, and a young easygoing manner.

"I lead a Jekyll and Hyde existence," he said as we galloped down the four flights of stairs rather than wait for the elevator. Ten years ago, as an escape from the tedium of running the business, Rimmer had turned to writing novels.

In addition to writing and the business, he lectures at colleges and at meetings of marriage counselors and psychologists. He hopes that Harrad College will be endowed, but he's not crusading for it or group marriage.

A group in Cambridge started a *Harrad Newsletter* to drum up interest in group marriage but suspended publication, charging that Rimmer had been uncooperative. Once during a speaking engagement, he was sharply questioned by a young psychologist who demanded that Rimmer reveal if his private life corresponded to his public advocacy of multilateral marriage. Rimmer's reply was his standard one: "All I've written is based on personal experience, but I can't say any more than that until social attitudes change. I still have to live in a society."

The psychologist denounced Rimmer as a fraud. Rimmer, who told me the story, shrugged it off, saying that young people are too prone to despise anything that smacks of hypocrisy.

Over lunch, I asked him what went wrong at Harrad West. He hadn't heard about the breakup; moreover, he'd never visited it. Why?

His explanation was vague—that he was a novelist and not the leader of a social movement. Though he wrote as if group marriage could save the world, he doesn't act or talk that way.

"A lot of group marriages get too ingrown. They spend too much time encountering and don't have any outside goals."

Could a group marriage succeed without any structured means of airing gripes, conflicts and jealousies?

Well, he conceded, six people were complicated. The constant adjustment didn't leave them much time and energy to seek goals, he admitted. Yet it could work if they were the *right* six. He said Harrad West was evidently the wrong six. They lacked the vital ingredient: "I understand that they weren't sexually attractive. Now take . . . [a mutual female acquaintance who was rather plain], now you wouldn't enter into a group marriage with her," he said. And pressing the point, he gestured across the table to Daisy, my attractive sister-in-law who'd come along for the interview. "Now, you and your wife might try it with Daisy and another man," he proposed, winking. But he was serious when he asked, "Why not?"

I didn't answer him fully (any more than he did my questions), but I tried to say that I thought group marriage a possible alternative for a small, tough-minded fraction of the population who still wanted to make it in the cities, but that I was convinced it wouldn't be as he described; rather, it would tend to resemble Herb's residence club of free swingers. Harrad West had failed, not for the lack of sexual allure or sexual jealousy, but because they had nothing *but* sex to hold them together— no common culture, no nonsexual forms of communicating and expressing love.

I told Rimmer that over the last year, I had come around to seeing my own marriage as one of the last refuges of romanticism. Two people who really worked at it could develop a deep, non-possessive love that satisfied both their egos and souls. The ultimate goal was to learn how to love. It didn't matter how. No doubt, group marriage was one of the strongest antidotes for possessiveness, jealousy and role-playing.

But as a permanent alternative to monogamy, I wouldn't consider it before I had first found a new community in which to set the expanded family—a new community with some objective higher than human love. Such a community would naturally relieve a lot of the emotional pressure and sexual monotony, as well as spiritual anxiety.

I asked Rimmer if he had heard of any group marriage living on a farm, close to the land. He hadn't.

VII

Virginia

Twin Oaks: A Walden Two *Experiment*

By the time I set out to visit Twin Oaks in August I had acquired many preconceptions about this *Walden Two* community located in Virginia. Relatively an older community (founded in 1967), Twin Oaks had been written up in *Modern Utopia*, the *New York Times Magazine* and other publications, and had attracted flocks of "commune watchers" like myself and visitors, both hip and straight.

Throughout my communal travels, I was always bumping into someone who had either visited or been one of Twin Oaks' many short-term members. Their reactions varied sharply. Hippies were repulsed by its emphasis on organization, behavioralism, and technology.

However, others—scientists, students and straight professionals—came away impressed that Twin Oaks was an exceptional example of social planning and technological efficiency, an encouraging contrast to the typical commune's disorganization, instability and insolvency. In these respects, Twin Oaks was praised as the one American community that could rival Israel's kibbutzim.

August 12

Twin Oaks is on the edge of the Piedmont region, about one hundred miles southwest of Washington, D.C. From Boston I took a train and headed down the Northeast Corridor, shimmering with midsummer fumes and humidity. I knew the trip too well. Miles of sidings, industrial stockpiles, abandoned passenger stations, whose cement platforms, covered with broken glass, had cracked and sprouted grass. After the first few miles, I pulled down the black, old-fashioned shade and turned to my file on Twin Oaks.

Like Harrad West, Twin Oaks was the outgrowth of a utopian novel—B. F. Skinner's *Walden Two*. B. F. Skinner, a psychologist, is known primarily for broadening the theory that behavior can be determined—"conditioned" is the word he used—by appropriate rewards and punishments. Although Skinner originally based his theories on experiments with rats, many other behavioralists have recently applied the principles to man's behavioral problems. Today conditioning is widely used to cure a host of ills ranging from homosexuality and alcoholism to claustrophobia.

In *Walden Two*, Skinner became one of the first to apply behavioral theory to man's institutions. In 1948 Skinner and many other social scientists saw utopia as within man's reach—if not utopia, then at least a *good* society in which starvation could be abolished, health and education guaranteed, and drudgery reduced by technology to a point where man for once could develop his "higher nature."

After two world wars, no one doubted that the technological and industrial power existed. The key was to put science and power in the service of humanity, to apply the scientific method to man's social environment, incorporating the findings of social science in the design of a new order that would avoid the environmental defects of the past. Neither inherently good nor bad, man was often the victim of his environment. Why couldn't he learn from his past mistakes and design a community with none of the structural flaws that had always created conflict, disorder and frustration? In part, *Walden Two* was Skinner's attempt to show it *could* be done; that the scientific method could be used to engineer a community whose structure would work to promote stability, cooperation and a maximum of leisure time.

No dry theoretical treatise, *Walden Two* is narrated by a visitor, a Professor Burris, who comes to Walden Two ten years after the colony's inception. Burris is an old friend of Frazier, who founded the community with a $1,000,000 endowment from an anonymous benefactor. With a population of one thousand and vast acreage, Walden Two is totally self-contained. It has its own school, farm, dairy, doctors, dentists and industry (producing and selling bricks of rammed earth). The community is apolitical. Policy decisions are made by six planners appointed from the ranks of managers. Members are bound by a code of moral behavior.

In the novel, *Walden Two*'s distinguishing feature is its labor credit system. On an equal basis, members can choose from a variety of jobs. Everyone benefits from the community's efficient planning, central purchasing, high technical productivity, and nonprofit structure. As a net result, the average workday has been cut to four hours. Much of the labor saving is due to the community's social environment. Rid of competition for status and profit, members work more productively than they would under capitalism. They use their free time to paint, make music and attend the community's full program of activities: concerts, theater and lectures.

The only overt conditioning is applied to the children, who are reared in a communal dormitory apart from their parents and under the constant guidance of a children's manager. At an early age, they are conditioned to develop positive social traits like courage, self-reliance and compassion. Skinner gives one example of how children can be taught self-control:

A group of children arrive home after a long walk tired and hungry. They're expecting supper; they find, instead, that it's time for a lesson in self-control: they must stand for five minutes in front of steaming bowls of soup. The assignment is accepted like a problem in arithmetic.

In the last few years, sales of *Walden Two* surged toward the million mark. Most of its readers are young people born in the early postwar years, when the novel was published. Their parents may have read it, but unlike them, the new *Walden Two* enthusiasts were going beyond the book, beyond theory.

I closed the underlined paperback edition I'd read in college and raised the blinds. Shopping centers and high-rise apartments reared out of the lush green of the Maryland suburbs. Time was running out for reading about utopias.

August 13

Hitchhiked the remaining twenty miles to the community. Deep green pastures, separated by thickets of scrawny pines stunted by the sandy soil, rolled gently to a hazy blue horizon. No rides. I turned off the highway and followed a dirt road, stopping along the way to pick handfuls of huckleberries to quench my thirst. Passing a church and a pre-Civil War sawmill that still used the river's power, I turned left and covered the last mile to the community.

Their driveway was marked by a mailbox bearing two oaks that branched from a common trunk. It led to a small clapboard farmhouse shaded by a grove of oaks. There was a swing on the gabled porch and around the house a collection of cars, trucks, buses, and dogs.

The community had named its three main buildings after earlier communitarian experiments. The farmhouse, which contained the kitchen and dining area, was called Llano, after New Llano, from 1914 to 1935 a cooperative community in California and later, Louisiana. From Llano, rock-lined paths connected two larger buildings. The nearest and newest was Oneida, a large two-story building containing the commune's offices, library, and an unfinished dormitory. Its second floor had ten windows all the same size and shape.

The more distant building was Harmony, a bulky asphalt-shingled structure that looked like a summer camp rec hall and that housed the community's one money-making industry, a hammock works. It had been named after New Harmony, Indiana (1825–28), a colony financed and planned by Robert Owen, the early Socialist thinker and reformer. Owen, who lost £40,000 in the venture, designed New Harmony as an alternative for the common man to the exploitative and diseased conditions of industrial cities. When the colony was wracked by disputes over religion and forms of government, he abandoned the project.

Samples of the hammocks were hung from the apple trees along the paths. To the rear of Harmony was a line of farm buildings, a barn and several sheds. They stood on the brink of a pasture that dipped down and rose again on a far hill edged by a uniform line of oaks.

The first person to whom I introduced myself immediately referred me to the community's official "visitor greeter," who, he thought, was Paul—this week. I found Paul. But he couldn't "greet" me because that had been his job last week. This week's greeter was Peggy, who was working at the community's store a few miles away. Nevertheless, Paul would show me around. He was a jovial young man in his twenties, dark-skinned, with close-cut black hair. Before coming here, he'd spent a year on a kibbutz.

He asked how long I'd be staying, gave me a booklet on the community, explained that the charge for week-long visitors was $1.50 a day, and told me my name would be placed on the labor credit system. He also advised me to "direct most of your questions to me or your greeter. Try not to pester the other members."

We walked down the path to Oneida. Outside, Walter, a tall young man, used an electric saw to cut boards. An air conditioner hummed in the lounge, where a few people were sunk in chairs, reading. In the office an older woman tapped an adding machine as she compiled a dietary study. Paul introduced me to another woman, who was typing a letter on an IBM Selectric. She was Kathleen "Kat" Griebe, one of Twin Oaks' eight founders. In her forties, she had short curly hair, worry wrinkles on her forehead, and was dressed in jeans and a flowered blouse. While chatting, we discovered a mutual acquaintance in Herb of Harrad West. Kat and Herb had been members of a Washington, D.C., cooperative—the nucleus of those who founded Twin Oaks. Before the group relocated to the farm, Herb had left the co-op because, he said, they were too sexually inhibited.

Kat recounted some of the changes that had taken place over the past three years, as Twin Oaks evolved from a group of eight social theorists, radicals and academicians to a community of thirty.

The community changed as younger members joined—many of them had never read of Skinner or Marx, but still fervently believed in an egalitarian social order. Kat referred to the period when a group cohesiveness began to emerge as the "socialization" of the community: "Intellectually, we met the fact that we had to think in terms of cultural changes on top of the superstructure of economic equality. Sexual freedom was the first and most important by far. Then we made our attempts at cooperative rather than competitive games. The youngest people were enthusiastic about these things, gave themselves to it wholeheartedly and helped us put it over. I didn't have much to do with it. I just watched and learned."

Kat paused to answer the questions of the woman nutritionist, who taught at a state university in Michigan and was here visiting her daughter. (I later observed that her daughter, Marnie, never referred to her as Mother, since that and other honorific titles—Doctor, mister, Dad—are forbidden by the first tenet of the community's credo, referred to as The Code: "All members are 'equal' in the sense that all are entitled to the same privileges, advantages and respect.")

While the women talked, I took mental notes on the room. A wall of books rested on board-and-brick shelves and were labeled by subject. The largest section comprised books on Communist China, and the smallest an ill assortment of fiction. The outside wall was made up of vertical slatlike windows of clear, heavy plastic. In the spaces between hung guitars and banjos. The overhead lights were fluorescent. The rug on the cement floor looked freshly vacuumed; in fact, a small sign on the wall informed me that THIS ROOM WAS CLEANED BY . . . and it gave three names and the date of the cleaning. In the corner,

next to the IBM, was an addressograph machine used to mail the community's newsletter, *Leaves of Twin Oaks*. A magazine rack contained issues of *Rat* and *Peking Review*. Opposite the windows, against a bare wall, was a row of desks. Behind a closed door and down a book-lined corridor were the small, private rooms of members. A flight of steps, unpainted two-by-sixes, went up to an unfinished second floor, temporarily a dormitory for visitors. The overall impression was of spare, utilitarian compactness.

"Have you had dinner?" Kat asked. No, I answered in dismay. I thought it was only 5:30. "But you're an hour behind Twin Oaks," she said, turning her wrist to let me verify the hour. She explained why the community had moved its clocks ahead. It had been too much of a shock for city workers to get up at 6 A.M. "Getting up at seven doesn't seem as bad, and being an hour ahead of the rest of the country is so symbolic."

I walked back to Llano, hoping to get some leftovers. Inside the front door, I passed a rack of envelope-sized cubbyholes for each member's mail and for intracommunity communications. A pencil dangling from a string and a stack of 3 by 5 index cards were provided for note writing. Other slots were marked "visitors' mail," "lost and found," "bills and labor credits slips," and a "bitch box" for complaints.

The first floor was divided into two cramped dining areas. The larger seated some sixteen people on uncomfortable blue seats that had been unbolted from a bus. Pots of food and plates were ranged cafeteria-style on a long table. I helped myself to overdone corn and turkey casserole (few vegetarians here), spinach and creamy milk from the community's three Holsteins. I passed up lime and grape Kool-Aid (each night two different flavors were offered alongside the milk).

As I stood getting my dinner at the counter, Carl introduced himself. A tall, gangly eighteen-year-old, who wears thick glasses, Carl dropped out of high school. "High school was boring. I was into science, and I knew more than most of the teachers." He left home to live with a group of young radicals in Wilmington, Delaware. After local police disrupted their demonstrations and busted them on various charges he came to Twin Oaks. In less than a year he's risen to one of the most responsible posts: manager of the hammock business.

Carl wanted to learn what I knew of spiritual communities, such as Lama, which he was considering visiting on his four-week vacation.

Vacation?

Briefly, Carl explained that the extra work points accrued by each member are credited toward vacation time, added on to the standard two weeks. "It's an inducement to do more than the quota." He wanted to visit places like Lama because he was one of the few at Twin Oaks interested in yoga and spiritual growth. Most of the others were atheists or agnostics, he said, who dismissed religion as "supernatural" and "irrational."

As we talked, he shoveled three heaping teaspoons of Quik into a plastic tumbler and filled it with milk. Two other visitors were trying to defrost the three refrigerators from instructions on a typed list of job descriptions on the kitchen wall.

The eight "outside workers" arrived in the kitchen from their jobs in Richmond. They were currently assigned to the two-month term of outside employment that rotates among the membership. They seemed grouchy and found fault with the dinners set aside for them.

Wages from outside employment accounted for half the community's income for 1970—around $32,000. Workers turn their checks in to Kat, the treasurer, and receive no more cash than the other members—the weekly 25-cent allowance, which Carl, for example, spends on chocolate footballs. The other half of the income comes from lectures and visitors' fees ($6,000), odd jobs, cattle sales, donations from incoming members, and hammock sales. The latter accounted for only $1,000. But the community hopes that eventually the hammock business and other "cottage industries" will bring enough cash so that members will no longer have to be dispatched to the outside economy.

We walked over to Harmony. In the dip of the pasture someone was bringing in the cows with calls of "cum-moose, cum-moose." A couple lay side by side in a hammock strung between two apple trees. Nearby, a girl picked up fallen apples and put them into a burlap bag. "She'll feed them to the hogs," said Carl. "It's one of the favorite jobs."

Harmony's cement floor and high roof reminded me of an airplane hangar. It smelled of sawdust and shellac.

A central work space was bordered by the rooms of members. The private rooms of members surrounded a central work space. Each door bore a Greek letter: alpha, beta, gamma, etc. "We wanted to avoid references like 'Kat's room' or 'my room,' " explained Carl, "to try to free people from thinking in terms of private property. It reinforces possessiveness." Though not private property, the rooms are guardedly personal. In fact, one of the tenets of The Code asserts that "individual rooms are inviolate," and it prohibits anyone from entering another's without permission. The door of Upsilon had been left ajar, revealing a 12-by-12-foot space, bare plywood walls, a mattress resting on cement blocks.

The upper end of the work space was blocked off by shelves of clothes and linens available for anyone's use. A large area was taken up by an offset press and photographic equipment. In one corner, a table was covered by tools and electric gadgets, with a list of dos and don'ts to follow in using them posted nearby. Most of the space was devoted to making hammocks. Stacks of them, wrapped in plastic bags, were ready for shipment. Shellacked oak frames were drying. There were large rolls of polypropylene rope, a synthetic fiber, which, Carl informed me, had proved stronger and more mildew resistant than natural rope.

Carl showed me the shuttle winder he'd invented to speed the measuring and marking of loop lengths for the hammocks. In the last year, Carl said proudly, man-hour labor had been nearly halved by the introduction of time-saving devices ranging from an electric drill press to a bolt holder used to tease rope ends through holes in the frames.

"Our biggest problem has been marketing," said Carl. "The manager before me had a nervous breakdown and left during the height of the buying season. No one else wanted to go around to the department stores. They felt it was too capitalistic." Carl doesn't look forward to the sales trip either, but he will do it "for the good of the community."

Carl left to do the evening milking. I strolled into the yard behind Llano. Laundry—the third batch of the day—hung on the clothesline. Someone was cutting the yard with a gas lawn mower. Paul was cleaning the parts of a Volkswagen bus. I sat down at one of three picnic tables, across from Rudy, the other founder still at Twin Oaks. He was talking with Dick, who'd just returned from his job as foreman at a Richmond factory. They discussed the community's newest offset printing industry. Twin Oaks had been given a contract to print a five-hundred-page textbook on behavioral psychology, and Rudy and Dick were trying to decide if it would be cheaper and faster for them to collate the book by hand or to lease a collating machine.

Hammocks and printing were just two of the industries and businesses attempted by Twin Oaks. Their first enterprise was directly borrowed from the fictional *Walden Two*. They bought a rammed earth machine for $175 to make building blocks of earth and 10 percent cement. Members spent hours shoveling and sifting the rocks from the red dirt. After making a few trial bricks, they computed the value of their labor at five cents an hour. The machine was sold for a slight loss.

Next, they manufactured electric film rewinders. But their sales distributors fell through. Last summer, on a grant from the Homer Morris Fund, a small foundation that assists intentional communities, they went into the veal-calf business. The idea was to buy the calves for $12 a head, nourish them off the commune's cows, and sell them for $100 each. The scheme was a complete flop. First, the cattle manager, the only one who knew much about animal husbandry, left the community. Due to the others' inexperience, the cattle weren't fed enough during the winter and came down with worms and other parasites. Two cows died. But even if it had weathered the winter, the business would have still folded. Unknown to the community, there was no local supply of day-old calves. The dairymen who used to sell them had gone into the veal business themselves. The community lost over $1,500 on the deal.

Nevertheless, Rudy is still confident that aspects of modern technology—like offset printing—*can* be adapted to make small-scale, decentralized industries profitable. Their press was the gift of a friend. "The rest of the equipment," Rudy said, referring to stencil cutters and silk-screen duplicators, "Can be leased almost anyplace in the U.S. at low prices."

Rudy, who's twenty-six, wears his long black hair tied back with a piece of rawhide, Indian-style. Today he had a STOP-THE-WAR button pinned to his blue chambray shirt. Reared in Atlanta, he has a mild accent and speaks cautiously and slowly. Though the acknowledged social theorist in the community, Rudy seems intently uncommunicative. I learned more of his views by reading a pamphlet of his, published by the Twin Oaks Press:

What if we just went ahead as though the revolution were over and we had won? What would a postrevolutionary society be like? A society committed to nonaggression, where one man's gain is not another's less, where work is minimized and leisure is maximized? . . . decentralized societal units of approximately 1,000 people or whatever size proves to be the most beneficial in terms of economic efficiency and sociopsychological health . . . [which] accepts active planning, active control of institutions of that society, active manipulation of the environment to produce the kind of life we really want. . . . They would be the vanguard of a federation of communes which would be the basis of a new society and they would serve as "propaganda by example."

Like *Walden Two,* Twin Oaks posts notices of evening activities. Tonight on the green chalk board in the kitchen was written "Oneida—Discussion." It didn't come off. Instead, the room was filled with readers and silent but for the air conditioner. In the twilight, I took off my shoes and walked toward the field. (I usually don't go barefoot, but Twin Oaks was affecting me.) A large area had been plowed, but was barren; early crops might have been harvested, but if so, nothing had been replanted. What crops there were looked neglected. I went down through the pasture. On the way back, I came across an empty root cellar inhabited by bats. Near the farmhouse was the plywood frame of an unused greenhouse. I stopped by the kitchen for a glass of milk and went to bed feeling down.

August 14

Wakened by the rustles and flaps of birds nesting under the eaves of Oneida, where I'd slept on the second floor. I didn't feel like getting up. For a while, I lay on my back regarding the functional wallpaper that covered the underside of the roof: "Owens-Corning Fiberglass . . . World's Leading Insulation . . . R-11, 3½. . . . Apply this side toward living space."

Like the rest of Twin Oaks' architecture, Oneida's style was starkly utilitarian. The room looked like a firehouse. Two rows of black poles thrust through the floor. They had been sunk into the asphalt foundation and supported the building's weight, relieving its interior walls. The advantage of pole construction, Rudy had told me, was that it saved lumber and allowed the interior walls to be moved at will.

The other visitors were already up. I went downstairs, stopping at the foot to read two typewritten pages marked "To the attention of visitors." They described the inner workings of the community—its meetings, "group rap" sessions, mutual criticism, and ended with the main point, that visitors should refrain from wasting members' time with "all-knowing" questions. We were warned not to expect personal treatment. I was not surprised. This wasn't a hip commune, and I hadn't come here expecting to be welcomed as a soul brother. Twin Oaks was determined to create a "viable alternative" to capitalism, and that was very *serious* business.

Breakfast was a make-your-own affair. Loaves of commercial "enriched" white bread, peanut butter, and a toaster were set out on a table. I sat down next to the nutritionist, who'd completed her study of Twin Oaks' diet. After analyzing the food consumption that a sampling of members had agreed to record, she'd concluded that the diet many chose was nutritionally weak, even though the farm offered a selection of balanced and nutritious foods. "There's plenty of fresh milk, but they drink Kool-Aid," she said, "and pass up greens that come right out of the garden."

At Twin Oaks the organic purity of foods is a secondary consideration. Cost is the main factor. I perused the shelves in the kitchen and cellar pantry. They were lined with gallon cans of fruit and vegetables that had been bought wholesale. There were cases of Chicken of the Sea, jars of Sampson's Instant Coffee, and boxes and boxes of Quik. Two freezers were full of frozen chickens bought on sale. Unlike most country communes, Twin Oaks grows little of what it eats. This is no matter of taste but of economic philosophy.

In 1967 they tried cultivating an acre of tobacco, as had the farm's previous owner. It sold for $500, but when they divided the profit by the great numbers of hours of inexperienced labor, the hourly wage rate came out to be less than 50 cents. The economic report for that year concludes, "It [tobacco] is not worth it in comparison to the dollar value of our labor in any other endeavor."

That same year, they tried to reduce costs by preparing dishes with homegrown food. They tried a breakfast of roasted corn, with sugar and cream, peanut soup and groundhog stew. But most members took one bite and left the rest, reported an issue of *Leaves*.

Over the last year, as younger members joined, Twin Oaks has moved toward greater awareness and appreciation of organic foods.* The last two years the community sprayed insecticides on some crops and used chemical fertilizer on the poor soil. This year they are considering the purchase of an organic viral deterrent to the Japanese beetles that attack soybeans. The main factor, Kat said today, was how much the

---

* As the national economy worsened and younger people joined, the community gave even greater attention to growing more of its own foods. After I left, shelves were added to the root cellar for vegetable storage, cheese curing and mushroom culture.

viral insecticide would cost per acre: "The trouble is that organic farming and foods are so damn expensive."

I helped Rudy with the morning dishes. It's one chore he likes to sign up for. After we started to work (he did the washing and I did the stacking), I got an inkling why. Possibly it was the idea that a man, and an intellectual and radical at that, could wash dishes more efficiently than most bourgeois American housewives. Steam clouded his heavy plastic-framed glasses. From his back pocket hung a Stanley measuring tape. He wore a khaki shirt and a fresh button: the POWER-TO-THE-PEOPLE insignia, an upraised, clenched fist.

Behind us, a girl who was baking cookies remarked that no one had baked for a long time. "We used to bake our own bread," Rudy said, but a cost-comparison study concluded that store-bought was cheaper, even if the wage rate for baking our own was zero . . . Once in a while, one of the girls bakes some bread, but it's more like—recreation."

Rudy plunged through the dishes like a human washing machine. First, he put all the plates into the first of three stainless-steel wells to which he'd added a detergent (nonbiodegradable). After a few minutes' soaking, he took them out and sprayed each one with a black plastic nozzle over the middle well, then dropped them into the third to rinse in water and germicide. Meanwhile, I took the plates from the rinse and slipped them between the plastic dividers of a dish tray. When it was full, I lifted it onto the top tier of a tall drying rack. After the excess water had dripped down to a drainboard, I carried the trays over to the cupboards. A third person was delegated to put the dishes away. The almost-mechanized efficiency of the operation was reminiscent of *Walden Two,* and I remarked offhandedly that in the fictional community all-purpose glass utensils had been invented to speed the washing and inspection. "So the inspector could spot food particles without turning it over," Rudy recalled.

As he talked, I screwed up my courage to spring a *question* (although I knew better than to distract a senior member in the heat and steam of his dish duties). Over the last three years, I asked, had Twin Oaks gravitated away from the ideals of Skinner's scientific utopia? There was a long silence before his answer, barely audible over the drone of the window fan: "Closer to *Walden Two*." And that was all, I came to realize, picking up the tray of dishes, that he was going to say.

In her capacity as greeter, Peggy reminded me to fill out a labor credit sheet and turn it in before lunch. Peggy is eighteen, the daughter of two Iowa City social workers. She's pleasantly plump, clear-skinned and very direct. She applied to only one college, Antioch, and when she was refused, decided to travel. "I lived in Berkeley for a while, but the whole hip subculture turned me off. It was just an escape. This," she said, motioning to the hammocks in Harmony, "is the answer."

Peggy helped me fill in my labor credits for the week on a mimeographed form. An unbroken row of numbers ran across the top, like a computer-punched card. Below were blanks for the week, August 14–20; NAME: Robert; and Quota. Someone had written "19.2" after the last (I'd decided to stay only three days). The quota for a full week was 38.4. Running vertically down the right side were the hours of the workday, 7 A.M. to 9 P.M. Horizontally across the top were the days of the week. Between them the two axes intersected to form a grid of 105 boxes, each one for a specific hour of a particular day.

I consulted a huge diagrammatic sheet that had been posted on a bulletin board. On it the community's entire work needs had been reduced to their smallest component operations. Listed next to each chore were the number of people required, number of credits per hour, number of credits per section (a job that must be done for a week), and total labor credits. The name of the game was to sign up for any combination of jobs to satisfy my 19.2 quota. The choice was great. For 2 credits, I could put away the groceries; for 1, draw up a menu, do auto repair or tractor maintenance. Under the large category of laundry, I could choose any one of four separate jobs: manning the automatic washer, ironing, overseeing the drying, or mending. Under the section "Animals and Farm," I could spray the cows; I could feed them hay; I could mind or milk them. There were many other jobs: the weekly buying trip to Louisa, greeting visitors, printing, skimming milk (twice a day), filing, typing and accounting.

The credits assigned each job varied from week to week. The more popular decreased in value; the less popular increased. The underlying philosophy was egalitarian. The system insured that everyone did the same amount of work and prevented a skilled elite from monopolizing jobs that could be learned and performed by anyone.

After deliberating, I chose "construction" from 10 to 11, 1.6 credits; making stretchers (hammock frames) from 2 to 5, 2.7 credits; doing the evening dishes, 1.5. To bring my total to 19.3, I signed up for one hour of gate and fence mending on Saturday. Dropping my form into a box, I fell into the lunch line.

Later in the afternoon the forms were compiled into a composite work schedule for the coming week. The compilation was done by Gabe, the credit manager, assisted by Eric and Denise. I sat in on the meeting.

First, Gabe went through the forms, reading the job requests aloud. Denise entered every request, using initials for each person, on a master form. The next step was to eliminate conflicting choices. Four people had signed up for construction, a section calling for only three. "Give me a number between one and four," Denise asked Gabe. "Two," he said. She struck out the second of the four names. Conflicts are resolved impartially; seniority doesn't exist at Twin Oaks. Example: Rudy and I had both signed up for evening dishes. Denise flipped a coin. Rudy lost, and I, a visitor of two days, won preference over a three-year veteran. Another conflict arose when two members, one of them the food manager, had signed up to cook the same dinner. Instead of flipping a coin, Eric proposed giving the manager his preference in his own area of management to "encourage greater specialization and efficiency." But Gabe ruled no, flipped, and the manager lost.

In every case where more than were needed had signed for the same job, Denise deducted 10 percent of its present value. Conversely, she added 10 percent as an inducement to jobs that attracted too few. Hammock making in particular seemed one of the least popular.

Surprisingly, there were few conflicts among the thirty workers—few instances when the labor credit manager had to make assignments to fill the blanks created by losing tosses. In making these assignments, he consulted the list of likes and dislikes each worker appended. For example, Wrenn wrote that she didn't want to cook any evening meals; so to satisfy her quota, Gabe filled the blank boxes on her form with jobs other than cooking.

Finally, the forms were filled and totaled on the electric adding machine. The new master work schedule was finished and hung on the bulletin board in the dining area. The individual forms were put in a box in Oneida to be picked up by the members. It had taken only two hours.

Before dinner, people crowded around the new master schedule. "Wow, the quota's *down* this week," someone noted. From week to week the quota fluctuates: up when members leave, down when visitors come. Since it's summer, there's currently an influx of visitors.

Because of the $1.50 a day charge and the work credit system, Twin Oaks, unlike New Buffalo, does not attract drifters looking for a groovy place to crash. Recent arrivals include John, on leave of absence from Swarthmore to seek "raw experience"; Don, a rich young ex-stockbroker, now a dog trainer in Manhattan, who wants to start a community; Dorothy, a tall blonde on her way to teach at a free school in New Hampshire.

My closest friend is Stephanie, twenty-one, who teaches modern dance to ghetto kids in the Philadelphia public schools. She has a lithe body, a turned-up nose and brown pigtails. In contrast to the women here, who wear gray-and-white bib overalls, Stephanie wears bright tie-dyes and tennis shoes without socks and wraps a green serape around herself in the evenings.

She arrived here with David. They are both members of a commune in Philadelphia. ("It's a kind of group marriage, but we have a lot to work out.") David was graduated with Stephanie from Washington University. He is more in love with her than she is with him and resents her other interests. One of Stephanie's reasons for coming to Twin Oaks was to observe how a "structured" community handled human relations, child rearing and the role of women. She doesn't expect their commune to last. "We have a lot of warm feeling and love but nothing to bind us together."

Women's liberation is very much a part of their postrevolutionary society. The labor credit system has abolished any possible job discrimination. Unlike many communes, Twin Oaks' women do much of the heavy farm labor, drive tractors, and shovel manure. They hold many of the managerships and have decision-making power. Susan, Kat's seventeen-year-old daughter, is one of the three planners, an executive board with staggered six-month terms. The women seem both shy and cool. Denise is a beautiful Mexican-Indian girl with honey-colored skin and dark glistening braids. She wears her bib overalls cut off above the knee, snugly around shapely hips. Denise shares the same pair of bibs with Kitty, a tomboyish girl with short hair, light eyelashes and a cool manner. On Kitty, the bibs are an asexual uniform. When I passed her this morning to breakfast, I half-expected her to greet me, "Good morning, comrade." But she didn't say anything at all.

After dinner this evening, Stephanie joined three of the women, Denise, Kitty and Christine, at one of the picnic tables. Unobtrusively, she asked them some of the same questions I would have. "Why don't you have any kids?"

The reason was partly economic, answered Denise. "We can't afford to build a children's dormitory. It's important to bring up children in their own house and to have professional care and supervision. Children's manager would be a twenty-four-hour job. Right now we can't afford the time."

"You've never tried having kids around?"

Yes, they'd had around eight for various lengths of time,

answered Christine, a two-year member. She dressed plainly in white shirts and had long black hair.

One of the first of the children to be raised by the community was Lisa, the daughter born to Rudy and Connie, his first wife. True to behavioral principle, Lisa slept in a Skinner air crib, which is sometimes and incorrectly referred to as a "Skinner box." (Skinner designed the box for experiments with pigeons and rats which were conditioned by a lever and food magazine.) The crib was designed by Skinner to provide a stress-free environment during the child's formative months, and thus promote the development of a secure personality. Lisa's was constructed of plexiglass and wood. It was thermostatically controlled; insulated against noise; moisture absorbent (no diapers needed); and wired for sound so that her cries could be monitored through a loudspeaker. However, Lisa spent only a few months in the crib and left the community when Connie left Rudy.

Communal child care became a source of conflict over Zandra, an eighteen-month-old. Initially, her parents agreed that she would be raised according to behavioral principles. They acknowledged the child to be the responsibility of the group, and not just theirs, the biological parents. Child care was put on the labor credit system and divided into shifts. The parents took one shift. The rest of the time, the child was in others' custody. After a while, the parents began to object to how the others treated Zandra.

They protested that Zandra shouldn't be allowed to run around barefoot or bathe with women members who might have venereal disease. On the other hand, members of the community criticized the mother for her "reinforcement" of the child's crying. "Every time Zandra was pissed at one of us," said Christine, "she'd 'cry for' her mother, who was pleased, thinking it proved that community care of children was against nature." The parents left, not only because of Zandra but also because they felt the commune was too dirty, disorganized and irresponsible. Another instance was Theron, the seven-year-old son of Donna, a divorced woman. Rudy, then child manager, allowed the boy freedom to stay up late at night, stay home from school and not brush his teeth. When Donna protested, Rudy answered that Theron's rebellion was part of a growth process. Donna took Theron and left the commune. These and other episodes convinced the planners to adopt a resolution temporarily excluding prospective members with children. Christine said, "We couldn't raise children who'd been so adversely conditioned already. . . . We're going to wait and have our own, and bring *them* up from birth according to behavioral principles."

"Who'll have the kids," Stephanie asked. "It will be the community's decision, of course," Christine answered. "Perhaps the biological parents would be paired eugenically. I'd like to see five women conceive around the same time. That way we could bring the children up together, and it would be more efficient to buy all their clothes at once."

How would they turn out? Would they be any different than if they'd been reared by two parents? Christine wasn't sure—it was an experiment. Thus far, the "evidence" indicated that the structure of the monogamous family engendered antisocial traits: competition and jealousy. "I don't think jealousy is an intrinsic characteristic of man."

Stephanie looked puzzled. Her own experience, she said, had convinced her that jealousy was deeply rooted. "I've tried loving more than one man, and someone always ends up feeling he's the one who's loved *less*. Do you really think that's because of social conditioning?"

Christine said that she had, in fact, conditioned herself not to feel jealousy when her lover began to sleep with other women. "I repeated to myself that psychologists say you can feel both unhappiness and happiness at the same time . . . I knew he was happy and I should be too. I kept repeating, 'I'm happy, I'm happy,' until I just *felt* happiness."

Stephanie shook her head. "It sounds like you're brainwashing yourself."

"No, it's just that jealousy's a very wasteful emotion. I'm easily satisfied sexually, so why shouldn't he have other relationships?"

August 15

It was close to ten, TO time, this morning, when Stephanie and I reported for construction. We were to cut and nail battens over Oneida's external siding. Rudy, the construction manager, was to give us our instructions. Organizationally, all work falls under the direction of thirty-five managerships held among fifteen people, slightly less than half the membership. There's a manager for animals, auto maintenance, the bus, the bees, the budget, construction, correspondence, the farm, hammocks, health, house, library, pets, recreation, safety, storage, visitors and labor credits. In return for their supervisory work, the managers receive a few more labor credits. But they have not become a managerial elite. The community is structured to keep skills from being monopolized. Under tenet two of The Code, managers are required "to explain their work to any other member who desires to learn it." Remembering this, Stephanie and I set off to find Rudy and get an explanation of our job: to nail the battens, stained strips of wood, across the vertical siding to prevent water from seeping through.

John was the third who'd signed up for construction. The three of us decided that two could do the work just as easily, and John went off to do his morning yoga. I checked out hammers, nails and a handsaw from the tool chest. Stephanie marked off lengths on the batten, and I was just about to saw when Carl came by. "Why don't you use the saber saw—save ya time."

Initially Stephanie dug the idea of an electric saw, but I persuaded her to stick with the handsaw. It was just as fast, safer and didn't need an extension cord. "The handsaw gives you a better feeling," I said. "Here, try it."

Stephanie gave me a half-amused, half-puzzled look. She sawed a few lengths; in no time, she was far ahead of my nailing. She was enjoying the work. Then Gabe walked by. "Why don't you use the saber saw?" he asked with a trace of irritation. "It's more efficient."

Stephanie kept on sawing. "We're doing all right without it." We had begun our small revolt.

Toward noon, we ran out of stained battens. Whoever had last done the job hadn't told the manager to order more lumber. It was one of the frustrating kinks in the system that inevitably result from division of labor and responsibility. My first impulse was to shrug my shoulders and moan, "It wasn't my responsibility. . . ." But then I considered the alternative— the open-ended commune where everyone was supposedly responsible and work was typically undelegated and the cows wandered off and two women were saddled with all the cooking. . . .

Though Twin Oaks' system was far more efficient and fair, it did however depress me; but this again was the reaction of a biased outsider.

After lunch, I sat in the smaller dining room. Above the telephone, directions had been posted on how visitors were to be received. An electric butter churn droned on a table, behind which was an old fireplace. The mantelpiece bore graceful scrollwork, but the opening had been sealed by a piece of tin flashing. In the corner, a small note stated: THIS ROOM CLEANED THIS WEEK BY ERIC, SUSAN AND GABE. There were no paintings or pictures.

I sat next to Kat. Before becoming interested in *Walden Two*, she'd been a legal secretary in Washington, D.C. "Most Americans put in no more than four hours of work a day, after you subtract all the coffee breaks and clockwatching." She read *Walden Two* and realized that there could be a rational way for "a small group of people to realize the benefits of technology without waiting around for a revolution." When she heard that a national convention had been organized to discuss the possibility, she attended. At the conference, held in August, 1966, at Walden Woods, Michigan, she met Rudy and some of the other founders. One member, Bud, put up the $30,000 to buy the farm. He left after a series of disputes, one of which involved his demand to be appointed a planner. He now leases the farm to the community.

Other land has been offered them, and Kat is hopeful that in a few years Twin Oaks will serve as a training ground for other *Walden Two* communities around the country. Several are now in the planning stages. A group in Providence, Rhode Island, is raising money to buy a dairy farm in Massachusetts to be called Walden Three. Neverland, an urban commune in Menlo Park, California, is planning another Walden (Walden Four?) "somewhere in the western United States." Yet another has been based on a photographic industry by East Street Gallery in Grinnell, Iowa; and Community Design, Inc., a group with two communal bases, one in Montrose, Colorado, and the other in Baltimore, is looking at sites in western Texas for "an international community" based on both Skinner and Israel's kibbutzim.

It was pleasant to have more than just the lunch hour between my two work shifts. From 2 to 5, I was assigned to making hammock stretchers. Meanwhile, I had my free time. Why did the phrase sound so strange? I took the first of my long escapist walks, along a small trail through the woods, to a half-lit clearing. Here I began to read Thomas More's *Utopia*—away from the sound of air conditioners, fans, vacuum cleaners, and the high whine of the new drill press.

I had to agree, it was a beautiful drill press. With managerial pride, Carl showed me how easy it was to change the bits and to adjust the crank. He taught me how to countersink the loop holes for the stretchers, and then he left. The two-foot stretchers were kept in a water bath to retain flexibility. I didn't have to decide where to drill and countersink. Across the stretcher someone had already drawn lines, three inches apart, for each hole—an efficient division of labor. Automatically, the drill intersected the middle of the lines. The first set was fun until I realized how inefficiently I was doing it. I was turning each stretcher over separately to be countersunk, so I had to push the "off" button and change the bit each time. I realized that I could increase my output per hour if I drilled a batch of stretchers on one side only, thus saving the time it took to change bits and to turn the machine on and off. Carl had given me no quota, but I still wanted to produce a respectable number so I could quit work at 5 P.M. and go swimming with a clear conscience. So my main consideration became efficiency. I adjusted my movements to the machine's well-oiled articulations. My mind disconnected and floated free. I remembered my father.

He was a time-study engineer for the Goodyear Tire and Rubber Company who spent his working life devising ways for men to operate machines with the fewest motions. For twenty years, as long as I can remember, he came home around 6:30 P.M., made a drink, picked up the Akron *Beacon Journal*, and quietly cursed his existence. He didn't quit the "salt mines," as he called Goodyear, but dreamed about the two weeks a year when we rented a cabin in Georgian Bay, Ontario. During his vacation, he was transformed into a happy, relaxed fisherman, a person. At those times we were close.

While in college, I worked two summers at Goodyear, in the offices and the factory. The factory jobs were interesting for a day or two, until the clocklike rhythm of the machinery took over my central nervous system and I began to operate mechanically, my disconnected mind, then as now, drifting into the past or the future. The air smelled of rubber in various stages of chemical composition. Carbon black uniformly covered the walls. So finely (for efficiency's sake) was the work divided, so specialized each action, that you worked like a robot. The thinking had already been done: time-study charts, quality analysis, foremen, supervisors, union work rules.

Soon you responded involuntarily to bells, sirens, and numbered requisitions. The rest of you tried to escape the vast pall of dinginess that hung over the dirty red brick factories, the strangely blue luminescent windows and the hot cinder parking lots. . . .

I had finished another batch of stretchers. I pushed the red "off" button, waited for the drill to stop spinning, loosened the bit, and adjusted the drill down until the bit met some resistance, then lifted the crank. . . .

There was no *one* thing about Goodyear that repelled me; that's why I grasp at poetic descriptions. Goodyear's dreariness didn't lend itself to sociological analysis or to reform. It was an all-pervasive consciousness that I had to reject outright, the way a man shakes himself out of a nightmare.

Before the Industrial Revolution what had work been like? Before the flaw cracked the once-clear crystal of man's consciousness. It must once have been clear and bright—suffused with more intense clarity and color. Some time between the Renaissance and the present, as man extended his intelligence through his tools and technology and altered his relation to nature, the quality of consciousness had changed. . . .

Into my mind flashed a picture of cutting hay last fall at Bryn Athyn: the hills, the rippled hay, the sky, Joshua's hair flying in the breeze; clear greens, yellows and blues, the staccato sound of the antique machine. . . .

A burning smell brought me back. I'd left the countersink in too long and it had scorched the wood. Little matter, the bit was all right, and if the hole was a trifle wide, no one would blame me; the hammock would still sell.

Toward the end of my shift, I was to take the drilled stretchers and force them into a frame which would give them a permanent bow. I put one end of the stretcher between two posts and bent it to fit the other end into the frame. I pulled and pulled, but the stretcher wouldn't bend. Then I called Carl. He tried, we both tried, groaned and pulled, but the stretchers wouldn't fit. "Shit, the guy must have sold me seasoned lumber," Carl said, and picked up most of the stretchers I'd drilled and threw them into the reject bin. For all of five minutes, the waste of my labor embittered me. Nevertheless, I'd fulfilled my day's quota and it was time to go swimming.

August 16

Slept late, unlike me. It was after ten by the time I got to the kitchen, gobbled some toast and coffee, and reported for construction. Stephanie and John were already hammering away. Had anyone noticed I was late? I asked, as if the long arm of Big Brother could at any moment tap my shoulder. No, they said, no one had noticed, complained or reported me.

It doesn't take long to notice that Twin Oaks operates with very little external supervision or compulsion. Rarely do managers check if the cows are being milked or the garden weeded at the right time by the right person according to the master schedule. The crucial supervision here is internalized social conscience. In a hip commune, the members work together out of shared consciousness. Here, however, people work apart. Yet the jobs do get done and with little griping. The system is equitable, and the quotas, averaging a little under six hours (compared to the four hours in *Walden Two*), are met with little sweat. The pace is relaxed and leisurely. Time passes quickly. Very rarely (as when drilling stretchers) do you feel trapped or bored.

I found an excellent vantage point on top of the ladder under Oneida's eaves. I was waiting for Stephanie to saw the battens. Out of the door below came the cleaning crew, pushing an industrial-sized vacuum cleaner. Behind the farmhouse, David and John hung out the first of the day's laundry loads. Rita, a visitor, watered the strawberries; Wrenn stopped picking up apples and chatted with Carl, who'd returned from the barn with pails of milk he'd just weighed and registered in the log by the stall. Up from the river came Kitty and Denise, their hair dripping and clean.

Every system of work has its unique strengths and weaknesses. The labor credit system's main advantage is flexibility. Why concentrate work into one single eight-hour shift, if it can be spread through the day and alternated with fun and conversation? Some members satisfy their quota by making hammocks after midnight while listening to music and talking. The point is to adjust work to each individual temperament. Kat prefers to work in the morning and evening and take a siesta in the afternoon. Here she can—but could not as a legal secretary in Washington.

The labor credit system is the mainstay of Twin Oaks' pleasant, well-ordered atmosphere. You have the satisfaction of knowing that if you turn your laundry in after breakfast, it will be clean, folded and ready before lunch, so you can count on a fresh shirt. Dinner will be served on time at 6:30. Your part of the work contributes to the whole. This community is small enough that you can see and feel the interrelationships. But in a community of 500 or 1,000—the size Rudy aims for—you're sure to lose the sense of wholeness and participation.

At lunch I sat next to Susan and was astonished to learn that she was Kat's daughter and only seventeen. She looks and acts much older. She had short blond hair, gray-blue eyes, and freckles. Aggressively intelligent and sometimes curt, she is aware of her bitchiness and often apologizes for it. She dropped out of high school, she said, because she felt uncomfortable trying to make friends. Twin Oaks became her substitute. Other members have tutored her in Spanish, geometry, chemistry, and behavioral psychology.

Not all of her last three years have been spent at the community, though. She was gone for a year, working and living with a man in San Francisco. The recurring pattern among the community's youngest members is these leaves of absence—time away that exceeds the standard two-week vacation. Some take jobs in cities and retain their membership by sending a minimum of $50 from their wages back to the community. However, the main reason for the leaves of absence, said Susan in a matter-of-fact tone, was "emotional."

There wasn't much to do in my "free time." I read the bulletin board, which is always a safe, predictable thing for a visitor to do, then wandered over to Harmony, where I read every word of the property manager's three-page policy statement on private rooms. Until the dormitory is completed, all rooms must be occupied by two members. Most of the policy dealt with the problem of couples who'd split up. Who gets the room? Apparently it's a recurring dilemma. Other sections of the bulletin board carried the headings OPINION-IDEAS and TRIVIAL POOP.

In the lounge at Oneida a new sign had gone up. THIS AREA CLEANED THIS WEEK BY . . . sure enough, the rug had been vacuumed. Certainly, Twin Oaks is the cleanest community I've visited. Regularly scheduled maintenance is one reason; another is the pervasive community conscience which makes me feel like Public Enemy Number One if I don't return a magazine to the rack. The omnipresent signs do the trick. It's also written in The Code (tenet nine): "We will clean up after ourselves after any private or individual project."

Inside the door had been posted a notice: GREAT LEAP FORWARD NOMINATIONS and a list of accomplishments that would be brought before the members to vote on during tonight's cadre meeting. The Great Leap Forward program was designed to motivate members to do more than their minimum—to invent more efficient ways of doing things or simply take initiative. The nominations mentioned Marnie's laying a cement floor in the barn and another's repainting the corn planter.

It was 2 P.M., time to report for construction. Rudy told me that Susan, the kitchen manager, had a project for me. She wanted me to build a spice shelf for over the huge gas stove. For a long time I contemplated the shelf space and planned how I'd suspend it. Meanwhile, Dorothy, a visitor, was starting to prepare dinner, as scheduled. Eagerly she began to whip up her tried-and-true spaghetti recipe, when a woman member clued her into the system, "You follow the menu."

"Menu?"

"Yes, the food manager fills the menu out for a week in advance." She gave Dorothy a 3-by-5 index card, the kind graduate students use. Under a heading "Dinner" and the date was an order for chop suey, using four frozen chickens, with a page reference to a cookbook, and a side dish of beets, "no vinegar."

"But I've never made chop suey before!" Dorothy protested. The other girl commiserated, but that was how the system worked. Cooking was, like many aspects of Twin Oaks, a collective effort. One person drew up the menu, another shopped, a third processed. "It sure takes out the fun," said Dorothy, frantically flipping through a cookbook.

Though women sign up for "food processing" (which has a high work credit), many do not like to cook here. Wrenn, a willowy readhead who was twenty-three, explained, "I'm probably the best cook, to be honest about it, but I won't cook here anymore. I'm a perfectionist, and I can't cook for a lot of people like I would for myself. There isn't time because it's such a large operation."

I cut the board and hammered it onto the supporting pieces on each side of the oven. From the counter, it looked rough and unfinished, but so did the other shelves that obviously no one had cared to sand, never mind staining. On the way to the tool shed, I passed Stephanie and David sitting in a hammock. They both looked disgruntled. Stephanie motioned me over, but when I came, she said, "Never mind . . . I was going to ask you, but it doesn't matter. Oh, well, are you going to paint the shelf?" Her eyebrows arched in an expression of the camaraderie that was growing among the visitors, and she answered her own question, "No, they don't paint anything around here." David added, "Except barns."

I thought awhile. Then I sanded the shelf; found some rags just where they should have been, in the rag pile on the back porch, and stained the shelves dark walnut. In place, stained and smooth, my new spice shelf looked absurdly, uselessly elegant.

The chop suey was good but not very suey. The beets were dull and canned. Near the end of dinner, the red Ford van pulled into the yard, bringing home the outside workers. Dick and John work at a factory that manufactures infrared heaters. Marnie is a lab technician, Christine a Kelly Girl, Gerrie a waitress at a Holiday Inn. The rest work as laborers for the Richmond Park Commission.

Every night they arrive uniformly grumpy. Among the stern "don'ts" posted to the attention of visitors is: "Never ask an outside worker how his day was."

The two-month stint that each member serves is the most depressing period of life here. Twin Oaks' original aim three years ago was to support itself through farming and home industry. Only eight months went by before two members had to volunteer to work outside. There's one good side to the system, though: In return for two months of rising at 5:30 A.M. and returning home to a warmed-over dinner at 7 P.M., the Twin Oaks member earns four to twelve months when he doesn't have to leave the farm.

Nevertheless, many have resigned from the community or had nervous breakdowns when faced with the prospect of working in the outside world, where, *Leaves* explained, many feel "isolated in a crowd of insane people who talk utter nonsense all day long." Some satisfy their work stint and avoid the two-hour-long daily commute by working in another city, living with friends and relatives. But they lose contact. One member returning from a job in a Detroit Steel mill was asked by a new member if he intended to stay long. He had been mistaken for a visitor—a cardinal sin.

Although less than $1,000 was invested during 1970 in machinery for home industries, some members are optimistic. Kat said, "A few more industrial contracts, a steady supply of lecture invitations, and an occasional professional who actually *enjoys* his outside job will leave us in fairly good shape. Best of all, if one of our manufacturing projects should find a steady market large enough to support the group, our financial worries would be over."

Other members are more skeptical. They believe that the community's economic woes go deeper than the problem of finding the right technology. "Twin Oaks could support itself without sending anyone to Richmond, by selling seventy hammocks a week," said Ben, Wrenn's husband, a disgruntled member working in Baltimore. "It's a victim of its own rhetoric. If we had a couple of good hard-sell salesmen, we could be self-supporting. But we're not capitalistic and we're not realistic."

I hurried, *very* efficiently, through the dishes to be in time for the cadre meeting. The word "cadre," French for "frame," refers in Communist society to small groups of farm or industrial workers. In China, workers' cadres have established their own working conditions and production goals. At Twin Oaks, a cadre meeting is synonymous with the open discussion of practical, usually economic problems. Cadre represents a divergence from Skinner's depiction of *Walden Two* as an apolitical and unideological technocracy. Following the novel, Twin Oaks began with three planners making most decisions. "We had very few open meetings," Kat recalled. "When we did, there were blowups. Someone would start screaming or walk out." At tonight's meeting the outside workers complained their car hadn't been serviced and gassed in advance of each morning's commute—as scheduled. They needed someone to wake them and make breakfast. The group reached a consensus: to offer Dick extra labor credits in return for waking the others. Susan volunteered to make breakfast, adding, "What you all really need is a wife." The decisions were made without consulting the planners.

The evening's main topic was a proposed change in the labor credit system. As an experiment, the membership could elect to join cadres, or groups of workers organized by specialization, for example, a food-processing cadre. Eric explained, "If you spend only one or two days a week in the kitchen, you never get a broad picture of all the different jobs. On one day, you might get an idea for a time-saver, but if you're away from the kitchen for a while, you forget. This plan encourages more specialization. I think it will make us more productive." All agreed it was a valid experiment.

But the change (it was later adopted as permanent) represents yet another divergence from Skinner, whose labor credit system was designed to promote variety and nonspecialization. I came away respecting the boldness of the community's experimental attitude. There's nothing sacrosanct here about Skinner. If one theory doesn't work, they'll try another. I guess Skinner would approve.

August 17

The country store is a few miles away on a hard-top, country road. The community leases the small cement-block store and Union 76 pumps for $35 a month from the owner, who eked a bare profit from it. Under Twin Oaks' management, business has remained marginal. The profit averages about $50 a week, coming out to 50 cents an hour in wages for the clerks who man it from 8 A.M. to 9 P.M. every day except Sunday. Like every other job, clerk is listed on the labor credit schedule; it's not particularly popular.

When I dropped by, Gabe was dusting the pharmaceuticals. "We're not in this to make money. We may put a ceiling on profits equal to the minimum wage for one clerk." Eventually they planned to turn the store into a cooperative, in which the area's poor blacks could hold stock and thus save money. That was a remote ideal, Gabe added. For the present, it's run like most other country stores: with a 25 percent markup.

Gabe looks like a Greek statue of Hermes. About 5 feet 10, he has broad shoulders, a tapering torso, and a strawberry-blond goatee, which matches his short, wavy hair. Under blond-white eyebrows his eyes are a frosty blue. He controls himself like a long-distance runner, pacing his dry humor so that you get a glint of it only now and then.

Gabe is one of the three planners. Before coming here two years ago, he attended Antioch College, where he turned on to Socialism and lost an earlier interest in the field of education. "Antioch is the epitome of liberal education. It's perfectly designed for the leisure class, to teach hip children of liberals how to live the gracious life—what records they should buy, what books to read. Antioch is too hedonistic."

When he received a high number in the draft lottery, Gabe, no longer needing a deferment, dropped out of Antioch and joined Twin Oaks. "It's the only American community close to being a kibbutz." We talked of the future, when Twin Oaks would have its own children and school. What subjects would they teach? Not decadent studies like the art of the Renaissance, Gabe said. "Much of history as it's now taught inculcates the values of the past." So does literature written in the moralistic belief that multiple sexual relationships are doomed by jealousy to destruction. "Rudy says we should create out own literature and write stories about triangular relationships which *do* work out." The curriculum of the Twin Oaks school would include skills like mechanics, mathematics, agriculture, electronics and animal husbandry.

A car occupied by a large black family pulled up at the pumps, and the father got out and lifted the hood. A fat boy came into the store, clutching a dollar bill. In an almost inaudible voice he ordered ice creams, pointed to candy, and got change for the soda machine. His little sisters, red ribbons around stumpy braids, came in and picked out more candy. Carrying a satchel that barely cleared the floor, the mother waddled in and bought a container of milk. Then the father got a quart of oil from behind the door and, as Gabe was busy, put it in himself. Not a word transpired, other than the monosyllables necessary to the tense, suspicious transaction. Gabe kept an eye out for candy pilferage and the children moved uneasily as if in the heart of enemy territory.

The scene underscored my doubts about the feasibility of Twin Oaks' political aims. I found it hard to imagine that educated Northern whites could soon overcome the racial and cultural gap between them and semiliterate Southern blacks. Some members talked as if they and the blacks might divide the country up into communes. First I'd like to see the cooperative work out.

Politics aside, Twin Oaks is on good terms with its neighbors, white and black, and has experienced no harassment. Unlike some communes, Twin Oaks respects the local climate of cultural and political conservatism and doesn't go out of its way to offend local mores. Drugs and alcohol are prohibited. Members don't dress or act freaky. They hold regular jobs. Marxist rhetoric is kept within the community.

Kat arrived to spell Gabe. Separately, Kat and Gabe are serious and businesslike. Together, the two, who are roommates, loosen up and joke around. But even when relaxed, neither is far from the problems of the community. This afternoon in the store, Gabe asked Kat's advice about a policy decision before the planners concerning "unwarranted" leaves of absence.

Currently, the policy is that members who leave without the planners' permission, or take more than their allotted vacation time, must pay a readmission fee of $200. One such member had returned, Gabe said, claiming not to have the $200. The planners must decide either to kick him out or waive the fee—which would undermine the system of applying extra work credits to increased vacation time. "If we let people take two months off that they haven't earned, it's unfair to the member who works hard all year round to get enough credits for an extra two weeks' vacation," said Gabe.

Kat was uncertain what to recommend. She recognized that the planners had made so many exceptions to the rule (her own daughter, Susan, had been one) that it was becoming meaningless. Kat wondered if enforcing the rule might drive away many potential members. According to Kat, forty members have left the community over its three years. "Perhaps we must accept the fact that young people today are mobile and restless and very few want to be pinned down to make the kind of commitment this life demands of them." When I left, the issue remained unresolved.

This afternoon Kitty left in a visitor's car for New York City —another unwarranted leave of absence. A member of the community for a year, Kitty had been making antagonistic remarks the last few days about male chauvinism. She was going to New York to devote herself to the cause of women's liberation. Denise was the only one who said good-bye as Kitty pitched her bag into the car. The two girls and Rudy had been a triad, one free of sexual jealousy. But the triad wasn't a reason for Kitty's decision to leave. There were no effusive embraces. The good-byes had been said in the privacy of the rooms.

There are two Twin Oaks. There is the external community that impresses visitors with an air of impersonality and efficiency. But a warmer, less formal community exists behind the doors of the private rooms. Only in contrast to the hip commune is this division unusual; for in most American communities—suburbs, cities, or small towns—the typical pattern is to have an inner circle of family and friends and an outer circle of less intimate acquaintances who meet in formalized situations.

Twin Oaks' members are aware that visitors who confront the community's frigid exterior leave with a mistaken impression. Tamar, a seventeen-year-old member, who was on vacation while I was at Twin Oaks, later sent me this explanation:

When you walk down the main street in your town, do you stop and talk with every person you pass? Do you even smile at all of them? How about every person in your local supermarket? What about the people who walk by your house? Don't you realize that they are all people—don't you feel cold when you ignore them? I mean really—don't you feel like a damned machine that doesn't have any time to waste? Or do you just feel like a human being who has a life to live and who doesn't have enough time to communicate with the people you love? I at least smile at every strange face I see and say hello—even if I'm about to go spend an hour with my roommate.

Another measure of the gap between the inner and outer aspects of Twin Oaks is artistic expression. Except for one amateurish painting on the drab walls of the dining room (the one with the unbolted bus seats), the rest of the public rooms were barren of art. On the other hand, some of the private rooms were artfully decorated with posters and murals. A few others were austere. Music fits the same pattern. Like the fictional Walden Two, with its nightly concerts and recitals, Twin Oaks has plenty of music and musicians. Members play guitars, the dulcimer, flute, autoharp, harmonica, clarinet, saxophone and recorder—but most often, in the privacy of their room (at least while I visited). There was a large record collection in the dining room, but the phonograph had been left broken and unrepaired for weeks.

Yesterday as Gabe and I talked of *Walden Two*'s emphasis on culture, he had observed: "Don't forget that Skinner was writing about the ideal—the Golden Age . . . right now, we're busy mastering the mechanics. Before we can write poetry, we've got to know how to fix a tractor."

Since my visit, members wrote that music had become more of a unifying activity. A choir had been organized and was being regularly attended. Singing lessons were held. And Gabe had written a musical comedy that was performed by the community.

This evening a reading was held at Oneida—yet another attempt at community-wide culture. The custom (which was later suspended) was to spend an hour taking turns reading books aloud—reading that has included *Winnie the Pooh*, *Kibbutz* by Melford E. Spiro and *Fanshen* by William Hinton, a documentary of the effect of the Communist revolution on one Chinese village.

Tonight's attraction was *The First Year of the Yangki Commune*. About fifteen people listened for an hour as the book passed from hand to hand. The chapter recounted how private landowners had been persuaded to pool their land and resources in the commune. They had been swayed by the party organizers' statistics—projections of the higher rice yields that would result from consolidation, by farming large tracts with machinery. A short discussion followed.

Kat said she was surprised that the individual farmers had responded to rational, statistical arguments appealing to their self-interest. Rudy commented that American radicals should make the same pitch. It was a fact, he said, that 50 percent of the people own only 8 percent of the wealth. By redistributing the wealth and the benefits of technology, the working day could be reduced to four hours.

I suggested that within the present system the shorter workday was coming about and cited Walter Reuther as a nonrevolutionary who'd led the drive. The American worker who owned a house, two TV's and a boat was hardly a disgruntled proletarian ready to rise and smash the system.

Rudy disagreed. Unions had sold out to capitalism: The affluence of the working minority who belonged to unions masked the poverty, hunger and privation of thousands.

Kat was less Marxist and doctrinaire. She doubted if Twin Oaks could advance the same kind of statistical, economic argument the Chinese commune had used to win members. Twin Oaks' agricultural yields and hammock output were anything but a convincing argument for the productivity of an American communal economy.

But the community had something *else* to offer, Kat said: "A quality of life superior to the cities, the rat race. They want a way out. These are people who have children or are going to have children. Six months ago, we couldn't have handled kids. Now the community's period of socialization is over."

August 18

Writing in a past issue of *Leaves,* Rudy suggested that Frazier, the theoretical architect of *Walden Two,* had wrongly assumed that psychological conditioning would be wasted on the community's first generation. Twin Oaks' experience indicated to Rudy that they *could* be socially engineered. Though the behavioral influence can be felt here, it is not institutionalized and is revealed mainly in what the members call "self-management programs." A self-manager can be recognized by his "counter." Tied to a loop in his jeans, Carl's counter was red and white plastic, like the ones housewives in supermarkets use to keep a running total of their purchases. He used to count every time he bitched at his girlfriend, Mindy. "I got into the habit of taking everything out on her . . . The counter makes me aware." Kat counted and graphed a set of habits and reactions to gauge her overall "quality of life." "No matter how depressed I may feel, it's encouraging to find that the net movement is upward."

The most systematic self-manager was Eric. Thin, blond and athletically trim, Eric wore a green Army cap, cut-off shorts, and comported himself with Nordic self-discipline, jogging and exercising daily. He is an excellent swimmer, a trained ornithologist, after whom a rare African bird has been named, and the son of fundamentalist missionaries. "I rejected religion when I was quite young. Biology satisfies me intellectually. I believe in science and hedonism—I guess that's what you'd call it—the belief that this world is all we can have of heaven, so we might as well make the most of it."

On one wrist, he conspicuously wears a gold-banded counter like the ones golfers use to count strokes; around his neck, a rawhide necklace composed of five rings of beads, each of which serves as a separate counter. "The basic idea of self-management is to force the individual to decide which aspects of behavior he wants to change, to make him conscious of the habit he wants to eliminate, and, finally, to set up a contingency system to decrease its frequency." Eric took me to his room (which he shares with Susan) to see his graphs.

It was comfortably untidy. Posters on the wall, clothes in the corner, and Susan sitting up in bed, wrapped in a sheet. He opened a notebook of graphs. Most had ascending lines. On the graphs he kept daily were plotted the number of times he avoided an argument, jogged, answered letters, had sexual relations, read, initiated conversations (a habit he would like to reinforce, since he is shy), kept promises, practiced guitar, lost his temper, argued irrationally, performed extra work for the community, and—graph of all graphs—filled out his graphs before breakfast.

Once he had graphed his behavior, Eric tried to alter it by setting up a system of self-rewards, termed "contingencies." "If I wanted to get into the habit of brushing my teeth every night, I could give Susan seven dollars at the beginning of the week, and every night after I brushed she'd give me back a dollar. After a few times, the habit would be so well enforced that I wouldn't need contingency." One contingency they tried was suspending sexual relations after days when they'd failed to resolve an argument by rational means. "It didn't work," Eric said, blushing.

Though it has few concrete applications, behaviorism exerts a pervasive influence on the tone of community life. It can be detected in members' conversations. For example, Paul, who doesn't believe in God, said, "Man is basically neutral. You can make anything out of him. What's usually taken for evil is really imperfect socialization." Walter, irritated by a visitor's remark that Twin Oaks had too much bureaucracy, exploded, "What evidence do you base your judgment on?" (overlooking the fact that the visitor had expressed his feelings, not his findings).

Skinner's influence is felt indirectly through the community's emphasis on structure. If the old flaws can be taken out of the social structure, assumed the behavioralists, then man will cooperate. One proven source of interpersonal friction is gossip: Psychologically, it's an avoidance mechanism that compounds misunderstandings. Twin Oaks attempts to prevent gossip by setting up alternative means for handling discontent (the bitch box). In addition, gossip is included in tenet three of The Code: "We will not discuss the personal affairs of other members or speak negatively of other members when they are not present or in the presence of a third party." There's no divine authority behind The Code. A member who breaks a tenet is not hauled before a tribunal but merely reminded that his behavior violated the community's empirically determined principles.

There are a few instances in which behavioral technique has been applied to the community at large. Cigarette smoking is one. The members unanimously decided that smoking was not only harmful to health but also an economic liability. Since the 25-cent allowance wasn't enough for smokers to supply themselves, the community purchased large tins of loose tobacco for them to roll by hand, but a "negative reinforcement" program was set up to curtail the use of the roller. The program was developed by Dick, the community's unofficial instructor in conditioning, who discovered behavioral psychology after being brought up a Christian Scientist. He was a graduate student of psychology at the University of Florida when he learned of Twin Oaks and came here.

The first step in his program was to put the tobacco tin and roller in Oneida's lounge, with instructions forbidding its removal. That alone cut down on consumption, said Dick. Anytime a smoker wanted a cigarette he had to go to Oneida—or else roll a supply in advance. Yesterday he upped the negativity of the reinforcement by moving the tin and roller up the stairs and into the visitors' loft—a hot and uncomfortable place during the day. On my way upstairs, I passed Dick and Walter, a smoker. "This is going too far," protested Walter, who'd just climbed up to roll some cigarettes in the loft.

Dick answered objectively, "Consumption hasn't decreased in two weeks. Let's try it awhile and see what happens."

Twin Oaks lends itself to easy generalizations and contradictory stereotypes (a Maoist's *Walden Two?*). Visitors come here for several days and leave with opposite impressions. The hip leave with *1984* on their lips. Others who've read *Walden Two* are disillusioned that the community is not as efficient and streamlined as its prototype. Preconceptions aside, Twin Oaks presents two faces. Its members fall generally into two groups. The older (twenty-three to forty) group includes the two remaining founders, Kat and Rudy, as well as Gabe, Eric and Dick. They've been members for a year or more and tend toward behaviorism and Marxism. The younger group (eighteen to twenty-one) is equally numerous, but more significant, since they are gradually taking the places of the departing older members. Many of the younger members disclaim Marx and Skinner alike. "I can't say that I buy all this Skinner stuff," said one young girl, "but if you're asking me if I prefer living in a community that has some kind of order or a hippie commune, well, the answer is order."

There must have been many people in the nineteenth-century Socialist communities who didn't believe in Socialism, phalanxes or cooperatives, just as there are people now who go to nude beaches without believing in nudism. "Remember the little old lady who spent most of her day in the rocking chair?" asked Wrenn, referring to the woman Skinner depicted in *Walden Two* as typical of the many who seek peace, contentment and security, regardless of the political or economic system imposed on them. "That's the kind of person I am. I'm satisfied living in a pleasant, orderly place."

The younger members of Twin Oaks live as they would anywhere, fall in and out of love, take unexcused leaves of absence, wonder about the future, and ignore ologies and isms. The older members are the first to concede the effect the new wave of young people has had. One change is a much more relaxed sexual atmosphere.

In its first year, from what I can gather, Twin Oaks was a community of ten, straitlaced intellectuals. Now, most are paired with roommates of the opposite sex. Every evening a skinny dip is held down at the river. A few triads have been attempted. Some talk of setting up a structured group marriage (like Harrad West) to retain good members "who had to leave because they couldn't find a sexual outlet."

This evening a "mutual criticism" was held in Oneida. The subject was Rudy, who had offered himself up. He sat on an ottoman, relaxed, his arms crossed on his knee. Surrounding him were fifteen members and five visitors. We knew better than to interject our own comments. The criticism went around the circle. Dick was first. He complained that Rudy, as maintenance manager, had neglected servicing the outside workers' car. Rudy jotted a note in a black notebook. Next, Kat made a more serious criticism. Rudy had overstepped his prerogative as construction manager and, without first consulting the planners, had made drastic alterations in the kitchen and installed a bathroom with "modern ideological overtones." She further charged that he had violated tenet three of The Code by saying that the planners often "passed fast ones" under the noses of the community. Also, he had sloppily abandoned construction of a concrete outhouse at the store, leaving the wheelbarrow and concrete behind. Rudy listened silently and continued to take notes.

After Kat, Paul spoke. "I can never tell when you've finished a sentence," he said, smiling and smoking a cigar. "I'll be going out of the room and you start talking again. Maybe you should put some 'and-uhs' between your sentences."

Gabe said he was disturbed by Rudy's laconic "I don't know" to many questions. "I feel you don't want to share your thoughts. When you do speak, you're usually right."

Peggy: "All I can say is that I haven't gotten to know you well enough to make any critical comment, and maybe that's my criticism."

Susan touched on his "erratic" periods of lethargy, alternating with peaks of enthusiasm. Eric chided him for sleeping late and recommended that he use his self-management techniques more diligently.

After the criticism completed the circle, Rudy glanced over his notes and answered deliberately in a low voice. It was part confession, part reply. Admittedly he hadn't done all his work or any "revolutionary thinking" or thought about the future of *Walden Two* communities. He explained why painting the barn had been so expensive and admitted he'd wanted to create a stir by redoing the kitchen. The community needed some drastic, overnight changes. He didn't know how to cope with the lethargy. "Some days it gets so bad I can't even do my graphs." However, the meeting had been a relief, he said. He'd volunteered in order to find out how his depression was affecting the others. "I'm glad to see that you all don't think it's so bad."

August 20

Didn't report for construction. After breakfast, I sneaked away, taking my escape route up the road, past the farm buildings, hopping a low place in the fence, and disappearing among the oak trees. In my favorite half-lit clearing carpeted with leaves and moss, I sat on my accustomed stump and resumed reading *Utopia*.

I didn't feel guilty of an anticommunitarian act. Yesterday I volunteered to go on a hay-cutting detail—backbreaking work above and beyond the quota. Also I take perverse pleasure in rebelling against the system, pilfering these minutes of privacy and seclusion. Of course, it is an irrational reaction. I am only a visitor here and it's not 1984 or Goodyear Tire & Rubber Company. I'm free to leave, and will, tomorrow. Yet I am reacting against something, or the lack of something. Here my consciousness seems driven back for comfort to the past. Thus I read of More's Utopians, an earthy, humble people who labored on large communal farms and lived in city "households"—comparable to some of today's urban communes—that had adjoining gardens of herbs and fruits. They had many religions; some worshiped the sun, others the moon, other planets or famous men. Despite their diversity, the Utopians shared common beliefs: The highest virtue was "living in accordance with nature." One Supreme Being was responsible for the Creation and the protection of the universe.

Such were the musings of a superfluous man, another Winston Smith as he puttered around the woods, rummaging through the antique shop of his mind for themes of Beethoven and lines of Shakespeare when he should have been at the drill press working for the collective good.

Tonight the members held their grouprap sessions. Once a week for an hour in the evening, four or five people get together in one of the private rooms to have a "scheduled conversation." The sessions were started, said Kat, in response to complaints that members lacked "a feeling of closeness . . . that we had descended to being only an aggregate of people with a common economic bond."

Meanwhile, the visitors sat on the porch, listened to the locusts and the squeak of the swing, and held our own rap session. We'd become united against the chilliness of the members. Tomorrow most of us would split. Tonight we exchanged addresses and held a group criticism of Twin Oaks.

Among us was Paul, who'd spent his summer here as a provisional member. Today he'd decided not to join. His chief complaint was ours: He didn't like the way the members treated visitors. "They use them."

Stephanie added, "They use themselves. If you were handicapped or mentally ill, they wouldn't let you join, because you wouldn't be useful to them."

We adjourned to the kitchen. After the rap sessions, a few members drifted in. Denise and Rudy got into a squirt-gun fight, chasing and ducking among the counters.

Kat came in and remarked that her group had discovered common childhood experiences: "We all had atheistic revelations and had our mouths washed out with soap."

In the members' presence, the visitors sustained their mood of open rebellion. There was talk of driving one of the cars into Louisa for a beer.

Some of the younger members appeared more receptive to visitors than the older group. They listened sympathetically to our criticisms and complaints. Most visitors appreciated the labor credit system's orderly and equal division of work. They granted that someday Twin Oaks would be self-supporting; surely *one* of its industries would come through. All were impressed by the members' determination and commitment, but equally depressed by a mood that none could isolate or define. It was something so subjective, said Stephanie, that all of us had separately wondered, "Perhaps it's just me?" But we'd compared notes and had found we all had the same reaction.

"I've got it." She brightened. "What the place lacks is *joie de vivre.*"

The younger members didn't answer immediately. Stephanie's last words had hit home. Bob, who grows his hair long and plays the guitar, said, "Sure, there's *joie de vivre* missing. I've seen a lot of changes since I've come here. Hip communes start out with a lot of joy, but the individual ends up being tyrannized by everyone else doing his own thing. Twin Oaks starts at the other extreme, with a lot of order, but it's moving in the other direction. It will never be a swinging commune, but stick around. It's going to be different."

Later in the year I sent a copy of the chapter to Twin Oaks. It was read aloud during a meeting, and soon after I received five letters. Most pointed out that I had collided with the frosty exterior the community maintains against the onslaught of visitors—who are the main source of its new members. "Two-thirds of our current membership were once visitors," Kat wrote. "Looks like we have to keep the door open."

Bob, the younger member I talked with last, wrote that I had visited at the worse possible time:

The summer itself is always a fluke time to observe our community because of the sheer number of visitors flying in and out. Some people come here because their life is so fucked up on the outside they are in emotional turmoil. It's summer. It's easy to split. So they run to Twin Oaks to get away from it all. Which in itself is not harmful. But they come by the hordes, day after day. People desperate for personal involvement, immediate friendship, and a sense of belonging. When it gets like that, you have to scrounge around for YOUR people, the people whose sensitivity and reinforcement you need to stay happy. But every day the faces keep changing. Everyday someone drops out of the sky and asks the same superficial questions you're tired of answering.

This particular summer's hordes were amplified by extentuating circumstances. It was the period of maximum growth and turnover. We were just finishing the second floor of the Oneida building, beginning to shuffle the kitchen all upside down to make more space for more members. The fenceposts, barn, garden, fields, industries, community clothes and labor credit system were under accelerated modification to match the expansion. The influx of members themselves was the biggest problem. . . . New ways of so many people getting to know and feel for each other had to be worked out. The old traditions (e.g., criticism) were beginning to lose their effectiveness. There was a lot of interpersonal friction and a tremendous amount of work to be done to boot. We tried to ease some of the strains of assimilation by experimenting with group raps and cadres. But it was too much at once. The community was a literal mess for weeks. We had to initiate clean-up campaigns to straighten things up enough so you could at least find tools and cooking utensils. It was hot in the kitchen besides, and no one was eager to spend the late afternoon slaving over a stove. I admit, our meals suffered slightly (our chop suey was no suey, catastrophic). Then there came the problem of distributing the work to so many people and still retain our love for equalitarianism. This all required a lot of fumbling. . . .

Most of the conditions for which you have criticized us were transitory. . . . The membership is much more together. The labor credit system is debugged to everyone's satisfaction. The farmhouse has been remodeled . . . paint, varnish, tables, shelves, curtains, complete to the last spice rack. . . . And we have completed Oneida in outstanding fashion and design, with a cosy "octagon" room for lounging and meeting upstairs and craft shop (with copper enameling kiln, electronics workbench, artists' supplies and lots of posters on the walls). We've also been doing a few minor projects in our space time . . . like planting a 250 fruit and nut tree orchard in our new beautiful 40-acre orchard grass and barley field, a community bathroom in Harmony, a combination indoor garage and workshop, improved hammock production, darkroom and printing press development. . . . Oh, yes, our meals are excellent these days. I do not mean to boast. But we would all be fat if it wasn't for the vast amount of work we've been putting out, work without exploitation, work with satisfaction. If you have any comments to make about our labor credit system, aside from the sign-up procedure seeming strange to you, let people judge our experiment by our results. They need no theoretical explanation.

May I leave you with the suggestion that if you wish to gain something truly meaningful from your experience with our community, take a more careful look at us. Perhaps you could write another chapter, "Twin Oaks Revisited." I'm not even certain your first chapter has any meaning. Aside from displaying your prosy critical style, and assuaging those close-minded people who are irrevocably prejudiced against organization, technology, and social experimentation, the only thing you could possibly accomplish is give many naïve and suggestible readers a downright bigotted distortion of what we are working so hard together trying to create. To wit: You would be working against our cause to explore a better way to

live, a way that must be found in the not-so-distant future if man
is going to survive on this planet. . . .

Should you decide to revisit, would you be so kind as to follow
the advice I gave long ago which you paraphrased into a close for
your chapter: "Stick around awhile."

VIII
Spiritual
Odyssey

New Vrindaban, Brotherhood of the Spirit, Lama and Baba Ram Dass

To hear the whole symphony one must
concentrate on the flow of notes and
harmonics as they come into being and
pass away, keeping one's mind continuously
in the same rhythm. To think over what
has passed, to wonder what is about to
come, or to analyze the effect upon one
self is to interrupt the symphony and to
lose the reality.
— ALAN WATTS, *The Spirit of Zen* (1958)

A few years ago, American students of Buddhism, Zen or Sufism
made the traditional pilgrimage to the East. By 1970 the direction had been reversed: The world's swamis, masters and gurus
were journeying West to the United States, which had become
the cradle of a worldwide spiritual revival.

One indicator was the new American spiritual communities,
which, since 1965, had made astounding leaps in numbers and
membership. By the fall of 1970, in cities alone, more than four
hundred and thirty new spiritual and religious groups had been
listed by the Liberated Church in America, a Berkeley-based
organization devoted to "hastening the extinction of the established denominations."

Fewer, but still hundreds had located in the country: from
the Meher Baba * Spiritual Center at Myrtle Beach, South Caro-

---

* Meher Baba, meaning "compassionate father," was the name later assumed
by an Indian master (1894–1969) of Persian parentage who was widely recognized
as having attained full "God realization." He and his disciples established a
spiritual colony, school, hospital and hotel for the poor near Ahmadnagar. A
thousand people were said to have journeyed in one day to the colony to
receive his *darshan*, or blessing. Meher Baba, who observed silence since 1925

lina, to the Zen Buddhist Mountain Center in a national forest, south of San Francisco.

Altogether, these communities covered the spectrum of spiritual ferment: from the Mennonite families who had founded Reba Place fellowship in Evanston, Illinois, to the hip members of the Fort Hill Community in Roxbury, Massachusetts, followers of Mel Lyman, who claimed to be the American avatar; from the radicalism and experimentalism of underground houses created by breakaway priests and nuns of the Catholic Church to the traditionalism of Hassidic communities formed by young Jews in San Francisco and Boston; from the complex theology and folk masses of Chicago's Ecumenical Institute to the fundamentalism of the evangelistic Jesus Freaks.

The origins and implications of this resurgence go beyond the scope of this book. What follows are sketches of the daily life and communal structures of three new and diverse spiritual communities. What they suggest, in common, is the future state of religion. Instead of the large, Sunday-only churches, there would be many smaller groups—ashrams, cults, lay orders—all taking different routes to the godhead. With little interest in dry theology, rational creeds or liberal sermons, they had sparked a return to the mystical core of religion—the individual's ecstatic apprehension that divinity is immanent not only in the cosmos and nature, but in man himself. Furthermore, these new com-

---

and communicated by means of an alphabet board, wrote several books and made six visits to Europe and the United States. Those who came into his presence were instantly convinced of his spiritual authenticity and that he was indeed what he said he was—the avatar and Messiah: "I am the New Christ/ You have waited and waited for me a long time./I am the real Guide./You will know me/You will see me./My word is Power./My thought is action./ I am the Truth." So great was his spiritual power that mere photographs of his smiling face, usually accompanied by his oft-quoted saying, "Be happy, don't worry," were enough to make ardent disciples, or "Baba lovers." Meher Baba followers included many hippies, who followed his teaching to give up drugs. Among them were several rock stars, notably Peter Townshend, the writer of the rock opera *Tommy*. Several societies have sprung up in this country: the Meher Baba Information, Box 1101, Berkeley, California, and a Meher Spiritual Center, located on a four-hundred-acre tract near Myrtle Beach, South Carolina.

munities had carried their faith over into every action of daily community life.

Of all the Eastern religions and disciplines that spread westward during the sixties, the largest, most organized was Hare Krishna. By 1970 there were fifty centers around the world and in the major cities of the United States, including San Francisco, Boston, Buffalo, Seattle, Columbus, Pittsburgh and New York. The national membership was estimated at 3,000. Funds and publication of *Back to Godhead* magazine (circulation 500,000) were controlled by the International Society for Krishna Consciousness, established by a seventy-five-year-old swami, A. C. Bhaktivedanta, who brought Krishna to the West.

In 1968, the swami instructed a group from the New York temple on Mott Street to set up an ashram in the West Virginia hills. It was to be, he wrote them, "a transcendental village . . . where people in the bona fide divisions of society will live independently, completely depending on agricultural produce and milk from cows (considered in the Veda to be man's second mother, and thus to be revered) . . . better to live there without modern amenities and a natural, healthy life for executing Krishna consciousness."

It was to be named New Vrindaban after Vrindaban, India, where Krishna is said to have first revealed himself.

I made two visits there: the first just months after it had been started; the other in August of 1970, after leaving Twin Oaks.

April 17, 1969

I drove south from Wheeling with Larry Kanevsky just after a cloudburst. Trapped behind a tractor trailer, we crept over the deforested, scarred hills, past small brick houses and JESUS SAVES billboards. At Limestone, we turned off the highway and wound through a valley, following directions to a small schoolhouse. There, at the foot of a road that came off the mountain and ended at a washed-out bridge over a muddy, swollen creek, we spotted a couple. The man, who had rolled up his pants, carried groceries; the girl, in a long dress, clutched an armful of roses. They were on their way to New Vrindaban. We joined them for the three-mile hike.

The young man was small, nearly bald and walked with a limp. He was Kirtanananda, appointed by the swami to be in charge of the ashram. The girl, who parted her black hair severely down the middle, was named Santybama. She was a few months pregnant and had spent most of her day in a health clinic waiting to be examined by a doctor. That the poor in America must wait interminable hours for health care she accepted with resignation. The swami had enjoined them to be poor and not to go on welfare. A friendly florist had given them the roses to grace Krishna's altar—three miles up the mountain.

Introductions completed, we began the hike. We crossed and recrossed the stream three times. Where it was waist deep, we passed the grocery bags and roses hand to hand over the coffee-colored water. As we climbed the rocky, slippery path, rose petals fell behind us, marking our progress in the mud. "The roses will make Krishna happy," Santybama said, smiling distantly as if recalling a long-lost lover.

Santybama said she'd been raised in a Jewish family on Long Island and had dropped out of New York University after taking many philosophy courses. "Judaism isn't a religion anymore, it's an ethic, a culture," she said, and lapsed into the mantra: *"Hare Krishna, hare Krishna, Krishna, Krishna, hare, hare; hare Rama, hare Rama, Rama Rama, hare hare."*

The path diverged from the creek and climbed the mountainside. As we walked, Kirtanananda told us about himself. He was the son of a Southern Baptist minister and had been a graduate student in history at Columbia. In the midst of writing his doctoral dissertation on Southern revivalism, he had dropped out. He said the Christian Church had lost touch with primal, firsthand spiritual experience and had substituted for it a rationalistic creed. "In this age of maya [material illusion] Western man must surrender his attachment to sense gratification by putting aside his reason, by training his consciousness to focus inward on the spirit. . . ." There was no contradiction between the basic teachings of Christ and those of the Bhagavad-Gita, he said; both Christ and Krishna were emanations of the same supreme unitary Being. "The Bible is only a partial guide. It tells you what to avoid, but not how to get there; it denies the senses, but it doesn't give you instructions on how to find bliss." His voice trailed off into the mantra, *"Hare Krishna, hare Krishna. . . ."*

We had come to the top. The road emerged into an open space and turned to the left. Across an open bay of space, on a peninsula that hung over the unpeopled hardwood hills, perched New Vrindaban—a small, plucky shack. "A man raised ten kids here," Kirtanananda said. The house appeared to have gone through several reincarnations. A tar-papered log cabin, it would have been ideal for a family of moonshiners.

Along the stretch of road small trees had been planted: two thousand white pines, as well as apple, pear and walnut trees. The community subsisted on a diet of fruit, rice and milk. "Krishna loves fruit," Kirtanananda said.

We entered through a cluttered kitchen and workroom, taking off our shoes inside the door. From there, bowing welcome, devotees dressed in saffron dhotis led us into a slightly larger room. Except for cushions, its floor was bare. The one window looked out on a chasm from which the evening mist was rising. Left alone, Larry and I dried and warmed ourselves in front of a small, crude fireplace of rock and mortar in which a few twisted pieces of locust wood baked.

In a few minutes, Kirtanananda reappeared. He'd changed into a dhoti and had dabbed gray clay on the bridge of his nose and forehead: *Telak,* the footprint of Vishnu and symbol of the body's spiritual dedication. He set a large tray down before us. On it were silver bowls of pineapple, dates, nuts, slices of orange, small folded cakes enclosing homemade blackberry jelly, and one bowl of water and rose petals.

Was this just for us?

Yes, Kirtanananda nodded, the custom, in India or West Virginia, was to serve guests *prasadam* (food) immediately upon arrival.

About a dozen devotees lived in the small house. Most were young men in their twenties. The unmarried men were called brahmacharis. The two married women in the ashram were brahmacharinis—sometimes called gopis, for short. They were Santybama and the wife of an English instructor at Ohio State University, Harvey Wheeler, who adopted the name of Hayagriva. Income from his teaching—he commuted to Columbus three times a week—was then the ashram's main financial support. Wheeler is a tall, muscular man in his early thirties. When I first met him, he dressed in jeans and a sweater. He and Kirtanananda had founded the ashram.

Reared a Roman Catholic, Wheeler was an agnostic until January of 1964, just after he'd received a master's in literature from New York University. "I'd read the mystical experiences of poetry—Blake and Whitman—but never connected them to myself."

While alone in a cabin in upstate New York, he ate several buttons of peyote. "It tore the doors of perception off their hinges to reveal a flaming Sistine vision . . . I actually left my body and journeyed into the universe to behold the Milky Way from an incredible distance. I discovered my real self extended beyond the body was eternal."

While teaching the following year, Wheeler delved into Buddhist literature and continued taking psychedelics. But his drug experiences had begun to repeat. In October of 1965, he and Kirtanananda boarded a freighter for India. They were searching for a guru and God. But they spent too much time smoking the hookah, got dysentery, and had to return to New York. There, in July on Houston Street, Wheeler met an Indian dressed in a saffron robe wearing pointed white shoes. He was his grace A. C. Bhaktivedanta, who had rented a storefront store at 26 Second Avenue to spread Krishna consciousness. The swami encouraged Wheeler to give up drugs. "You don't have to take anything for your spiritual life," he said in an authoritative manner that convinced Wheeler. It worked. "As I walked down the streets of Manhattan, chanting, I began to notice that the buildings, the people and the sky all looked very beautiful . . .

the sound of the Supreme Lord of the Universe was passing through my body, coming upon me like a delightful exhilarating song that had somehow been dormant, choked in me for centuries. . . . It was the same song (*kirtan*) that you can hear in the St. Matthew Passion."

It was time for the evening *artrik* (food offering) which would be followed by the *kirtan*—an hour or more of chanting. *Artriks* are held before each meal at 5:30 A.M., noon and 6:30 P.M. The morning and evening *artriks* are followed by *kirtans*.

Santybama took her roses behind a curtain alcove that held the altar. Instruments were distributed: hand cymbals, drums, and conches. Kirtanananda sat cross-legged before a small organ. Hayagriva held a large gong. Suddenly the curtains were jerked back, spotlights flashed on (one of the community's few conveniences was electricity) and the chanting began. It took my senses a moment to recover. The altar was covered with painted figurines, small pictures of gurus, incense, camphor, flowers, a fan of peacock feathers, and a conch shell. We stood, swaying and chanting, for about an hour. The *prasadam* was offered up to Krishna.

At the conclusion, the curtains were drawn across the altar. We sat on the floor, quiet and smiling. The two women brought bowls of rice and vegetables from the kitchen and served the men. When the meal was over, the women cleared the dishes, then sat down and ate separately.

I chatted with Sachisuta. Like the rest, his head had been shaved except for a *sika* (steeple)—a small clump of hair tied by a rubber band at the back of the head. Born a Roman Catholic in Memphis, Tennessee, he went to New York when he was fifteen. He served in the Coast Guard and later became a merchant seaman. Like many of the other devotees I interviewed, he had been a heroin addict. "I tried to squeeze the last drop of pleasure I could . . . until I got to the very end, when I was so run down that I couldn't feel pleasure anymore, only escape from pain."

In his lap lay a string of 108 prayer beads. He carried them around in a cloth bag that hung around his neck. For each bead, he chanted the Hare Krishna mantra. "It makes you very happy and it's so easy. Try it."

Kirtanananda walked quietly among the seated, chanting members, telling them that it was time to sleep. When he pointed out places on the floor for Larry and me, we realized he was indeed in complete charge, a kind of father superior. As Ronidhir, another devotee, remarked: "It's good to learn to be obedient."

April 18

I slowly awoke to hushed voices, the soft tinkling of raga music on the stereo, the crackling of the fire, the swish of a broom as a devotee swept the back room. Outside the window all was black.

A conch was blown, announcing that it was time for the morning *kirtan*. My stomach empty, still sleepy, I fell into the chanting and songs, which this time took over my weakened consciousness. The altar seemed to pulsate. I watched Santybama in spasmodic dance, her face radiant. I lost all sense of time. When the *kirtan* ended, I sat down before the window. The outer world emerged from gray: a corncrib, a wrecked truck, a light going on in the farmhouse on the opposite hill.

August 18, 1970

Over a year elapsed before I returned. This second time I came from Twin Oaks, making the journey from one extreme of the communal movement to the other: from faith in science and technology to faith in mantras and transcendent being.

I hitched from Wheeling. When night fell and no cars stopped, I started to walk. A gentleman by the name of Chuck McCombs, to whom I am grateful, picked me up and drove out of his way to drop me at the schoolhouse. There I ate a Mrs. Wagner's Pie and drank a carton of chocolate milk before beginning my ascent.

The road was the first thing I saw that had changed. It had

been widened by a crawler, which was parked above the bridge. Mile markers on the trees pointed the way. When I arrived, around ten, everyone was asleep. In front of the one small house stood the frame of a pavilion. Under the half-finished roof I could discern by moonlight a dhoti-clad figure stretched out on a work table. I pitched my bag on a square of plywood and slept.

Around four thirty, I was awakened by joyous shouted greetings: *"Haribol! Haribol!"* It was time for *kirtan.* I was one of the last ones inside the temple. No longer a humble shack, it had been completely and rather expensively redecorated. The walls had been smoothly plastered and painted blue. Light came through translucent panels on the ceiling. The fireplace had been rebuilt to twice its size and now bore an ornately carved mantel. Against the far wall, where once the old altar had been, stood a chair with a velvet seat, and over it hung a large photograph of the swami.

The room was crowded. The ashram now had forty members, many of them *gopis,* and fifteen children. The younger boys wore dhotis and *sikas.*

During one part of the service, Hayagriva read and interpreted a sacred text. It was impossible, he said, for man to worship God directly, since God could not be grasped through the senses or intellect; hence, he needed lesser incarnations—enlightened men who have been able to "see God." The service seemed studded with many more laudatory references to the swami, "his divine grace, A. C. Bhaktivedanta, Prabhupada."

Breakfast followed the scripture reading. Styrofoam cups containing a mush of rice, milk and raisins were distributed. Next on the schedule was *japa,* a period between breakfast and the beginning of work which is devoted to chanting on the prayer beads. Between 7:30 and 8:30 A.M., devotees sit on the temple floor and chant to themselves, letting the beads slip through their fingers. Others chanted as they walked over the hillside. Meanwhile, the supervisor of the ashram and his assistants went about delegating the day's work.

That weekend the ashram was busily preparing to host a festival for devotees and representatives from the temples on the

Eastern Seaboard. Some of the women sat on the temple floor weaving garlands of flowers. I began to speak to one of them. She was saying, "It's possible in this age to attain full realization without having to pass through all the lesser incarnations . . . ," when she stopped and looked up. A brahmachari hovered over us. First, he made some domineering comments on how she was making the garland. Then, he turned to me with his list of jobs. I stood and walked out into the morning. The brahmachari said that Ronidhir was now in charge of the ashram, having replaced Kirtanananda, who was touring India with the master. Each morning, Ronidhir got together with two of the other brahmacharis and drew up a list of what had to be done. No one questioned the job assignments. Since I hadn't had much sleep, I requested a less strenuous task than splitting wood to be used for cooking outdoors. The brahmachari smiled and slapped me on the shoulder. "But when you work for *Krishna,* he gives you all the energy you need."

It must have been only six, New Vrindaban time (like Twin Oaks, they set their clocks an hour ahead), but the ashram bustled with activity. A temporary shelter was being constructed to house the weekend guests, and devotees who had changed from their dhotis into jeans were nailing a tin roof to the frame. One group harnessed two horses to a cart. They would drive it down to the schoolhouse and from there take a community car into Wheeling for goods. (As yet, no automobiles could make it up the road.) One group was dispatched to the second floor of the main building to package incense, the ashram's main money-making activity. Another contingent went off to dig two extra outhouses to accommodate the guests, in addition to the two regular outhouses—one for each sex.

Behind the small house, kettles hung over fireplaces. Wood I split was picked up and fed into one of the fires by a burly young man, who reminded me of Friar Tuck. Striking up a conversation, he said he'd been a rock singer in New York. "I used to think in terms of dualities," he said, "and I wondered why life didn't have any continuity . . . New Vrindaban is the perfect Vedic life. We are Prabhupada's army, but no one minds if others give orders; we're all working for Krishna, to please him and make him happy." He quoted the Bhagavad-Gita: "You have no right to the fruits of work. Desire for fruits of work must never be your goal."

After I had split a large pile, enough to keep the fires going for a while, I told Friar Tuck that I was taking a break and would return. I walked by the door of the kitchen. Outside were posted the "rules of the kitchen," below the inscription "Next to the deity room, the kitchen is Krishna's favorite dwelling."

1. Remove shoes before entering.
2. Wash hands, feet and mouth.
3. Do not smell, taste or lustfully enjoy Krishna's foodstuffs.
4. Speak with reverence while preparing the holy *prasadam*.
5. Clean mess, returning items to proper places.
6. Always think of Krishna.

I continued my walk. Over the year, the community had built a dozen houses, several of them domes. The married couples lived together in separate cottages. Generally, the brahmacharis lived two to a cottage. One of the new buildings was a one-room school. When I dropped in, there were from seven to twelve children and two teachers, both men, in the plywood building. The children seemed well behaved. They were taking turns reciting legendary episodes from Krishna's life. Often, the teachers would interrupt their recitations and instruct them to "stand up straight."

One of the children told me his name was Nathan. He had a Southern accent. "I'm not old enough to have a spiritual name," he said. During his recitation, he used the word "expand."

"What does that mean?" questioned a teacher.

"To grow bigger."

"How can Krishna do that?"

"Krishna can do anything."

On the way back, I met Hayagriva. He told me they'd have to install toilets before the state would accredit the school. "We'll do it their way, but I doubt that anyone will use the toilets even after they're installed."

Following Indian custom, they do not use toilets, or even toilet paper. Instead, they wipe with their hands and wash themselves with water from small plastic containers carried to the outhouses. (A few communes which are ecologically aware do the same.)

While I visited, Hayagriva was still teaching, but only half of his salary was going to support the ashram. It was steadily becoming more self-sufficient by selling incense bought from its sister temple in San Francisco. "Last weekend we made over one thousand dollars at Miami U [in Oxford, Ohio]," he said. The ashram sends out groups in a bus to chant, convert and sell incense at campuses throughout the Midwest.

As we talked, Santybama came along the path, carrying her baby. I introduced myself as the writer she'd met more than a year ago walking up the muddy trail. She remembered and asked why I was writing a book. "Krishna relieves you of all karma and responsibility. Once you turn to Krishna, you don't have to worry about yourself, your family, or society."

Santybama was in charge of the duties which the swami had assigned to women: all cleaning, darning, sewing, cooking, and churning of butter.

During lunch hour, scriptures were read over an outdoor loudspeaker. The men sat on the lawn listening, while the women carried out bowls of soup that contained corn, peas, tomatoes, potatoes, and broccoli. Before eating, each devotee prostrated himself before his bowl and prayed. I sat next to Santybama's husband, who said he'd been reared a Jew and then had been an atheist. They are one of several married couples, or grihasthas, who live here. They take a "regulative" attitude toward sex. Following the swami's advice, they have intercourse not for pleasure but for procreation and only during the woman's ovulation period.

I took the remaining portion of my soup back to the kitchen and poured it into the soup pot. I'd been instructed to do so; since food was a manifestation of Krishna, it must not be wasted. Then I returned more willingly to splitting wood, which had become a favorite skill of mine. One devotee working nearby bugged me by repeatedly warning me to keep my eye on the ax head, watch my backswing, not swing too hard or the ax would glance off. I was annoyed until I noticed that the others gave and took constant criticism. Sometimes the reprimands were sharp: "Who told you to mix the paper and the garbage?" Ronidhir rebuked a devotee who was assigned to clean up the grounds. "No one," he answered meekly.

"Do only what you're told."

I began to realize how different my consciousness was from theirs. They had subordinated their egos to pleasing Krishna, and there was no place for hurt feelings or rebellion in "Prabhupada's happy army."

Members of other temples began to arrive. Four of them, who'd come from New York and were members of the Sanyassi, a renounced order, held prominent positions in the society's hierarchy. Because of their spiritual progress, they had been relieved of administrative and business responsibilities such as publication of the society's magazine. Like the swami, their only duty was to teach. They were barefoot and carried staffs. As they came into view, devotees lifted their arms in an ecstatic V and welcomed them with shouts of *"Haribol! Haribol!"* prostrating themselves along the path. The four seated themselves in the shade of a large tree to the side of the house. The women, after prostrating themselves, served *prasadam*.

One of the four was a chubby young man who wore a wristwatch. He inquired why I was visiting the ashram. When I explained that I was doing a chapter in my book on spiritual communities, he asked, "Communities? There is only one spiritual community, only one God and one divine grace—A. C. Bhaktivedanta, Prabhupada." Each syllable of the swami's name rolled sonorously off his tongue.

I said that my reading of the Bhagavad-Gita had led me to assume there were many paths to the Godhead.

"Which version of the Gita did you read?"

The one translated by Christopher Isherwood.

"But that's not an authorized edition. There is only one edition," he said, producing a paperback version which had been translated by A. C. Bhaktivedanta. All other versions were full of "mental deceptions" and "mental speculations."

"If you do not put aside your mental analysis, you will never understand," he said.

Toward the end of the afternoon work stopped. I joined a party of men who were going down to the gorge to bathe in the creek. During the summer, baths are a regular part of the day. They are segregated; the women bathe between 4 and 5, the men from 5 until the conch is blown for the evening *kirtan*.

The pool was beautiful. It lay underneath a waterfall that dropped eight feet over the edge of a layered rock formation. The sides of the gorge were densely foliated, tropically green. I sat on a rock enjoying the light and colors. A devotee sat down beside me and delivered the soft sell: how he'd gone through Zen and drugs and how Krishna was the way. Krishna was bliss, freedom from desire, care and ego. You had only to chant the mantra. . . .

But I was deaf to his proselytizing, immersed in the maya of the waterfall. I was alone in this enjoyment, which only increased the sense of alienation similar to what I'd felt at Twin Oaks. Here, however, it was even more severe.

I doubted whether I could stay another day.

That evening after *kirtan* two outsiders wandered up the road, an Ohio State student and Reno, a hippie hitchhiker the student had picked up. The student was mildly interested in the ashram; the hitchhiker content to crash there. I greeted them like long-lost brothers. Reno took out his tobacco pouch and began to roll. I warned him that the society forbade the use of drugs and alcohol, as well as tobacco. He shrugged and put it away. At my suggestion we walked down the road and shared a smoke. It felt as though we were back in high school stealing a smoke in the john. Lightning danced on the horizon. If it weren't for the approaching storm, I told them, I'd leave that night. They asked me why. I could only quote Kesey in reply: "You're either on the bus or off the bus." And I was off.

When, around four thirty, the early rising devotees came rousting through the pavilion crying *"Haribol!"* I lay motionless. I heard the others getting up and staggering to early *kirtan*. I knew I must be the last left sleeping. A devotee shook my shoulder: "Hurry, brother, you'll be late for *kirtan*." I turned my head so he could see my beard, groaned, and turned over. After he abandoned me, I went back to sleep with a clear conscience.

Although it showed signs of incipient institutionalization, there could be no doubt that Hare Krishna was prospering and growing into one of the major religions of the subculture. Since I last visited, Hayagriva wrote me that the ashram had purchased a ninety-acre farm that bordered on the main road. Now cars can drive directly and easily to the ashram. They had also begun to manufacture their own incense in Pittsburgh. Devotees now alternate between the mountain retreat, the incense factory and a new temple in Pittsburgh, about fifty miles away. With the ashram completely self-supporting, Hayagriva quit his teaching post and was planning a trip to open more centers in South America.

The only other movement equal in numbers and influence to Hare Krishna was the Jesus Freaks—the loose term given to the many small bands of street evangelists who'd couched their fundamentalist message and appeals to personal revelation in the hip colloquial: "Get stoned on Jesus!" Like Hare Krishna, the Jesus movement originated on the West Coast in the mid-sixties. Most of its members were young hippies who had hit bottom on drugs—like some of the people I had met at Living Waters (Book Three). By 1970 Jesus Freaks spread throughout the country, setting up storefront centers, newspapers and communes in Kansas City, Ithaca, New York, Worcester, Massachusetts, Detroit, Cleveland and Denver. They held "Bible raps," "Jesus teach-ins" and Jesus rock concerts (many were musicians).

They could be dogmatic. One leader referred privately to Steve Gaskin, a well-known hippie priest, as the "white devil." Jesus Freaks in Berkeley accused the Krishna devotees of ransacking one of their communes. Scuffles broke out between the two groups on Sproul Plaza at the University of California, where every day the Krishna people went to chant and do their jogging-in-place dance while the Jesus Freaks shouted their message over the cries of the burrito venders.

Unlike the tightly organized Krishnaites, the Jesus Freaks splintered into many small groups, which moved from storefront to storefront with no tie to any established denomination. Their largest West Coast organization was the World Christian Liberation Front in Berkeley. WCLF publishes *Right On,* a newspaper, translates portions of the Gospel into modern idiom, distributes the tracts at peace rallies and in front of pornographic movies. Though the Jesus Freaks joined nonviolent demonstrations—picketing the offices of a slumlord—some regarded them as reactionaries. Lawrence Lipton, columnist of the Los Angeles *Free Press,* described them as the "finks of capitalism and the status quo whose job is to dilute and neutralize and ensnare potential dissent."

Most of their crusading zeal goes into the hippie ghettos. Runaways, addicts and disturbed young people have taken overnight refuge in their hostels. Many of them took to heart the message that Jesus is a real force in the world and stayed, living with their brothers and sisters in the communal houses that spread over the West Coast: the House of David in Seattle; the House of the Risen Son, in Eugene, Oregon; The Jesus Christ Light & Power Company, Los Angeles. Following the communes, many had begun to move to the country: to Antioch Farm outside Mendocino, California; to Emmanuel Farm, near Sumas, Washington.

By living communally, the Jesus Freaks saw themselves as the modern counterparts of the early Christians described in Acts: 3:43

All whose faith had drawn them together held everything in common. They would sell their property and possessions and make a general distribution as the need of each required. With one mind they kept up their daily attendance at the temple, and breaking bread in private homes, shared their meals with unaffected joy, as they praised God and enjoyed the favor of whole people.

The Jesus Freaks and Krishnaites represented the injection of new wine into old wineskins. However, the spiritual movement also witnessed the appearance of new eclectic forms of worship, liturgy and ritual that drew on Christianity, the Eastern disciplines, ESP, psychedelics and hip pantheism.

The Church of the Awakening, the Neo-American Church and the Church of the Clear Light held communion using peyote and LSD as sacraments. George Hurd, the former guru of Oz and now Father George, who had taken vows in an offshoot sect of the Greek Orthodox Church, wrote and conducted an Aquarian Mass that was held in The Center, Santa Fe. It opened with ten minutes of oming and included a recitation of the Nicene Creed, as well as reference to the "god who dwells within each of us—be he called Christ, Krishna, Buddha; be he called I AM . . ." and concluded with a "kiss of peace" passed among the communicants.

A liturgy of "voluntary primitivism" was the basis of the Ahimsa Church established at Wheeler ranch. It asserts four truths: (1.) The truth is forever one, naked, nameless and homeless. (2.) The truth is thy own self. (3.) Love (Life=Light =Consciousness)=Love. (4.) O Lord: Everything + Everyone + Everywhere=God. The church's four missions were to preserve the purity of the air and water and to abolish ownership of the land and sources of energy. Every Sunday members attended a "love feast" and practiced yogic eating: "hold one mouthful of food for one hundred relaxed breaths, then chew only with front teeth." Other recommended yogas were shitting in the garden, thumbsucking, and candle gazing.

There were hundreds of small esoteric cults. Satanists, posing as a Christian brotherhood, who sold high-priced religious tracts on Harvard Square; an order of Episcopalians who believed in reincarnation; and many groups, like the Here and Now Commune in San Francisco, who shared a cosmology that involved flying saucers.

The largest of the contemporary spiritual communities of young people is the Brotherhood of the Spirit.* Composed of two hundred members in Warwick and Northfield, Massachusetts, the Brotherhood is a unique spiritual order—the unlikely combination of mystical elements of Christianity and Hinduism allied with extrasensory perception and the idiom of rock music.

The society was envisioned and begun by a charismatic high school dropout and ex-Hell's Angel, Michael Metalica. To the community, Michael represents a latter-day John the Baptist who has been endowed with prophetic powers to lead the Brotherhood and the world out of the "negativity" of the Piscean Age into the pure light of the Aquarian.

Michael grew up on an upland farm outside Leyden, Massachusetts, a tiny village founded in the eighteenth century by God-fearing Puritans. When he was six, his parents, both Episcopalians, punished him by sending him to bed early one night. It was then, he recalled, that he had his first apocalyptic vision: the earth, seen as from a spaceship, undergoing titanic upheavals and energy transformations. During his childhood, waves of "spontaneous energy" made him feel joyfully whole. But as he grew into adolescence, these visions and sensations faded. In high school Michael was a competitive and popular

---

* In contention as the largest new community, spiritual or otherwise, is The Family, a group of two hundred and seventy who in March of 1971 relocated from San Francisco to a 580-acre farm near Pegram, Tenn. They made the move together in a caravan of thirty buses. Their spiritual leader was Steve Gaskin, an ex-college teacher who used to draw up to 2,000 listeners at rock auditoriums on Monday nights. Within the Family were fourteen four-person marriages. One involves Gaskin. "We practice a kind of householding yogi," he said.

student, who did honors work. But a deep frustration gnawed inside. At first, he didn't know what he wanted. When he read a *Saturday Evening Post* article on the Hell's Angels, a rebellious brotherhood "who would have died for each other," he dropped out of school, left home and went to California to join them. After a stint with the Angels on the coast, Michael returned home. Disillusioned, he took a job as superintendent of a pickle factory. Then in May of 1968, feeling empty, not knowing what to do, he quit his job and built a tree house not far from his parents' home in Leyden.

He lived alone in the tree house, meditating and working without pay for neighboring farmers. "I was trying to find some way to get back that spontaneous energy." One day at the town dump he met Elwood Babbit, a bus driver in his fifties who was a medium and the local counterpart of Edgar Cayce. The meeting was crucial. Until this point, Michael hadn't trusted his visions. Was he sane? But Elwood confirmed that his experiences were real and convinced Michael that his karmic role was to found a spiritual cult. (Later, Michael told me, "The truth is I was once Saint Peter.")

Like a magnet, Michael's tree house attracted visitors. By the fall of 1968 Michael was joined by eight other young men— high school and college dropouts from the dreary, red-bricked industrial towns of the Connecticut Valley. Most of the nine original members had all been heavy drug users; more significantly, they shared a profound spiritual discontent—a craving to find meaning outside themselves. One of the original members was Chris, the son of a doctor. In high school he felt stifled by conservative dress codes and uncreative teachers who assigned dull topics. "Instead of drilling you with dates—like when Washington was inaugurated—teachers should be guides to helping you learn from experience." Socially, Chris was shy to the point of paranoia.

One night in the college library he read a commentary on the life of Jesus. "I started thinking what would happen if Jesus would walk down the main street of my hometown. Most people would laugh in his face. But a part of me said, 'I'd know who he was and I'd want to follow.' And then I realized that what I wanted to do was to change the world, and that if I wanted it bad enough, I could do it."

When Chris visited the tree house, Michael left him alone in a tent to listen to a cassette recording of one of Elwood's "transmissions." (In his trances Elwood acts as a medium for the voices of the prophets and gods.) This recording was of Moses. "I didn't know if it was Moses or not," Chris said later, "but there was something in it that spoke to me." When he left the tent, Chris was high.

The society went through trying times. While they were away on a visit, local ruffians burned down their tree house. Undaunted, they built a lean-to cabin in the mountains. There they spent the winter, meditating individually and together, eating nothing but brown rice, tamari sauce, and drinking melted snow.

That was the winter of my first visit. My impression was of incomprehensible kooks who spoke darkly of disasters and vaguely of positive and negative energies. For almost two years I didn't return. But while I was traveling elsewhere around the country, the society steadily grew and moved. From February to June of 1969, twenty-one of them (now almost half women) lived in shacks, tents and tree houses in Johnson's Pastures, Vermont. But they didn't get along with the hedonistic, hippie members of the adjoining commune at Guilford. For the summer of 1970, the society—now numbering thirty-three—moved to a summer camp near Heath, Massachusetts. By April they had grown to seventy. New members were required to turn over their worldly possessions to the society. And when members who had small inheritances joined, the society bought a country restaurant-nightclub in a wooded section of Warwick, Massachusetts, four miles away from Elwood Babbit's house.

When I first revisited the society—now called the Brotherhood—in early November of 1970, their growth astounded me.

In contrast to the nine of them in the lean-to cabin, they were now one hundred and fifty strong. The shutters and doors of the sedate clapboard inn had been repainted purple. The old restaurant kitchen had been enlarged and redecorated with brick, barn beams and indirect lighting. From a large shed-shaped building emanated amplified, live rock music of Spirit in Flesh, the Brotherhood's band. The group had just signed a recording contract with Metromedia. Young girls with clean, long hair and light in their eyes quartered cabbages to make a crock of sauerkraut. Beyond the house stretched neat, 100-foot rows of a well-harvested garden. A brigade of members unloaded wood from one of several trucks. Another group dug a sewer line. At the other end of the property rose the nearly completed frame of a 100-by-31-foot dormitory—three stories high. Standing in front, directing crews of workers nailing panels to the top floor was Brian Smith. I remembered Brian from two years before as a pale, wasted young man, the son of a Quaker carpenter, who had hit bottom. "We've already spent five thousand dollars on this building" he said in the tone of a man who knows what he's about. "We've got a house with fifty people over in Northfield—mostly the members with kids (about fourteen). We hold the school there . . . After our membership hits five hundred, we'll begin to spread out to other areas," he said, and I began to wonder if the Brotherhood might indeed become the largest spiritual order since the Shakers. "When it gets to be heavy," he went on, "thousands will come to us. Then we'll have to do a little more sifting. . . ." What did he mean? "Well, selecting out those who come to drain us and those who can fully give energy."

Indeed, the Brotherhood was Messianic, dynamic, growing, materially successful; still, I couldn't quite understand what they were about. And in November, I couldn't stay to learn. For one reason, they prohibit visitors from remaining overnight; secondly, I felt, as I had at New Vrindaban, alienated and threatened by a group consciousness my intellect couldn't understand.

I drifted over to a group who had taken a break from digging the sewer line. They were talking about Elwood's latest transmission from Vishnu and were discussing auras, progressions and astral planes. While I stood there, rather uncomfortably, a tall young man with curly hair introduced himself. Ted had been graduated from Yale with a major in psychology and philosophy, done graduate work and taken thirty trips. As he talked, he blew up balloons and tied the ones that didn't burst into a cluster. "If you try to understand this place intellectually, you won't ever know what it's about," he said. "I've searched through all the philosophies trying to find an answer, and all of them—well, except Socrates—they've forgotten the most important thing." He pointed to a young man directing the sewer crew. "That's Bear. He's wiser than all the philosophers because he's learned how to love. It's really quite simple."

Bear asked Ted to bring his crew some apples. We started toward the main building. Suddenly, a group of men started chasing Dale, a redheaded member, one of the founding nine. They were playing tag like seven-year-olds. Dale jumped over bundles of stacked lumber.

Ted and I went inside the washroom addition, which houses the sinks, washer and dryer. We were engaged in some sort of theological discussion when Dale came through. He paused and picked up my negative intellectual vibrations. When he learned I wasn't a prospective member but a writer, he said, "You might find out more if you weren't so intellectual. If you could just be like another kid, then I'd feel like a brother to you," and slapped my back and went back to work and play.

I didn't return to the Brotherhood until the following spring. In the meantime, I read the only book that approaches the Brotherhood's beliefs and practice, *The Aquarian Gospel of Jesus the Christ* (L. N. Fowler & Co., Ltd., London, 1964). It was read and studied by the children who attended the Brotherhood's school and is acknowledged by Michael Metalica to be the only spiritual tract that corresponds "to the truth. We believe in it."

Written in the late nineteenth century, the gospel purports to be a transcription of the Akashic Records, that is, the Universal Mind from which Oriental scholars and Hebrew masters intuitively derive spiritual truth. The transcriber was Levi—

Levi H. Dowling (1844–1911)—a dissenting minister who wrote
the gospel in a trance. The gospel depicts Jesus as man with
extraordinary psychic powers that enabled him to become totally
realized—one of many christs who have appeared throughout the
astrological ages. The first third of the gospel covers the "silent
years" between Jesus' (nonimmaculate) birth and his appearance as a prophet in his thirties. According to Levi's transcription, Jesus spent these years traveling through the Far East,
where he assimilated the teachings of Hinduism, Buddhism,
the Persians, Greeks and the seven initiated mysteries of the
Egyptian hierophants.

Compared to the New Testament, *The Aquarian Gospel*
most closely resembles The Gospel of John in its stress on love
and the mystical process of man realizing the kingdom of God
within himself. Potentially, every man can attain christ-consciousness by transmuting his lower carnal self into pure spirit.
But the process often takes more than one lifetime. In itself, sin
exists only as a negative imbalance of the seven creative attrib-
utes that man, over several lifetimes, must master. Thus, sin
or disharmony is relative to each man's stage of spiritual progress. *The Aquarian Gospel* teaches that love is the "golden
cord" that runs through all Ten Commandments and is the
force by which man can transmute the illusion of his flesh or
separate ego. The fifth postulate to be mastered is brotherhood:
"A selfish faith leads not to light. There is no lonely pilgrim
on the way to light. Men only gain the heights by helping others
gain the heights." Jesus came to earth not to found a church:

Man is not far enough advanced in sacred thought to comprehend the Universal Church, and so the work that God has given me
to do is not the building of that church. I am a model maker, sent
to make a pattern of the church that is to be—a pattern that the
[future, Aquarian] age may comprehend. . . . The perfect age will
surely not require priests, and shrines . . . forms and rites and carnal
sacrifice. In the age of Aquarius, the world will hear and comprehend the seed of his teaching . . . [and] on the day of Pentecost a
new christ will again be manifested.

I returned to the Brotherhood with special permission as a visitor to live with the prospective members on the second floor of the completed dormitory. The prospective members, or PM's for short, are at the base of the Brotherhood's hierachy. Michael makes all major financial and spiritual decisions. Directly under him in the chain of command is a group of seven elder members, who supervise work and have full responsibility when Michael, the band's lead singer and composer, is away. Next are the members; below them, the prospective members, a group that varies from fifteen to thirty as new people arrive every day and others depart. The PM's must live in the community for two months before qualifying for full membership. Anyone who agrees to the community's rules—no drugs, no smoking, no sexual promiscuity—can be admitted as a prospective member. However not all are accepted. At the end of the two months the membership votes on each candidate—a vote which Michael can overrule. At any time, Michael or the inner seven can expel or suspend members or PM's. During their probation, the PM's go through an intensive experience that winnows those who cannot overcome their negativity. After a few days the chaff separates itself from the wheat. Many can only tolerate one day at the Brotherhood and leave at a fast pace. Those who do stay insist they can't live elsewhere.

Initially, I felt as I had before—trapped. The dorm was designed like the archtypal tree house—to promote a group consciousness. About twenty-five people, two-thirds men, slept on bunks made of two-by-fours in one large undivided room. We worked together, meditated together, and excreted side by side in a coed outhouse. One group of PM's got up at dawn to do calisthenics, chanting "I am spirit! I am spirit!" as their hands clapped overhead. Group meetings were called any time of the day or night. Once Michael awoke a group of PM's by playing a Beatles record at high volume. It was a test. For a while no one protested—intimidated by Michael's authority (he insists he has none). When one girl finally complained, Michael replied, "I wondered how long it would take you," switched off the record, and left. The continual meetings are the only activity which verges on ritual. "One of the sages in *The Aquarian Gospel*," Chris pointed out, "predicted that the future church wouldn't need forms and rituals."

The main purpose of the meetings is to draw out the PM's negativity. Chris began one session by saying, "Just one look at you drags me down. Can't you understand why we don't let you into the members' meeting? You drain off all our energy! I mean, you've got to commit yourself totally—you can't get through the gates of heaven with two dollars in your back pocket." He turned to Mark, a young black. "Right now, I wouldn't vote you in. Half the time you're bullshitting everyone. I'm not asking you to give up your identity, just be more open and grow."

The PM's included: Steve, a shy University of Massachusetts dropout, who used to eat four McDonald hamburgers a day because he felt "so empty"; Doris, a thin girl, who had been strung out on speed; Kathy, the mother of two, who separated from her husband and came to the community to find a selfless way of loving; and Gordon, a young redheaded Canadian, who was undoing the "cultural conditioning which makes us think we're just material."

The PM's were encouraged to exorcise their negativity as if it were an evil spirit. "Say what you feel, even if it's rotten—get it out of you," Chris urged, "and then take a look at it and you'll see that it's not really you." Unlike encounter groups, they do not analyze or probe for the roots of neurosis but seek catharsis and spiritual reinforcement.

In the few days I began to see positive results. Steve, who was much less withdrawn, said: "With so many people around me who are concentrating on the positive, I forget about my problems." He stopped eating compulsively. The Brotherhood's spiritual therapy so impressed a psychiatrist at the Bronx State Hospital that he referred one of his patients to the community; however, the experiment failed because the community couldn't provide him the constant supervision needed.

The first afternoon I helped two PM's get the water out of the flooded basement of the dormitory. Lynette poked her head in the doorway. "Are you back?" Her eyes smiled and looked into mine.

I remembered the first time we had met. It was in the kitchen of the main house and we had stood for about fifteen minutes, eyes locked in an embrace. "I know you from somewhere," she had said softly, her lips slightly parted. We groked. In a while I began to see her face change, as if her "one" face were really a composite of multiple exposures that flashed on and off subliminally, undetected by normal vision.

After the mood was broken, I told her what had happened to me. She wasn't surprised. The Brotherhood shared the ability to see into each other's spirit with the "third eye," the center of spiritual insight located in the forehead. "What you saw were the forms my spirit took in other lives. I was the wife of a soldier, who left me to go off to the French and Indian War, the mistress of an English baron. Once I lived on the American prairie. And I'm sure that I was a milkmaid in Switzerland. My father was born there." We concluded that I had known her during one of my previous lives in Switzerland.

"Most of the people are here to work out the karma left undone," she said. "Some of us were lovers who got hung up on sex and never learned to love with nonattachment."

Lynette gaily helped us push the water toward the clogged drain. She sloshed it with the side of her boot and sang "By the sea, by the sea, by the beautiful sea." There was light in her eyes. And I began to slosh, too. What had begun as a chore became a game. The water all went down the drain.

Standing in line for dinner, I was approached by a towering member who inquired if I had been Henry David Thoreau. He was about the fourth to ask me that. He was Ralph Waldo Emerson. In front of me in the line a Cardinal Wolsey chatted with a Chinese mogul, who had allowed his house to collapse rather than break off his elegantly long fingernails in repairing it. Thus in this lifetime he must work through personal vanity. "Wow, this is such a high-energy day," someone remarked, as if he were noting the humidity or temperature. A group of us joined arms and rocked together. Down the line another group let out Indian war whoops. "Oh, John, you have such a beautiful blue aura," a girl told her companion. An aura, I learned, was energy discharged by each spirit and visible as a silhouette around a person's head. The color and intensity of auras varied according to one's spiritual progress. Michael Metalica, Elwood Babbit, and a few other members of the community were said to be able to read auras.

A hush fell over the line as Michael came down the passageway. He is tall, muscular; has blond-red hair; a hawklike nose; wears tight pants and a velvet tunic over a thermal underwear top. Around his wrists are wide leather bands. Lynette rushed up to him. "Oh, Michael, I've been high all day!" He laid both hands on her shoulders so that only inches separated their faces and said slowly in his commanding, resonant voice, "keep on working on it and you'll be high all the time," and strode off.

While waiting for dinner, I was greeted warmly by five or six people who have known me in previous lives. "You've got a very old spirit," said Karen, who is twenty and was sure I had been her grandfather. "I feel so close to you. I can say anything to you and it feels right." Before joining the community (in this life), she had been a young concert violinist, who had committed herself to a mental hospital. Very openly she told me about her troubles, and I told her mine.

The line led down a long passageway past the shower room, toilet room (both mixed) and an inscription on the wall:

> I Am Spirit
> I Am Vibrating Creative Energy.
> I Vow to Do, Be and Obey
> The Will of the Creative Energy.
> I Vow to loose myself
> From My Carnal Self. So Be It.

Standing behind what was once a bar, three members doled out portions of brown rice, beans and applesauce. Over the bar, a ladder led to a small room made of scrap lumber. On it in black paint, someone had scrawled MIKUL'S TREE HOUSE. The ceiling of the main room was vaulted and divided into panels. Inscribed in golden letters within them were the Brotherhood's Seven Universal Laws: Order, Balance, Harmony, Growth, God-Perception; Spiritual Love and the highest and final law, Compassion.

I sat down next to Ralph Waldo and discussed reincarnation. "Whether it's true or not, reincarnation gets our attention away from the carnal self," he said. "A lot of people's problems have nothing to do with how their parents toilet-trained them. For example, I don't get along with a person here because I died in a concentration camp and he was one of the Gestapo. The main thing is to keep focused on the spirit. We're all one family of spirits who have been going through time together. The one thing in common is we all at one time were persecuted for our religions. Some of us were heretics who were burned at the stake. A lot of us were the early Christians."

Another member, once a Tibetan lama who had been executed by the Communists, told me that the Brotherhood was karmically selected to play some role in ushering in the Aquarian Age. I hung on his every word. "At one meeting, we got into communication with a spirit who may have been Christ. He said that he was going to materialize again right here. Wow—there's this guy who has no social security or draft card. If that doesn't blow your mind. . . ." It did.

I crawled into my bunk. I could hear everything on the floor. Mark was hustling a girl (which he was always doing), "just working out my negativity," he told her. She answered, "Well, I wish you'd hurry up and get off this sexual vibration." On another bunk a couple sat face-to-face in the lotus position, meditating.

Not only is sexual promiscuity contrary to the Brotherhood's code, but it's almost impossible for the PM's and most of the members because of the cramped quarters. Married couples and those who have established a spiritual rapport sleep together in small curtained alcoves of the main building. But if a man begins sleeping around with several of his "sisters," the word inevitably gets out. Guilty parties have been privately and publicly confronted with evidence of their philandering, and a few have been expelled or suspended from the community.

But no one considers the promiscuity rule repressive. One woman member, who had once been married, told me, "There's one hundred percent less balling here, but not because of the rule. Most couples try to reserve sex as a ceremonial occasion to coincide with their spiritual highs. When you make love every night, you get into a pattern that closes you off from each other and other people. . . . Here, I don't have to get uptight when a man comes up to me and looks into my eyes and have to think fast how I can be nice to him without putting a dent in his ego. Because he's not putting the make on me. This way we're free to love many more soul brothers and sisters."

I woke at dawn and took a walk—alone. Still felt a little trapped but vowed to open myself up to whatever the Brotherhood offered. For breakfast, millet, *chapiti* bread and yogurt. I sat across from Jackie, a young girl with black eyes that fixed on mine. After breakfast, we groked for a long time. The rest of her face seemed to dissolve until there was just her eyes. It was like making love, perhaps more intimate. Some secret of our natures seemed to transpire. Later in the day when we passed, I could feel the bond between us. Perhaps we had once been lovers.

Someone asked if I would help tear down a shed and sort the lumber. Within the community work is accomplished with great spontaneity and initiative. Michael lets the membership know what needs to be done, and the word trickles down. Many times I saw members initiate projects and find the tools and the manpower without any apparent supervision.

We'd been silently sorting the lumber a few minutes when one member called a meeting. We sat in a circle on small logs. "Something is wrong," the member said. "It doesn't feel right today. Klondike, I think you're oppressing me." Klondike, a tall, reflective man, didn't answer. The other member continued: "Let's try working not so hard or seriously . . . and do it with less attachment." Everyone agreed—we'd try it. Then a girl came over. "They're going to slaughter the hog and need lots of water." So we dropped work on the shed and formed a water brigade. We built fires under three ash cans and filled them with water. Others had set up a table, sharpened knives, and built a pen. John and Jeff were nailing a huge beam high between two pines, from which the slaughtered pig would be hoisted. Everyone worked with phenomenal energy. Jeff shimmied up and down the tree, ran off to get an ax, ran back, and hammered furiously. I'd never seen anyone work with such total commitment.

Artie, a local farmer, and Wally, a member who had grown up in rural Virginia, slaughtered and dressed the hog. Artie shot it twice between the eyes and then gouged a knife into its throat, slashing a main artery. Wally held the hind legs, which thrashed until the blood pumped out. "Very heavy," said John, a curly-blond-haired young man, with clear blue eyes and a calm manner. "A year ago, we couldn't have done it. Now killing our own meat seems right. If an animal gives itself to be sacrified for man, its spirit will move on."

In the afternoon I returned to my bunk to read mimeographed copies of the transmissions which Elwood Babbit had received. Most were from Vishnu, the second of the three principal Hindu deities, regarded as the preserver of the world.

In conversation No. 4, August, 1970, Vishnu communicated that infinitude is composed of seven rings. The first and lowest is composed of the grossly material. The seventh and highest is pure spirit—"bright, etheric light." At the fourth ring, spirit and materiality are finely balanced. Each ring has its unique vibrational setting that corresponds to seven chokras, or energy centers, in man's body. As man becomes aware of these centers, he progresses upward. Most men are on the fourth progression, struggling to balance spirituality and materiality, the positive and negative. Because Vishnu in this age has increased the overall vibration of the cosmos, men are making swifter progress through the rings.

Each man, Vishnu declares, is a free agent. He can freely elect to stay where he is, or to move on by opening "wide the door of spontaneity, where each moment is a listening device for the next vibration that is nudged within the brain itself, and there acted upon without fear and pride or the repressions of a material discipline. The child exemplifies the true spontaneity of spirit which is needed when you open the true way to the true Self."

As I read, a small redheaded girl sat beside me. We shared energies for a while; then she went to the window and looked out on the woods. "Oh, God, every day it gets more wonderful!"

I joined a crew who was shoveling layers of clay from the yard in front of the house. The clay had been deposited there from a newly dug waterline. Members who noticed that I was beginning to groove on the community approached to ask if I'd decided after all to become a prospective member. Most couldn't understand why I planned to leave the next day. "Don't you feel what a high charge this place has?" Yes, it did, but I would have to find the same high on my own—outside. Impossible, they said.

Finally had a meeting with Michael, a very busy superintendent, rock star and prophet. Face-to-face he is sincere, direct and not at all taken with his image. But there's never a doubt who's in charge. If a car is to be borrowed or a hog slaughtered, the word comes from Michael. When he found out a band member was sleeping with a prospective woman member, he broke up the affair. Henceforth members don't get sexually involved with PM's, Michael ruled. And yet, he doesn't seem infatuated with power. "I'm just an illusory leader," he told a meeting. "We're all leaders. I just realize my karma more."

And what a karma! No less than Saint Peter's—to awaken the spirit of the world with a new gospel. "The medium of the Aquarian Age is going to transcend the verbal—it's music. . . .

Man, when people sitting in front of their TV's drinking beer hear the band, they're going to flip out into a new consciousness."

I felt high for the rest of the afternoon—definitely a contact high. Karen and I stood at the end of the long boardwalk that runs over the mud between the dorm and the main building. I told her of emotional problems that had been dogging me before coming here and now had been mysteriously dissolved. She said, "It's all growth. When it hurts, you've got to keep steady and have faith that life expands and contracts. When you become like a small child, you're very vulnerable. People can hurt you more, but they can also love you. But first you love yourself. You say I AM and you know the fullness. It's very simple. We're simple, you and I."

From the shed we could hear the band practicing. Around us, members sang a song written by Michael as they worked, walked and played:

> If you look to those above you
> I'm sure that you will find
> That in their quiet moments they're afraid
> That they might lose their fortunes.
> They'd rather lose their minds,
> And they will, unfortunately.
> Yes, they will, it's not up to me.
> They're going to fulfill the prophesy
>
> THE MEEK SHALL INHERIT THE EARTH
> WE WHO WERE LAST SHALL BE FIRST
> THE MEEK SHALL INHERIT THE EARTH.

The pig was roasted over an open spit and served for dinner. I got one piece of pig fat—alas, karma. The main room was packed and looked like a college mixer. But it felt quite different. Here I could talk to anyone, about anything, or could simply sit alone on a bench without feeling awkward or left out. Just BE. "We're reflections of each other's souls," Gordon said. "We just need to polish the mirror a bit." Lynette sat on the floor in front of us. Tonight she was Heidi, the Swiss milkmaid. Then she let her hair down and was someone else and beautiful.

Mitch, a member who'd lived at Drop City, told me that he believed I should stay at the community. "Communes don't have any purpose. . . . You and I have so much to tell each other and to learn. . . . It's not like that on the outside. The Brotherhood is an island of positive energy. The first day you leave you'll stay high for about twenty-four hours. And then you'll come down—hard."

Did he mean that one man alone couldn't resist the world's negativity? "Everything that happens in the world affects us. The only way we can counteract the negativity is by staying together. I've known so many people who left here and said they could make it on their own, you know, by doing yoga and meditation. They couldn't."

I left the next morning, catching a ride with a van into Greenfield, where I would hitch down 91 to New York City. Dan, who worked for the band, drove. I sat next to Fran, who was going to a dentist appointment. She and her husband had come to the community guided by its "nucleus of energy," but her husband had left because "he couldn't give up his old roles. . . . Sometimes I'm not sure if the Brotherhood is real or not," she said, "it's so far ahead of the time. Maybe New York City *is* real."

I looked into her eyes. Yes, they had that same brightness. The glance might be my last charge of positive energy for the day, I thought. The van passed by the historic markers and upright Georgian houses of Northfield and pulled into a gas station. Two attendants were seated in the window of the station. One of them glanced up—he was just a few feet away from me, and for an instant his eyes crossed mine and then in a spilt second averted. God, I thought, they *are* different.

Of the three groups contained in this book, the one that properly deserves the name "spiritual community" is the Lama

Foundation, outside San Cristobal, New Mexico. It has none of New Vrindaban's religious organization and orthodoxy; none of the Brotherhood's almost therapeutic togetherness. By choice, Lama does not want a permanent guru, an inclusive ritual or the growing membership usually synonymous with "successful" church institutions.

Here, the spiritual emphasis is individual—each member follows those exercises or yoga which work to guide him on his journey toward enlightenment. Lama's structure is distinctly that of a community in which work, decisions and membership are carefully regulated toward the spiritual.

Lama was founded in June of 1967 as a nonprofit foundation —"school for basic studies." Since then, it has evolved a more distinct spiritual framework.

The foundation was started by Steve and Barbara Durkee, a couple in their late twenties. Previously, Steve had been an artist, one of a circle in New York who create huge, unsigned futuristic works. After a two-year search and with $25,000 from an anonymous donor, the Durkees bought the 130-acre site on a high (9,000 feet) wooded slope overlooking a vast plain bounded far to the west by a spectacular mountain range. The foundation took its name from a local village, now all but deserted.

Lama's structure makes it difficult to join. Since the population is held to a maximum of twenty-five, there's seldom a vacancy, and if there is, new people must be accepted unanimously by the membership. One applicant not accepted was Crazy Paul, a spaced-out young man who had visions and who eventually found his way to New Buffalo. His membership, he was told, would be contingent on his taking a bath—something that evidently conflicted with Paul's principles. One member recalled that "he stood there looking up at the shower head for hours." Then, without turning it on, he left the community.

Once approved, new members must live for six months away from the community. The rationale is twofold: to deter those who go from one community to another to "find themselves," and to attract those who have already acquired skills and an identity apart from Lama. "We don't want to be a psychological refuge from the world," one member explained. The community also permits a limited number of month-long visits in the summer. Again, my short stay was an exception to the rule.

Unlike the two orders I visited previously, Lama assesses each adult member $60 a month. Consequently, members must either have independent incomes or return periodically to outside work—usually in the winter. Most are college graduates in their late twenties, including a few couples with children who are bussed to a private school in Taos.

As at Libre, vehicles are parked at a distance, far out of view of the community, which must be approached by foot. The buildings are the finest examples of contemporary communal architecture in America. The main one is composed of a breathtaking dome, flanked on either side by flat-roofed adobe wings —a perfect blend of old and modern styles. One wing houses a Japanese bath large and deep enough to accommodate most members at once. It is encircled by a Japanese garden on the inside. Light streams in through large uncovered windows. To one side of the dome is a brick-floored library, heated by its own fireplace and indirectly lighted by opaque pipes jutting through the walls like portholes.

Above the main complex, a rock-lined path rises to a combined kitchen-dining room, a two-story octagon topped by a peaked dome resembling a Tibetan yurt. On the outside, the two stories are connected by a flight of stairs. Food, prepared below, is hoisted upstairs on a dumbwaiter which emerges in the center of a low octagonal table.

Though meals are taken communally, most of the members (who vary in number from around twenty-five in the summer to some fifteen in the winter) live in separate cabins and A-frames scattered over the slope among stands of ponderosa pine. There is one dormitory, which houses a maximum of about six.

A small garden is intensively cultivated and enriched by droppings from the community's goat herd and chickens.

Experimentally, they raised a special strain of mountain wheat from which they ground flour and baked their own bread.

However, because of its poor soil and dedication to spiritual development, Lama purchases most of its food. No one uses food stamps.

Their best known innovation has been the "grow hole" (described in Book Five). It furnishes the community with greens and vegetables throughout the winter. The results of Lama's application of solar heat and other experiments are disseminated through the Cookbook Fund. Its major publications have been Steve Baer's *Dome Cookbook* and *Cookbook for a Sacred Life,* a collection of spiritual writings.

Lama's atmosphere contrasts sharply with the two religious communities I've described. At New Vrindaban and the Brotherhood of the Spirit decisions emanate from a definite leader, tradition and group consciousness so that little individual deviance is permitted. At Lama, work is delegated and organized by an impersonal, egalitarian schedule, a version of Twin Oaks' labor credit system. Each week, members sign up for six chores; one person is temporarily appointed "hawk," or abbot, to check that everyone does what he signs up for. Similarly, decisions—such as the selection of new members—are made by consensus.

Lama has no one spiritual path, or tao, plotted out. Its central purpose is to provide a community structure which encourages individuals to develop their *own* routes of spiritual growth. "We are not religious," Barbara Durkee told me. "We have a basic core belief in God—Christ, Meher Baba, the Buddha, Mohammed—and in the transitory illusive nature of life: the fact that you can only work on yourself, no one can do it for you; and that there is no meaningful goal other than enlightenment."

The first up in the morning at Lama is the "janitor," who performs the morning duties. The job rotates among the members. First he builds a fire in the meditation room, a low, windowless room on one side of the dome. Then he rings the first bell of the morning at 5 A.M. by striking empty gas cylinders and the exhaust tube of an ICBM (found in an Albuquerque junkyard) that hang suspended from a gracefully carved crosspiece between two posts in front of the kitchen-dining hall. The first bell is optional, for those who want to spend the dawn in quiet meditation. A general wake-up bell is rung at 6:30 and another at 7 to announce the daily prayer meeting usually attended by all members.

Members sit in a circle on cushions and, during the cold months, wrap themselves in blankets. The janitor selects the prayers and chants, which are alternated with ten-minute periods of silence. Readings are drawn from the Bible, the Koran, the writings of the Essenes, and the Bhagavad-Gita. The meeting ends in time for breakfast at 8 A.M.

In contrast to New Vrindaban, where devotees pass most of their day in group chanting, Lama members spend much of their time alone and often silent. Trivial banter is avoided. The main pursuit is contemplation—the slow withdrawal and concentration of consciousness inward to the calm center of being. It's called "centering." After an opening grace, many meals are eaten in silence, the only sound being the tick of chopsticks.

One afternoon, I talked with Barbara Durkee as she sat before a loom weaving a rug. A large, handsome woman in her early thirties, she wore a cross over a tanned, wool sweater and gray-checked bib overalls. "A lot of people come here expecting some far-out community; actually we're funky, middle-class." She herself came from an upper middle-class family and graduated from Stanford. Steve, her husband, is a tall, commanding Renaissance man—artist, architect, inventor. After marrying, the Durkees lived in four communes. One was USCO, a multi-media silk-screening group. For eight months they shared a house in New Mexico with Richard Alpert, Timothy Leary's associate. Meher Baba, who became their first guru, told them not to use drugs and not to permit their use in the community.

The first year, Lama's main community ritual was the encounters held every week-night. "After a while, we saw they weren't getting us anywhere," Barbara said, "except deeper into neurosis and avoidance of the real, individual problems. Everyone became convinced that it did nothing to raise our level of consciousness. You can't get along with other people unless you're at peace inside."

Members spend a day or several days a week alone in the

hermitage, a cabin for silent retreat located a small distance from the main buildings. While there, a member is relieved of all chores, even child care; baby-sitters are appointed on schedule. "A servant to the hermit" tends the fire in the cabin and brings food to him if he's not fasting. "It was the first time in my life that I've been absolutely alone and at peace," recalled Barbara, the mother of three young girls.

The community's one common ritual is the Sufi dances held every Sunday, visiting day. The Sufis were an austere mystical sect within Islam. Sufi dervishes were beggars whose whirling dances transported them into states of ecstasy. The art of these dances was taught to Lama members by Samuel Lewis who died in February of 1970 at the age of seventy-four, and who was considered a Sufi saint (his remains are enshrined at Lama).

On Sunday, Lama members started the dance by forming a large circle around one couple. Hands joined, the circle twisted clockwise as the central couple raised their arms overhead and spun in the opposite direction. Everyone chanted *Zee Allo Hoo, Zee Allo Hoo!* Then, the circle dissolved to couples and finally to individuals doing their own twists. At the end everyone collapsed onto the ground in a state of dazed bliss.

The dances are the most striking instance of the parallel between the Sufis and Lama.

Like the early Christians, the Sufis reacted against the dry theology and orthodoxy of established religion—specifically Eighth Century Islam. They sought personal illumination through their dances, night-long vigils, music, poetry and meditation. Representing a fusion of many spiritual influences, the Sufi borrowed elements of Buddhism, Zoroastrianism and Judaism. One Sufi prophet was decapitated by Moslem authorities for declaring, "I am Truth," i.e. God.

Similarly, members of Lama are syncretic and have incorporated the truths and practices of many religions and teachers: Jesus, Rama Krishna, Hari Dass Baba, Ouspensky, Gurdjieff, Thomas Merton, Ghandi and de Lubiz. They try whatever techniques further their spiritual progress—from Zen meditation to communion at a local church on Sunday.

Most spend at least an hour a day doing hatha yoga, learning to control their bodies by assuming any one of eighty-four statue-like positions, or *asanas*. The most simple one is the corpse position: lying flat on your back, completely relaxed. One of the most difficult is the spiral twist which involves looping your left armpit under the right knee and above your left thigh, joining hands and twisting the head over the right shoulder. A few have tried Tai Chi Chuan, a Chinese meditative exercise involving one hundred and eight motions. Others do Zen, meditate for long periods and clear their minds by chanting mantras.

A mantra is a spiritually charged phrase. If repetitively chanted, the mantra resonates one of the seven chakras or energy centers of the body, mind and soul. In contrast to New Vrindaban's single mantra, the spiritual air of Lama is filled with many mantras, each tailored to the individual's needs and position on the road to enlightenment. There are Sanskrit mantras for taking showers, toileting, washing clothes and cooking. Vernon, one member, explained, "Mantras help me detach my ego from my action, and keep from identifying with the doer of the act."

Christian mantras in English are also used. Barbara first tried the Sanskrit mantras, but they didn't work for her. She visited Herman Redneck, a mystic and teacher who lives in Taos and is consulted by Lama members and spiritual seekers from all over New Mexico. "When I told him I was raised an Episcopalian, he gave me a Christian mantra. It works. The words are a great balm. Whenever I feel the old tension, the mantra returns me to that calm center."

In the two days I spent at Lama, I did not experience the psychological estrangement I had at New Vrindaban. For certain people, Lama offers a delicate balance between the monastic, contemplative life, necessarily a lonely pursuit, and the vitality and natural flow that come from being involved in a community. "I never feel like leaving here," said Barbara, "not even to go shopping. For me, there's no difference between the community and the world. Everything we do here is a kind of karma yoga. Chopping wood or carrying water, done in the right spirit, are meditation. Simple tasks keep me focused, centered on what's real. We praise God by building domes."

On a chilly April night, the community held an outdoor steambath. A huge fire was built to heat a pile of rocks that were then carried by shovel into a tepee. When water was dashed on the rocks, the tepee filled with penetrating steam. One by one, we left the tepee and dived into a man-made pond a few steps away which reflected the night stars; then we stood around the fire, wrapped in blankets, and sang, "Row, row, row your boat, gently down the stream. . . ."

"Hey, you know something?" said Vernon after our voices and their echoes receded into the forest. "That's a mantra!"

The next morning at prayer meeting, in place of the usual chants, Eric announced, "Let us regenerate ourselves by greeting the new day." Wrapped in an Indian blanket, he led the way into the woods patched with snow and up through the ponderosas. There were about twenty of us stretched out in a file that curved over the mountain. Some chanted to themselves and walked slowly, oblivious to the branches that whipped back. Others, like Steve, strode upward and were waiting on an open ridge when the rest of us arrived, puffing.

The west-facing crest was on the edge of the foundation's property, which was bordered by national forest land. The site had been proposed for another hermitage. Pines on the sharp slope thinned to piñon. Miles below, in the gray morning light, the arid floor was streaked by a small white line, the highway. Nothing moved there, not a car, not a sign of human life. The mountains behind were dark against the slowly brightening sky.

Eric, an ex-Marine, sat in the lotus position. Others knelt, backs straight. I sat with my legs crossed and my hands on my knees. We all faced west. As the sun climbed behind the mountains at our backs, the tops of the farthest mountains brightened. The light dropped down, driving before it the receding shade. I could hear it coming, like the first wave across a still ocean: first a rustling moan, then gaining force, coming up the mountain, rustling the tops of the trees, until it swept over us, the sound and light of a new day.

Eric walked toward the edge of the slope, arms raised. The rest of us got up; stretched, and walked over the knoll. Some embraced. Others smiled and said, "Good morning. Good morning."

By the time I got down to the kitchen Eric had a batch of pancakes sizzling on the gas stove. We ate them with raisins and honey. There was no coffee, since it was felt here that it destroyed B vitamins, so I made a cup of Pero, a German coffee substitute made from grains. The new copy of *Time* was circulated and voraciously read. "They want to impeach Douglas," said Steve, "because he wrote an article comparing Nixon to George III." Barbara came in dressed in a robe. She'd just gotten up. "How can you read *Time* after meditation?" she asked.

Carolyn appeared, wearing a white flared skirt. An attractive English girl, she had been at Millbrook with Timothy Leary and Richard Alpert. She and five other members regularly attend different churches in the area. Before leaving, she signed up for chores on the work schedule and conferred with Barbara about packing the children's school lunches. "Be sure you make the sandwiches out of white bread," warned Barbara. "Last week someone made them out of brown bread, and the other kids made fun of them."

At Lama, I sensed a certain distance between members. They do not seem as spontaneously and as emotionally involved as members of some communes. I expect the difference is due to the community structure, as well as to the spiritual purpose. As Lama developed its spiritual tone, the group curtailed the regular encounter meetings. Interpersonal conflicts became an individual concern. As they gained greater honesty, compassion and frankness, individuals were able to solve problems themselves without involving the entire community. "I've become much more honest with myself," Carolyn said. "When some people make me uptight, I look into myself to see why. I try to check the uptightness before it gets too far. Most problems are worked out one by one, as they happen."

Later I found a secluded log just above the main buildings and sat down to think and take notes.

"*Mujer!*" I looked up. Steve Durkee stood at the top of the path that sliced down the hill to the garden. At its far edge sat the Durkees' small cabin. He was about to take the truck and go on an errand. "Barbará!" he shouted, accenting the last *a* as in Spanish. She came to the door.

"Good-bye, I love you!" he yelled.

"That's nice," she returned.

"I love God almost as much as I love you," he declared.

"It should be equal," she answered. "You should love God as much."

"Shalom. Peace. Love." He turned to leave.

She called after, "Don't stay forever."

Apart from the flow of its community life, Lama's spiritual approach cannot be capsulized. Instead of having one central creed and guru, the community imports a host of teachers who, during the summer, lead two-week to two-month-long ashrams.

Of all its teachers, no one better embodies the community's syncretic approach than Baba Ram Dass, the former Richard Alpert. The ashram he led during the summer of 1969 "crystallized into a real experience all the different practices we had been experimenting with," Barbara said. "It upped the level of Lama and helped us to withdraw from our own melodrama."

With $25,000 Baba Ram Dass raised from lectures around the country, he commissioned Lama to publish and distribute free *From Bindu to Ojas,* a guide to the spiritual journey. It may well become the new testament of a growing generation of post-drug spiritual seekers. Like the people to whom he addresses his teaching, Baba Ram Dass began his own quest through psychedelics.

In 1961 Baba Ram Dass was a psychologist who held four departmental appointments at Harvard. He maintained a bachelor's apartment full of antiques in Cambridge; a Mercedes-Benz sedan and a Cessna 172 airplane. He believed that a rational application of science would cure most of man's problems.

Then, on March 6, at the house of a Harvard colleague, Alpert took a dose of Psilocybin, a synthetic derivative of the sacred mushroom of Mexico. The colleague was Dr. Timothy Leary. The story of how Leary and Alpert began their investigations into LSD, first experimenting with themselves, then with prisoners at the Concord Reformatory and Harvard students, is now legend. The Harvard experiments led to their dismissals from Harvard—the first firings in the history of the university faculty.

Renegades from the academic community, Alpert and Leary wandered. They went to a commune in northern Mexico, to a tropical island, and finally to the mansion in Millbrook, New York. There, locked for days in the mansion's own bowling alley, they took 400 microgram dosages of LSD every four hours in an attempt to raise and permanently change their consciousness. But they always came down. After Millbrook folded into a $50,000 pile of unpaid bills, Leary and Alpert separated. Still the Messiah of acid, Leary was sentenced to prison, escaped, and fled to the Middle East, endorsing violent revolution.

In 1967 Alpert left for India and returned a year later, transformed. He was no longer Richard Alpert, PhD, but Baba Ram Dass, "servant of God." He renounced drugs and sexuality and dedicated himself to translating his newfound insights of ancient spiritual truths into terms the present generation could dig. Three months after visiting Lama, I interviewed him at his parents' summer estate on Webster Lake, near Franklin, New Hampshire.

July 18

From the lake, the long driveway ran back to a stately green-shuttered clapboard house shaded by gnarled maples. Baba Ram Dass came to the door—a lean, bearded six-footer dressed in white slacks and white jersey, over which he wore a set of sandalwood prayer beads. His hair, which receded from a high brow, was tied in a clump at the back of his head. He smiled as I explained the purpose of my visit: Having made a superficial odyssey through the new spiritual communities, I needed his guidance. Where was the movement going? What community should I emphasize? What sources should I investigate?

While he finished some writing, I waited for him in the barn —actually, a recreation hall and Alpert family museum. In the center were a billiard table and a ping-pong table; a pipe organ at the far end. Displayed on the walls were old photographs of Williston Academy graduations, a Dartmouth banner, and cover stories and testimonials to Baba Ram Dass' father, George Alpert, lawyer, Jewish philanthropist and former president of the New Haven Railroad.

When he returned and found me pondering the family mementos, he suggested, "Let's talk elsewhere—this is all my father's trip." Barefoot, he walked ahead through the house— glimpses of pewter and hooked rugs over hardwood floors—to a large, screened-in porch. He sat in a lounge chair, crossed his legs beneath him, and held his back straight. The porch looked out on a pair of unused tennis courts, a flagpole flying the Stars and Stripes and a raspberry patch, where his father, now retired, spent the cool evenings picking berries.

Baba Ram Dass stretched one arm out, its palm cupped and upraised. "If it wasn't for all of this"—meaning his family's wealth—"I wouldn't have got to where I am. . . . The need for sensory involvement has to be satisfied. You have to go through all the maya."

Were we entering a new age? A period of widespread spiritual revival? I asked. No doubt, he answered. America would soon rival India as the world's spiritual center. "The consciousness of fifteen-year-olds in this country has evolved—something fierce!" After he returned from India the summer of 1969, thousands of young people flocked to the Alpert house to be near him. "I met some kids whose heads are in a completely different time-space matrix," he said, explaining that their consciousness was less cramped by the imprinted dimensions of Western society and philosophy. "Television does some of this—it speeds them through materiality. A kid who sees a moonshot doesn't have to do it himself. He's already been to the moon."

Drugs had the same effect—of accelerating experience and sensual involvement and ultimately freeing youth to go on to other "planes of consciousness."

Of his experiments with acid at Millbrook, Baba Ram Dass said that the drug repeatedly took his awareness to the same point, but no farther: "I could see the shadow of something; but I couldn't get beyond. I always came down to base-level perception."

Alpert didn't go to India expecting to be changed at all: Allen Ginsberg and Leary had gone before and returned apparently unaffected. Alpert made the typical Westerner's tour, too—sleeping in Hilton Hotels and traveling in a Landrover outfitted with a tape deck. His companion was a thirty-five-year-old genius who'd made five million by selling the company he'd started to Xerox, and now was intent on becoming a Buddhist. One day, while dining in a Nepalese restaurant, Alpert and his friend were approached by a 6-foot-7 blond American wearing a dhoti. He sat down opposite Alpert and stared. He didn't say anything, but there was something in the recesses of his eye that told Alpert: *He knew what it was—it,* the ultimate being, the shadows of which Alpert had only glimpsed during his highest acid trips.

"It was like meeting a rock. It was just solid, all the way through. Everywhere I pressed, there he was!"

His name was Bhagawan Dass. At seventeen, he'd dropped out of Laguna Beach High School and had spent the last six years hitching around the world, and had become an initiate of the Theravada Buddhist cult. Alpert parted from his wealthy friend, who went on to Japan, and began to travel by foot with Bhagawan Dass. His new companion wasn't interested in any of the fantastic stories Alpert could tell of Harvard or Millbrook. "Don't think of the past," he would tell Alpert. "Just be here and now."

One day, Alpert borrowed a Landrover so that they could

visit the temple of Bhagawan Dass' guru—an old man who weighed 90 pounds and scarcely ate. He sat on the temple floor surrounded by attendants. Bhagawan Dass prostrated himself, sobbing, and touched his master's feet. The guru's attention turned to Alpert, who remained standing. At first, the holy man teased him, asking if he would give him his car—which wasn't Alpert's to give.

Then he asked if Alpert had any drugs. Alpert traveled well supplied with a box of mescaline, STP, DMT, Librium and several tabs of redoubtable "white lightning" acid. One 305-milligram tab could deliver a psychic shock that would shake the faith of Job. The guru pointed to a tab. Alpert gave him one. He popped it and held out his hand for another, and another—bringing the dose to 915 milligrams. Alpert waited. An hour passed. Nothing happened. The guru remained placid and self-controlled. Then he spoke: "Each country creates an avatar in whatever form the people believe in. Americans believe in science. So the avatar that first came to America came as a pill."

That night, wandering alone under the stars, Alpert experienced an hallucination, his first without drugs. He saw the face of his mother, who'd recently died of cancer—cancer of the spleen. It was another part of Alpert's past he hadn't revealed to Bhagawan Dass.

The next day, the guru addressed Alpert: "You walked under the stars last night and saw something?"

Yes, Alpert replied, feeling a constriction in his chest.

"Your mother?"

Yes, the constriction tightened.

"She . . . dead?" asked the guru, moving his hands over his stomach to indicate a swollen belly.

Yes. . . .

Up to this point, the guru had put his questions in a dialect immediately translated into English by his attendants. Now, he uttered one devastating word in English: "Spleen?"

With that, Alpert's mind "burned out its circuitry in its zeal to have an explanation. I needed something to get closure at the rational level and there wasn't anything. There just wasn't a place I could hide in my head about this. And at the same moment I felt this extremely violent pain in my chest and a tremendous wrenching feeling, and I started to cry. The only thing I could say was it felt like I was home. Like the journey was over, like I had finished." *

During the next months at the temple, Alpert rose before dawn, bathed in the river, performed his purification rites, and read Sacred Scriptures—not only the Vedic literature but also the New Testament. And he was happy. He'd attained a spiritual high without drugs. Rather than "getting" high, he had "become" high by detaching himself from illusion, from the causal plane, from the sensual. He had discovered that the kingdom of God was within the self. Though he wanted to stay at the temple, his guru said his mission was to return to the United States and publish a book that would serve as a guide for others.

On a philosophical plane, Baba Ram Dass teaches that the cosmic journey is a movement from the metaphysical illusion of duality (good/evil, spirit/flesh) to a very high awareness that transcends the ego's time-space conceptions, a state of being "here and now."

The ultimate destination is not to be "good" in the Sunday school sense, but to detach one's innermost, divine being (the guru and God within the heart of the soul) from his outer wrappings—like a snake shedding its skin.

"You must see that all beings are just beings . . . and that all the wrappings of personality and role and body are the coverings. Your attachments are only the coverings, and as long as you are attached to someone else's covering you are stuck, and you keep them stuck in that attachment. Only when you can see the essence, can see God in each human being do you free yourself and those about you. It's hard work when you've spent years building a fixed model of who someone else is to abandon it.

---

* Quote taken from *Our-Story, My-Story, Your-Story, His-Story*, which includes details of Alpert's experiences in India. Published by Lama Foundation, Box 444, San Cristobal, New Mexico.

But until that model is superceded by a compassionate model, you are still stuck."

From his checkered background as a psychologist, pioneer of LSD and spiritual discoverer, Baba Ram Dass has drawn together a new model for guiding man toward full realization. The model is similar to that intuitively followed by the Brotherhood of the Spirit, in that it assumes the existence of the seven ascending energy centers or chakras. Baba Ram Dass asserts that man has been trapped in models based on the lower chakras. Freud based his model exclusively on the second chakra, sexual energy; Adler, on the third, power. But Baba Ram Dass' model begins with the fourth chakra, compassion. The model, he admits, is a device. Imagine, he says, that within the heart of the soul there exists a "witness"—an ever calm, non-judging, detached observer. He sits there like a director watching the illusion of life with *"Unbearable compassion"* in the darkness beyond the footlights. The actors come and go on the stage of our conscious and unconscious mind: sexuality, power, money, egos, super-egos, ids. Often when the director sleeps, they fight among themselves, waste energy and turn the play into a vain melodrama.

The first step toward enlightenment must be to awaken the witness, the director. Meditation, hatha yoga and celibacy are also means of breaking the attachment to the body and establishing that calm center. But eventually, even the witness must go. "The goal is non-dualistic. The means is dualistic. Such a means is a sturdy vessel to get you across the ocean of *samsara* (illusion). Once you reach the far shore, you leave the boat behind."

He does not try to convert. Though he has spoken at colleges around the country, he doesn't offer any one way—there *is* no one way to enlightenment. "I can only work on myself. . . . If I help you at all it's because I am helping my own consciousness."

Toward the end of the interview, I was affected by Baba Ram Dass' aura; his face was a magnet to my eyes. I'd experienced the effect before—from the altar at New Vrindaban, from the girl at the Brotherhood of the Spirit who felt we had known each other in a past life. Baba Ram Dass had something, he knew. . . .

Sensing the shift in my thoughts, he said to me, "Someday, we will get to those questions you're not ready for now. You're writing a book on communes and I can give you the answers you need. I'm here to give what people want, whatever level they're on."

I returned to my prepared questions: How did the communal movement fit into the spiritual evolution? What one community best exemplified his teaching? He answered metaphorically. "The spirit grows like a small tree. A fence must be placed around it for protection. But after it's grown roots, the fence must be taken away so it can grow more." At the beginning, spiritual growth must be guided. The seeker must find his teacher—whose very presence imparts spiritual knowledge; at the outset, he must have faith in his teacher—be he Christ, Mohammed or a yogi. The structures of the community help the seed's nurture. But ultimately, the fence must be removed; the servant must leave the community and his master. "We make the way alone. After a certain point, no one else can help you."

Baba Ram Dass' parable suggested another metaphor, an image that occurs throughout religious writing—the doorway ("straight is the gate"). At the beginning of faith, the seeker must believe that his door—Christ, Mohammed, Buddha, Krishna—is the only door, because on his approach he cannot see any other entrance. But after going through, the path of the seeker opens outward. Looking back, he becomes aware that his was one of many doorways. At this point, the seeker no longer needs the framework, the doorway, the walls of religious institution.

Baba Ram Dass saw signs that the same process was expanding the structures of the new spiritual orders. "They are much more involved with the world than the monastic orders of the past. The Zen mountain monastery (in California) has begun to admit married couples. Lama is determined not to fall into the ego trap of religious institutionalization."

Ultimately, the movement in spirituality would erase the metaphysical we/they fence that separates the "utopian" community from the rest of the world.

Baba Ram Dass conceived that a Wall Street broker could become a mystic without quitting his job or leaving Manhattan if he'd attained the transcendent consciousness of being here and now and of realizing that nothing happens by accident—that by being a broker, he was working out his karma. "It was no accident that I was born a Jew. Someday I may even go back to the university and go to temple." He sat forward a little, lightly clapped his hands—a sign the interview was over.

Driving home, I felt happy and relieved. Baba Ram Dass' presence had induced a mild contact-high. He had ended my quest for the spiritual community. There were many taos, doors and gurus. And many communities—waystations, temporary retreats—in the journey of consciousness which would eventually carry us back into the world, transformed by consciousness into *one* world. In that age to come, the wall between church and the secular world would disappear. Liturgy would become life itself, karma yoga—doing what you must do—with full awareness and art. It didn't matter whether you wrote a book, sold stocks, or dug up potatoes. You do what you must do, be what you must be—here and now.

Though I could only understand the shadows of Baba Ram Dass' words, the interview had brought a journey to an end. But another had just begun. "Nothing happens by accident," he had said, like so many others on my trip had told me. But where was this chain of "accident" leading?

IX

Back to Vermont

*Consciousness, Friends and a
New Community*

Later we realized that this country, this land, this clearing in the woods, was the place we had been seeking for so long, eyes open, souls closed, to find; and that we had come to it quite accidentally after we had given up hope, only after we had been driven to instinctive escape and saving blindness.

The end to all our stories is that we come home. To keep the journal's chronology straight, I return twice to Vermont: the first time in May, after covering the West; the second time in September, after a much shorter trip to Twin Oaks.

Both times, I felt that my journey, life, and part in the communal movement had turned back like the somersaulting curve of a wave against a cliff and had come almost full circle.

The Yaqui master of Castenada's *Don Juan* teaches that every man has his appropriate spiritual and geographical spot in the world, a destined location where he should stand to attain his highest being. Mine was Vermont. I had not been seduced by Oregon's mountain forests or New Mexico's colossal spaces. Feet reinstated on Green Mountain soil, walking along the golden dappled roads under the green arches of maples, I knew that this was my place: This was where I once belonged and was to begin again.

In May, after five months in the West, I began moving eastward. I flew from San Francisco to Sioux Falls, South Dakota, and hitchhiked through Minnesota. I stopped over at George-ville, where I picked up a ride with Barbara and Tracy, who were on their way to a farm they had just bought in northern Ontario.

As the miles of interstate unrolled over the flatness of Minnesota, I began to feel that our moving east, back to where America historically began, had a deeper meaning. The trip was over. The youngest generation of pioneers had taken the well-marked road west—in search of a "new life." Disaffection, rebellion and radicalism drew them into the city's hippie villages. Drugs pushed the frontier of discovery into consciousness. What they discovered, finally, was not "new": It hadn't existed beyond the western horizon, in Berkeley, thirty acid trips, or in the fabled communes. At the end of the search the first of the pioneers were led back into themselves, souls, heritage, and to the land.

Tracy and Barbara were two of many examples. With all their worldly possessions in the back of a new Datsun pickup, they looked very straight, like any other American family on the move. Barbara held their sleeping baby. Tracy was clean-shaven. Before leaving San Francisco, he'd gotten his hair cut. "I don't think of myself as a hippie anymore. For a while, long hair was a uniform that I wore to tell everyone I was one of them. But now, it's something that just gets in my way."

Tracy was striking out on his own. He planned to start publishing the Canadian version of *Whole Earth Catalogue*. A few years ago, he was down and out on New York's Lower East Side. He fled to Maine and isolated himself to get clean. After he met Barbara, they lived together in several communes.

While in San Francisco, they both worked for the *Whole Earth Catalogue*. Tracy became involved in scientology, a discipline for detecting and unraveling psychological hangups. After months of analysis, he registered a "clear" reading on the E-meter, a galvonometer-like device that purportedly gauges the clarity of your mental state. "Scientology doesn't help everyone. It did help me, but every person has to find his own thing—either a therapy or a religion that works."

They saved their money for the truck and a down payment on land in Ontario. They were not going into political self-exile. Their decision resulted from having found the right land, the right place, the right people. "The first time we got into the town, we felt at home. The people there are down-to-earth. They don't care who you were or where you've been. They'll talk all day to you like they've known you all your life."

The movement was filling in the hinterlands. Couples, families and groups—some who'd lived in communities for years—were moving to Wyoming, Montana, Tennessee, West Virginia, Vermont, Maine, where prices were lower, longhairs fewer, and natives much less uptight.

The new settlers of New England and Appalachia wanted more, of course, than bargains and safety. They sought roots and traditions which would sustain the evanescent hip consciousness. They went to learn the arts, skills, crafts, the lore of a nearly vanished America—to build on the past, to restore the family homestead abandoned by their great-great-grandfathers, who had gone west seeking greater opportunity.

To America's forsaken heritage they brought a new spirit from which they would fashion a new cultural alloy, a way of life and a code for them and their children to live by—consistently and faithfully.

From Minneapolis I flew to Montreal and hitched the last hundred miles home. At the border, a young customs agent emptied my pockets and kept me waiting while he waved fat car after fat car through the station.

Scarcely anyone in the village recognized me. I was tanned, bearded and had lost fifteen pounds. When I arrived at the cabin, Pud, the puppy I'd left behind, was a full-grown dog who yapped at my heels. My son, David, cried. Susan, five, looked at me shyly. How was I to get my two lives together? At first, I couldn't.

Five months ago (an abridged lifetime) Robert the Writer had sallied forth to observe the communes of America, to capture their quintessence. But throughout the trip, the communes, the people he'd met, the baptisms and rebirths he'd undergone (good copy, of course) had forced the whole Robert to put away his mental notebook. For the first time in too many years of deferred humanity, he had lived fully, immediately.

Through it all, Robert the Writer had remained detached and sometimes amused. But now home, he reasserted himself. It was time to sit down and write The Book in my *own* house, to be served dinner by my faithful Penelope. No more brown rice and lentils.

It wasn't that easy. Soon enough, the changes caught up.

The first week, Mary and I went on a shopping trip to the nearest city, Newport (population 5,000). At the turn of the century, Newport had been a bustling rail terminus. Every spring railroad cars full of Bostonians and New Yorkers arrived to fish for trout and salmon on Memphremagog, the lake that runs from Newport 30 miles north into Quebec.

The town's trade fell off as the railroads died. Now it depends on the winter skiers and the weekend French Canadians, who cross the borders to snatch American "bargains." On Moratorium Day last fall, every lamp post along Main Street flew U.S. flags put up by the local American Legion chapter. Meanwhile, the lake is being choked with algae fertilized by the effluent from the city sewage plant.

So with some surprise, but mixed emotions, I noticed the new faces along Main Street and in the laundromat—hippies, not many, but a few. Two girls in long velvet dresses caught glares and stopped cars. A couple parked in a Landrover told me they'd come into an inheritance and were looking for land to settle on. They asked directions, giving names of communes I'd never heard of, which made me feel foolish. Here I had covered some 10,000 miles tracking down communes from Oregon to New Mexico and returned to find them rampant in my own county.

Had I heard about Earth People's Park?

They must be kidding—in Vermont?

A few days later, I got a newsletter from EPP (I'd contributed $3) which jubilantly announced: "We've done it, Earth People, just what we've all talked about! The first Earth People's Park has been purchased and set free! . . . a wooded piece of virgin land of approximately 600 acres in northern Vermont." To be exact, it was in Norton, about 20 miles up the pike. Egad, hippies! I envisioned another New Mexico scene: publicity, police crackdowns, vigilantes. Hippies were a fine subculture to visit, but I wouldn't want one living next door to me. . . .

Until May we lived in the cabin on a knoll. I bought the property five years ago in partnership with Bill, a fellow reporter on the Newark News. On long weekends he and I built his cabin—the one we'd been living in for a year and half. Now Bill was planning to build an addition. So we found an elongated (40- by 12-foot) shack down the road on the edge of our property. We rented it for $10 a month from a man who had raised eight kids under its low, sloping roof and, most recently, chickens. It came with an uncluttered view of hills, a hayfield and a brook providing constant background music. Inside the door, over the peeling wallpaper, Mary stapled a saying of Bertrand Russell: "It is preoccupation with possessions more than anything else that prevents man from living freely and nobly." For Mary, it was home—the Brook House. For me, it was temporary until we built our own house on the knoll or in a community. As I wrote the book, I'd make plans and then do it: very logically, very orderly.

Quentin, nineteen, showed up first. He was Bill's brother-in-law and had just dropped out of Rutgers. Next came Michael, twenty, referred to us by his brother, Larry, the photographer. Michael needed a quiet wholesome place—far from drugs and dealers in Philadelphia.

One day as we hauled rusted bedsprings and pieces of sheetrock out of the house, a brown and white Scout pulled into the yard. Out bounded Susan and Ron, the couple I'd said goodbye to at New Buffalo and invited to visit Vermont. And they did, looking around for a farm to buy.

The Brook House became a *de facto* commune—the last thing in my mind. I had wanted to spend the summer writing about communes, not living in one.

All told, Mary took the situation in stride. She hadn't lived in a commune before. But while I'd been gone, she had read the periodicals. She liked living in the country without electricity, a telephone, and with water that runs only seasonally when the spring is full. The rest of the time, she takes two five-gallon plastic jugs down to the brook, stopping along the way to pick wildflowers or note a pileated woodpecker or a possum track: things I don't see. She's more in tune with the earth than I; a woman of natural grace who continually amazes and fascinates.

From Susan, Mary learned how to stir-fry vegetables and bake beans, beginning with real beans. Ron, a jack-of-all-trades, who can do almost anything from mine blasting to automotive design, taught her how to bake bread. She'd tried using recipes, but bread is another thing to be learned from people.

She got along well with Michael and Quentin. Half the time, she played their housemother, cooking breakfast, lunch and dinner, making sure their laundry got cleaned. The rest of the time she was their boon companion and peer. She enjoyed being ten years the younger and listening to Quentin tell how he stole signs off the New Jersey turnpike and about Ron's adventures in the Hell's Angels. They brought out Mary's other sides (at twelve, she had been the toughest tomboy in Scarsdale, New York).

Mary grooved on everyone. And I, the supposed expert on communal life, was tense, selfish and, sometimes, jealous.

When Quentin slaked his thirst by drinking cans of Hi-C cherry juice (2/94 cents), I mentally chalked up my increased grocery bill. One day I wrote a commandment in indelible Magic Marker across the door of our Servel (gas) refrigerator: JUICE FOR KIDS (UNDER 7). This only increased juice consumption and provided Quentin with hours of banter: "Hey, Bob, does seven mean seven feet?"

I was obsessed with the overuse of the car. Since Ron and

Susan's truck had broken, the Opel was the only operating vehicle among six adults. It always seemed to be running somewhere—the phone booth, to buy beer, to get milk from the drivers, and always shuttling between the Brook House and the Hill House (where Quentin and Michael slept). I began to keep a record of the mileage and the mounting gas, oil and repair bills which were sucking up the last of my advance. Finally, I declared a lot of the trips with the Opel "unwarranted." Immediately "unwarranted trips" crept into Quentin's every other sentence.

Unable to write in the confusion and clutter of the Brook House, I reverted to my previous pattern of dividing my work from family. I commuted to and from my mother-in-law's fully applianced house two miles away on the big lake, going to my office, as it were, at 10 A.M. and coming back around 5 P.M. When I returned for dinner, Pud rushed out barking. Then I'd go inside and pointedly ask what had been "accomplished." (I'd bought several bundles of cedar shingles to cover the cracks in the outside walls. By winter one section was left uncompleted, for which I blamed Michael.)

Big Susan and I became antagonists. We were too much alike —that was our problem. She and Ron had just come from the Southwest communes. In comparison, the Brook House was dull, middle-class. They arrived to find us eating store-bought food full of preservatives and listening to the top 40 on the radio.

When I spread out my New York *Times* on the table, I felt guilty—still tied into the mass media. One evening Susan dragged us outside to hold a circle om. I felt embarrassed and unmoved.

She made me see that I was doing the same thing to my own daughter, Little Susan as her father, a doctor, had done to her: Wrapped up in my book, I was ignoring my daughter's need for attention and love. It was all true, part of me. But there was nothing I could do.

Defensively, I said the Brook House was no commune, only a temporary arrangement. We had no structure, I argued, no way of dividing up the work, sharing expenses, no long-range goals. "How can you feel that way?" asked Susan, convinced my trip to the communes had failed to touch me.

Mary began to side with the others. I was annoyed she was so palsy with Quentin and Michael. Ignoring my "law" against overusing the car, she took them to get Dairy Joys and one night, to a drive-in movie. Why did she want to hang out with teen-agers? I took it out on the dog. One night, when I lifted a board to whack him, Mary screamed at me. I left the house for days, retreating to my "office" across the lake.

By August no one enjoyed the house. Susan and Ron decided to split, heading off to look for land in Canada. Quentin, who found the country a drag, went back to New Jersey to work and reapply to college. Michael visited Larry and his wife in Philadelphia.

Once again, Mary and I and the kids were a single family. We slunk back to our old habits: turned the radio back on and unashamedly ate white spaghetti. After dinner we read by kerosene light. Our old, comfortable, unchallenged existence. And after a while, we both agreed it was dull.

But I was no less uptight. Writing was strained and forced. Even the Vermont landscape seemed flat. The journal entries I'd made in the communes were another man's insights. The difference wasn't the magic of communal structure, per se. The Brook House was just as planned as any commune. The difference was me. Robert the Writer was trapped; he couldn't check out after a month. Instead, he had reacted like any other human to a real-life situation: defensively. I was unwilling to let go of what was mine, my car, my money, my wife.

Self-psychiatry only made it worse. My ego was a cancer. The more attention and stroking it got, the more malignant it grew —secreting some strange tension into my brain that blocked out impulses and locked my awareness into a narrow band of objectivity like a radio stuck at one frequency.

Somehow, drugs could release this lock, opening consciousness into a world of greater depth, sonority and brighter color

—like that of childhood. But the glimpse was always fleeting. Similarly, communes were not, in themselves, an alternative. As a social form, they could sustain, even heighten, the consciousness of individual. But the consciousness was somewhere beyond the ego, through a narrow doorway. We must go through it alone and unaided. Once on the other side, we may be able to get together.

So in August I left on another trip. My destination was Twin Oaks, New Vrindaban and Georgeville. But I had a deeper purpose: to be alone again and free float, to get myself back together. How, I had no idea.

While hitchhiking, I had the first of several interior experiences that still puzzle me but undoubtedly changed me.

I was stranded outside a small town on Route 69 in northern Iowa. According to my "schedule," I was to be in Minneapolis that night. I had to check my uptightness. Hitchhiking does enforce a kind of faith. And if you're without it, you go back to Greyhound. Briefly, my code was to love whoever picked me up for the time, have faith that I would get somewhere (don't carry a sign), and never to refuse a ride. And so after an hour of being passed by, I resigned myself and began to play a game. A fool's game. Forgetting my plight, I waved at each car that roared, lagged, or cruised by, tailoring the wave to the character of the car and its occupants. I V-signed the ones that gave off good vibes, respectfully saluted the state police, bowed to an elderly couple in an air-conditioned Chrysler, and let my arm drop like a flagman at the Indianapolis 500 for a souped-up Chevrolet. For once in my life I was an utter fool—and some cars even made U-turns to come back for an encore. Then it happened.

The sun hovered low over the fields of corn, wheat and alfalfa flat to the horizon. At its edge, a line of telegraph poles. A freight train came first into hearing and then sight, the sunlight glinting on the orange diesel. It strung out the horizon, rumbling on, its sound muffling all others. I felt the sun warming the side of my face. The back pack lightened. My feet connected to the earth. No more time; the train would rumble on, and the cars would pass by, but I was not waiting. I was not *I* but being here and now.

This kind of experience has happened again. And I have slipped back a few times, but the slips don't bother me so much. Write them off to evolution. Some new journey had begun, to some farther frontier. Sure, the first doorway had been an illusion. There were an endless perspective of doorways as in the image of two opposing mirrors. Who knew where it would lead? Some speak of spirit, God, infinite energy and love that passeth human understanding, but just knowing life was a journey was some consolation—like knowing a virgin forest exists—to those who have to make all the karmic rest stops and detours. Each step becomes less important. As Justin said, "We're all going to make it."

When I got back from the last trip, I moved my work over to the Brook House. For once, I'd try to live and write in the same house, same room. I didn't know if I could.

Mary came back from a farm auction with an old Singer sewing machine table for a desk and an Underwood Noiseless typewriter, *circa* 1925, both for bids of one dollar. I adopted the sturdy Underwood and shelved my sleek Olympia. Michael came back. He couldn't stand Philadelphia—the soot, speedy vibes and trapped people. He was hooked on Vermont.

In September Lucy arrived. Five years ago, during summer vacations from Bryn Mawr, she'd been our baby-sitter. Since, she'd taught public school, gone to art school, and worked as a waitress at Max's Kansas City in New York. Now she didn't know what to do, except to go to Berkeley. Instead, she stayed with us.

The four of us (more depending on the season) get along amazingly, though as many human hangups and hassles are there, inseparable from the good. Mary still bottles up her feelings and doesn't complain enough, but that's her; always the conciliator, yielding and loving when I can't. Michael still has his down days when a great pillow of apathy comes out of nowhere and lays him low; but then, the next day, the playful genius descends and he's patched the car muffler with tin cans, shoveled the roof, and almost killed himself felling an elm.

Lucy and I love to stay up through the night (something Mary and I used to do before the kids came. Now she flakes out around 8 P.M.). The other night we made a screenplay for a movie to be called *Those Bleached Bones* starring Jack Nicholson, as an archaeologist who discovers Christ's bones (subsequently stolen by the Vatican) and is turned on by an international drug dealer played by Dustin Hoffman. If we can't get to a movie, we make them up.

But at times, Lucy drives me up the wall. She has a pair of Swedish clogs (which I've hidden several times) that clomp, clomp, clomp and drive me Sane!

As for me, everyone knows better than to grab the *Times* before my breakfast ritual or to put a ball of yarn on my sacred shelf. At first, living in one room brought out all our quirks; they bumped into each other but gradually found their niches like the customary seats at the dinner table.

For me, the main difference is that I don't care so much anymore—not about them, but about me ("Teach us to care and not to care."). Ray Mungo, a friend has said it simply in *Total Loss Farm* which is about his own communal experience in Vermont: "No more me, no more you."

September

> My object in living is to unite
> My avocation and my vocation
> As my two eyes make one in sight.
> Only where love and need are one,
> And the work is play for mortal stakes,
> Is the deed ever really done
> For Heaven and the future's sakes.
> —"Two Tramps in Mud Time," ROBERT FROST

A beautiful morning. The days have their own seasonal rhythm. I get up around eight and, first thing, walk to the edge of

the garden in my long john bottoms, commend the corn's overnight growth, and piss. Mary, a dawn ariser, makes weather
entries in her log. The fresh smell of coffee. It takes me back to
other mornings in the blue-tile kitchen of my grandparents' big
house in New Philadelphia, Ohio, getting up early to go bass
fishing on Leesville dam. Today where can you get coffee beans
and a hand grinder?

I wear the same outfit today as every day: blue- and black-
checked wool shirt frayed and soft from use. Next, the bibs,
loose hanging, with all kinds of pockets for all kinds of things:
the zippered one on the bib itself, a special pouch over the heart;
to each side, long narrow pockets, good for pens, pencils or the
stem of a corncob pipe; and the long pocket down the right leg
for screwdrivers, wrenches. We've all got bibs now (ordered
from Sears) and have dubbed ourselves the Bibs family. But
names don't mean anything anymore.

Spent the afternoon picking raspberries; Mary and I took
turns carrying David in a backpack. Got a headache. We went
down to West Charleston and bought a bottle of wine. By the
time we got home the headache was gone. Such a simple, high
day.

For the first time in my life, I'm free of having to prove anything. What a relief not to *become* somebody. To be. Yet I must
be someone, must do something.

I've decided to be a farmer.

I'd like to be an ordinary, probably sloppy farmer. Something
of a fool, a regenerate intellectual, happy to walk through mud
in high rubber boots and dump the slop to the hogs. I'd like to
think with my hands, to cover them with grease and learn how
to fix a tractor, get drunk with the Driver Brothers and stand in
their yard outside their garage and listen to stories of outwitted
game wardens and state police . . . and laugh and tell some of
my own.

Have lots of bills, no cash. Write poems on the backs of en-
velopes. I'd be content to come home to lunch in the high heat
of noon and eat ham (our own) on Mary's brown bread and
smear it with very cold, homemade corn relish. Content to cut

wood during those quickening weeks of fall, counting each cord as it mounts the side of the house, thinking ahead to how it will keep the stove burning through nights when the freezing trees crack like gun shots and Mary and I will make love under layers of quilts, and then, deep sleep.

Two things enter into my decision to be a farmer. One is the utterly absurd and romantic intimation that in a former life I was an American farmer during the eighteenth century. I have glimpses of clear sunlight, deep blues, of Monticello growing like a silver bubble out of the green forest that once stretched unbroken from Virginia to Maine—the natural limitation of man's intelligence like the restrained lyricism of a Mozart piano concerto.

The other is on a more rational level. I want to remain self-employed; stay at home for most of the time near my wife and children; and do something useful in God's country. Don't think I'll write another book for a while. Something immoral about a full-time writer, like being a full-time minister. The early Christians, I've read, were tent-making ministers. Better to be a full person: a farmer, but not one of those industrialized farmers who are written up in the farm bureau journals and own $100,000 in machinery and put five hundred acres in soybeans. But a farmer like Robert Ashton Spaulding.

Our mentor, hero, and almanac, Robert Ashton Spaulding is a keen and wiry eighty-three. The other day he paid us a visit, as he does from time to time, to check on our agrarian folly.

He rode down on his miniature horse, Daisy, flanked by his great nephews, Daryl and Dalton, nine and six. He is a slight man, with a square chin and bird's-foot wrinkles in the corners of his ice-blue eyes. His hands are large and like tanned leather. He sticks close to his land, a high upland farm with a splendid stand of sugarbush. His house sits on a bluff protected by venerable maples whose wood matches its unpainted clapboard—a ruddy brown. The fall-foliage tourists drive past without noticing his house or admiring the fine pilasters at each corner.

When he leaves, it is only for short jaunts on foot or horseback to the general store. On town meeting day last March I encountered him walking along a back road dressed in his Sunday duds, intent on covering the five miles to cast his vote.

He's sugared since "o four," (1904) but each year he scatters a few less buckets. Last year he was thrown from a wagon and broke a bone. All I know of maple sugaring he's taught me. He'd never think of using plastic pipe or burning oil in his evaporator. He's made taps by hand out of wood. He intuitively respects the divinity and mystery of nature and bends with the wind.

Whenever I question him—how deep to drill for the tap, when to expect the first run, how many gallons a tree produces —he exasperates me. He always answers vaguely. "Now some folks drill a half inch and wait a spell 'n see how it runs. Others may drill seven-eighths inch. T'ain't so patient. . . ." (a meaningful smile). And he usually concludes, "I reckon you should just *try* and I'll come down and see how you do." There's no formula for instant success in sugaring any more than in making a commune. Sugaring is an art that depends on man working through nature. It turns on the weather: the clear, sunny days followed by cold freezing nights, when the sap magically runs long and fast. Why, no one knows.

A few years ago, Robert said sadly, his post office box used to be crammed with various farm publications. Like the old journals, the yeoman farmers have expired under the crush of mechanization and big money. They've been succeeded by the businessmen—the ones who have begun to use computers to correlate the amount of feed with the milk production of each cow, each having a magnetic number. Robert can't understand why folks buy milking machines and thermostats, when his hands and a round oak stove suit him fine. Neither can we. For Christmas, we plan to get him a subscription to the *Whole Earth Catalogue*.

The new rural society taking root in Vermont is one that Robert Ashton Spaulding might recognize and feel at home in. In the last year the number of communes has jumped from around twelve, concentrated in the south, to around fifty, all over the state. No one knows for sure how many. Within a twenty-mile radius of us, there are three communes. In addition, unknow numbers of hip couples have bought land and built houses in the hills of Montgomery or West Corinth or East Brighton. Sometimes, the only clue is their flowered mailboxes and their cars, beat-up Saabs with New York plates.

So far, the hub of the society in the north country is Hatch's Natural Food Store in St. Johnsbury, about forty miles away. Hatch's is the way the general store used to be in the days of cracker barrels, barn raisings and corn huskings. From Hatch's we pick up rice, soybeans and announcements: classes in the Lamaze method of childbirth, in St. Johnsbury; a health-food conference in East Ripton; the Wednesday night Women's Liberation meetings in Putney; seminars at the Tail of the Tiger, a Buddhist community in Barnet, conducted by a Tibetan lama, Chogyam Trungpa Rinpoche.

From communes all over the state, Hatch's receives sundry news and requests for help, which, by agreement, are pooled into a newsletter called *Freedback*. An extract:

Earth, Air, Fire and Water need one flatbed truck, source of leather and scraps; horse-drawn farm equipment, money, clothes for newborn baby and kids, especially size ten; info on cheap building supplies; barrels, and a recipe for cheap brine pickles. Green Mountain Collective is doing a radio show one hour a week on a Burlington FM Station. Cliff and Paula Greenberg have some hand tools and a weird assortment of bits and pieces of information and talents. . . . Quarry Hill would like children from different communes to visit. . . . Bert Muzzy has knowledge of organic farming, logging, carpentry, masonry, water systems. . . .

The new society resembles pluralist, provincial America as it had been under the Articles of Confederation. It is intently decentralized. What organization exists is based on the anarchist principle of voluntary sharing or mutual assistance: There has been discussion of setting up a ham-radio network, a medical service, and a school bus that would circuit-ride between the communes.

This fall we exchanged our surplus beets for some of Mullein Hill's kale. We became members of a food cooperative set up by the West Burke commune.

Get-togethers are seasonal. Hatch's held a Christmas party. The Mount Philo Collective in North Ferrisburg hosted a winter solstice celebration. There isn't much intercommunal visiting. For one thing, the cars don't go over forty miles at a stretch. And if your family is large and interesting enough, there's no Saturday night compulsion to "go someplace" or "do something." Although we've borrowed a lot from the past, we've also learned not to repeat some of the mistakes. For example, what's happened to the one-family farm in Vermont. The sons and daughters go downcountry for jobs and to escape the farm's isolation. The old folks are left in a large farmhouse with a barn full of cows. Every week in Vermont twenty-five farms are sold.

So a large family is a necessity, though it needn't be a family related by blood. They can be our friends and our friends' children. Life on a farm needn't be lonely anymore. Modern communications help. I like taking the transistor radio, with a Beethoven quartet playing, to our outhouse and letting the music blend with the subdued colors of the woods. And I still read the New York *Times* when someone thinks to pick up the back copies at the general store. The world's not as far off for us as it was for farmers twenty-five years ago. Besides, we don't cut ourselves off from our neighbors.

For the most part, hippies who come up from the city quickly become self-proclaimed Vermonters. They lose the Woodstock complex and don't want a hip scene. They're more paranoid about a hippie influx that might spoil their haven than they are about the state police. With few exceptions, the climate of the new rural society is apolitical, actively opposed to talk of revolution. *Freedback* flatly refuses to print any "separationist political information that furthers the we/them division."

The reference was probably to the Putney commune, which publishes *Free Vermont*. Editorially, the newspaper urges Vermont hippies to unite, as if they were the Vietcong, and "liberate" the state from an oppressive economic and power structure.

Free Vermont sent out an invitation for a statewide conclave of communes and tribes which read:

We've been isolated from each other too long; brothers and sisters are getting ripped off in Vermont as well as across the nation. We've been harassed for our music, drugs and our revolutionary spirit, media, clothes & long hair and ideas of communism; we've been threatened with building codes, health laws, eviction, guns, narcs, all sorts of shit. To survive and grow stronger we must gather together to share our skills and communal vision.

However, the conclave itself turned out far differently from what the invitation had suggested. It was hardly a war council. More than two hundred attended, camping out for the weekend in a meadow on Earth, Air, Fire and Water commune near Franklin. The women formed a circle to discuss their problems. A barn was torn down. The newsletter was organized. And we all stood in a huge circle of linked hands and sang "Amazin' Grace."

By its close the Putney people were exasperated by the nonradical drift. They began to cite some of the incidents of harassment that had been mentioned in the invitation. But none of the members from other communes could agree that Vermont was coming down that heavy. "My mother used to tell me," someone quipped, "if you look for trouble, you'll find it." On that note, the conclave adjourned. The up-country hippies had called their Putney cousins paranoid. And they had called us naïve: Sooner or later, the long arm of repression would seek and destroy us.

For a few weeks in the fall, I was afraid that the Putney people might have been right. One night Michael and Lucy went out to visit Earth People's Park in Norton. A friend who had offered to drive them took a wrong turn and crossed the international border into Canada. Ever vigilant, federal customs agents swooped down, searched the car, and uncovered a little hash and one roach. This "bust of the century" was reported all weekend on the local radio and given headlines in the newspapers, including pictures of the Brook House.

The bust revived my nightmarish fears that the same country backlash that had struck the family of Oz would wipe us out, too. We did attract more gawkers than before; a few shouts but no night riders or vigilantes. If anything, our local relations improved. Some of the village gentry snubbed us. But we had many more friends from the backcountry—folks who lived like us, off the hard-top, drank spring water, and harbored their own resentment against the establishment. Moreover, they could see how we were trying to live.

Our experience was borne out by reports that other communes in the country had achieved coexistence with their neighbors. Bloodshed did occur as feared in New Mexico, but it could have been far worse had not the hip influx abated.

A vigilante posse of Chicanos attacked the Kingdom of God commune near Guadalupita, killing one member, wounding another. The rest fled into the mountains. Otherwise, an uneasy truce prevailed in the land of enchantment. Minor Van Arsdale wrote me that those who decided to stay "have shaved and cleaned up and look straight. And they stay home."

From Oregon, I got a report from Harry L. Elliot, editor of the *Daily Courier* in Grant's Pass. "I'd say relations between the straights and the hips have calmed somewhat. The militancy of the earlier days [1968], shortly after the hippies arrived, has cooled, and there seems to be a realization that they are here to stay."

I had wanted to go back to Meadville to see if that All-American weathervane of opinion had altered. Rather, I wrote Ken Williams, former managing editor of the Meadville *Tribune*. His reply was optimistic.

"If a commune resembling Oz were to move into Crawford County today, I doubt whether it would precipitate either extreme interest or revulsion . . . [none have]. "Meadville had become more tolerant of youthful life-styles," Williams said, due to "the widespread cultural changes" affecting the entire country. "There is an acceptance today which just might lead to greater tolerance of another commune."

The barometers seem to point to a climate of peaceful, even friendly interchange between the hip communes and their straight neighbors. Quite a difference from 1968. Our neighbors see that we're not plotting a revolution or enticing their kids into immoral pursuits. But a large part of the change is due to the communes' own evolution toward a more tolerant attitude to the outside world. The we/they division has given way.

October

Revisited the Wooden Shoe on its new farm in New Hampshire. What a change from a year ago (Book One). Then they were renting the house in Hartland over Interstate 91 that had gas heat and the Che Guevara poster over the knotty-pine walls. And they talked of anarchism and radicalizing Dartmouth. Now their home is a drafty old farmhouse restored from sills, on up to the attic, where most sleep (with hot-water bottles). Instead of the Revolution, they talk of slaughtering and dressing Willis, their hog. That's another change: fewer vegetarians.

When Larry and I arrived, Carol was making a frame for a French door in the kitchen "To let the air in and the children out." While she hammered, Jesse, her child, played outside among the woodchips. Odessa, pregnant, put up storm windows. Like Carol, she would have her baby at home with a seventy-year-old local GP who still made housecalls standing by.

Ralph and Pearl, an elderly couple who live on the farm up the road, came by to celebrate Pearl's birthday. Carol baked a cake using a natural chocolate substitute. It had been Ralph, the commune's adopted grandfather, who had shown them how to block and replace the sills.

The Wooden Shoe still supports itself by working as a crew, advertising for jobs in the local paper. The women work alongside the men; a few times, just the women have reported for ditch-digging jobs.

They have no more paranoia about being busted in the dark of night. "The local selectman lives up the road," said Jake Guest, who visits us from time to time. "People know that we work, not that hard, you know, but we work . . . and we have nothing to hide."

*   *   *

I'm learning how to follow David, my two-year-old. This afternoon he embarked fearlessly down the road. I stayed a few steps
behind while he plunged ahead, at a speed between a walk and
run, looking over his shoulder now and then to see if I was
tagging along.

The road goes down into a hollow and over the brook. Day
and night, we hear its rushing. It comes down a wooded canyon
and is channeled under the road through a metal pipe; on the
other side, it emerges and relaxes into a pebbly four-foot-deep
pool.

Some instinct draws both of us to the pool's edge; daringly,
David steps as close as he can. His face reflects his twin apprehension of the danger and beauty swirling beneath. He picks up
a stone from the road, steps to the edge, and pitches it into the
pool. He laughs. Then he goes back for another stone. I sit on
the cement abutment. The current pushes out from the tube,
sending a white flume directly ahead, branching back in counter-
waves as from the trunk of a tree. Beside the mouth of the tube
are still backwaters, the safe habitat of water striders. Onto the
brownish-gold floor of the pool that is always shifting light and
dark they cast fantastic shadows, which in size and beauty sur-
pass their own reality; they are just black insects with long
spidery legs that nervously flex and propel them in short spasmodic spurts of blackness, each encircled by an orange corona,
like small bobbing suns in total eclipse.

David has come to the other side of the pool, to the muddied
bank where every morning one of us fills the water jugs. I am
jarred out of the hypnosis of the lulling interplay of light,
shadows and windy, constant rush of water into action: I take
off his shoes so he can wade in the cool mud and icy water. He
goes slowly into the ankle-deep water, a little scared and excited.
"Look." I point to the golden deep center of the pool where
foot-long shapes have been stirred into alert, darting movements.
"See the trout." Now, for the first time, he sees them and points
himself—"trout, trout!" For a change, I have taught him something of the mystery of elusive fish who you know are always
there, hiding beneath rocks under the blurred surface, lying,

noses pointed upstream, holding themselves gently against the current, their square tails twitching; but my eye can never capture them in distinct focus, camouflaged as they are, with their black backs and dappled sides, whose spots shift and move among the water striders' orange-ring shadows. Like the deepest currents of our minds, they cannot be grasped without killing them, only glimpsed in their quick darts and explosive rises.

David crosses to the other side of the road, led by something, and finds a small path down under low branches on the upper, wilder side of the brook. The light sifts through green needled boughs. He splashes awhile and begins to wade upstream, pointing ahead to where the brook disappears in a dark, sinister thicket of fallen logs and underbrush. I realize what he wants to do: follow the stream to its source, to pursue its mystery. I've never gotten around to following the brook up the two folds of hills that close into a deep canyon of tumbled, car-sized boulders, so inaccessible that the white pines there are first growth. With hushed reverence Albert Driver refers to the canyon as a hideout for bears. He has seen their tracks and droppings and heard them crashing around, and he says he carries a shotgun when he fishes the brook. But David wants to go and I promise him that someday we will.

My own father had been unable to keep a similar promise to me. Outside Massillon, Ohio, there's a cliff rising high above the Ohio Canal—the kind of cliff a five-year-old associates with *The Last of the Mohicans*. When we drove past, my father used to point it out, recalling his Boy Scout days when he had climbed and camped on its summit; but he had never gone beyond. There were too many deep ravines and dense woods. Someday, he promised, he and I would scale the cliff and sleep out overnight. That was in the 1940's. We never did. The last time I was through Ohio, the cliff had been flattened for an interstate highway.

Daisy, Mary's sister, brings us a carload of city wares from Boston that we'd placed on order from her, goods we can't produce, buy locally, or do without: a case of chunky peanut butter purchased through a food cooperative; a quart bottle of

Tamari sauce bought at Erehwon, the big organic food distributor; a paperback copy of Gurdjieff's *Meetings with Remarkable Men;* a set of nut drivers Michael wants so he can put an outside antenna on the radio; a leg of fresh lamb; and Dylan's *New Morning,* even though we don't have a record player.

We do need the outside world, then—no apocalyptic delusions about that. But we like the freedom of being able to pick what little we require and leave the rest; at this distance, to take the best of the economy without having to live with its less desirable by-products.

A few years ago we were safe in Vermont (so we thought) from the urban monster. Now, we're not so sure. Almost everyday, the ominous rumblings. South of us, Interstate 91 is being blasted through the hills. In a year, it will be open all the way south to Boston and New York. The interchange has already been built between Derby and Newport. There a shopping center highlighted by a Mammoth Mart has arisen. At night part of the sky glows an eerie green from the towers of light over its parking lot—"the biggest in Orleans County," someone boasted the other day on local radio. In the meadow below, a retired couple bought a trailer and erected a tall arc lamp. Yet another intruder on the night, the Orleans County Airport installed a beacon to make 180-degree swipes at the sky and detract from the northern lights.

And then there are the snowmobiles, the all-terrain vehicles that carry their fumes, noise and infernal combustion everywhere.

> In wildness is the preservation of the world
> —HENRY DAVID THOREAU

We talk of moving away into the last reaches of the wilderness, far off the hard-top. Our friends in the cities, still fighting the good fight within the system, regard us as escapists. To them, we are repeating the American error: doing what our parents did in fleeing to the suburbs, turning our backs on the real problems and issues.

To the New Left, we are naïve romanticists.

In an issue of *Ramparts,* David Kolodney asserted:

No one should imagine that by eating organically grown—even communally grown—vegetables, he will help the starving nations locked in a U.S. economic straightjacket. No one should be so stupefied by universal love as to think that some phalanx of amaranthine flowers is going to stop the war machine.

Instead of starting with war, exploitation and imperialism, we begin at the center—ourselves—and work outward. A matter of interlocked priorities: The self needs a community; a community needs a culture; and a culture—here's the rub—needs spirit. Without it, a society falls flat like bread without yeast. For me, shopping centers and industrial parks (what a strange term) and freeway ramps are man's dull mirror: a dead end, a closed system, a cul-de-sac.

Somewhere the spirit lives; through the woods, over the hills there lies some unknown pond in the lap of mountains reflecting the infinite sky. . . .

There is definitely a "lost river" in New England. I know that from the bumper stickers on the cars that have supposedly found it, just as they have "discovered" the "Catskill Game Farm," or the "Ausable Chasm." Of all such places, lost river's irony sticks in my mind as what we must *not* do: civilize the wilderness. Then we will indeed lose ourselves, our children and their heritage.

So we plan to beat a strategic retreat, a few steps back into the woods. But we can't go alone. We need others—maybe a dozen families. A simple example. I've always wanted to resurrect the old-fashioned icebox. But who cuts ice anymore? And just think of doing it alone! First, I'd need an icehouse and a team of horses to pull the sled loaded with blocks of ice off the pond. But one step at a time: To keep a team of horses in this climate, I'd need a barn; and to feed them, acres of oats and hay. To cut the oats and hay, I'd need . . . and so on. It would take one lifetime to work up to cutting one block of ice.

And we needed others around for the less practical reasons: friends, lovers, parents, teachers—people who know how to repair a four-wheel-drive, devise a windmill and a gristmill.

As I wrote the book, the pieces of a plan came together for a wilderness village of farmers, craftsmen and artists. It would be large and structured enough to have the stability of a community and the vitality of a commune. It's not that clear. I've learned well enough not to overplan.

Better to let the land do most of the planning.

I'd like about one thousand acres back in the mountains, inaccessible to the builders of ski chalets. Key item: We'd build our own road. Possibly, some of the development costs could be paid for through a grant or loan under the New Communities section of the U.S. Housing Act of 1968. I'm not opposed to using the federal government. Wanted: one lawyer.

Like Libre, we'd keep the private cars parked at the gate. The village-owned truck would be the only vehicle to make (scheduled) trips in and out. Ideally, the village would be clustered around a high-altitude pond or one we would make by building a dam. Wanted: one engineer. Each family would be responsible for building its own house—all out of sight from each other and interconnected by trails.

In November I went down to Tunbridge to sound the plan out on Mark and Martha (the couple from Bryn Athyn of Book One). They were living in a former schoolhouse. After Woody had repossessed the farm and turned it into his hard-work commune, they had spent the winter in Lyme, New Hampshire, and then recrossed the Connecticut to live at Toad Hall, a farm owned by Michael Martineau, the heir of a railroad fortune. Michael wanted to start a Summerhill-type school on his property. But Mark and Martha decided to go their own way, having learned that communities dominated by one person are programmed for conflict. They moved into the schoolhouse, got jobs, and saved money for the land they would look for in the spring.

After dinner we sat in the tattered armchairs in front of the fire and discussed my scheme. Later they asked the questions. How about money? Who would own what?

I would have liked to deed it over to God as Lou Gottlieb had urged; but, short of God, I would put the land in the hands of a nonprofit corporation. It would be composed of stockholders who would hold varying amounts of shares in the land. But no one individual would separately own land. The larger stockholders would be given leases on enough for their house site and garden, say ten acres (I'd need to lease more to do farming). Those who couldn't afford to buy stocks could lease on a yearly basis, maybe $500. That money would be used to pay back the low interest on stock possibly acquired by foundations or by individuals looking for a good cause to invest in.

"What would happen if someone wanted to leave?" asked Martha.

They wouldn't be able to sell their house on the open market, I answered; only back to the corporation, at a fair assessed price. Similarly, the corporation would buy back its stock to maintain financial control.

Mark was distressed by the legalistic sound of my plan—a corporation, federal grant, leases. "You mean we have to kick people out if they don't pay their leases?"

I doubted if it would come to that. If someone couldn't make the payment, or if he had an expensive illness—well, the members would decide. One thing at a time.

"But it sounds so complicated."

I agreed. Though it wasn't simple, the framework did provide an escape hatch. Many communal experiments had boxed themselves in, not by structure but by ideals: They *had* to live under the same roof, *had* to work together, *had* to get along. There had to be some alternate structure so that the village could withstand human stress. The structure was open enough to allow for the growth of a common building and enterprises (a vineyard? a trout farm?). Surely, we'd build a school, have a food cooperative and a place to meet.

I hoped we could build a hermitage like Lama's and hold morning meditation. But the spirit would have to grow. It couldn't be planned. If some people wanted to form a group marriage, fine. If another family (in the broad sense) wanted to import a swami, groovy. But the point of the village structure was that it wouldn't depend on the success of the school, the group marriage or the swami. It would rest securely on the land. The only rules would be ecological: outhouses mandatory. No outboards on the pond—just canoes and rowboats; no pesticides on the land.

Martha commented that it sounded like a resort for the privileged few who could afford stock. I pointed out that some would only need to scrape up the $500 for the lease. I didn't want a cloister: Was there anything wrong with being able to make a little money? On the contrary, the village would probably be more diverse than most communes; perhaps it would attract a retired, older couple, along with freaks who would live primitively, craftsmen, artists and professionals, all of whom would shuttle between the "outside" and the village. It would be easier to leave the village, though it was in the heart of the wilderness, than a one-family farm. I was going to farm. But ultimately, the economic problem was left to the individuals.

"Where on earth are we going to find people?"

We already knew quite a few. Once the option on the land was taken, the rest would find us, maybe beat a path to our doors —so convinced was I that we were just a few hundred miles and several months ahead of the stampede.

Mark didn't like the bigness of the plan—too many acres, people and too much money.

But for me, the village struck the right balance of men, resources and land: between freedom and stability, individuality and cooperation, tradition and innovation. Admittedly, one thousand acres was a lot for twelve families, though we would use only part of it. Ideally, we could buy or lease lumbered-out land that could be reforested. The idea was to use as little land and resources as humanly possible and leave the rest—alone.

January, 1971

We've been effectively snowbound most of the month. The school bus manages to get in and pick up Susan; on 30-below mornings the Opel groans under a frozen engine. Lacking an electric dipstick, standard equipment up north, we find that a tray of hot wood coals under the motor thins the oil, so it turns over easily. We are an island surrounded by fields and woods of waist-deep snow. The solidified path to the house is several steps higher than the base of the door. Stepping down, you get the sensation of entering a bunker that has been dug out after the white holocaust. Snow shoveled off the roof has begun to block the clear-plastic-covered windows. If we don't clear the snow from the roof, a thousand leaks appear on the first sunny day the temperature gets up to 20.

Our supply of dead elm is holding out. Amaryllis, the cat, has found the warmest sleeping spot—on the snowshoes that straddle the rafters. As the money runs out, we make the necessary accommodations. We disconnected the refrigerator. Perishables are kept on the floor at various distances from the front door. The bottom drawer of the sink is a freezer locker. We cook on the top of the wood and kerosene stoves. When the pipe from the spring froze, we reverted to hauling water from the brook, taking along an ax to bash a hole large enough for the five-gallon plastic jugs that are pulled home on a tote sled.

I spend most of the day at the typewriter. Lucy retypes the final draft. Michael keeps the woodbox full, shovels snow, bakes bread, reads catalogs (*Hudson Vitamins, Sears, Roebuck, L. L. Bean, Whole Earth*) and makes plans. The long insular winter has him down; he can't wait until the thaw to get outside, build a shed, sugar, and start the garden. We're all restless for the spring. Then we can go scouting in the mountains for the community site. For the time being, surrounded by a sea of snow and temperatures that can kill, the six of us must wait.

It helps to get *Mother Earth News, Good Times, Rolling Stone* and the other publications that periodically reassure us there *are* others just as crazy. Yesterday Mary quoted from a letter printed in a *Whole Earth Supplement*. A young woman wrote in bemoaning the end of the hippie movement, or her conception of the movement—presumably the antiwar years, when Yippies danced nude on Wall Street and tossed dollar bills onto the floor of the Stock Exchange. Now the letter writer's friends were retreating to the country, paired as old man and old lady, and taking refuge in gardens, pets, children and macramé.

"It sounds like us," Mary commented.

True, we don't look much like a movement. Someday, though, we hope to be part of a community, one of hundreds that will change history by example. For the time being, we're a small, funky family out here in the snow tending the fire through the night.

During the winter of waiting, we're not alone. There are many more, members of a greater community extending through pine forests, mountains and plains. Over these distances that we have transcended, we are together, though apart.

Every day brings a letter from the others. The Oz family is scattered. Father George writes that the Center, the spiritual-hippie hostel he founded in Santa Fe, was forced to close. George was arrested for "creating a public nuisance." The city council met to air numerous complaints that the Center was a hub of drug peddling and promiscuity and an invitation for more hippies to crash into Santa Fe. Later George was hired as the director of Outreach, a drug abuse program in Santa Fe. In many ways, the program continued the work of the Center in providing "positive alternatives to drugs—other ways of turning on," George wrote. Despite the harassment that has dogged him and his family the past two years, George remains "positive. . . . Not that we don't have a lot of shit to shovel through, but the brotherhood of man is a given—our awareness of it evolves."

As for other Oz people: Josh is living with an elderly woman in the Sierras and has collaborated with Morgan to produce a humorous tarot deck. Nevada is still on the lam. After reaching the Coast, Kathy and Michael split up. She went into a mental institution, came out with short hair, and the last I'd heard, was a librarian in a small Iowa town. I often wonder, Whatever happened to Kathy?—probably a question that has haunted her life. Maybe I'll go back to Iowa someday to find out.

From High Ridge Farm I get word from Reuben, Jack,

Elaine, Maureen, and Laura. They all give versions of how Claudia had her baby, Bree Tokiti Neal, in the A-frame after ninety minutes of labor. "It was the most beautiful, far-out thing that ever happened to me," Claudia wrote. "Bill delivered him and cut the umbilical cord and almost everyone else was there, breathing with me, oming, very together, very intense, and, oh, so joyous."

The family made a gravity feed irrigation system, fed by a hand-dug well 30 feet deep, "which is a hell of a hole," Jack wrote. "We got no more water than we did at ten feet. So next summer I guess we will dig some more." The major project of the summer was the 45-by-30-foot building with a tall stone fireplace. It will contain a central kitchen, dining room and children's room. For income, to make up for the food stamps they no longer take, one couple a week work at a greenhouse-nursery 80 miles away, planting and harvesting Easter lily bulbs.

Except for staph and eye infections, "we are all well," reports Elaine, who wrote a warm letter telling of the changes she's gone through. Maybe she'll come to Vermont one of these days. Little Roland and Matthew, now "Chip," are going to public school. So are Kathy and Susan, who now live with Maureen in a house a few miles away from the farm. Maureen split up with Roland but still visits the commune. Peter is planning to buy land with a couple who live in the valley.

Laura left the farm. She writes from Oakland that she is living in a storefront, going to art classes twice a week, and composing songs. Woody is with her. He has changed his name to Smokey.

We kept in touch with Ron and Susan who lived with us last summer. They send postcards and letters. After leaving Vermont, they traveled through Canada but didn't settle there—too cold for Ron's Oklahoma-Cherokee blood. They spent the winter in Oakland, California, where they were legally married and had their baby, a girl, to whom they gave a Cherokee name, Ama Selu, meaning "corn and water woman." In Oakland they saw a lot of Big David and Barbara, who had decided after all to leave New Buffalo. They were saving money for land in British Columbia. Ron and Susan attended when Barbara had her baby, squatting over a rubber mattress, encouraged by a midwife and David, who sang peyote songs in her ear. The baby was named Yana Oma.

But Susan's letters also brought news of a tragedy that befell George and Joyce. After leaving New Buffalo, they lived for a short time in Aspen, Colorado. There a car struck and killed little Jamil, Joyce's son by Max Finstein. Joyce is pregnant again, and they are living as a separate family a few miles down the road from New Buffalo.

Cave David sends happier news: Mary has married Richard. "I gave them a Sioux peace pipe as a wedding gift. . . ." His letter continues:

The corn harvest was poor due to a shortage of water, a very early September frost and an excessive lack of attention to menacing weeds. The squash did better, though, and the garden vegetables (cabbage, carrots, onions, lettuce, turnips, and Swiss chard) did excellent. The area apple harvest is good and two of our trees produced bountiful fruit. We have prepared the greenhouse for winter by mudding the sides and roof and covering it with straw. . . . Using the Morningstar team of horses, we plowed the old bean field and planted winter wheat last week. Also an acre of rye. I hurt my back carrying mud buckets, and a young yogi named Judge has been taking care of me. She teaches us important breathing exercises at dawn and rubs my back morning and night. Tom and Henry and I are still the main gardeners, but Tom just left for a two-week vacation to New York to see his father. We have a young Indian boy living with us. He is just back from Vietnam, and we really like him, although he's pretty confused and gets into a lot of fights.

New Buffalo's "permanent population" is still about thirty and we have somehow managed to keep our gates open to visitors all summer. Little Doug is in jail on $10,000 bail for armed robbery (a past offense), and Tonio is putting up a prayer meeting for him this Saturday.

All the buildings have been mudded and repaired. An artist painted Indian pictures and murals on our Circle wall. I feel good about living here now; only a handful of drunk neighbors remain unfriendly. The pasture is finally completed and the herd of goats stands. Things are slowly getting together but the improvement is very gradual. Our meetings are run more orderly now and we respect each other more.

Morningstar is also improving. They have built a new kitchen and dining room above similar to Lama's. Reality is down to ten people. The valley is just about filled to capacity with Chicanos, Indians and hippies. Too many more will cause the melting pot to boil over.

Blond Larry and Marilyn are still here. Torah makes really good wheat bread. Taylor is still here, although he and Tonio and Aquarius Paul work every day in Arroyo Seco. Susan is teaching in town four days a week. . . .

Justin lives on the other side of the valley and is an accepted road man at prayer meetings. One old man from Oklahoma stays in my room and is teaching me much about their ways. These old fellows are our teachers and we try to care for them as best we can. He has been like a father to me, telling us many stories. He thinks I should marry one of these young girls here—maybe the yogi. The only permanent child here is still Nancy Warak (Mary's daughter).

Ira and Maureen live in Arroyo Seco and Andrea is one of Susan's pupils. George and Joyce live down the road.

The outside world appears pretty shaky, so I have been doing some heavy praying lately. I am a bit anxious but not worried. *Yana huia—wana huia na hu!*

Love,
CAVE DAVID (NEFER REN)

February

Ron and Susan and Ama Selu and Definitely, their cat, have returned for a visit.

As I sit at my desk in the corner and try to finish this book, the small room is filled with people, things, words, animals, kids. From the rafters hang socks, ice skates, hats, gloves, scarves, baby pajamas, snow pants, and boots with laces tied together. On the bench in front of the kerosene stove, Lucy knits a pink vest for Susan and sings "Drill, ye tarriers, drill. . . ." Susan and

David are playing monster. Big Susan is cleaning the debris off the table. Michael adjusts the bar on the chain saw. Mary cooks rice and watches Ron make sukiyaki.

And Robert: well, he sits here, still wondering how he's changed so that he can type and at the same time groove on what's going on.

We've all changed, very quickly these past years. Big Susan and I, once antagonists, are now close. She no longer sneers at neurotic middle-class life or puts down anything that falls short of her ideals. She's softer, more relaxed, at home with both her past and present. She has on an old sweater she last wore in graduate school: an orange wool turtleneck from Saks. Over the heart, she's embroidered a thunderbird as an emblem of her New Mexico years.

Having Ama brought her into closer contact with her own body and feelings, she says. Continually she fondles and holds the baby. Her own parents rarely touched her. "Can you imagine mothers putting on plastic gloves to change a diaper?" When she goes for a walk, she snugly wraps Ama in a ruana sling. The baby sleeps beside her and Ron.

They've decided to buy a farm in West Virginia. It won't be a commune, though two or three other friends might eventually live with them. Ron is planning a hexagonal house around a dome-enclosed greenhouse. They will leave in a few days, stopping over in Washington, D.C., to stay with her parents and timing their arrival in West Virginia with the first birds and mud of spring.

We say good-bye for now. Someday I'll go on another trip to visit them and the other families in Oregon and New Mexico— all members of the new community taking roots all over this, our land. For the time we write across these distances, though distance cannot separate us anymore, for their joys are our joys, their sorrows ours. And their healthy, wild children—Sol Ray, Cedar, Sammarah, Shantih, Abraham, Yama Oma, Ama Selu, Red Pony, Sarah, Julia, Jesse, Aurora—they are our children.

GETTING BACK TOGETHER
by ROBERT HOURIET

With photographs by Lawrence Kanevsky

A GREAT migration is under way across the continental United States. In the last five years tens of thousands of young people—and some adventurous over-thirties—have begun new lives in communes and communities in pine forests, on mountainsides, on arid mesas and open plains. They have turned their backs on the old America. What is it they hope to find in the new?

When Robert Houriet set out in 1968 to explore the texture and direction of communal life in America today, the movement was regarded by media and public alike as a "freak scene"—dropouts who hadn't decided what to drop into, open-ended communes of drifting hippies with no purpose, no traditions, no tomorrow. They knew what they *didn't* want of plastic American culture, but not what they did. Everywhere, he found "hassles and marathon encounter meetings that couldn't resolve questions like whether to leave the dogs in or out. Everywhere, cars that wouldn't run and pumps that wouldn't pump because everybody knew all about the occult history of tarot and nobody knew anything about mechanics. Sinks filled with dishes, cows wandering through gates left open and no one to blame. Everywhere, in-